Insurance Company Operations

LOMA (Life Office Management Association, Inc.) is an international association founded in 1924. LOMA is committed to a business partnership with its worldwide members in the insurance and financial services industry to improve their management and operations through quality employee development, research, information sharing, and related products and services. Among LOMA's activities is the sponsorship of the FLMI Insurance Education Program—an educational program intended primarily for home office and branch office employees.

The ***FLMI Insurance Education Program*** consists of two levels— Level I, *Fundamentals of Life and Health Insurance,* and Level II, *Functional Aspects of Life and Health Insurance.* Level I is designed to help students achieve a working knowledge of the life and health insurance business. Level II is designed to provide a more detailed understanding of life and health insurance and related business and management subjects. Students who complete Level I receive a certificate. Students who complete both levels earn the designation Fellow, Life Management Institute (FLMI) and receive a diploma.

Statement of Purpose: LOMA Educational Programs Testing and Designations

Examinations described in the *LOMA Insurance Education Catalog* are designed solely to measure whether students have successfully completed the relevant assigned curriculum, and the attainment of the FLMI and other LOMA designations indicates only that all examinations in the given curriculum have been successfully completed. In no way shall a student's completion of a given LOMA course or attainment of the FLMI or other LOMA designation be construed to mean that LOMA in any way certifies that student's competence, training, or ability to perform any given task. LOMA's examinations are to be used solely for general educational purposes, and no other use of the examinations or program is authorized or intended by LOMA. Furthermore, it is in no way the intention of the LOMA Curriculum and Examinations staff to describe the standard of appropriate conduct in any field of the insurance and financial services industry, and LOMA expressly repudiates any attempt to so use the curriculum and examinations. Any such assessment of student competence or industry standards of conduct should instead be based on independent professional inquiry and the advice of competent professional counsel.

Insurance Company Operations

Gene Stone, FLMI, ACS, CLU

Information That Works ®

FLMI Insurance Education Program
Life Management Institute LOMA
Atlanta, Georgia
www.loma.org

FLMI 290 Text

Author:	Gene Stone, FLMI, ACS, CLU
Manuscript Editor:	Harriett E. Jones, J.D., FLMI, ACS
Exam Editor:	Sean Schaeffer Gilley, FLMI, ACS, ALHC, HIA, CEBS, AIAA, PAHM, MHP
Project Manager:	Jane Lightcap Brown, FLMI, ALHC, ACS
Production/Editorial Manager:	Stephanie Philippo
Copyeditor:	Robert D. Land, FLMI, ACS
Production/Print Coordinator:	Michelle Stone Weathers, ACS
Permissions Coordinators:	Catherine E. O'Neil Iris F. Hartley, FLMI, ALHC
Index:	Robert D. Land, FLMI, ACS
Cover Design:	Kathleen Ryan Michelle Stone Weathers, ACS
Typography:	BJ Nemeth, Puffin Typography

FLMI 290 Quik Review

Author:	Tom Lundin Jr., FLMI, ACS, AIAA, AIRC, PAHM
Editor:	Barbara Foxenburger Brown, FLMI, ACS
Project Manager:	Gene Stone, FLMI, ACS, CLU
Production/Editorial Manager:	Stephanie Philippo
Technical Development:	James Eldridge
Production Coordinator:	Allison Ayers

ISBN 1-57974-081-2

Library of Congress Catalog Card Number 00-131139

Printed in the United States of America

Contents

PART 2

Preface

As part of the increasingly complex financial services industry, life insurance companies have unique characteristics. The purpose of *Insurance Company Operations* is to explain how life insurers operate within the financial services industry.

Life company operations is an extremely broad topic incorporating many specialized disciplines, such as marketing, actuarial work, underwriting, claim administration, investment management, information management, and many others. Indeed, you could read entire books on each of these specialties. This book presents a substantive, meaningful discussion of each company operation as a part of an ongoing process. As you read, you will learn that this process begins with the formation of an insurer and proceeds through the development, distribution, and administration of life insurance products. We also discuss some of the strategic decisions insurers face that affect their long-term success. By the time you reach the end of *Insurance Company Operations*, you will have a solid understanding of how and why life insurance companies take the actions that they do.

Acknowledgements

Completing a project of this magnitude would be impossible without the contributions of a great many people. Ensuring that the material is current, accurate, and relevant involved the time and talents of many experts within LOMA and throughout the financial services industry. I wish to express my gratitude to them all.

Insurance Company Operations is a new textbook, but it draws on the outstanding work of Kenneth Huggins and Robert D. Land in *Operations of Life and Health Insurance Companies, Second Edition.* That text, which for many years was the principal textbook in LOMA's FLMI Course 290, provided me with a road map for approaching this vast subject. I am grateful to the authors for their efforts.

Textbook Development Panel

I would like to recognize the work of the members of the textbook development panel who helped to shape the text outline and who reviewed and commented on each chapter of the textbook. Working under a rigorous deadline, this group of industry professionals made countless valuable suggestions, answered my numerous questions and requests for advice, and helped to ensure that the finished work is accurate and complete. I am indebted to this review panel, whose members are listed on the following page:

- Robert Ahlschwede, FLMI, CLU, Compliance Manager—Investment Products Group, CNA Life

- Robert E. Beckoff, FLMI, ACS, Assistant Vice President, New York Life

- John F. Brancato, FLMI, Assistant Vice President of Systems, New York Life

- Roger W. Jolliffe, FSA, FCIA, FLMI, ACS, CFP, Vice President and Senior Actuary—Corporate, London Life Insurance Company

- Bruce Lovett, FSA, MAAA, Second Vice President and Actuary, The Guardian Life Insurance Company of America

- Lawrence B. Ruark, Ph.D., FLMI, ACS, AIAA, AIRC, CLU, Senior Compliance Analyst—Individual Markets Compliance, Sun Life Assurance Company of Canada

- Lloyd M. Spencer, Jr., FSA, Assistant Vice President, Financial Services, Lincoln National Reassurance Company

- Patricia E. Stevenson, FLMI, ACS, AIAA, AIRC, Compliance and Product Specialist, The Baltimore Life Companies

- Linda Theodore, ASF, AIRC, Actuarial Administrative Manager AEGON—Special Markets Group

- Sandi L. Weinberg, FLMI, ACS, AIAA, AIRC, HIA, Supervisor, New Products/New Markets Division, Physicians Mutual Insurance Company

Selected Text Reviewers

Many industry professionals reviewed selected chapters in their areas of expertise. This group of reviewers also provided me with valuable feedback, suggestions, and information. These reviewers and the subject areas that they reviewed are listed below.

Information Management

- Barry B. Buner, Second Vice President, Information Technology, Transamerica Life Companies

- Mary Claire Sheehy, FLMI, ACS, HIA, Systems Director, Allstate Life Insurance Company

- James V. Standaert, FLMI, National Secretary, Modern Woodmen of America

Marketing/Product Development

- Jack L. Baumer, FSA, MAAA, Assistant Vice President—Variable Products, Allianz Life Insurance Company of North America

- John A. Boni, RHU, Lead Product Design Analyst—New Products/New Markets Division, Physicians Mutual Insurance Company

- Jeff Mohrenweiser, FSA, CFA, Assistant Vice President, CNA

- Mark S. Nelson, FSA, MAAA, Assistant Vice President and Actuary—Finance Division, Physicians Mutual Insurance Company

Product Distribution

- Tommy H. Jackson, CLU, FLMI, HIAA, Manager, Multi-Life Marketing, UnumProvident Insurance Company

- Frank D. Memmo, Jr., Vice President—Operations, AIG Life Companies (U.S.)

Underwriting

- Christopher C. Cook, FLMI, FALU, Vice President of Underwriting, American General Life Companies

- Joe W. Dunlap, FLMI, CLU, ChFC, ACS, Vice President, Policy Administration, American Amicable Life Insurance Company of Texas

- John Harold Jones, Jr., FLMI, AALU, CLU, ChFC, Senior Underwriter, CNA

- Ann M. Wenzl, FLMI, ALHC, ACS, HIA, MHP, AIAA, AIRC, Assistant Vice President, Credit Insurance Division—Administration, Central States Health & Life Co. of Omaha

Customer Service

- Gary J. Coles FLMI/M, ACS, Vice President, Individual Administration, National Life of Canada

- Stacy B. Ketcham, FLMI, HIA, Project Manager, Special Projects, World Insurance Company

Claim Administration

- Judy Freeman, FLMI, ALHC, ACS, Administration Officer, Fortis

- James B. Hiers, III, FLMI, ALHC, HIA, ACS, Assistant Secretary, Munich American Reassurance Company

Financial Management/Investments/Accounting

- John C. Di Joseph, MAA, FSA, Senior Vice President and Chief Actuary, J.C. Penney Direct Marketing Services, Inc.

- Gary Hickman, FSA, Associate Actuary, J.C. Penney Direct Marketing Services, Inc.

- Marjorie G. Kennedy, FLMI, CLU, Sr. Accountant, Security Financial Life Insurance Company

- Ellen I. Whittaker, FLMI, Senior Investment Officer, Berkshire Life Insurance Company

- Rodney Wilton, FLMI/M, FCIA, FSA, MAAA, J.C. Penney Direct Marketing Services, Inc.

Legal Operations/Regulatory Compliance

- Billie Jean Baldwin, FLMI, ACS, Director of Compliance, Paradigm Insurance Group, Inc.

- Francine Cardon, FLMI, Director of Compliance, CNA

- John B. Gould, FSA, MAAA, FCIA, Assistant Vice President & Actuary, CNA

Other Industry Contributors

Many other industry experts lent their time and experience to help me with selected portions of the text. These contributors include the following:

- Susan F. Brandon, Account Executive, The Benefit Company

- Mary K. Bryant, ACS, Project Manager—Quality Department, First Colony Life Insurance Company

- Robert Harvey, Associate Vice President—Client Services Department, First Colony Life Insurance Company

- Peter Lawson, FLMI, ACS, ALHC, Manager, Life Claims, London Life Insurance Company

- Susan H. Mott, Ph.D., Marketing Officer, Nationwide Financial Services

- Mark A. Parkin, FLMI, Partner, Deloitte & Touche LLP

- Calvin Robinson, Vice President and Associate General Counsel, Woodmen of the World Life Insurance

- Janice F. Spradlin, FLMI, ACS, ALHC, Director—Training, Standard Insurance Company

- Frank Zinatelli, FLMI, LL.B., Associate General Counsel, Canadian Life and Health Insurance Association

LOMA Staff/Consultants

Textbook authors at LOMA are fortunate to have many fellow staff members who are knowledgeable about industry trends and practices in a diverse array of subject matters. Many past and present LOMA employees took part in the development and production of this book.

First, I would like to thank Harriett E. Jones, J.D., FLMI, ACS, Senior Associate, Education & Training (E&T), and Sean Schaeffer Gilley, FLMI, ACS, ALHC, HIA, CEBS, AIAA, PAHM, MHP, Senior Associate, Examinations, who reviewed the entire text during its development and made innumerable suggestions. This book could never have been completed without their time and energy. Jo Ann Appleton, FLMI, ALHC, HIA, and Ernest L. Martin, Ph.D, FLMI, reviewed later drafts of the chapters and helped me shape them into final form.

Next, I would like to recognize the following LOMA staff members who reviewed selected chapters and gave me much useful feedback: Stephen W. Forbes, Ph.D., FLMI, Senior Vice President, Research; Jennifer W. Herrod, FLMI, ACS, AIAA, PAHM; Elizabeth A. Mulligan, FLMI, ACS, AIAA, ALHC, PAHM, Senior Associate, E&T; and Ann M. Purr, FLMI, CSP, ACS, PAHM, AIAA, Second Vice President, Management Services. Other LOMA staff members who made contributions to textbook development include Mary C. Bickley, J.D., FLMI, AIRC, ACS, AIAA, PAHM, Associate, E&T; John P. Burger, FLMI, ACS, AIRC, AIAA; Susan Conant, FLMI, CEBS, HIAA, PAHM, Senior Associate, E&T; Nicholas L. Desoutter, FLMI, ACS, Senior Associate, Examinations; and Jean C. Gora, Manager of Research.

I wish to thank the following people for graciously fulfilling my daily research requests: Olivia Blakemore, ACS, Information Center; Mallory Eldridge, Research Analyst/Writer; and Janet Smith, Information Center Researcher.

Robert D. Land, FLMI, ACS, copyedited the manuscript and compiled the index, and Iris F. Hartley, FLMI, ALHC, secured the necessary permissions. On the production side, Stephanie Philippo, Director, Editorial/Production/Intellectual Property Management, managed the entire production process; Michelle Stone Weathers, ACS, Production/Print Coordinator, coordinated the typesetting and printing; and Catherine E. O'Neil, Editorial/Permissions Coordinator, coordinated the copyediting and indexing. Aurelia Kennedy-Hemphill, Administrative Assistant II, E&T, provided excellent administrative support throughout the project.

I would also like to recognize the work of Tom Lundin Jr., FLMI, ACS, AIAA, AIRC, PAHM, Associate, E&T, who authored the lessons for the *Quik Review for FLMI 290—Insurance Company Operations* CD-ROM that accompanies this text, Barbara Foxenburger Brown, FLMI, ACS, Associate, E&T, who edited the *Quik Review*, and James Eldridge, Programmer Analyst, who handled the technical development of the *Quik Review*.

Dennis W. Goodwin, FLMI, ACS, Second Vice President, Education Division, and William H. Rabel, Ph.D., FLMI, CLU, Senior Vice President, Education Division, lent their interest, guidance, and words of encouragement to the project. Last, but by no means least, I am indebted to Jane Lightcap Brown, FLMI, ALHC, ACS, Director, E&T, who managed the entire project. She reviewed the manuscript, kept the project pointed in the proper direction, and made sure that the light at the end of the tunnel was not an oncoming train.

Gene Stone, FLMI, ACS, CLU
Atlanta, Georgia
2000

Introduction

Insurance Company Operations describes how life insurance companies in the United States and Canada carry on their businesses. The text, which is designed for students who are preparing for LOMA's FLMI Course 290 examination, is divided into two parts.

- Part 1 (Chapters 1–10), describes how life insurance companies are formed and organized, and how they design, develop, and distribute insurance products.

- Part 2 (Chapters 11–19) describes how life insurance companies administer their products, service their customers, and take steps to help ensure long-term business prosperity.

Several features have been included in each chapter to help you organize your studies, reinforce your understanding of the materials, and prepare for the examination for this course. As we describe each of these features, we give you suggestions for studying the material.

- **Learning Objectives.** The first page of each chapter contains a list of learning objectives to help you focus your studies. Before reading each chapter, review these learning objectives. Then, as you read the chapter, look for material that will help you meet the learning objectives.

- **Chapter Outline.** The first page of each chapter also provides an outline of the chapter. Review this outline to gain an overview of the material that will be covered; then scan through the chapter to familiarize yourself with the presentation of the information. By looking at the headings and the figures, you will get a sense of how the various subjects relate to each other.

- **Key Terms.** This text assumes that you have a basic knowledge of the key terms and concepts associated with life insurance principles and products. In some cases, these basic terms are also reviewed and explained in this text. Terms associated with insurance company operations are highlighted in ***bold italic*** type when they are first used or defined. These terms are included in a list of key terms at the end of each chapter, and you can also find a comprehensive list of all key terms in the glossary at the end of this book. As you read each chapter, pay special attention to these key terms.

- **Insights.** Excerpts from industry publications and other sources appear throughout the text and are designed to amplify the text's descriptions of certain topics. These Insights should help you get a better understanding of the day-to-day operations of a life insurance company.

- **Best Case Scenarios.** This text contains a running series of features known as Best Case Scenarios. These scenarios guide you through life insurance company operations from the point of view of a hypothetical insurer, the Best Friend Life Insurance Company. In each chapter, you will read how Best Friend handles a particular problem or situation related to the subject of that chapter. You will also see how the company manages its relationship with a family of insureds. The Best Case Scenarios are intended to synthesize the material and improve your understanding of life insurance company operations.

- **Focus on Technology.** A special series of insights called Focus on Technology illustrates some of the ways that new technologies are affecting life insurance company operations. Each chapter includes at least one Focus on Technology that is related to the chapter topic.

In addition, the text contains numerous figures and "Fast Facts," which are interesting statistics or thought-provoking facts intended to round out the presentation of material and enhance your learning experience.

Using LOMA Study Aids

LOMA has prepared study aids designed to help students prepare for the FLMI Course 290 examination. LOMA recommends that you use all of the study aids available for this course. **Studies indicate that students who use LOMA study aids perform significantly better on FLMI Program examinations than students who do not use study aids.**

Using the Prep Pak for This Course

In addition to this book, LOMA's *Prep Pak for FLMI 290* is assigned reading for students preparing for the FLMI Program examination. Used along with this textbook, the Prep Pak will help you master the course material. Included in the Prep Pak are chapter review exercises, practice exam questions, a full-scale sample examination in both paper and electronic format, and answers to all of the questions in the Prep Pak.

The Prep Pak may be revised periodically. To ensure that you are studying from the correct text, check the current LOMA Insurance Education Catalog for a description of the texts assigned for the examination for which you are preparing.

Using the *Quik Review* CD-ROM Accompanying This Text

The CD-ROM found on the inside back cover of this text contains a *Quik Review for FLMI 290—Insurance Company Operations,* which gives you an overview of the materials found in this text. The *Quik Review* is designed for instructors and students studying for the FLMI 290 examination.

Life Insurance Company Operations and Ethics

Providing life insurance protection and wealth accumulation tools for millions of policyowners in the United States and Canada requires the skills, energy, and creativity of the many people who work for life insurance companies. A *life insurance company* is a company that underwrites and issues life insurance. Many insurance companies that sell life insurance also sell other insurance products, such as health insurance, annuities, and even property/casualty insurance. However, the purpose of this book is to describe how U.S. and Canadian life insurance companies operate: how they are formed and organized; how they conceive, develop, distribute, and service products; and the steps they take to ensure corporate success.

By reading this book, you will learn what life insurance companies do and how they do it. You will understand the big picture of life insurance company operations and also many of the details that make up the big picture. If you are an employee of a life insurance company, this book will help you see how the work you perform fits in the entire scope of your company's business. You will learn how your individual efforts affect your company's service to its customers and its overall performance.

This chapter provides an overview of life insurance company roles and operations, and the ethical environment in which insurers operate. As you will see, life insurers occupy an important position of public trust, so they have a legal and moral responsibility to conduct their business fairly and honestly.

To help illustrate some of the concepts involved in life insurance company operations, this book includes a series of narratives involving a hypothetical insurer—the Best Friend Life Insurance Company—as well as its employees, agents, and policyowners. We call these narratives Best Case Scenarios. These scenarios are not meant to portray actual events or the specific procedures of any particular insurance company. The scenarios demonstrate typical activities of life insurance companies, home office personnel, and agents as they provide financial protection for their customers. For an introduction to Best Friend and certain characters whom we will revisit throughout the book, read Best Case Scenario 1-1.

Best Case Scenario 1-1.

Introducing the Carpenters.

Tom Carpenter, age 31, is an airplane mechanic for a major commercial airline. His wife, Maria, is a 31-year-old optometrist. Their combined annual household income is $93,000. They own a home on which they make a monthly mortgage payment. Fifteen months ago, Tom and Maria had their first child, Christina. Each work day, the couple places the child in a day care center.

Prior to Christina's birth, Tom and Maria had not given much thought to the possibility that one of them might die unexpectedly. They had also taken only a few steps toward organizing their finances and planning for their retirement. Occasionally, they deposited money into a bank savings account, which they periodically used for household improvements and vacations. Through their respective employers, Tom and Maria received group term life insurance coverage with a benefit amount equal to two times their annual salaries. Also, both of their employers offered a 401(k) salary reduction plan, to which Tom and Maria each contributed 5 percent of their gross salaries. Maria owned a few shares of stock that she had inherited. But neither Tom nor Maria had ever purchased individual life insurance.

Christina's arrival into their lives changed Tom's and Maria's view of their finances. What if either of them died suddenly? What financial hardships would the surviving spouse and child endure? Would the surviving parent be able to support himself or herself and the child on only one salary? Could the surviving parent afford to send Christina to college? Tom and Maria decided it was time to address these concerns.

Through a referral from another parent at Christina's day care center, the Carpenters obtained the name of Louise Chen, a career agent with the Best Friend Life Insurance Company. During a meeting with Louise, Tom and Maria provided her with personal and financial information about themselves. Louise analyzed their financial needs and presented information about Best Friend and its products. Tom and Maria decided to apply for Best Friend life insurance policies covering each of their lives. The protection provided by these policies eased their concerns about an uncertain financial future. •

The Roles of Life Insurance Companies in the Economy

Life insurance companies play a number of essential roles in the economies of many nations. These roles include operating as market-driven organizations, providing financial security to consumers, serving as financial intermediaries, and employing a great many people.

Market-Driven Organizations

At one time, life insurance companies tended to be largely *product-driven organizations*, which place great emphasis on selling sound products at competitive prices through strong distribution systems. Essentially, product-driven organizations develop certain products and then attempt to sell them to the public, without focusing on the public's needs, tastes, and preferences. A classic example of a product-

driven organization was the early Ford Motor Company, whose founder, Henry Ford, once quipped that customers could buy his Model T automobile in any color as long as it was black.

Most life insurance companies today have evolved into **market-driven organizations**, meaning they respond to the needs of the marketplace and the consumers who make up the marketplace. A market-driven organization determines the needs of its customers and develops products, services, and distribution methods to satisfy those needs. Because insurers are able to satisfy customer wants and needs, the market operates efficiently. New ideas and products continually appear in the market, and prices remain reasonable.

The operations of market-driven organizations require coordination and input from many departments and functional areas. Staff members from all areas of the insurance company must work together to develop and distribute products that customers want, at prices that are both attractive to the consumer and profitable for the company.

A market-driven life insurance company is generally better able than a product-driven life insurance company to compete in today's business environment. Market-driven companies take the lead in developing marketing strategies and products, whereas product-driven organizations generally lag behind the marketplace. Because they predominate in the life insurance industry, market-driven organizations are the focus of this text.

Providers of Financial Security

Central to any discussion of life insurance and life insurance companies is the concept of *risk*, which is the probability of financial loss. Life insurers develop products and services that help people and organizations manage some of the financial losses they may face. For example, a family faces the chance that if one of its principal wage earners dies, the surviving family members will experience serious financial consequences. Life insurers provide protection from the financial losses associated with certain types of perils, thus offering financial security to policyowners, insureds, and beneficiaries. People who are adequately insured can pursue their goals in life, knowing that if they die or become disabled, their families or businesses will avoid undue financial hardships. When people feel confident that insurance will provide in the event a loss occurs, they do not need to tie up an extraordinary amount of money in savings in order to ensure that they can provide for these uncertain risks. Thus, this money goes back into the economy for investments.

Life insurers offer a wide range of financial products designed to meet various consumer needs. (See Figure 1-1 for a list of common uses

> **FAST FACT**
>
> In 1998, $14.47 trillion of life insurance was in force in the United States, and $1.85 trillion of life insurance was in force in Canada.[1]

FIGURE 1-1. What Life Insurance Can Do.

- Pay final expenses after a death
- Liquidate a mortgage or pay rent
- Maintain a standard of living
- Establish a cash reserve

- Fund a bequest
- Establish business continuity
- Pay for education
- Provide supplemental retirement income

---

of life insurance.) Products such as term life insurance, whole life insurance, medical expense insurance, disability income insurance, long-term care insurance, dental insurance, vision care coverage, and group life and health insurance protect consumers from the economic risks associated with death, disability, and illness. Other products, such as annuities and mutual funds, help consumers accumulate money for future needs and increase their personal wealth. Furthermore, life insurance companies manage a large portion of the retirement funds of U.S. and Canadian residents, thereby helping people to accumulate wealth for their retirement years and to protect themselves against the risk of outliving their financial resources.

Financial Intermediaries

Life insurance companies are among the most important financial institutions in the world. A *financial institution* is a business organization that collects funds from the public and places these funds in financial assets, such as stocks, bonds, insurance policies, annuities, real estate, bank accounts, and loans to businesses and consumers. At the beginning of 1999, U.S. and Canadian life insurance companies held approximately $3 trillion of financial assets.[2] Financial institutions include insurance companies, banks, credit unions, mutual fund companies, finance companies, and securities firms.

Life insurance companies are also important *financial intermediaries*, which are institutions that move money from people and businesses that have excess funds (lenders) to people and businesses that have a shortage of funds (borrowers). In the process of moving funds from lenders to borrowers, financial intermediaries generate income for themselves. Life insurance companies are financial intermediaries because they take a portion of the money that their customers pay in the form of insurance premiums and invest that money in business and industry. Insurers' investments provide funds that these businesses need to operate and expand. As shown in Figure 1-2, life insurers are among the most important sources of funds provided to businesses.

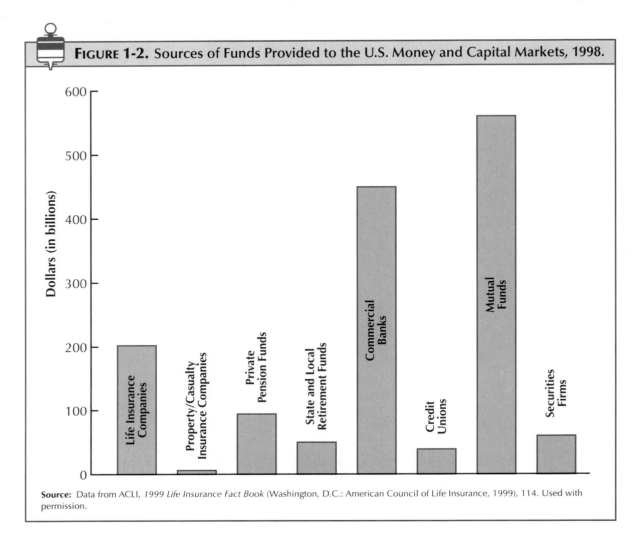

FIGURE 1-2. Sources of Funds Provided to the U.S. Money and Capital Markets, 1998.

Source: Data from ACLI, *1999 Life Insurance Fact Book* (Washington, D.C.: American Council of Life Insurance, 1999), 114. Used with permission.

Large Employers

Besides fulfilling market needs and offering financial security to the public, life insurers also strengthen the economy by providing jobs. In 1999, about 1,690 North American life insurance companies provided jobs for 1.5 million people, not including the sales force. Life insurance sales functions provided another 792,000 jobs.[3]

Life Insurance Company Operations

In the context of commerce, an *operation* is an action or a process that a company performs to conduct its business. The specific life

insurance company operations that we will discuss in this book are as follows:

- **Forming and organizing the insurance company.** Before an insurance product can provide financial protection, a company must exist to develop and distribute the product. Forming a life insurance company in the United States or Canada requires an enormous amount of capital, as well as compliance with many legal and regulatory requirements. In Chapters 2 through 4, we will discuss how life insurance companies are formed and organized to operate most efficiently and to meet their corporate objectives. We discuss insurance regulation, procedures for commencing business, typical organizational structures of insurance companies, and staffing considerations. In Chapter 5, we discuss the information systems that life insurers use to manage the information that is a crucial component of all of an insurer's operations.

- **Assessing customer needs.** Market-driven organizations (1) define market segments on which they focus their marketing efforts and (2) study the market segments to determine the types of products customers need and are most likely to purchase. In this phase of life insurance company operations, the company considers many factors that influence the tastes and preferences of its target consumers. Chapter 6 addresses market segmentation and identifying customers' needs.

- **Developing products.** Once the insurer has identified its target markets and determined the types of products those markets want and need, the insurer develops appropriate products. Product development includes generating and screening product ideas, testing ideas for feasibility, and designing the products. Under the guidance of the company's actuaries, the insurer establishes a premium scale for the product that is both financially sound and competitive in the marketplace. For each new product, the company also develops a marketing strategy, a distribution system, underwriting guidelines, and customer service and claim administration procedures. The insurer also ensures that the new product complies with all applicable laws and regulations and that the insurer has adequate information system support to sell and administer the product. Chapters 7 and 8 provide an overview of these many aspects of product development.

- **Distributing products.** Distributing insurance products has historically taken place through the personal selling efforts of insurance agents. Many insurance companies engage tens of thousands of agents to sell their products. Insurers also use a number of

distribution systems that do not involve face-to-face selling. In Chapter 9, we discuss the characteristics of various distribution systems, including agents, broker-dealers, direct response, Internet sales, and bank distribution, and explain the company's relationship to each system. In Chapter 10, we examine home office support for each distribution system.

- **Administering products.** *Administration* in this context includes underwriting and application processing, policy issue, policyowner service, and claim administration. Life insurance companies develop underwriting guidelines so that underwriters can make fair and consistent risk selection decisions. Once a policy is in force, insurance companies respond to many types of customer service requests. Companies also develop procedures to handle claims submitted under insurance contracts. Chapters 11 through 14 describe these aspects of product administration.

- **Ensuring corporate success.** An insurer has an ethical and legal obligation to operate responsibly and to remain in business so that it will be able to fulfill its financial commitments to its policyowners. Insurers also have a duty to attempt to provide their owners with an acceptable return for their investment in the company. An insurer that breaks the law or allows its financial condition to deteriorate places its policyowners at risk. Life insurers take many steps to ensure the company's continued success, including managing investments, maintaining solvency and profitability, fulfilling financial reporting requirements, complying with applicable laws and regulatory requirements, and effectively managing strategic (long-term) issues that affect the entire company. We discuss these aspects of insurance company operations in Chapters 15 through 19.

All life insurance companies carry out each of the above operations in *some* way. However, not every insurance company undertakes each operation in *the same* way. Insurers have their own products, cultures, modes of organization, and management styles, and these differences are reflected in the specific ways in which companies operate.

Integration Among Functional Areas

The operations we've introduced are conducted by people working in a variety of functional areas. Figure 1-3 contains a list of typical life insurer functional areas. One theme you will notice throughout this book is that effective life insurance company operations require a tremendous amount of integration and coordination among an insurer's

---

FIGURE 1-3. Typical Functional Areas in Life Insurance Companies.

Actuarial: Ensures that the company conducts its operations on a financially sound basis, and assists with pricing and product development.

Underwriting: Ensures that the company classifies insureds such that their mortality experience, as a group, falls within the range of the mortality rates assumed at the time of product design and pricing.

Marketing: Is involved in numerous aspects of the development, pricing, distribution, and promotion of insurance products.

Customer Service: Provides assistance to the company's policyowners, agents, brokers, other employees, and beneficiaries.

Claim Administration: Assesses and handles claims presented by policyowners or beneficiaries.

Investments: Manages the company's investments according to the guidelines established by the company's management.

Accounting: Summarizes the financial affairs of each of the company's businesses and files required financial statements with appropriate regulatory bodies.

Legal: Represents the company in all legal matters and drafts the policies and other contracts that insurers use in the course of business.

Compliance: Ensures that the company's operations comply with federal, state, and provincial general business laws and with insurance department regulations.

Human Resources: Manages matters relating to the company's employees.

Information Systems: Develops and maintains the company's computer systems and oversees information management throughout the company.

---

functional areas. For example, employees who establish underwriting guidelines and risk selection classifications cannot do their work without statistical information from the actuarial staff. Actuaries need investment and economic assumptions from the investment area in order to develop premium rates and manage the cash flow of existing business. Investment officers need technological support from the information systems staff so they can best analyze the company's investment portfolios. And onward the connections go. Insurers that have a high level of coordination among functional areas will be in the best position to operate smoothly, to provide customers with outstanding products and services, and to prosper long into the future.

Risk Management in Life Insurance Companies

In providing insurance protection to the public, life insurance companies are exposed to many types of risk—such as product design and

pricing risk, underwriting risk, credit risk, market risk, operational risk, liquidity risk, legal and regulatory risk, and strategic risk. Figure 1-4 provides a description of each of these risks. To operate productively and to avoid undue financial losses, insurers must manage these risks. ***Risk management*** is the practice of identifying risk, assessing risk, and dealing with risk. Failure to identify and effectively manage risks hinders an insurer's chance of success, and severe mismanagement can even put the company out of business.

Managing the risks a company faces is at the heart of insurance company operations. Figure 1-5 lists examples of each of these types of risks that affect an insurer's operations, the potential consequences of these risks, and steps an insurer can take to manage each risk. Keep in mind that this list represents only a small sample of the risks in the insurance business. In subsequent chapters of this book, we discuss additional risks that challenge the operation of an insurance company and the techniques insurers use to manage those risks.

FIGURE 1-4. Types of Risks Faced by Insurers.

Product Design and Pricing Risk—The risk that the insurer's actual experience with mortality or expenses will differ significantly from expectations during product design, causing the insurer to lose money on its products

Underwriting Risk—The risk that the insurer will approve an inappropriate amount of coverage for an applicant or approve coverage for unacceptable applicants

Credit Risk—The risk that a debtor of the insurer will be unable or unwilling to fully meet a financial obligation

Market Risk—The risk that changes in market interest rates, securities prices, or foreign currency exchange rates will result in financial losses for the insurer

Operational Risk—The risk that the insurer will experience problems in the performance of business functions or processes, such as internal control breakdowns, technology failures, and human errors

Liquidity Risk—The risk that the insurer will be unable to obtain necessary funds to meet its financial obligations on time without incurring unacceptable losses

Legal and Regulatory Risk—The risk that the insurer will suffer financial losses as a result of noncompliance with laws, rules, regulations, and ethical standards

Strategic Risk—The risk that the insurer will not implement appropriate business plans and strategies needed to adapt to changes in its business environment

Source: OSFI, *Supervisory Framework: 1999 and Beyond* (Ottawa: Office of the Superintendent of Financial Institutions, 1999), 15–16.

FIGURE 1-5. Risks to an Insurer's Operations and Risk Management Techniques.

Insurance Operation	Risk	Consequence	Risk Management Technique
Analyzing markets	Market risk—Failure to properly identify consumer needs	Company markets products that do not appeal to consumers	Conduct comprehensive marketing research; carefully study demographic trends in market segments
Product development	Product pricing risk—New product is priced too low	Company has inadequate funds to pay claims under the product	Use mathematical models to test the adequacy of numerous pricing assumptions and develop an appropriate pricing scale
Distributing products	Operational risk—Slow policy delivery system	Customers are frustrated by excessive wait to obtain products applied for	Require agents to attend periodic field underwriting seminars; require home office adherence to policy issue timeliness guidelines
Underwriting applications	Underwriting risk—Overly conservative underwriting guidelines	Insurer accepts only proposed insureds that pose extremely low risk and, consequently, loses business to competitors	Develop underwriting guidelines to accept proposed insureds of varying risk; charge premium rates based on the amount of risk each proposed insured presents
Providing customer service	Operational risk—Long turnaround times on customer service requests	Customers leave company because of frustration over customer service delays	Upgrade technological capabilities so that customer service representatives are able to quickly fulfill customer requests
Administering claims	Operational risk—Inadequate claim fraud detection system	Insurers mistakenly pay fraudulent claims, leading to a rise in the insurer's operating costs and an increase in insurance prices	Train claim analysts to identify potential claim fraud; adequately investigate claim cases in which fraud is possible
Managing finances	Liquidity risk—Rising market interest rates	Insurer's bond investments lose value, policyowner withdrawals rise, and insurer may be forced to sell bonds at a loss to meet demand for cash	Manage assets and liabilities effectively; design insurance products with features that minimize policyowners' demand for withdrawals
Managing investments	Credit risk—Defaults on low-quality bonds owned by the insurer	Insurer loses anticipated bond interest income	Evaluate potential investments carefully; invest a large percentage of company funds in high-quality investments
Accounting and financial reporting	Legal and regulatory risk—Accounting transactions not recorded according to accounting standards	The company's financial statements are incorrect and misleading	Communicate the policies and procedures for recording financial transactions; train employees in these procedures
Ensuring compliance	Legal and regulatory risk—Agents' use of advertising and promotional material that do not comply with state laws	The company could be subject to fines and regulatory sanctions	Require that the home office approve all sales materials before agents can use them
Managing information	Operational risk—Unsecure internal computer network	Unauthorized people can access the company's network and vital company information and records	Install computer firewalls and other security measures to restrict access to the company's computer network
Strategic decision-making	Strategic risk—Failure of a corporate merger to produce desired returns	The value of the company will decline, and the value of owners' interest in the company declines	Perform careful and extensive evaluation and investigation of the target company, its financial condition, and its potential risks before entering into a merger agreement

© 1998 Tim Peckham. Used with permission.

Ethical Decision Making

In the 1980s and 1990s, the public's trust in life insurance companies faded because of some widely publicized unethical and illegal actions—policy illustrations that misled customers, prominent life insurance companies that became insolvent, "vanishing" premiums that did not vanish when agents said they would, and acts of questionable behavior. Although the companies that committed these intentional and unintentional misdeeds were the exception rather than the norm, the image of the entire industry was affected. Life insurance companies have worked hard to restore and maintain the public's trust and confidence by actively training employees and sales agents in the highest standards of ethical business conduct and decision making and by promoting and demonstrating cases where these standards are upheld.

In this text, we define *ethics* as a system of accepted standards of conduct and moral judgment that combines the elements of honesty, integrity, and fair treatment. Making ethical business decisions involves behaving in accordance with accepted legal and moral principles of right and wrong. Acting ethically means, among other things, upholding promises to customers, operating in a responsible manner, treating customers equitably, doing high-quality work in a timely

fashion, and keeping confidential information private. Virtually every move an insurer makes has ethical implications. Focus on Technology 1-1 discusses the ethical issues that life insurance companies face with respect to online collection of information about their customers.[4]

Life Insurance Companies and the Fiduciary Relationship

When a company operates ethically, the company gains the trust of its constituents—the employees, owners, customers, vendors, competitors,

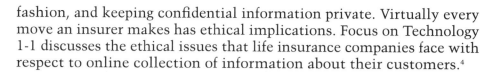

Focus on Technology 1-1.   **Peeking Through the Electronic Keyhole.**

Invasion-of-privacy concerns are accelerating as the insurance industry increasingly uses computers and Internet tracking to collect data on policyholders and prospective clients. For every technological advance, there can be an invasion-of-privacy concern.

Legislatures and courts have wrestled with defining "invasion of privacy." In determining whether an intrusion is highly offensive, the test is the degree of intrusion, as well as the intruder's motives and objectives, the setting in which the intrusion occurs, and the person's expectation of privacy in that setting. To prove an actual intrusion, there must be an unwarranted access to data that a person had reason to expect would remain private.

Internet technology allows easier collection, storage, transmission, and reuse of personal information than ever anticipated. Insurers have taken to the World Wide Web, posting home pages and beginning data collection efforts. Insurers may use an online questionnaire or a

registration form on its Internet site to collect and collate information. The user is generally not told how that information will be used or if it will be resold. "Cookies," which send information to a user's Web browser and store it in their computer hard drive, track visited sites. That information can be used to profile users anonymously.

The potential for invasion of privacy arises because of the conflict between the user's right to privacy and the money made by reselling the data to third parties. Further clouding the issue is the ease with which computer hackers can penetrate company databases that contain personal information.

The insurance industry, which is on the forefront of electronic collection of information, needs to consider the potential exposure for invasion-of-privacy claims from consumers who did not agree to allow collection or resale of their personal information.

Assume an insurance company collects information based on

"cookies" sent to a user's computer. The user does not realize that the cookies and click-stream information are transmitting data about him. This information is collected, sorted, and sold to a third party without the consumer's knowledge. What if, during the transfer process, information containing false, derogatory statements is erroneously recorded, resulting in the denial of a contract, financing, credit, or life insurance? Is there a potential invasion of privacy claim or similar tort?

Previously, personal information was gathered at great expense, or not at all. Now it is routinely collected, analyzed, packaged, and distributed instantly and at trivial cost. Secrets now fly around the globe at the speed of light, preserved indefinitely for recall from computer memories. These changes make it more essential to preserve privacy.

It is better to be proactive and address the potential invasion-of-privacy claims related to data collection than to defend the policy in court. •

Source: Excerpted from Peter A. Lynch, "Peeking Through the Electronic Keyhole," *Best's Review,* Life/Health ed. (August 1999): 72–74. © A.M. Best Company. Used with permission.

and other parties in the company's business environment. A company that operates unethically destroys trust, and, as a result, hinders commerce; without trust, people and organizations become wary of being deceived by other parties and may avoid engaging in business with them.

While trust is important in all industries, the nature of the life insurance industry makes trust vital. When a person buys a policy from a life insurance company, the person exchanges premium payments for the insurer's contractual promise to pay benefits if a covered loss occurs. By entering into an insurance contract with a policyowner, an insurance company becomes a *fiduciary*, which is an entity or individual that holds a special position of trust or confidence when handling the business affairs of another and that must put the other's interests above its own. A life insurance company acts as a fiduciary because policyowners entrust the insurer with specific amounts of money that the insurer manages for the benefit of the policyowners. Policyowners expect the insurer to safeguard this money and to pay promised benefits.

Before a person will buy a life insurance policy from an insurer, the person must trust that

- The insurer will remain financially healthy and stay in business long into the future

- The life insurance policy, a relatively complex legal contract, contains no hidden or inadequately explained provisions

- The sales agent's statements and illustrations of the policy are clear and accurate

- The actions of the sales agent and the insurance company are fair and honorable, and are taken in the best interests of the policyowner[5]

Because of the nature of the fiduciary relationship, life insurance companies and the people who work for them have a responsibility to act ethically and to make correct ethical decisions. To do otherwise would violate the covenant of the fiduciary relationship and could cause harm to a policyowner or a beneficiary.

For example, in Best Case Scenario 1-1 you met Tom and Maria Carpenter. By purchasing life insurance, the Carpenters feel comforted in the knowledge that, if one of them should die suddenly, the Best Friend policies will provide financial security for the surviving spouse and child. If Tom dies and Maria files a claim for the policy proceeds, she trusts that Best Friend will fulfill its obligations to her.

What would be the financial consequences to Maria and Christina if a claim administrator at Best Friend could decide arbitrarily to deny this claim? What if Best Friend had carelessly invested premium payments in high-risk ventures that failed, and now the company cannot pay its contractual obligations? What if during the course of the sales process, Louise Chen had not provided the Carpenters with all the information they needed to make a purchase decision that was in their best interests, and Maria now learns that this policy does not provide the benefits she thought it did? Each of these examples of unethical behavior could be devastating to Maria and her child.

Ethical Dilemmas

An insurance company expects its employees to behave both legally and ethically—to act in accordance with accepted legal *and* moral principles of right and wrong. In many situations, the difference between right behavior and wrong behavior is obvious. But employees of life insurers often face complex business situations where the best ethical resolution—the right decision—is not so clear. An **ethical dilemma** is a situation in which a person is uncertain about the best ethical decision. This uncertainty arises because there are good reasons to take a particular action but also good reasons not to take it.

Consider the following scenario: An insurance agent helps a married couple finalize a financial plan for their future. The next day, the husband calls the agent to make changes to the financial arrangement. The man says he has a mistress that his wife is unaware of, and he wants provisions made for the mistress in the event of his death. He tells the agent that his wife does not pay close attention to the family's financial details, and she need not know about this change in the financial plan. What is the agent to do? Both the husband and wife are his clients. How can the agent handle their conflicting interests?[6]

Generally, ethical dilemmas are complex problems that contain more than one possible solution. Insight 1-1 suggests strategies for resolving ethical dilemmas.

Improving Ethics in the Life Insurance Industry

Life insurance companies can take several measures to improve their own ethical conduct and thus to enhance ethics within the industry. These measures range from establishing codes of conduct and corporate ethics offices to offering ethics training for industry employees. Insurers can also encourage consumer education and endorse published industry standards.

Insight 1-1. **Strategies for Resolving Ethical Dilemmas.**

Ethical dilemmas require sophisticated and thorough analysis. The world has become so complex, with so many interrelationships, that it is not simple to decide who owes what to whom. Ethical theories can suggest some decision-making procedures. What follows is an attempt to blend the best features of these procedures in deciding how to resolve an ethical dilemma.

1. *Learn as many of the facts as possible.*

2. *Determine who has a stake in the activity and who is affected by it.* Most times when we judge the worth of an activity, we limit our considerations to how it will hurt or help us. Since ethics concerns being fair to others, getting beyond self-centered considerations is important.

3. *Examine existing options and/ or determine new options.* Rushworth Kidder, a noted ethics consultant, points out that two options for action are not enough in problematic situations. A dilemma is a situation in which only two courses of action *appear* to be possible, and there are reasons for and against either course. Since reasons exist not to follow either course, you are said to be "caught on the horns" of a dilemma. The trick is to find your way through the horns by finding a third option and resolving the dilemma.

4. *Evaluate the options.* This is the heart of the ethical enterprise, for the primary task for ethics is the analysis and evaluation of human actions, past or future. But how

does one evaluate actions? First, judge whether the action is good (i.e., beneficial). Second, determine whether the action is fair (i.e., just). Third, ask whether one has a responsibility to perform the action because of a previous commitment or promise. Finally, determine whether the options are legal.

Applying these questions to any proposed action will help evaluate that action. If an action is beneficial, fair, consistent with commitments, and legal, then we have every reason to perform it. If it is harmful, unfair, requires us to break our word, or violates laws, we have every reason to avoid the action. ●

Source: Adapted from Ronald F. Duska, "Insurance Ethics: The Right Training at the Right Time." Adapted, with permission, from the *Journal of the American Society of CLU & ChFC*, Vol. LII, No. 4 (July 1998): 26, 28. Copyright 1998 by the *Journal of the American Society of CLU & ChFC*, 270 Bryn Mawr Avenue, Bryn Mawr, PA 19010. Distribution prohibited without publisher's written permission. For copies of this article in its entirety, contact Norine Pigliucci at 610-526-2524.

Establishing Codes of Ethics

A starting point for improving corporate ethics is for life insurance companies to formulate ethical codes that set guidelines for appropriate values and standards of ethical business behavior. These codes state broad ethical standards and guidelines. A life insurance company should regularly review its ethical guidelines to ensure that they continue to cover all business interactions and comply with all applicable laws.

Codes of ethics can help employees evaluate the appropriateness of various responses to a given situation. The codes of ethics of many life insurance companies include examples of ethical dilemmas that may be encountered in the course of the company's work. Each example is followed by explanations of what the company believes would be the proper response to the dilemma.

Insight 1-2 examines ethical codes for insurance companies that expand internationally. This information is important because insurers are more willing and able than ever before to expand their operations into other countries.

Insight 1-2. Insurers Need Global Policy for Ethics.

U.S. insurers, eager to develop global growth strategies, need to develop universal ethics standards and understand the costs of following "best ethical practices" when trying to grow business in cultures with different customs and standards.

The task is not easy. The ethics landscape can be uneven and complex. Acceptable business practice in one culture may not be acceptable in another. Employees may face dilemmas in which a code of conduct is not consistent with the normal business practices of a culture, or a custom is not consistent with the code.

The potential cost of unethical behavior, or even the appearance of unethical behavior, is high— damaged corporate reputation, legal liabilities, reduced profitability, workforce demoralization, and perpetuation of corruption and economic decline in the host country.

Corporate ethics—implicit or explicit codes of conduct—are the values that define corporate reputation and relations with employees, customers, suppliers, competitors, and host governments. A formal ethics policy clarifies the gray areas as much as possible and prescribes appropriate and inappropriate business practice.

Respect for human dignity and life, freedom from pain, integrity, honor, compassion, and generosity are all common values. Are they enough for a global company to standardize ethics for worldwide operations? If not, how does the company deal with the potential ethical inconsistencies across different cultures?

In the process of gathering "cultural intelligence," senior management must seek to (1) adopt a code of ethics that deals in a straightforward manner with a country's cultural practices or conventions and (2) implement and maintain the code through employee education and training.

Honesty is the best policy. True global business champions are not only leaders in market share, revenue, technology, and influence but also in ethical conduct. Such companies set ethics standards without creating cultural conflict. They define and continuously reexamine ethics rules to improve conduct and ensure consistency. They do not turn a blind eye to bribery or corruption in areas where it is common.

Insurers pursuing global growth strategies must not only understand differing laws and regulations, but also recognize the implications of the laws for their dealing with unethical government officials who seek payments to advance company business administration, customers who might not pay their bills, client companies that go bankrupt, weak banks and capital markets, and employees who misrepresent the value of their products. •

Source: Excerpted from Alexandra Zakak and Steve Douvas, "Insurers Need Global Policy for Ethics," *The Journal of Commerce Online*, 19 March 1999, http://www.joc.com/issues/990319/iInsur/e28865.htm (11 May 1999). Used with permission.

Professional societies and government regulators also identify standards of conduct for members of certain professional groups. For example, the National Association of Insurance Commissioners (NAIC), a nongovernmental organization composed of insurance regulators from all U.S. states, has developed a series of model laws that incorporate a number of practices considered ethical in the insurance and financial services industry.

Establishing Corporate Ethics Offices

Another way a life insurance company can help make ethics an integral part of company operations is to establish a corporate ethics office. A *corporate ethics office* is a department or unit in which employees

can (1) receive advice or counsel to help resolve ethical dilemmas and (2) report ethical misconduct. An employee who seeks advice about an ethical matter sometimes wishes to remain anonymous. For example, an employee facing a complicated ethical dilemma may not want to ask a supervisor for assistance for fear of being perceived as a poor decision maker. A corporate ethics office can provide the desired anonymity. Also, an ethics office is an outlet for an employee who witnesses misconduct but either is afraid to report the incident or believes that no action will occur if the incident is reported to a supervisor.

Providing Employee Training in Ethics

Ethical performance needs to be trained, managed, and evaluated. Training employees to make proper ethical decisions is as important an aspect of employee development as is the technical training involved in an employee's job function. In training sessions, students are placed in ethical dilemmas and coached on how best to resolve them. Opportunities for ethics training in the life insurance industry include the following:

- Including ethics training in company conventions, agents' and agency managers' meetings, company training conferences, and continuing education programs.

- Requiring at least one face-to-face ethics discussion each year between agency managers and sales agents. This discussion could include a review of the company's guidelines for ethical conduct.

- Integrating ethics programs into meetings of industry organizations, such as LOMA, LIMRA International, American Society of Financial Services Professionals, LUTC (Life Underwriters Training Council), Society of Actuaries, Canadian Institute of Actuaries, ICA (International Claim Association), CLHIA (Canadian Life and Health Insurance Association), ACLI (American Council of Life Insurance), NALU (National Association of Life Underwriters), and others.

Offering Consumer Education

Well-informed consumers are prepared to recognize and confront unethical behavior that occurs during product marketing or administration. To enhance consumers' knowledge, the life insurance industries of the United States and Canada have taken steps to educate consumers about life insurance products. The goal of consumer education is to improve consumers'

- Understanding of the basic features of insurance policies

- Ability to select the most appropriate plan of insurance to meet their needs

- Ability to evaluate similar plans of insurance

In addition, laws in most U.S. states require insurers to give prospective customers a Buyer's Guide and a policy summary. The Buyer's Guide includes general information on life insurance, whereas the policy summary contains information about the specific policy being sold. In Canada, consumers are furnished with booklets such as "A Guide to Buying Life Insurance" and "Retirement: As You'd Like It."

Insurance Marketplace Standards Association (IMSA)

Efforts by the U.S. life insurance industry to improve its image and to maintain high ethical standards have resulted in the ***Insurance Marketplace Standards Association (IMSA)***, an organization established by the American Council of Life Insurance (ACLI) in 1997 to implement a voluntary market conduct compliance program for the life insurance industry. IMSA is built on an integrated set of ethical principles, a code of ethics, and a program of self-assessment and independent assessment. IMSA's goal is to help insurers improve their market conduct practices and strengthen consumer confidence in the life insurance industry. To qualify for IMSA membership, a life insurer must first adopt the ACLI's Six Principles of Ethical Market Conduct (shown in Figure 1-6), which are designed to assist insurers in developing strategies for market conduct compliance programs.

FIGURE 1-6. ACLI's Six Principles of Ethical Market Conduct.

An insurance company that adopts the Six Principles commits itself to

1. Conduct business according to high standards of honesty and fairness and to render service to its customers which, in the same circumstances, it would apply to or demand for itself

2. Provide competent and customer-focused sales and service

3. Engage in active and fair competition

4. Provide advertising and sales materials that are clear as to purpose and honest and fair as to content

5. Provide for fair and expeditious handling of customer complaints and disputes

6. Maintain a system of supervision and review that is reasonably designed to achieve compliance with these Principles of Ethical Market Conduct

After adopting the Six Principles, the insurer undergoes a two-step assessment program. In the first step, the insurer conducts a self-assessment using the IMSA *Assessment Questionnaire and Assessment Handbook.* To satisfactorily complete this step, an insurer must respond affirmatively to 27 questions dealing with procedures and processes the company has in place to ensure that all aspects of its operations are conducted ethically. In the second step of the assessment process, the insurer engages an independent, IMSA-approved assessor to review the insurer's self-assessment report. The assessor also performs an independent assessment to determine whether the insurer had a reasonable basis for its responses in the questionnaire.

Any life insurance company that satisfactorily completes the two steps in the assessment program qualifies for a three-year membership in IMSA. To maintain its membership, an insurer must undergo the two-step assessment process every three years.

Key Terms

life insurance company
market-driven organization
risk
financial institution
financial intermediary
risk management

ethics
fiduciary
ethical dilemma
corporate ethics office
Insurance Marketplace
    Standards Association (IMSA)

Endnotes

1. ACLI, *1999 Life Insurance Fact Book* (Washington, D.C.: American Council of Life Insurance, 1999), 1; CLHIA, *Canadian Life and Health Insurance Facts,* 1999 ed. (Toronto: Canadian Life and Health Insurance Association, 1999), 3.

2. "U.S. Life/Health Earnings Declined in 1998," *BestWeek—Life/Health Statistical Study* (April 12, 1999): 1; ACLI, 158.

3. ACLI, 81; CLHIA, 3.

4. Technology—from the increasing power and speed of computers to the expanding usefulness of the Internet—has a significant effect on the operations of life insurance companies. In chapters throughout this book, we have included Focus on Technology insights that relate technology issues to the chapter subject matter.

5. Harold D. Skipper, Jr., "Market Conduct Issues and the Transformation of the U.S. Life Insurance Business," *Journal of the American Society of CLU & ChFC* (March 1995): 37.

6. Example adapted from Ronald F. Duska, "Ethics in Estate Planning," *Journal of Financial Services Professionals* (January 1999): 22.

Insurance Regulation and the Financial Services Industry

Life insurance companies are subject to extensive regulation designed to protect insurance consumers, who are considered to be the less-informed party in the contractual arrangements between insurers and consumers. In this chapter, we will briefly discuss the regulatory systems that govern the operations of life insurers in the United States and Canada. We provide this information early in this textbook so that you will understand the legal foundation of life insurance industry operations.

Besides being members of the life insurance industry, life insurers are also important members of the larger *financial services industry*—the industry comprised of financial institutions that help consumers and business organizations save, borrow, invest, and otherwise manage money. The financial services industry has undergone substantial change in recent years. This chapter also provides an overview of the current financial services industry and shows you the typical life insurance company's place in it.

We begin by describing the regulation of life insurance companies in the United States and Canada. Then we look at other businesses that compete with insurers for the sale of life insurance products. Finally, we examine recent changes to and the possible future direction of the U.S. and Canadian financial services industries.

Regulation of Life Insurance

From the moment a life insurance company is formed, almost every phase of its operation is subject to regulatory supervision. The functions that the life insurance industry performs—providing consumers with protection against financial loss and offering consumers opportunities to accumulate wealth—have placed the industry in a special position of public trust. In both the United States and Canada, governmental authorities regulate insurance companies to ensure that they uphold that trust.

Insurance laws can be classified into two broad categories: solvency laws and market conduct laws.

- In general terms, *solvency* is the ability of an insurer to pay its debts, policy benefits, and operating expenses when they come due. *Solvency laws* are designed to ensure that insurance companies are financially able to meet their debts and pay policy benefits on time. Solvency laws regulate an insurer's capitalization, policy design, and policy reserves.

- *Market conduct* is all of the actions taken in the performance of an organization's business operations. *Market conduct laws* are designed to ensure that life insurance companies conduct their businesses fairly and ethically. These laws govern insurance company management, marketing, advertising, underwriting, policyowner service, complaint handling, and claim administration.

Regulation of Insurance Companies in the United States

Life insurance regulation in the United States is principally concerned with the financial soundness and the business practices of insurance companies. Individual state governments are the primary regulators of insurance. However, insurers are also subject to a number of federal laws and so must adhere to certain federal regulation.

State Regulation

Each state has established a system of law to regulate the insurance business within that state's borders. Each state has its own insurance department that is directed by an *insurance commissioner* or a *superintendent of insurance.* State insurance departments have the primary legal authority to oversee the solvency and market conduct of insurance companies operating within their jurisdictions. Among its responsibilities, a state insurance department

- Licenses insurance companies to conduct business in the state

- Licenses agents to sell insurance in the state

- Reviews the Annual Statements of insurance companies conducting business in the state. The *Annual Statement* is a document that reports information about the insurer's operations and financial performance. Insurers operating in a state must file an Annual Statement with the state insurance department and with the National Association of Insurance Commissioners (discussed below). Many states require an insurer to file an abbreviated form of the Annual Statement every three months. Insight 2-1 illustrates how insurance regulators use the Annual Statement to monitor the financial condition of insurance companies.

- Reviews policy forms to ensure that they include the required provisions and are printed according to specific standards. A

Insight 2-1. **Using the Annual Statement to Monitor Insurer Solvency.**

Red flags went up immediately at the Oregon state insurance department as the financial analyst examined one insurer's Annual Statement. Some of the assets reported weren't admissible under insurance accounting rules. The company's surplus was overstated. It was losing money.

The analyst reported the discrepancies to her supervisor, and within two days, examiners from the Oregon Insurance Division were on the scene conducting an investigation of the company.

The case is a good example of the team approach utilized by the Insurance Division's Company Regulation Section. It also illustrates the importance of moving quickly when solvency questions arise.

Financial analysts review all quarterly and Annual Statements filed by the Oregon domestic insurance companies. They perform a detailed review of the balance sheet, income statement, analysis of surplus, and all support schedules included in statements filed on behalf of each domestic insurer. They also make sure each company complies with Oregon insurance law.

The staff does a comprehensive examination of each domestic insurer every three years and does an extensive review of the source documents that were used to create their financial statements. •

Source: Excerpted and adapted from "Experienced Staff and Team Approach Key to Successful Company Regulation," *Oregon Insurance Regulator* (Winter 1999): 2. Used with permission.

policy form is a standardized form, drafted by an insurer and filed with insurance regulators, that shows the terms, conditions, benefits, and ownership rights of a particular insurance product.

- Makes periodic, on-site investigations of insurance companies to examine their financial condition and market conduct practices

- Maintains an office for receiving and acting on consumer complaints

- Ensures that insurance companies observe state rules affecting policy reserve maintenance and investment activities

- Influences the prevailing tax environment for insurance companies located in that state

Federal Regulation

Although a state insurance commissioner is the primary regulator of insurance companies operating in each state, insurers must comply with a variety of federal regulatory requirements. For example, federal laws that regulate the sale of securities also apply to variable life insurance. Other aspects of insurers' operations that are affected by federal laws include interstate advertising, employment practices, welfare benefit plans provided for company employees, and the care and handling of personal information about customers.

The National Association of Insurance Commissioners (NAIC)

The **National Association of Insurance Commissioners (NAIC)** is a nongovernmental organization composed of insurance commissioners or superintendents from every state. The NAIC fosters uniformity in state regulation and cooperation among state insurance departments by developing **model laws**, also called *model bills*, which are pieces of sample legislation on which states may base their own insurance laws and regulations. Although the NAIC has no regulatory authority, the recommendations of the NAIC and the actions taken at its meetings carry great weight with state insurance commissioners, state legislatures, and the insurance industry.

A recent challenge for the NAIC has been to develop model laws to help state insurance regulators deal with several issues related to the distribution of life insurance via the Internet. For more on this topic, see Focus on Technology 2-1.

 Focus on Technology 2-1.   **Old Regulations, New Issues.**

The Internet is moving commerce ahead at almost light-speed, but the ability of insurance regulators to match that pace continues to present challenges.

In 1997, the National Association of Insurance Commissioners (NAIC) was in the process of trying to define the regulatory issues related to the Internet. The time since then has been spent trying to figure out which regulations apply to the Internet and which do not. With the publication of the NAIC's white paper, "The Marketing of Insurance Over the Internet," the issues have been solidly defined in order to allow states to amend laws that may impede electronic commerce (e-commerce) in insurance.* Standardization of state laws—in electronic concepts, document issues, and licensing procedures—ultimately will pave the way for the growth of e-commerce. "Our goal," says Robert Large, co-chairman of the NAIC's electronic commerce working group, "is to harmonize laws across states and across electronic and paper processes."

In order to achieve this goal, says Large, "the NAIC will issue a self-assessment framework to states, allowing them to see why it is important to change their laws and how certain regulations impede industry growth."

Statutes that states are asked to evaluate include those impacting the use of credit cards to pay for insurance premiums; "wet" (pen-and-ink) signature requirements, as opposed to electronic signatures; body fluid sample requirements for the issuance of life insurance; co-signature requirements; advertising and disclosure regulations; fraud; and consumer privacy.

The goal of being able to complete the entire insurance sales process online would be unattainable without legislation permitting electronic signatures. An electronic signature is a series of encrypted key strokes known only to the user, and is just as binding as a wet signature. About half the states have enacted or initiated bills related to electronic signatures. State legislatures have been careful to author bills based on existing legislation with the goal being to establish something closer to a national standard on electronic signatures. •

* An NAIC *white paper* is a publication that explains an aspect of insurance regulation.

Source: Excerpted and adapted from Johannah Rodgers, "Old Regulations, New Issues," *Insurance & Technology* (June 1999): 23–24. Used with permission.

Regulation of Insurance Companies in Canada

As in the United States, life insurance regulation in Canada is primarily concerned with (1) the safety, soundness, and solvency of insurers (known in Canada as *prudential regulation*), and (2) the fair and ethical conduct of business (known as *marketplace regulation*). Canada also has a third component of regulation—*self regulation*—which is a body of insurance industry standards and guidelines that complements federal and provincial regulation. Generally, a life insurance company doing business in Canada must

- Obtain from the appropriate regulatory agency an authorization to carry on business and a license to sell insurance

- File an **Annual Return**, which is a report of each insurer's operations and financial performance, similar to the U.S. Annual Statement

- Submit to on-site examination by insurance regulators

Whereas in the United States most solvency and market conduct regulation are handled by state governments, in Canada the federal government and the provincial governments jointly manage life insurance regulation.

Federal Regulation

The federal **Insurance Companies Act**, which took effect in 1992, sets forth federal insurance laws and the regulatory system for federally regulated life insurance companies. Federally regulated insurance companies, which include (1) all Canadian insurers incorporated by the federal government and (2) the Canadian branches of all insurers incorporated in other countries, must comply with the provisions of the Act.[1] Administration of the Act is ultimately the responsibility of the Minister of Finance, who is the head of the Department of Finance Canada, the federal agency that provides the federal government with analysis and advice on the broad economic and financial affairs of Canada. However, the **Office of the Superintendent of Financial Institutions (OSFI)**, headed by the *Superintendent of Financial Institutions* (a civil servant who reports to the Minister of Finance), is the primary regulator of insurance companies, as well as of banks, trust companies, loan companies, *caisses populaires* (similar to U.S. credit unions), and pension plans. OSFI's primary focus is on the solvency of these federally incorporated financial institutions.

With respect to federally regulated life insurers and other financial institutions, OSFI serves two broad functions—regulation and

supervision. Regulation involves providing input into developing and interpreting legislation and regulations, issuing guidelines, and approving requests from insurers. Supervision involves periodically examining federally regulated insurers to assess their safety and soundness and taking corrective action against life insurance companies whose ability to satisfy their policy obligations is threatened. In 1999, OSFI began revising the way it supervises and determines the financial soundness of federally regulated financial institutions, including life insurers. As Insight 2-2 explains, the new supervisory framework emphasizes evaluating the quality of each insurer's risk management practices based on the risks it faces.

Another role of OSFI is to encourage federally regulated life insurance companies to adopt sound business and financial practices. Insurers must abide by the *Standards of Sound Business and Financial Practices,* jointly developed in 1997 by several regulatory bodies, including OSFI and the Canadian Life and Health Insurance Association (CLHIA), an industry association of life and health insurers. The Standards set forth minimum guidelines in several categories such as capital management, credit risk management, securities portfolio

 Insight 2-2. **New Supervisory Framework for OSFI Focuses on Risk Management.**

In August of 1999, the Office of the Superintendent of Financial Institutions (OSFI) announced a change in the way it supervises financial institutions—including insurance companies—and determines the soundness of their financial condition. Under the new supervisory framework, OSFI focuses its efforts on evaluating each institution's material risks and the quality of its risk management practices. OSFI identifies areas of high risk and then investigates further to determine what steps the institution is taking to manage the risks. Previously, OSFI's supervisory approach was more general and focused on examining each functional area of a financial institution.

Key principles of the new framework include the following:

• The supervision of Canadian financial institutions is conducted on a consolidated basis, using information from other regulators as appropriate. Supervision includes an assessment of each institution's subsidiaries, branches, and joint ventures both in Canada and internationally.

• The exercise of sound judgment in identifying and evaluating risks in an institution is essential to the effectiveness of the new framework.

• The level and frequency of supervisory scrutiny depends on the risk assessment of the financial institution. Institutions that are well managed relative to their risks require less supervision.

• Supervision includes reviews of major risk management control functions, such as Financial Analy-

sis, Compliance, Internal Audit, Risk Management, Senior Management, and Board oversight.

• Communication of findings and recommendations to each institution must be timely.

The new supervisory framework helps OSFI address new challenges arising as a result of measures to increase competition in the Canadian financial services sector (see Insight 2-3 later in this chapter). According to John Palmer, Superintendent of Financial Institutions, measures to increase competition among financial services providers are beneficial to consumers and to the economy as a whole, but they may increase risk to the financial system. •

Source: OSFI, *Supervisory Framework: 1999 and Beyond* (Ottawa: Office of the Superintendent of Financial Institutions, 1999), 2–5.

management, product design and pricing, underwriting, and internal control. All insurers subject to the Standards must be able to demonstrate compliance with the minimum standards by performing a self-assessment test and filing a confidential annual report of their test results with federal or provincial regulators.[3]

Provincial Regulation

Each province and territory has enacted laws regulating insurance within that province. The insurance laws of a province are usually contained in that province's Insurance Act and are enforced by an administrator usually known as the *Superintendent of Insurance.*[4] All insurance companies incorporated under the insurance laws of a particular province are subject to prudential regulation and examination by the insurance department in that province, rather than by the federal government.[5] Provincial insurance laws also govern marketplace regulation of all federally incorporated *and* provincially incorporated insurers operating in that province. Such marketplace regulation addresses the conduct of companies and sales agents in their marketing, distribution, and administration of insurance products. Provincial regulators also license all insurers and all insurance agents doing business in the province.

Self Regulation

The life insurance industry in Canada has elements of self regulation. With respect to marketplace conduct, an insurer must abide by the code of ethics of the CLHIA as a condition of membership in the CLHIA. Figure 2-1 shows the CLHIA code of conduct. Member companies also abide by more than 50 CLHIA guidelines concerning many aspects of insurers' operations and marketplace conduct. Guidelines do not have the force of law, but insurers are expected to abide by them. In addition, provincial insurance departments may adopt any guideline as law.

The Canadian Council of Insurance Regulators

The *Canadian Council of Insurance Regulators (CCIR)* is a committee of provincial insurance regulators that is similar to the NAIC in the United States. The CCIR looks at emerging industry and business trends and works toward harmonizing legislation through model codes and standardized reporting requirements. The Council's efforts help make insurance regulations uniform in the common law provinces, which are those provinces with laws based on English common law. All Canadian provinces except Quebec are common law provinces. Quebec law is based on the French Civil Code rather than on English common law. Consequently, basic insurance laws in Quebec have differed from

---

FIGURE 2-1. CLHIA Code of Ethics for Member Companies.

All CLHIA members have committed themselves to conduct their business in accordance with the following principles:

• To engage in keen, fair competition so that the public can obtain the products and services it needs at reasonable prices

• To advertise products and services clearly and straightforwardly, and to avoid practices that might mislead or deceive

• To ensure that illustrations of prices, values, and benefits are clear and fair, and that they contain appropriate disclosure of amounts that are not guaranteed

• To write all contracts in clear, direct language without unreasonable restrictions

• To use underwriting techniques that are sound and fair

• To pay all claims fairly and promptly and without unreasonable requirements

• To ensure competent and courteous sales and service

• To respect the privacy of individuals by using personal information only for the purposes authorized and not revealing it to any unauthorized person

Source: CLHIA, *Canadian Life and Health Insurance Facts*, 1999 ed. (Toronto: Canadian Life and Health Insurance Association, 1999).

---

those in the rest of Canada, but, since 1977, the Quebec Insurance Act has brought Quebec insurance law closer to the insurance statutes of the other provinces.

The Financial Services Industry

The financial services industry is comprised of a number of types of financial intermediaries, which, as you learned in Chapter 1, move funds from entities that have excess money to entities that have a need for money. As shown in Figure 2-2, financial intermediaries traditionally have fallen into three general categories: depository institutions, contractual savings institutions, and other institutions.

• A ***depository institution*** is a financial intermediary that accepts deposits from individuals and businesses and makes loans. Depository institutions allow customers to maintain savings and checking accounts and obtain mortgage loans, business loans, and consumer loans. Examples of depository institutions are *commercial banks* and so-called *thrift institutions*—federal

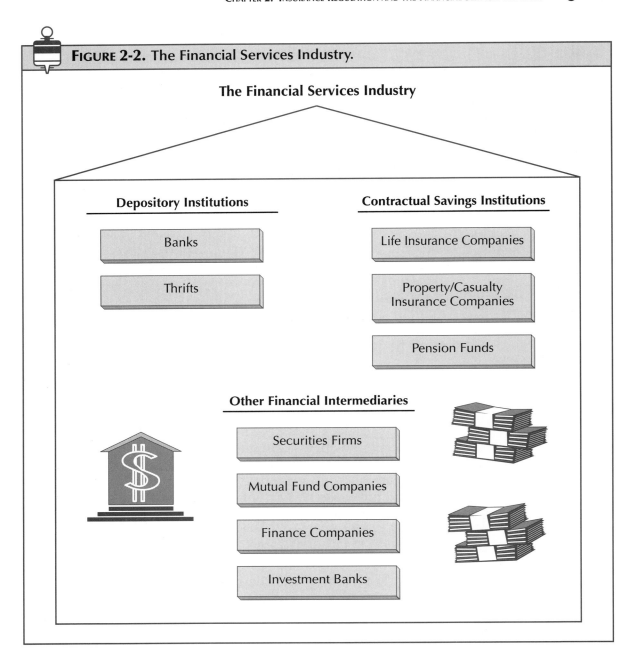

FIGURE 2-2. The Financial Services Industry.

savings banks (formerly called savings and loan associations), mutual savings banks, credit unions, and *caisses populaires.*

- A ***contractual savings institution*** is a financial intermediary that acquires funds at periodic intervals on a contractual basis. Contractual savings institutions help provide financial security to their customers. Examples of contractual savings institutions

are *life insurance companies, property/casualty insurance companies,* and *pension funds.*

- Other institutions serving as financial intermediaries include *finance companies,* which issue short-term debt securities and use the proceeds to make loans to business and consumers, and *mutual fund companies,* which pool the funds of many small investors and use the proceeds to buy stocks, bonds, and other financial instruments. Securities firms and investment banks, while not considered true financial intermediaries because they do not move funds from savers to borrowers, are also important players in the financial services industry. *Securities firms* consist of securities *brokers* (who link the buyers and sellers of securities), and securities *dealers* (who are principals in securities transactions and buy and sell from their own accounts). *Investment banks* assist corporations and governments with the initial sale of securities to the public.

Changes in the Financial Services Industry

Traditionally, the financial services industries in the United States and Canada have been distinctly segmented. Numerous laws and regulations have prevented affiliations between firms in different segments of the financial services industry and clearly defined the boundaries of each segment's business. Generally speaking, commercial banks and thrift institutions accepted deposits and made loans. Insurance companies sold insurance products and annuities. Securities firms facilitated the purchase and sale of stocks and bonds. Investment banks helped businesses and governments raise money through new issues of stocks and bonds.

In recent years, however, the various institutions have entered each other's traditional businesses, obscuring the distinctions among institutions and creating an intensely competitive and integrated financial services industry. (Figure 2-3 summarizes some of the new competitive opportunities among different financial institutions.) Several factors driving the changes in the industry include

- Removal of legal and regulatory barriers that prevented affiliations between different types of financial intermediaries. We will discuss new financial services laws in more detail later in this chapter.

- Improvements in technology that facilitate the development and delivery of new types of financial products

FIGURE 2-3. New Opportunities for Traditional Financial Institutions.

United States

- Insurance companies enter the banking arena by acquiring federal thrift institutions.

- Insurers and banks sell mutual funds, once the sole domain of mutual fund companies.

- Commercial banks, securities firms, and mutual fund companies sell life insurance and annuities.

- Mutual fund companies, banks, and securities firms compete with insurance companies for employer-sponsored pension plans and management of the public's retirement savings.

- Securities firms and mutual fund companies offer money market mutual funds in order to compete with commercial banks for consumer deposits. A *money market mutual fund* is a mutual fund that invests in short-term securities and that typically offers check-writing privileges.

- Insurance companies compete with banks for the management of *trusts,* which are fiduciary relationships in which one party (the *trustee*) holds legal title to property and manages that property for the benefit of another party (the *trust beneficiary*).

Canada

- Banks can own insurance companies, and, with limitations, insurance companies can own banks.

- Insurance companies compete with banks in lending money to businesses.

- With limitations, banks can sell insurance.

- Insurance companies compete directly with banks for *registered retirement savings plans (RRSPs),* which are tax-advantaged retirement accounts for individuals.

- Competitive pressures from foreign financial institutions. Specifically, a number of large European financial services firms have purchased U.S. insurers to gain entry into the U.S. market.

- Pressures to increase revenues and improve profitability

Other Providers of Life Insurance

As shown in Figure 2-3, financial institutions and organizations other than life insurance companies can sell life insurance products. These organizations include fraternal benefit societies, commercial banks, securities firms, and mutual fund companies. Like insurance companies, any of these organizations wishing to distribute insurance must obtain a license to conduct an insurance business in each state or

province in which they plan to sell policies. Also, people soliciting insurance on behalf of these organizations must obtain the appropriate state license to sell insurance.

The entry of other institutions into the life insurance industry has created many competitive challenges for life insurance companies, but it has also created new opportunities for insurers, as Best Case Scenario 2-1 illustrates. For example, many insurance companies have formed alliances with fraternal benefit societies, banks, securities firms, and mutual fund companies to distribute the insurers' products. Insurers have made a significant effort to provide training and other resources to the organizations willing to sell their products.

Fraternal Benefit Societies

Approximately 160 fraternal benefit societies operate in the United States and Canada. *Fraternal benefit societies* are organizations formed

Best Case Scenario 2-1. Expanding Distribution and Product Offerings in the New Financial Services Industry.

Two strategic goals for the Best Friend Life Insurance Company were to expand the distribution of its term life insurance product line and to increase its mix of products. To achieve the first goal, Best Friend entered into a joint venture with a bank. To achieve the second goal, Best Friend acquired an institutional money manager that sold mutual funds.

Best Friend Entered Joint Venture with a Bank
Mighty Bank was searching for ways to increase its sales revenue and to offer more products that could meet the needs of its customers. Executives from Best Friend and Mighty Bank entered into a mutually beneficial joint venture whereby Best Friend used Mighty Bank as a distribution channel; Best Friend provided Mighty Bank with term life insurance products that the bank could sell through its network of bank branches. Mighty Bank

received a commission on each policy sold, and Best Friend kept the profits generated by the policies.

To help improve the probability of the venture's success, Best Friend helped train Mighty Bank employees about insurance concepts and the specific features of the Best Friend policies sold through the bank. Best Friend also assisted the bank employees in meeting insurance licensing requirements. Proper training enabled Mighty Bank employees to become better insurance salespeople and also protected the brand names of Best Friend and Mighty Bank from being tarnished by improper insurance sales tactics.

Best Friend Purchased a Money Management Company
Executives at Best Friend decided that the company should offer investment products to its customers. This strategy would allow the insurer to cross-sell numerous financial products to customers, thereby

increasing sales and enhancing customers' loyalty to the company.

To achieve its goal, Best Friend purchased Davis & Co., a money management firm with its own line of mutual funds. Following the acquisition, Best Friend sold the Davis mutual funds through its own agency force. Best Friend agents were trained to sell mutual fund products and were required to pass licensing examinations in order to be eligible to sell the funds.

Purchasing Davis & Co. not only provided Best Friend with a quick entrance into the mutual fund business, but also paved the way for the insurer to expand its product mix in the future. For example, Best Friend could develop and sell a range of other investment-type products, such as variable life insurance, variable annuities, and 401(k) thrift and savings plans, and use the Davis funds as investment choices for each product. •

to provide social and insurance benefits to their members. In such societies, members often share a common religious, ethnic, or vocational background, although membership in some fraternals, including some of the largest, is open to the general public. Each fraternal is managed by a governing body elected by the members in accordance with the society's bylaws.

Fraternal societies operate through a lodge system whereby only lodge members are permitted to own the fraternal society's insurance. Some fraternal societies offer insurance to people who are not society members at the time of application, but the applicants automatically become members of the society once their policies are issued. In 1998, fraternal benefit societies in the United States and Canada received approximately $2.9 billion in premiums and annuity considerations.[7]

In the United States, the National Fraternal Congress of America, in conjunction with the NAIC, has developed a Uniform Fraternal Code that applies to the insurance operations of fraternal benefit societies. This code defines a fraternal benefit society and includes regulatory requirements for life insurance policies issued by fraternals. In Canada, fraternal insurers, like commercial insurance companies, may be registered (and therefore regulated) under federal law or provincial law. The majority of fraternal benefit societies in Canada are federally regulated.

Each fraternal society operating in the United States and Canada is required to file an annual valuation report issued by an actuary, who must certify that the fraternal's policy reserves are adequate. U.S. and Canadian fraternal societies are subject to the same laws regarding investments as are commercial insurers.

Commercial Banks

Bankinsurance is insurance coverage that is manufactured and underwritten by a commercial bank's own insurance company and distributed through the bank's distribution channels. Changes to U.S. laws in 1999 (discussed later in this section) permit bankinsurance in the United States, while banks in Canada can engage in a more limited form of bankinsurance. We discuss the insurance-related activities of U.S. and Canadian banks in this section.

U.S. Banks. Until relatively recently, credit life insurance and savings bank life insurance were the only avenues for most banks into the sales of life insurance.

- *Credit life insurance* is a type of life insurance designed to pay a debt to a creditor if the debtor-insured dies. Banks throughout the United States have been allowed to manufacture and sell credit life insurance since the early 1900s.

- For many years, savings banks in Connecticut, Massachusetts, and New York were the only U.S. banks allowed to underwrite and sell life insurance other than credit life insurance. Employees in these banks sell *savings bank life insurance (SBLI)* policies over the counter in the bank branch to people who live or work in the state.

The source of a U.S. bank's authority to sell life insurance other than credit life insurance and savings bank life insurance depends on whether the bank is a state-chartered bank or a federally chartered bank. State-chartered banks, called *state banks*, are regulated by state banking authorities. Federally chartered banks are called *national banks*. The federal Office of the Comptroller of the Currency (OCC), an agency of the U.S. Treasury Department, charters, regulates, and supervises national banks. National banks and state banks in most states have the authority to sell many forms of insurance, such as term life insurance, permanent life insurance, property/casualty insurance, dental insurance, vision care insurance, disability income insurance, long-term care insurance, and group health insurance. Banks sold $8.6 billion of insurance and $22.5 billion of annuities in 1998.[9]

Canadian Banks. All Canadian banks are federally incorporated and are regulated by the Office of the Superintendent of Financial Institutions. OSFI also regulates all non-Canadian banks doing business in Canada.

As in the United States, banks in Canada have long been allowed to sell credit life insurance through their branch offices. However, affiliations between banks and insurance companies were prohibited until the revisions of the federal Bank Act in 1992. Currently, banks are allowed to own insurance companies, and banks can operate in life insurance and property/casualty insurance through their own insurance subsidiaries that they create or purchase. However, the following restrictions limit Canadian banks' insurance activities:

- Banks are prohibited from selling most kinds of insurance through their branches.

- The use of bank customer data by insurance companies, including the banks' insurance affiliates, is strictly limited. A bank may not use customer data to target only selected customers; any insurance solicitations must be sent to *all* of a bank's customers.

Securities Firms and Mutual Fund Companies

Since the 1990s, securities firms (broker-dealers) and mutual fund companies have sold life insurance products with much success. These firms may offer both term life insurance and permanent life insurance, provided that their sales representatives are properly licensed.

Securities firms and mutual fund companies cannot create their own insurance products. Instead, they may own a life insurance company, or they may also enter into a distribution arrangement with one or more insurance companies. In either case, an insurer assumes the risk on the insurance coverage that the securities firm or mutual fund company sells. The insurance policies may be sold exclusively by the securities firm or the mutual fund company.

Securities firms and mutual fund companies usually offer life insurance through their retail branch offices and via their Internet sites. Insurance can be offered only in jurisdictions where the underwriting insurance company is authorized to conduct business and where the securities firm and mutual fund companies are licensed to sell insurance. In Canada, most insurance companies, securities firms, and mutual fund companies carry on business nationwide.

Reforming the U.S. Financial Services Industry

The U.S. financial services industry changed considerably with the passage of the *Financial Services Modernization Act (FSMA) of 1999.* This federal law advances integration of financial services providers by permitting banks, insurance companies, and broker-dealers to affiliate in a holding company structure. A **holding company** is a company that has a controlling interest in one or more other companies, known as **subsidiaries**. Generally, **controlling interest** of a company is ownership of more than 50 percent of the company's voting shares of stock.[10]

The FSMA allows the establishment of financial holding companies that can own many types of financial institutions. (A large holding company that controls many different types of subsidiary financial institutions is sometimes referred to as a *financial conglomerate.*) Financial holding companies are permitted to conduct activities that are financial in nature or incidental to financial activities, such as insurance activities, securities activities, merchant banking, real estate

development, and investment and financial advisory services. Insurance companies may establish or become part of financial holding companies, and insurers may acquire or establish banking affiliates.

Functional Regulation

The FSMA provides for the functional regulation of financial institutions. ***Functional regulation*** is the principle that similar financial activities should be regulated by a single regulator, regardless of which type of financial institution engages in the activity. Thus, the law preserves state regulation of insurance and clarifies that any entity engaged in the business of insurance must be licensed according to state insurance law. Similarly, all banking activities are regulated by bank regulators, and all securities activities are regulated by securities regulators. Overseeing this system of functional regulation is the responsibility of the Board of Governors of the Federal Reserve System. The Federal Reserve Board relies on functional regulators' examinations of financial institutions, but the Board is authorized to intervene if it believes the health of a bank affiliate is threatened.

Multistate Insurance Licensing

The FSMA prohibits a person or an entity from providing insurance in a state as principal or agent unless the person or entity is licensed as required by the insurance regulator of that state in accordance with state insurance law. In addition, states have three years from the date of enactment of FSMA (November 12, 1999) to enact agent licensing laws that are uniform from state to state. The state licensing laws also must allow agents to obtain a single license to transact business in numerous states rather than require them to obtain a separate license for each state.[11]

If the majority of states fail to harmonize agent licensing requirements within the three-year period, the FSMA calls for the creation of the National Association of Registered Agents and Brokers (NARAB). The NARAB would provide a clearinghouse through which uniform agent licensing, appointment, continuing education, and other sales qualification requirements and conditions would be adopted and applied on a consistent basis.

Bankinsurance Activities

A bank generally may sell insurance as an agent, but the bank cannot assume the risk on insurance policies. Such activities must be conducted by a financial holding company or by an insurance affiliate of the bank. A financial holding company can engage in all forms of insurance activities, including selling and assuming the risk on insurance policies for the holding company or its subsidiaries.

Consumer Privacy

Financial institutions must establish written procedures for protecting consumers' private information, and they must disclose these privacy policies to their customers each year. Customers cannot block a financial institution from sharing their personal data with companies the institution is affiliated with under a holding company structure. However, customers have the right, by written request, to block the sharing of confidential data with third parties, such as telemarketing firms, outside the holding company structure.

Reforming the Canadian Financial Services Industry

Since 1992, federally chartered insurance companies, banks, trust and loan companies, and *caisses populaires* have been supervised by a single federal regulator: OSFI. (Securities brokers and dealers are regulated primarily by provincial securities departments.) This single federal regulatory regime has made the Canadian financial services industry fairly well integrated.

As discussed in Insight 2-3, the Minister of Finance in 1999 announced a new policy framework to further promote competition and integration within the Canadian financial services industry. The purpose of this framework is to serve as the basis for future financial services legislation.

Key Terms

financial services industry
solvency
solvency laws
market conduct
market conduct laws
Annual Statement
policy form
National Association of
    Insurance Commissioners
    (NAIC)
model law (model bill)
Annual Return
Insurance Companies Act
Office of the Superintendent of
    Financial Institutions (OSFI)

Canadian Council of Insurance
    Regulators (CCIR)
depository institution
contractual savings institution
fraternal benefit society
bankinsurance
credit life insurance
savings bank life insurance
    (SBLI)
state bank
national bank
holding company
subsidiary
controlling interest
functional regulation

Insight 2-3. Reforming Canada's Financial Services Sector.

In June of 1999, Minister of Finance Paul Martin announced a new policy for reforming all of Canada's financial services sector. The new policy, outlined in *Reforming Canada's Financial Services Sector: A Framework for the Future,* is based on the recommendations made by a federal government task force that spent two years interviewing Canadian citizens and organizations and studying the financial services sector. Recommendations in the new policy framework serve as the basis for future financial services-related legislation introduced in the House of Commons.

The new policy framework is guided by four fundamental principles:

• Financial institutions must have the flexibility to adapt to the changing marketplace and to compete and thrive, both at home and abroad, in order to retain their role as critical sources of economic activity and job creation.

• Competition is necessary to provide a dynamic and innovative financial services sector and to ensure that individual and business consumers have a range of choice at the best possible price.

• All consumers and individual businesses should receive the highest possible standard of quality and service.

• The regulatory burden on financial institutions should be lightened wherever possible, consistent with prudential and public interest objectives.

Under the new policy framework, banks have greater flexibility to engage in strategic alliances, more flexible ownership structure, a new holding company option, a broader range of permissible investments, and a streamlined regulatory process and merger review process. Life insurance companies have access to the payments system, a new holding company structure, and streamlined regulatory processes. Trust companies have a broader range of permissible investments, a commitment to examine capital taxes with the provinces, and streamlined regulatory processes. Credit unions have improved ability to restructure themselves to enhance their national presence. •

Source: Adapted from Department of Finance Canada, "Minister of Finance Announces a New Policy Framework for Canada's Financial Services Sector," *Department of Finance Canada,* 25 June 1999, http://www.fin.gc.ca/newse99/99-059e.html (13 September 1999). Reproduced with the permission of the Minister of Public Works and Government Services Canada, 2000.

Endnotes

1. Federally regulated insurers, along with fraternal benefit societies, account for more than 90 percent of the life insurance business written in Canada.

2. Department of Finance Canada, *Report of the Task Force on the Future of the Canadian Financial Services Sector* (Ottawa: Department of Finance Canada, 1998), 174.

3. OSFI, *Standards of Sound Business and Financial Practices for Life and Health Insurers* (Ottawa: Office of the Superintendent of Financial Institutions, 1997), 1–3.

4. The actual agencies overseeing provincial insurance regulation go by various names, such as the Treasury Department (Alberta), the Department of Justice (New Brunswick and Saskatchewan), and the Financial Institutions Commission (British Columbia).

5. Five insurance companies are exceptions to this rule. These five insurers were incorporated in Nova Scotia prior to 1989 when that province's *Insurance Act* required provincially incorporated insurers to register at the federal level under provisions of the *Canadian and British Insurance Companies Act.* When the *Insurance Companies Act* replaced the *Canadian and British Insurance Companies Act* in 1992, these five insurers were brought under the new federal legislation and continue to be subject to federal regulation.

6. David Greising, "$1,000,000,000,000 Banks," *Business Week,* 27 April 1998, 32.

7. ACLI, *1999 Life Insurance Fact Book* (Washington, D.C.: American Council of Life Insurance, 1999), 79; Canadian Life and Health Insurance Association.

8. Trevor Thomas, "Banks Expand Array of Products, Assn. Finds," *National Underwriter,* Life & Health/Financial Services ed. (19 July 1999): 15.

9. Michael O'D. Moore, "Banks' Sales of Traditional Insurance Grew 35% Last Year, A Survey Shows," *American Banker Online* (6 October 1999), http://www.americabanker.com (8 October 1999).

10. A less than 50 percent interest can be controlling if the remaining shares of stock are widely dispersed or not actively voted.

11. In January 2000, the NAIC adopted the Producer Licensing Model Act, which allows licensed agents to obtain licenses from other states through reciprocal agreements between states. The model act enables uniformity of agent licensing among the states that pass the model act.

Formation of Life Insurance Companies

LEARNING OBJECTIVES

After reading this chapter, you should be able to

🌐 Compare the procedures for incorporating and licensing an insurance company in the United States and Canada

🌐 Describe the differences between a stock insurance company and a mutual insurance company

🌐 Describe the steps involved in the process of demutualization

A life insurance company, like most organizations engaged in commerce, must first be legally established as a business before it can begin selling its products. In this chapter, we will look at how insurance companies are incorporated and the steps life insurance companies take to establish business operations. We will study the two basic forms of life insurance companies: stock companies and mutual companies. We will also examine how insurance companies change from one form to the other.

The Corporate Structure of Life Insurance Companies

Because of the need for insurance companies to be permanent and stable, insurance laws in the United States and Canada require that all commercial insurance companies be organized and operated as corporations. A *corporation* is a legal entity, separate from its owners, that is created by the authority of a government and that continues beyond the death of any or all of its owners. According to this definition, corporations have two important characteristics that protect their stability and permanence:

- The characteristic of limited liability. Because corporations are distinct legal entities, a corporation can be a party in a legal action. Any legal actions involving a corporation affect the assets and liabilities of the corporation, but do not create personal liability for any of the corporation's owners.[1] Moreover, the owners of a corporation are not personally liable for the debts of the corporation. If a corporation goes bankrupt, the corporation's creditors must be satisfied with the assets of the corporation only. The creditors cannot legally require the owners of the corporation to pay the corporation's debts from their personal property.

- The characteristic of continued existence beyond the death of any or all of the corporation's owners. This feature gives a corporation stability, because a corporation that is well-managed can also survive the personal misfortunes of any of its owners.

Incorporating in the United States

The exact requirements for incorporating an insurance business vary from state to state. The usual procedure is for the people who want to form the corporation to file proposed articles of incorporation with the appropriate state official. The **articles of incorporation** make up a document that describes the essential features of the proposed company. These features include the

- Company's name and location

- Names of the company's officers

- Type of business in which the company will engage

- Amount of the initial investment being made in the company

- Number of shares of company stock initially issued (stock companies only)

The organizers of the corporation must also pay a filing charge to the state. The corporate filing then becomes a matter of public record.

In many states, state insurance laws contain the requirements for the incorporation of life insurers, and the state insurance department handles all aspects of insurance company incorporation. In other states, state laws that govern the incorporation of all businesses also govern the incorporation of insurers. Regardless of whether an application for incorporation is filed directly with the state insurance department or is filed with another state administrative agency, such as the office of the secretary of state, the incorporation of a new insurance business is subject to the approval of the state insurance commissioner.

In reviewing an application for a proposed life insurance company, state insurance officials investigate the moral character of each of the company's organizers, the company's business plan and financial projections, and its plans of organization and operations. If no objections are raised to the application and articles of incorporation, and if the organizers have complied with all legal requirements, the state then issues a certificate of incorporation, also known as a *corporate charter*. The **certificate of incorporation** is a document that grants a corporation its legal existence and its right to operate as a corporation under the terms specified in the articles of incorporation. All pertinent state laws regarding incorporation of an insurance business automatically become a part of the certificate of incorporation. If the corporation, once in business, violates any condition included in its articles of incorporation, it breaches its contract with the state and risks losing its certificate of incorporation.

An insurance company incorporates only once, in the state of its choosing. The state in which the insurer incorporates and has its principal legal residence is known as the insurer's **domiciliary state**. The company is then said to be *domiciled* in the state in which it was incorporated. An insurance company usually locates its home office in its domiciliary state. The **home office** is the headquarters of an insurance company and is often the location of the company's executive offices. From the point of view of any state, a **domestic corporation** is an insurer that is incorporated under the laws of that state, a **foreign corporation** is an insurer that is incorporated under the laws of another state, and an **alien corporation** is an insurer that is incorporated under the laws of another country. These distinctions play an important part in the manner in which states regulate insurance companies.

Licensing of Life Insurance Companies in the United States

Before an insurer can begin to transact business in any state, including its domiciliary state, the company must obtain from the state insurance department a **license**, also known as a *certificate of authority*, which is a document providing legal authority for the insurer to conduct an insurance business in the state. An insurer must obtain a license from each state in which it plans to transact business, and the insurer can sell only the lines of business authorized by the license. For more on state licensing of insurers, read Focus on Technology 3-1.

In order to obtain a license in any state, an insurer must meet the state's licensing requirements. Most licensing requirements help to ensure that insurers are (1) financially sound and able to meet their obligations to policyowners and (2) directed by managers who are knowledgeable and capable of running an insurance company.

The specific financial requirements within a state depend on whether the insurer will be organized as a stock company or a mutual company. A **stock insurance company** is owned by the people who purchase shares of the company's stock, whereas a **mutual insurance company** is owned by the policyowners of the company. We will discuss stock companies and mutual companies in detail later in this chapter.

A state's financial requirements govern an insurer's assets, liabilities, and capital and surplus. *Assets* are all things of value owned by the company, such as bonds, mortgages, cash, and computer equipment. **Liabilities** are the company's debts and future obligations, such as policy benefits that will become payable in the future. **Capital and surplus** refers to the amount by which a life insurance company's assets exceed the amount of its liabilities. **Capital** represents the funds that a company's owners have invested in the company. **Surplus** represents

Focus on Technology 3-1. Streamlining State Licensing of Insurance Companies.

Going through a complete licensing procedure in each state in which an insurer wants to do business can be time consuming, especially for insurers wishing to operate in many states. Each state has its own licensing requirements, lengthy application forms, and licensing procedures.

A working group of the National Association of Insurance Commissioners (NAIC) has attempted to streamline the company licensing process with the development of the Uniform Certificate of Authority Application (UCAA), a standardized licensing application that an insurer can submit in participating states. Under the UCAA program,

an insurer files one copy of the license application in its state of domicile. If the insurer wishes to obtain a license in other states, the insurer files only a "short form"—a simplified version of the original application—with the insurance department of each additional state. In fact, a single short form can be filed with numerous states simultaneously. The state of domicile that issued the original license forwards a certificate of compliance to other states indicating that the insurer has been approved in the state of domicile.

Each participating state insurance department still performs its own independent review of the license

applications, and individual states retain the right to reject applications. The advantage of the UCAA is that it eliminates the need to file a full-length application in a unique format for each state.

The UCAA program would also eliminate other licensing requirements and procedures, such as (1) the requirement that the fingerprints of an insurer's officers and directors be on file with the state insurance department, and (2) seasoning rules that require insurance companies to be in business for a minimum number of years before becoming eligible to obtain a license. •

Sources: "Uniform Certificate of Authority Application," National Association of Insurance Commissioners, http://www.naic.org/ucaa/ (13 October 1999). Alex Maurice, "NAIC Unit OKs New Insurer Licensing Plan," *National Underwriter*, Life & Health/Financial Services ed. (15 March 1999): 3.

the total net profits that have been earned from a company's operations and left to accumulate since the company's inception. For mutual insurers that do not issue stock, capital and surplus is known simply as *surplus*. Capital and surplus—or just surplus—is also referred to as *capital funds.*

The primary purpose of financial requirements is to ensure that new companies entering the life insurance business have enough assets to meet liabilities during normal operating conditions, and enough capital and surplus to guard against adverse conditions. Two basic financial requirements that states impose on insurers are capital funds requirements and trust deposits.

Capital Funds Requirements

All states require that, upon incorporation, insurance companies must have at least a minimum level of capital funds. The exact minimum varies from state to state. For example, Figure 3-1 shows the minimum capital funds requirements for stock insurers and mutual insurers in the state of New York.

The New York capital funds requirements mentioned in Figure 3-1 are among the most rigorous in the United States. Other states may require a lower amount of initial capital or surplus for an insurance

FIGURE 3-1. Minimum Capital Funds Requirements—State of New York.

Stock Life Insurers

- Initial capital of at least $2 million from the sale of stock

- Initial surplus of at least $4 million or 200 percent of the company's capital, whichever is greater

Mutual Life Insurers

- A minimum of 1,000 applications for life insurance, each application being for a face amount of at least $1,000

- The full amount of one annual premium from each applicant, with the sum of all premiums equaling at least $25,000

- Initial surplus of at least $150,000

Source: New York State Consolidated Laws, Chapter 28, Sections 4202 and 4208.

company to be licensed. In practice, insurance companies usually have levels of capital funds in excess of the minimum initial requirements. A company that has excess amounts of capital funds is able to demonstrate that it has enough funds to operate an insurance business in a financially sound manner. After commencement of business, the minimum level of capital funds an insurer must maintain varies with the amount and nature of risk assumed by the company.

Trust Deposits

An insurer must deposit in trust with the state of incorporation a specified minimum amount of securities. Laws in other states in which the insurer intends to obtain a license may require the insurer to maintain trust deposits in those states as well. The securities held in trust must be of a certain type that each state specifies. The securities are used for the benefit of the insurer's policyowners should the insurer become unable to pay its promised policy benefits.

Best Case Scenario 3-1 reviews the steps involved in establishing an insurance company in the United States.

Incorporating in Canada

In Canada, a life insurance company may choose to incorporate under federal law or under the laws of a province. Most Canadian insurance companies are federally incorporated. Whether seeking federal or

Best Case Scenario 3-1.

Steps in Establishing a U.S. Life Insurance Company.

A group of organizers decided to incorporate the Best Friend Life Insurance Company, a stock life insurer, in State A and sell insurance in State A, State B, and State C. The organizers planned to raise initial capital of $5 million by issuing 500,000 shares of stock in the company and selling the shares to investors for $10 per share. The organizers have also arranged to borrow the funds needed for the company's required initial surplus.

The figure and time line below show the sequence of steps that Best Friend's organizers took in order to incorporate in State A and become licensed to solicit business in States A, B, and C. No dates are included in the time line because times varied from state to state.

Best Friend applied for licenses in other states later by depositing the required securities in trust and filing with the state insurance department an application for a license. •

	State A Domicile and Place of Business	State B Place of Business	State C Place of Business
TIME LINE ↓	File Articles of Incorporation		
	Apply for Certificate of Incorporation		
	Apply for license to transact insurance business: • Raise initial required capital through issuance and sale of shares of stock • Borrow amount equal to required initial surplus • Deposit securities in trust	Apply for license to transact insurance business: • Deposit securities in trust	Apply for license to transact insurance business: • Deposit securities in trust
	Obtain license— Best Friend licensed as domestic insurer	Obtain license— Best Friend licensed as foreign insurer	Obtain license— Best Friend licensed as foreign insurer
	Begin soliciting business	Begin soliciting business	Begin soliciting business

provincial incorporation, a company must conform to laws and regulations regarding minimum required capital funds, ownership structure, board of directors' powers and duties, and payment of dividends. In Canada, a company incorporated under Canadian law is known as a **resident corporation**, and a company incorporated under the laws of another country is known as a **foreign corporation** or a *nonresident corporation*.

Federal Incorporation

To incorporate at the federal level, a new insurer must comply with the terms of the federal Insurance Companies Act. The Act establishes the business and investment powers of Canadian insurance companies, their corporate governance, and the procedure for making changes to their corporate structure. To apply for federal incorporation, a proposed company must file with the Office of the Superintendent of Financial Institutions (OSFI) an application for **letters patent**, which is a document certifying that the government has given an insurer the right to incorporate. The application for letters patent identifies the company's name and location, the manner in which it will acquire capital, and whether the insurer will be a stock company or a mutual company. In considering each application for letters patent, the Superintendent of Financial Institutions takes into account the sufficiency of the applicant's financial resources, the soundness and feasibility of its future plans, its business record, and the competence and experience of the individuals who will operate the company.

Provincial Incorporation

To incorporate in a particular province, an insurer must, depending on the province, conform to the requirements of either a provincial Insurance Act (such as the Quebec *Insurance Act*) or a general business corporations act (such as the New Brunswick *Companies Act*, the Ontario *Corporations Act*, and so forth). In some provinces, an insurer seeking incorporation files an application for letters patent with the appropriate provincial governmental authority. An insurer wishing to incorporate in other provinces files an application for a **memorandum of association**, which is a document similar to letters patent that contains the fundamental terms for registering for incorporation.

Order to Commence an Insurance Business

Within one year after incorporating, a federally incorporated life insurance company must apply to OSFI for an **order to commence and carry on insurance business**, a document that authorizes the insurance company to begin insuring risks in Canada.[2] To obtain such an order, the applicant insurer must meet minimum financial requirements. For example, a stock insurer must have a minimum of $10 million in capital. A mutual insurer must have a minimum amount of surplus as prescribed by the Minister of Finance. If the Superintendent of Financial Institutions authorizes the insurer to commence its insurance business, the insurer can write only the classes of insurance that the Superintendent's order specifies.

Provincially incorporated insurers must also obtain an authorization to carry on insurance business. However, provincially incorporated insurers obtain such authorization from the superintendent of insurance in their province of incorporation. In provinces in which an insurer incorporates under an Insurance Act, the order to carry on business is obtained during the process of incorporation. In other provinces, an insurer first incorporates under the provincial general business corporations' law and then applies for authorization to commence business under the provincial Insurance Act.

Licensing of Life Insurance Companies in Canada

After receiving the appropriate governmental authorization to commence business, a Canadian insurer or a foreign insurer wishing to operate in Canada must obtain a license from the provincial insurance department of each province in which it will transact business. Although the licensing requirements differ somewhat from province to province, an application for a license typically must be accompanied by (1) documentation proving the insurer's incorporation, (2) a statement of the insurer's current financial condition, and (3) payment of a licensing fee. The statement of the insurer's financial condition is required to prove that the company is maintaining at least the minimum amount of capital funds required by law. A final requirement for obtaining a license in most provinces is that the insurer must file all of its proposed policy forms with the provincial superintendent of insurance. If any form does not comply with all applicable statutes and regulations, the superintendent may require the company to amend the form until it complies.

Stock and Mutual Life Insurance Companies

The two most common types of commercial insurance companies are stock companies and mutual companies. As you learned earlier, a *stock insurance company* is owned by the people who have purchased shares of the company's stock. **Stock** is a security that represents an ownership interest in a company, and the holders of stock—called **stockholders** or *shareholders*—are the owners of the stock company. Stockholders are eligible to receive **stockholder dividends**, which are periodic distributions of the company's net profit. Stockholder dividends generally are paid quarterly and may be paid in cash or in additional shares of the company's stock. The price per share of a company's stock can rise or fall, resulting in gains or losses for a stockholder when selling the stock. Figure 3-2 describes two classes of stockholders.

FIGURE 3-2. Common Stockholders and Preferred Stockholders.

Common Stockholders

- Usually receive voting privileges in company elections—one vote per share of common stock owned
- May or may not receive stockholder dividends
- Are not guaranteed that each dividend will be a certain amount

Preferred Stockholders

- Do not ordinarily receive voting privileges in company elections
- Receive stockholder dividends before any dividends can be paid to common stockholders
- Are guaranteed that dividends will be a fixed amount

Although stockholders are the owners of a stock company, they typically are not involved in the company's day-to-day operations. Instead, most stockholders are granted the right to vote in elections for members of the company's board of directors (the organization's governing body). The directors then appoint executives to control the company's day-to-day operations.

We have previously mentioned that a *mutual insurance company* is owned by the company's policyowners—people who have purchased policies from the company. Policyowners have both membership rights and policy rights in the mutual company. **Membership rights** are ownership rights in the company, such as the right to vote in elections for the company's board of directors on the basis of one vote for each policyowner, regardless of the amount of insurance or the number of insurance policies that the policyowner owns. **Policy rights** are contractual rights, such as the right to the policy values, the right to assign the values to another party, the right to designate the beneficiary of the policy proceeds upon the death of the insured, and the right to participate in annual distributions of excess surplus.

As with a stock company, a mutual company's board of directors appoints executives to manage the company's day-to-day operations. Because a stock insurer can issue stock that represents ownership in the company, the stock company itself can be owned by another company (a stock insurer, a mutual insurer, or a company outside the insurance industry). A mutual insurance company, on the other hand, does not issue stock and cannot be owned by another entity. A mutual company can, however, own a stock subsidiary company.

Participating and Nonparticipating Policies

All mutual insurers and some stock insurers in the United States issue a type of insurance policy called a **participating policy**, or *par policy*, under which the policyowner shares in the insurance company's surplus. The amount of surplus that is available for distribution to policyowners is called the **divisible surplus**. A policyowner's share of the divisible surplus is a **policy dividend** and is payable to owners of participating policies at the end of the policy year. Policy dividends are considered a return of part of the premiums that these policyowners paid to keep their policies in force for that year.

Policy dividends should not be confused with the stockholder dividends paid to owners of a company's stock. Policy dividends are refunds of excess premiums, whereas the dividends paid to stockholders are distributions of net profits.

Most of the policies sold by stock companies in the United States are **nonparticipating policies**, or *nonpar policies*, under which the policyowners do not share in company surplus. In rare instances, a mutual company can sell nonpar policies along with its par policies. More commonly, mutual companies offer nonparticipating policies only through subsidiary stock insurance companies that they own. Canadian insurance companies, whether stock or mutual, generally offer both par and nonpar policies.

Proportion of Stock Companies to Mutual Companies

Virtually all newly formed life insurance companies in the United States and Canada take the form of stock companies, primarily because stock companies are easier to establish than are mutual companies. To establish a mutual insurance company, the company's organizers must find a specific number of people who are willing to apply for insurance and pay the first annual premium to an insurer that does not yet legally exist. Finding investors who are willing to purchase the stock of a new stock insurer is much easier and more practical. The founders of a stock company can raise the money needed to establish the company by selling shares of stock in the firm that is being created. After commencing operations, a stock insurer can raise additional funds by selling more shares in the company.

At the beginning of 1999, 1,563 life insurance companies were doing business in the United States. Of these, 1,457 insurers—93 percent of the total number of companies—were stock companies, while the remaining 7 percent were mutual companies. Mutual companies, however, held about 32 percent of the assets of all U.S. life insurance companies, whereas stock companies held about 65 percent of the assets.[3] The reason that the small percentage of mutual companies holds a disproportionate share of the assets of insurance companies is

that the average mutual company is much older and larger than the average stock company. Figure 3-3 compares the number of companies, amount of assets, and amount of earned premium income of mutual and stock companies in the United States. Figure 3-4 provides the same information for Canada, where 107 of 129 life insurers are organized as stock companies.

Changing the Corporate Form

Under some circumstances, a stock insurance company may become a mutual company, and a mutual company may become a stock com-

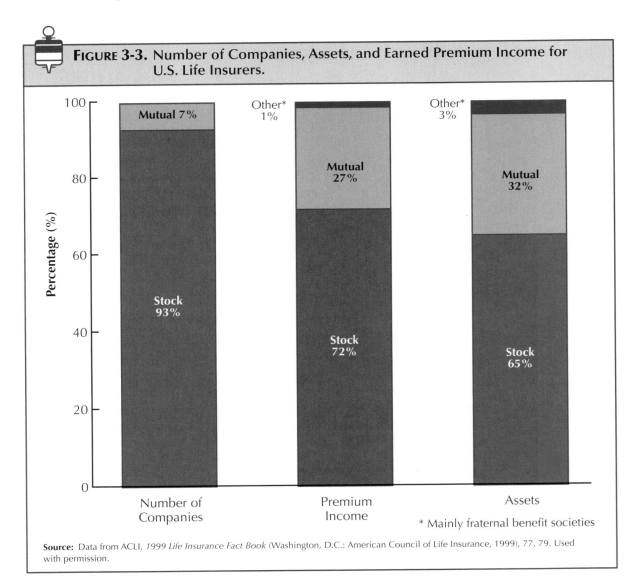

FIGURE 3-3. Number of Companies, Assets, and Earned Premium Income for U.S. Life Insurers.

Source: Data from ACLI, *1999 Life Insurance Fact Book* (Washington, D.C.: American Council of Life Insurance, 1999), 77, 79. Used with permission.

FIGURE 3-4. Number of Companies, Assets, and Earned Premium Income for Canadian Life Insurers.

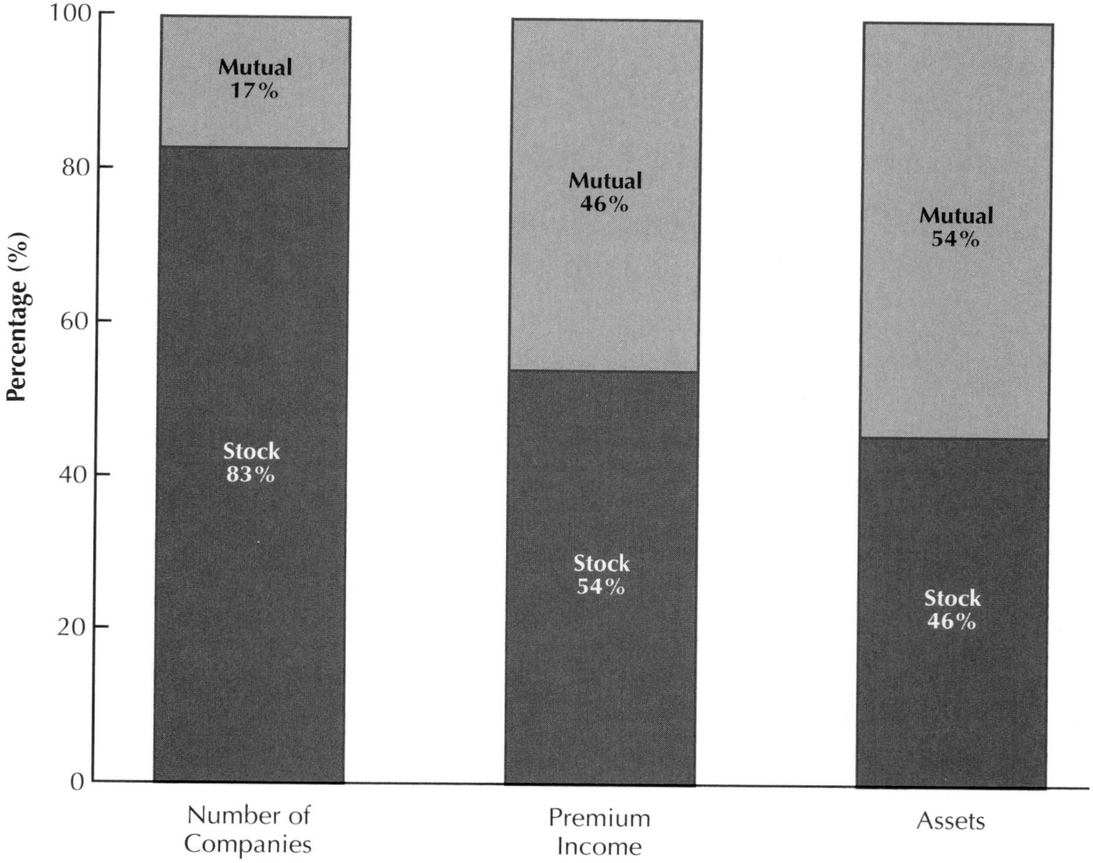

Percentage (%)

Number of Companies: Stock 83%, Mutual 17%

Premium Income: Stock 54%, Mutual 46%

Assets: Stock 46%, Mutual 54%

Source: Data from CLHIA, *Canadian Life and Health Insurance Facts,* 1999 ed. (Toronto: Canadian Life and Health Insurance Association, 1999), 25–26.

pany. In both cases, the changeover process is time-consuming and expensive, but for various reasons companies sometimes decide to change their corporate forms.

When a stock life insurance company converts to a mutual insurer, the process is known as ***mutualization***. During the 1950s, several Canadian stock insurance companies converted to mutual companies in order to avoid being taken over by foreign firms. (As noted earlier, a mutual company cannot be acquired by another company.)

Today, however, a more likely change of corporate form is for mutual company to convert to a stock company through a process called

demutualization. Between 1930 and 1987, 125 U.S. mutual companies—most of whom were relatively small—demutualized. Since then, a number of other mutuals, including some of the largest insurance companies in the United States, either demutualized or began the process of demutualization.

Demutualization regulations in the United States are inconsistent from state to state. Almost all states allow some form of demutualization, but the laws of some states are quite restrictive while others are not. In Canada, demutualization by federally incorporated insurers was not permitted until 1992 when the passage of the Insurance Companies Act allowed small life insurers (those with less than $7.5 billion in assets) to demutualize.[4] In 1999, an amendment to the Act permitted large insurers to demutualize, and several Canadian mutuals, including each of Canada's four largest mutuals, began the process of demutualization.[5] Ironically, some Canadian insurers that converted from stock companies to mutual companies in the 1950s were among those that decided to demutualize in the late 1990s.

The Process of Demutualization

Demutualization in the United States is essentially a three-step process. First, the mutual insurer draws up a plan of demutualization that must be approved by the company's board of directors. This plan provides details of how the company will demutualize. Most importantly, it identifies the economic benefit—such as cash, shares of stock in the new company, or additional policy benefits—the company will provide for its policyowners.

Second, the plan of demutualization is filed with the insurance department in the insurer's domiciliary state. The insurance department reviews the plan for fairness and compliance with various requirements of state law. Usually a public hearing takes place to allow interested parties to comment on the plan. Typically, the plan must be approved by the insurance department of each state in which the insurer does business.

Third, the plan is presented to the mutual insurer's policyowners for their approval. While state requirements vary regarding the degree of policyowners' support needed, typically two-thirds of voting policyowners must approve the plan for demutualization to proceed.

In Canada, a mutual insurer seeking demutualization must develop a plan of demutualization and obtain the approval of

- The company's board of directors

- Regulators in Canada and in foreign jurisdictions in which the company operates

- Two-thirds of the company's voting policyowners

- Canada's Minister of Finance

In addition, Canadian law requires that the entire value of the demutualizing company must be given to the company's voting policyowners.

Once demutualization is complete, eligible policyowners of the mutual company typically become shareholders of the publicly traded stock company. Policyowners have the opportunity to retain their shares of stock or sell them. All policyowners' benefits and insurance coverages are preserved in the new stock insurer. The stock insurer also offers new shares of stock to investors for the first time, a process known as making an ***initial public offering (IPO)***. An IPO enables a stock company to raise additional capital for a number of reasons, including expansion, acquisition, and improved solvency. Shares of stock, whether held by policyowners or by the public, can subsequently be traded on the open market.

Key Terms

corporation	letters patent
articles of incorporation	memorandum of association
certificate of incorporation	order to commence and carry on insurance business
domiciliary state	stock
home office	stockholder (shareholder)
domestic corporation	stockholder dividend
foreign corporation	membership rights
alien corporation	policy rights
license (certificate of authority)	participating policy (par policy)
stock insurance company	divisible surplus
mutual insurance company	policy dividend
assets	nonparticipating policy (nonpar policy)
liabilities	mutualization
capital and surplus	demutualization
capital	initial public offering (IPO)
surplus	
resident corporation	
foreign corporation (nonresident corporation)	

Endnotes

1. However, the members of a corporation's board of directors—who may also be company stockholders—are not always immune from individual liability. In some court cases, a corporation's board members have been held personally liable for the actions of the corporation and have been assessed heavy penalties by the court.

2. Companies holding unexpired certificates of registration under the old federal insurance legislation—the *Canadian and British Insurance Companies Act*—are deemed to have obtained this approval.

3. The remaining 3 percent of assets were held by fraternal benefits societies and savings banks that are permitted to sell life insurance.

4. Mutual Company Conversion Regulations, SOR/93-205, pursuant to Section 237(2) of the *Insurance Companies Act.*

5. M. Christian Murray, "Canadian Insurers Now Free to Demutualize," *National Underwriter*, Life & Health/Financial Services ed. (5 April 1999): 3.

6. William N. Pargeans and Robert L. Adams, "Canadian Demutualization: Form or Substance?" *BestWeek—Life/Health Special Report* (6 July 1999): 1.

7. Lynna Goch, "1998: The Year in Review," *Best's Review*, Life/Health ed. (January 1999): 39.

The Organizational Structure of Insurance Companies

LEARNING OBJECTIVES

After reading this chapter, you should be able to

- Describe the basic activities in each functional area of a typical life insurance company

- List four factors that are essential for an effective organizational structure

- Explain what kinds of information are contained in an organization chart

- Compare the duties and responsibilities of a company's board of directors, officers, managers, and supervisors

- State the differences between insurance companies that are organized by function, product, territory, and profit center

- Discuss new alternative configurations to the traditional organizational pyramid

- Explain why committees are important to a company's operations

To effectively accomplish its core operations, a life insurer must coordinate the activities of its various functional areas. **Coordination** is the orderly arrangement—that is, the structure—of the activities of various parts of a company so that the company can achieve its goals. The ability of an organization to coordinate its activities depends on how effectively the organization is structured. The structure defines the tasks assigned to each job position within the company and identifies who reports to whom. Although there is no "right" way to set up an insurance company and its organization, insurers strive to structure their organizations in a manner that best enables them to meet their corporate objectives.

The purpose of this chapter is to describe how life insurance companies generally organize their operations. We begin by identifying and describing the specific functions performed within life insurance companies. Then we describe some components of the organizational structure of life insurers and the types of organizational structures that life insurers typically adopt. We examine committees and discuss their purpose in an insurance company. Finally, we discuss the importance of employee training and employee development.

Functional Areas in a Life Insurance Company

Carrying out the core operations of a life insurance company requires the efforts of a great many people who perform specific functions. The word **function** generally describes a distinct type of work, an essential step in a process, or an aspect of operations or management that requires special technical knowledge. The functional areas found in a typical life insurer include marketing, actuarial, underwriting, customer service, claim administration, investments, accounting, legal/compliance, human resources, and information systems. As we show you throughout this book, most of these functional areas are involved in more than one of the company's core operations. The information systems function, for example, has a role in all of an insurer's operations.

Insurers organize themselves in many different ways and vary their organizations to fit their own specific needs. They use terms like *department, unit, division, group,* and *section* to designate various collections of people who perform related activities. Although in this text we sometimes refer to a specific department or unit in an insurance company, keep in mind that we are actually referring to a functional area within the company.

Marketing

Marketing in a life insurance company has the following responsibilities:

- Conducting research to identify the company's target customers

- Working with other departments in the company to develop new products and to revise current ones to meet customers' needs

- Establishing and maintaining distribution systems for the company's products

- Preparing advertising campaigns and promotional materials

The type of distribution systems an insurer uses helps determine which activities its marketing department performs. For example, an insurer that uses only a brokerage distribution system has different marketing activities than a company that sells through ordinary agencies, worksite marketing, an Internet site, or partnerships with commercial banks.

Actuarial

Actuarial is responsible for ensuring that the company conducts its operations on a financially sound basis. Actuaries play an important role in designing a company's insurance products. The actuarial department establishes premium and policy dividend rates, determines what the company's reserve liabilities should be, and calculates nonforfeiture and loan values. Actuaries conduct research needed to predict mortality and morbidity rates, help to establish the company's underwriting guidelines, measure the profitability of the company's products, and help negotiate reinsurance agreements, through which an insurance company transfers some or all of an insurance risk to another insurance company. Actuaries usually participate in the company's relations with insurance regulators, and a designated actuary annually renders an opinion as to the adequacy of the company's policy reserves.

Underwriting

In life insurance companies, underwriting is responsible for making sure that the company accepts insureds whose actual mortality rates, as a group, do not exceed the mortality rates assumed when each product's premium rates were calculated. To do so, the underwriting department

works with the actuarial department and with medical personnel to establish criteria for accurately evaluating and classifying proposed insureds according to the degree of mortality risk that each one represents. Then the department selects insureds according to the guidelines established for each product. Underwriting may also participate in the negotiation of reinsurance agreements. Most insurers establish a separate group or unit that submits cases for reinsured coverage and administers the many details associated with reinsurance.

Customer Service

As its name implies, customer service provides assistance to the company's customers. A company's customers include agents, brokers, other employees, and beneficiaries, as well as the company's policyowners. Customer service representatives fulfill requests for information, help interpret policy language, answer questions about policy coverage, and make changes requested by policyowners, such as address changes, beneficiary designation changes, or mode of premium payment changes. The customer service department may also calculate and process policy loans, nonforfeiture options, and policy dividend payments.

Claim Administration

Evaluating and handling claims is the duty of claim administration. Claim analysts review claims presented by policyowners or beneficiaries, verify the validity of each claim, calculate the correct benefit amount, and authorize the payment of benefits to the appropriate person.

Investments

Investments examines the economic and financial marketplace and manages the company's investments according to the guidelines established by the company's management. Together with the actuarial area, the investments department manages investments to produce returns that match—in timing and amount—the company's policy obligations. Authorized members of the investments department buy and sell stocks, bonds, mortgages, real estate, and other financial assets. They also act as advisers to the company's top management when the company is considering or carrying out a merger or an acquisition.

Accounting

Accounting maintains the records that show the financial results of a company's numerous business transactions. The accounting department manages the company's general accounting records, prepares financial statements for management decision making and to meet financial reporting requirements, controls cash receipts and disbursements, oversees the company's budgeting process, and works with legal/compliance to assure that the company is complying with government regulations and tax laws.[1]

Legal

The legal department handles all legal matters for the company. Company lawyers advise claim examiners when claims are disputed; work with accountants to determine the company's tax liabilities; represent the company or supervise outside attorneys in any litigation involving the company; handle investment agreements, policy assignments, and title searches; and develop policy forms, agency contracts, and other legal documents used by the company. Some companies combine the legal and compliance functions into one department, and other companies have separate departments. Even in companies that separate the departments, a strong relationship exists between legal and compliance.

Compliance

Compliance ensures that the company's operations comply with federal, state, and provincial laws and with insurance department regulations. Responsibilities within the compliance area include studying current and proposed legislation to determine their effects on the company's operations, educating company employees about applicable laws and regulatory requirements, monitoring the conduct and sales practices of the company's producers, overseeing the company's internal control procedures, and working with insurance regulators when they conduct examinations of the insurance company.

Human Resources

Human resources (HR) is responsible for matters relating to the company's employees. The human resources department helps formulate company policy with respect to hiring, training, and dismissal of employees; determines levels of employee compensation; plans for

training and developing employees; and assures company compliance with federal, state, and provincial employment laws. HR also administers the company's employee benefit plans, such as group insurance, tuition reimbursement, employee pension plans, and paid leave.

Information Systems

Information systems (IS) is in charge of managing information throughout the company, chiefly by developing and maintaining the life insurance company's computer systems. Because computer systems are used in all areas of insurance companies, the IS department affects every part of the organization. IS helps other departments in the company to develop, buy, and use the computer systems and software they need to provide information, maintain records, and administer products. The IS staff also manages the company's computer networks, maintains company records in computerized files, and conducts analyses of the various computer systems used in the company.

Components of the Organizational Structure

An insurer coordinates the activities of various parts of the organization so that the company can achieve its goals. Coordination of activities takes place through the organizational structure of the business. An effective organizational structure has the following benefits:

- Enables the business to assign responsibility throughout the organization. **Responsibility** is a duty or task assigned to an employee. Effective organizations are successful at ensuring that all employees understand their responsibilities.

- Provides employees with the proper authority to meet their responsibilities. By **authority** we mean the right of an employee to make decisions, take action, and direct others in order to fulfill responsibilities. For example, a manager who is responsible for seeing that all policyowner correspondence is answered within a predetermined service response time should be given the authority to hire enough people, rotate workers, assign overtime, and take other appropriate action to meet the assigned deadline.

- Provides a process for holding employees accountable for their job performance. **Accountability** means that employees are answerable for how well they use their authority and how effectively they carry out their responsibilities. An effective company

is organized so that specific accountabilities are clearly assigned to individuals or groups.

- Sets clear guidelines for the delegation of authority and accountability. ***Delegation*** is the process of assigning to another employee the accountability for completion of a specific task. The performance of many functions within a life insurance company requires the work of many people, and effective managers are successful at delegating sufficient authority and accountability to employees so that everyone's time is used most efficiently in accomplishing the organization's goals.

The Organization Chart

The formal internal organization of a company is exhibited in its organization chart. An ***organization chart*** is a visual display of various job positions in a company and the formal lines of authority and responsibility among company employees. Figure 4-1 shows an example of a hypothetical organization chart. Organization charts can be simple representations of only the major functional areas or complex drawings of all job positions within a company. An organization chart also shows the company's ***chain of command***, or the structure of authority that flows downward in the organization from the higher levels to the lower levels. The chain of command identifies who reports to whom in the company. Management continually revises the way the company is organized in order to improve the company's efficiency and ability to compete.

Organization charts use solid lines to signify direct reporting relationships between managers and employees. An organization chart may also show dotted lines to indicate when there is some degree of reporting relationship between staff, though it is not a traditional manager-employee relationship. Dotted-line relationships are most common when an employee reports to a manager in one functional area but also has responsibilities in another area. For example, a marketing associate has a direct (solid-line) relationship with her marketing manager and also has a dotted-line relationship with the product manager whose product she is responsible for marketing.

According to the principle of ***unity of command***, each employee should receive authority from only one person and be accountable to only that person. Traditionally, insurance companies tended to avoid situations in which an employee had a solid-line reporting relationship with one manager and a dotted-line relationship with another manager, because these situations violated the unity of command principle. In such situations, the employee is answerable to two people; as a result, all three parties could become frustrated and confused. In

FIGURE 4-1. Sample Organization Chart.

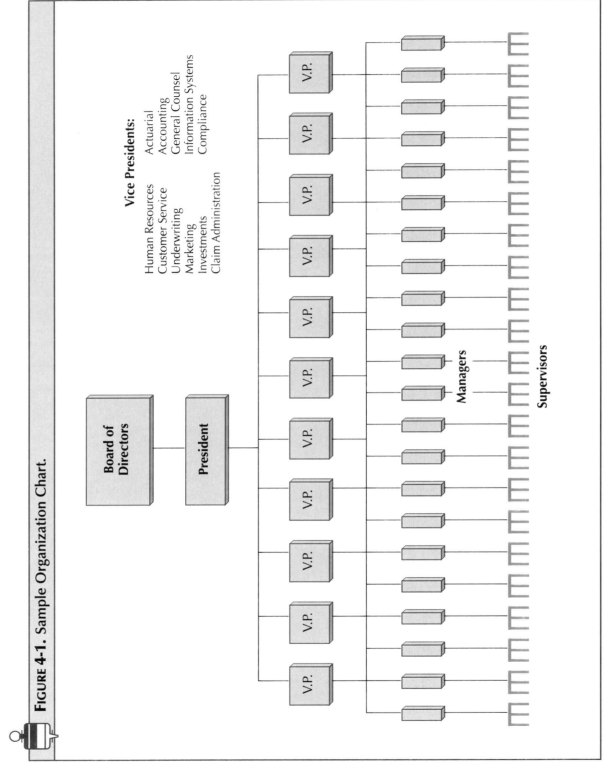

today's organizational environment, however, insurance companies typically cannot adhere strictly to the unity of command principle.

Pyramidal Structure and Levels of Authority

The organization chart in most insurance companies resembles a pyramid, such as the one shown in Figure 4-2. The pyramid structure illustrates that the authority in a company starts at the top with one person or a small group of people. Authority is then distributed through the chain of command to ever-larger numbers of people throughout the company.

Policyowners or Stockholders

The owners of a company—the policyowners in mutual companies or the stockholders in stock companies—are the ultimate source of authority for a life insurance company. Theoretically, then, the owners would occupy the top line of a life insurance company's organization

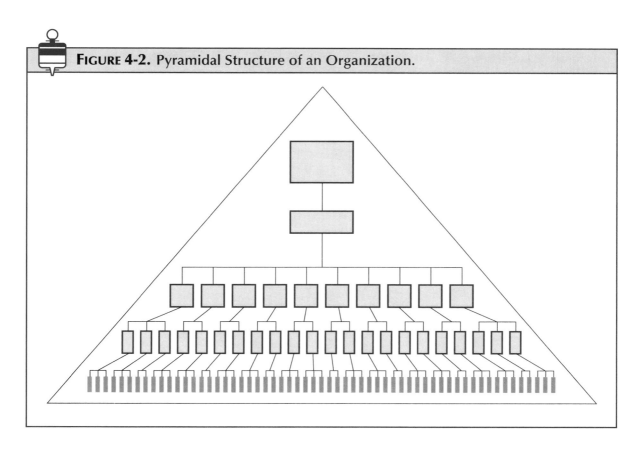

FIGURE 4-2. Pyramidal Structure of an Organization.

chart. However, the owners do not usually direct the operations of the company; therefore, generally they are not shown on the organization chart. Instead, the owners elect a board of directors and delegate their authority to the board.

Board of Directors

The **board of directors**, elected by the owners and shown on the top level of the organization chart, is the primary governing body of a corporation. In representing the owners of the corporation, the board has a primary responsibility to review the activities and finances of the company and to set company policies. The board of directors appoints the chief executive officer and other officers of the company and holds these officers accountable for the company's operations.

Usually, several of the company's senior executives are also members of the board. Board members who hold positions with the company in addition to their positions on the board are known as **inside directors**. Board members who do not hold other positions with the company are known as **outside directors**. Outside directors of life insurance companies are usually business people, professionals in academia and health services, and community leaders. In most companies, the board of directors meets either monthly or quarterly, although it may hold special meetings when necessary. Figure 4-3 lists some of the duties that directors perform during board meetings.

Company Management

Employees whose primary responsibility is to guide the work of other employees are said to be members of *management*, whether they are officers, managers, or supervisors. Their major functions involve

FIGURE 4-3. Duties of the Board of Directors.

- Setting the major policies for the firm
- Evaluating the firm's operating results
- Authorizing major transactions, such as mergers and acquisitions
- Declaring the dividends to be paid to stockholders or policyowners based on the recommendations of management
- Appointing the officers who operate the company
- Setting the compensation for the firm's top-level executives

planning what should be done, *organizing* the human and technical resources to get the job done, *influencing* and *directing* the people doing the work, and *controlling* the work process so that the work is performed in a satisfactory manner.

The most senior manager in a company, and the person located just beneath the board of directors on the typical organizational chart, is the chief executive officer (CEO). In most companies, the CEO is also the company's president. (In this textbook, we will generally use the term *president* rather than *CEO*.) The board of directors entrusts the president with broad administrative powers.

Some companies also have a *chief operating officer (COO)*, who manages the day-to-day operations of the company and reports to the president. Also reporting to the president are executives known as *vice presidents*. Each vice president supervises a major division of the company. In addition to coordinating the activities of their respective divisions, vice presidents also stay informed about trends in the industry and advise the president on company operations. A company's president and vice presidents are considered the company's *officers*. Under the direction of the board of directors, officers are intimately involved in **strategic planning**, the process of determining an organization's major long-term corporate objectives and the broad, overall courses of action that the company will follow to achieve these objectives.

Below vice presidents in the chain of command are the company's middle-level *managers*. Managers are generally in charge of departments within divisions and are responsible for translating company policy and strategic plans into plans for day-to-day operations. Managers are less involved in strategic planning and more involved in **tactical planning**, also called *operational planning*, which is the process of determining the specific tasks that need to be performed to carry out the organization's strategic plans.

Next in the chain of command are people at the *supervisory* level of management. Supervisors are generally in charge of sub-units of departments and are responsible for implementing the tactical plans made by middle management. Supervisors have less latitude in interpreting the directives of top management and spend more time in the direct supervision of non-management employees than do managers higher in the organization.

Variations Among Companies

Most insurance companies have employees at each of the levels depicted in Figure 4-2. Many large companies also establish subdivisions of the categories shown. For example, the category of vice presidents often includes executive vice presidents, senior vice presidents, vice presidents, and assistant vice presidents. Large companies may also

have senior managers, managers, assistant managers, supervisors, and assistant supervisors. Even the terminology used to describe various positions varies from company to company. In one company, a person at the managerial level in charge of the accounting department may hold a title such as *accounting manager*. In another company, the person holding a job with the same duties may be called the *chief accountant, controller,* or *comptroller.*

Centralized and Decentralized Organizations

The organizational structure of many businesses can be described as having characteristics of centralization or decentralization. In **centralized organizations**, top management retains most decision-making authority for the entire company. In **decentralized organizations**, top management shares decision-making authority with employees at lower hierarchical levels.[2] In decentralized organizations, top management typically makes decisions regarding general company policy, and authority for other types of decisions is delegated to middle- and lower-level managers.

Centralized and decentralized organizations each have certain benefits that the other does not. For example, company policies and actions in a centralized organization tend to be consistent because one central, high-level authority makes the decisions. Also, centralization reduces certain administrative costs because a single centralized department usually handles administrative services for the entire company. One advantage of a decentralized organization is that managers can respond quickly to situations because they have more authority to make decisions. Having this authority can increase managers' morale and provide them with career development experience. Also, a decentralized approach can lead to personalized decisions more closely attuned to specific customers' needs. However, decentralization can lead to inconsistencies in policy from one area of the company to the next.

In reality, centralization and decentralization are two ends of a continuum, and no organization is ever completely centralized or decentralized. Each insurance company tends to be positioned toward one end or the other on this continuum, and each company may periodically adjust its position. Although there are no absolute guidelines to determine whether a centralized or a decentralized approach is more appropriate, decentralized organizations tend to be more flexible and quicker to respond to changing environments. Therefore, the greater the complexity and uncertainty involved in an organization's external environment (factors outside of the company), the greater the tendency for the organization to be more decentralized than centralized.

© 1997 Frank Monahan. Used with permission.

Line Units and Staff Units

You may have heard the terms *line unit* and *staff unit* used to describe functional areas of an organization. **Line units**, also called *production departments* or *operating departments*, are areas of an organization that produce and administer the firm's products or services. In a life insurance company, the major line units are marketing, actuarial, underwriting, customer service, claim administration, and investments. **Staff units**, also called *service departments*, are areas that provide support services to line units and other staff units but do not themselves produce or administer products and services. Insurance company staff units include accounting, legal, compliance, human resources, and information systems.

Insurance company operations require line units and staff units to work closely to coordinate their activities. For example, one responsibility of an insurer's underwriting department (a line unit) is to evaluate the risk presented by each applicant for insurance. The underwriting department relies on the information systems de-

partment (a staff unit) to provide the computer and other technical support that will help the underwriters evaluate risks and select the premium rate corresponding to each risk.

Line Authority, Staff Authority, and Functional Authority

Three important types of authority in an organization are line authority, staff authority, and functional authority.

- *Line authority* is direct authority over workers. Line authority corresponds directly to the chain of command, beginning with the board of directors and extending down through all levels in the organization. Both line unit managers and staff unit managers exercise line authority over the employees that they directly supervise, and, in general, these employees do not have the option of disregarding or ignoring direct line authority.

- *Staff authority* is authority held by staff unit personnel to advise or make recommendations to line unit personnel. Staff authority is less concrete than line authority and is frequently directed upward. For example, an insurer's vice president of human resources may possess staff authority to advise the company president regarding the impact of a proposed merger with another insurer. However, the president is not obligated to act on the advice.

- *Functional authority* is a staff unit member's formal or legitimate authority over line units in matters related to the staff member's functional specialty. An example of a staff member exercising functional authority is a compliance officer who requires an individual life product manager to change the wording in a new policy form so that it conforms to state insurance regulations.

Typical Ways Insurers Organize Work Activities

Providing insurance products to the public is a complex endeavor involving many people and work activities. Insurers must organize these work activities into an integrated structural plan. Among life insurance companies, the traditional ways to organize activities are by *function*, by *product*, and by *territory*. More recently, *profit centers*, *strategic business units (SBUs)*, and *matrix organizational structures* have evolved.

Organization by Function

An insurance company that is organized by function differentiates its major divisions by the work that the divisions perform. Each functional area is usually a separate unit that performs its function for all of the company's products. For example, all actuarial activities for the company take place in a single actuarial area, all group life underwriting activities take place in a single area, and so forth.

Organization by Product

A life insurance company that is organized by product distributes work according to the company's lines of insurance. A major division of the company administers each line of business and handles most of the functional activities for that line of business only. However, a few functions, such as investments, legal, compliance, and human resources, may be handled through a centrally administered department. Despite these few centralized departments, organization by product tends to decentralize a company, allowing more decisions to be made by the employees who are most closely involved with a particular type of product.

Organization by Territory

A company that is organized by territory determines its major divisions according to the geographical areas in which it operates. An insurer operating in several countries may have a separate division for each country. A company doing business in only one country may divide its operations according to states, provinces, or regions.

The top executive of a regional office is usually a senior vice president who reports to the president of the company at the home office. The typical insurance operations conducted at regional offices include underwriting, policy issue, premium billing and receipts, customer service, claim administration, and the supervision and support of the marketing activities in the designated region. The regional offices may also have their own human resources units, as well as small legal and actuarial staffs that consult with the home office staffs as needed.

Best Case Scenario 4-1 illustrates organization by function, product, and territory.

Best Case Scenario 4-1.   **Choosing an Organizational Structure.**

After the Best Friend Life Insurance Company incorporated and obtained the appropriate authority to begin transacting business, the company's executives had to determine the most appropriate way to organize the company. Best Friend was authorized to sell individual life insurance, group life insurance, individual disability income insurance, and group pension products in the United States and Canada. Best Friend's executives considered three basic organizational structures: by function, by product, and by territory.

Organization by Function

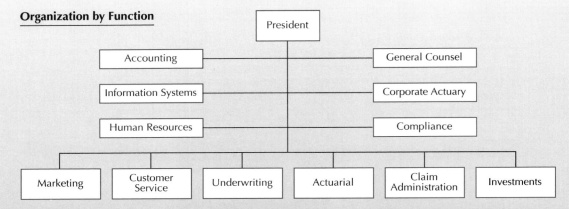

If Best Friend were to organize the company by function, staff in each department would perform one function for all of the company's products. For example, Best Friend's underwriting department would handle all of the underwriting activities for each of Best Friend's individual life insurance, group life insurance, individual disability income insurance, and group pension products. The claim administration department would handle claims for each of the four product lines, and so on.

Organization by Product

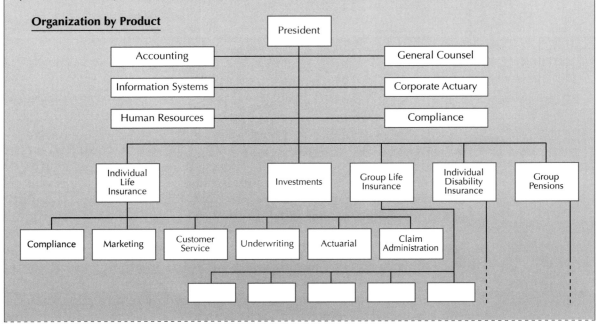

Best Case Scenario 4-1. Choosing an Organizational Structure (continued).

If Best Friend were to organize its operations by product, each of its lines of business—individual life, group life, individual disability income, and group pensions—would take care of its own actuarial, marketing, underwriting, customer service, and claim administration activities. Other functions would be handled by centralized departments.

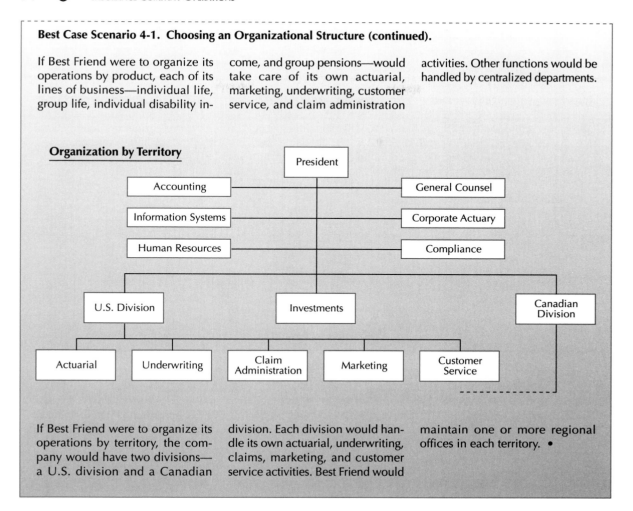

Organization by Territory

If Best Friend were to organize its operations by territory, the company would have two divisions—a U.S. division and a Canadian division. Each division would handle its own actuarial, underwriting, claims, marketing, and customer service activities. Best Friend would maintain one or more regional offices in each territory. •

Organization by Profit Center or Strategic Business Unit

Another way to organize a company is by profit center. A ***profit center*** is a line of business that (1) is evaluated on its profitability, (2) is responsible for its own revenues and expenses, and (3) makes its own decisions regarding its operations. Life insurers that use a profit center approach resemble companies that are organized by product because a company's product lines are typically the main areas of the company that generate revenues. For example, an insurer organized by profit center may have an individual life insurance profit center and a group life insurance profit center.

Each profit center is responsible for its own revenues and expenses, and the person in charge of each profit center has control over most

aspects of the profit center. In a company organized into profit centers, units or departments that are not themselves profit centers but that perform activities to support profit centers are known as *cost centers*. Cost centers are responsible for costs but not for revenues. Typical insurance company cost centers are human resources, accounting, legal, compliance, and information systems.[3]

In some companies, particularly large companies that operate in many geographic areas, profit centers are considered strategic business units. A *strategic business unit (SBU)* is an organizational unit that acts like an independent business in all major respects. An SBU (1) serves a specific market outside the parent corporation, (2) faces outside competition, (3) controls its own strategic planning and new product development, (4) has its own management and support functions, and (5) is responsible for its own costs and revenues. Each strategic business unit resembles a complete company in miniature.

The head of a profit center or SBU (usually a division vice president) is held accountable for the center's profitability. The profit center/SBU structure allows a company's upper management to easily identify the profitability of each line of business and therefore single out lines of business that are performing above and below expectations. Profit centers can also allow employees to become more involved in decision making. Because each profit center is responsible for its own performance, the primary direction provided for each profit center comes from the head of the profit center rather than from the board of directors or a company's executive offices. As a result, people lower in the organizational chain of command can have more influence on operations than they would if the company were organized more traditionally.

A disadvantage of the profit center/SBU approach is that it may produce a certain amount of duplication of effort, particularly among support personnel. For example, if each of two SBUs—individual life and group life—has its own information systems unit, the company may be spending more money than necessary by maintaining two separate computer systems and IS staffs.

Matrix Organization

In the traditional organizational pyramid, lines of authority flowed only vertically. A *matrix organization* is an organization with a structure that includes both vertical and horizontal lines of authority. As shown in Figure 4-4, a matrix organization chart has a checkerboard configuration. In a matrix organization, project managers borrow technical specialists from various departments to work on projects temporarily. Project managers have only limited, dotted-line authority over the specialists, who otherwise report to their line unit or staff unit managers.

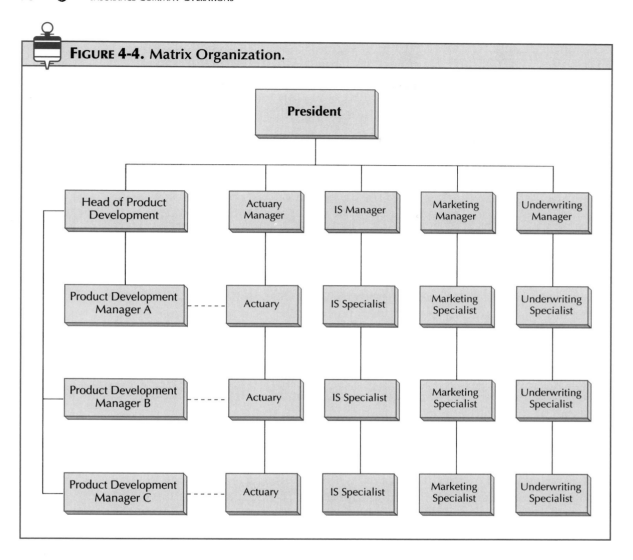

Figure 4-4. Matrix Organization.

Some insurance companies use the matrix structure to a limited extent, but few use it exclusively. An advantage of matrix organization is increased coordination; the manager of a project is in position to coordinate the interrelated aspects of a particular project, such as developing a new type of insurance product. Other advantages of a matrix structure are a greater exchange of information among functional areas, increased organizational flexibility, and in many cases, enhanced commitment to a project from people involved in the matrix. A disadvantage of this structure is the possibility of power struggles caused by overlapping authority and responsibility. Also, this structure often violates the unity-of-command principle; that is, in a matrix structure, employees may report to more than one manager.

New Organizational Shapes

In recent years, many companies have reshaped the traditional organizational pyramid. New structural trends include removing layers of management, creating teams, and creating many small sub-units within a larger organization. These trends have spawned new organizational shapes. We discuss three of these shapes—the hourglass organization, the cluster organization, and the network organization—which are shown graphically in Figure 4-5.

- **Hourglass organization.** This structure consists of three basic layers, with the middle layer being much narrower than the top and bottom layers. The top layer contains executives who are responsible for formulating the organization's strategic plan. The middle layer consists of a small group of middle managers who coordinate the functions of the bottom layer, which typically consists of a diverse group of technical/professional employees. A distinguishing characteristic of the hourglass organization is that the middle managers are generalists, rather than functional specialists. Traditional managers, such as marketing managers or underwriting managers, are functional specialists.

- **Cluster organization.** This structure is comprised of a number of work teams. Employees do not have permanent job responsibilities.

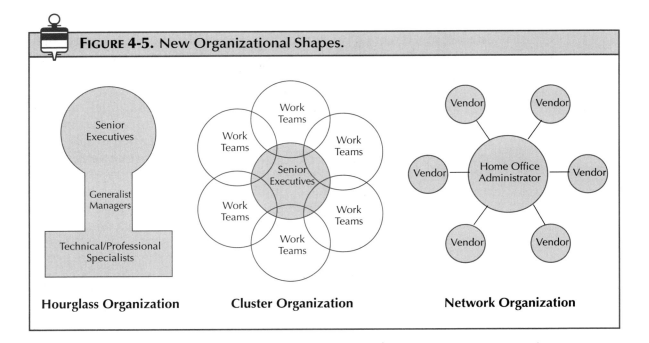

FIGURE 4-5. New Organizational Shapes.

Hourglass Organization

Senior Executives

Generalist Managers

Technical/Professional Specialists

Cluster Organization

Work Teams

Senior Executives

Network Organization

Vendor

Vendor

Vendor

Home Office Administrator

Vendor

Vendor

Vendor

Instead, they progress from team to team as projects warrant. Key to the success of a cluster organization is hiring employees who have a wide range of technical skills and who can handle flexible work assignments.

- **Network organization.** This structure is designed for the coordination of subcontracted production and marketing operations. The company itself contains only a handful of employees whose primary responsibility is administrative oversight. Network organizations have been called "virtual corporations" because their employees do not actually produce the products and services they sell. Instead, the company outsources most or all of its production, marketing, and support activities. ***Outsourcing*** is the process of hiring a vendor to provide a service rather than having the company's own employees provide the service. Focus on Technology 4-1 describes one virtual company in the life insurance industry.

Committees

Some aspects of a company's operations do not fall within the jurisdiction of any single department. To address these cross-jurisdictional operations, most companies establish special committees to bring together a number of people, each of whom has other responsibilities within the firm. A ***committee*** is a group of people chosen to consider, investigate, or act on matters of a certain kind. Committees exist at all levels of an organization and are used when a particular problem or task is best tackled by individuals with different talents and perspectives.

Permanent committees that company executives use as sources of continuing advice are called ***standing committees***. Companies establish other temporary committees, which may be called *ad hoc committees*, *project teams*, *work groups*, or *task forces*, for a specific purpose, such as planning a new information system, establishing a subsidiary company, developing a new product, or revising the company's accounting system. Once an ad hoc committee's purpose is accomplished, the committee is disbanded. Standing committees and ad hoc committees usually consist of a project chair or project director and several committee members. During the project, the committee members are responsible to the committee chairman, although the members do not completely sever ties with the departments from which they came.

A company's key executives and members of its board of directors make up several of the most important standing committees of any

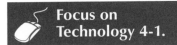

Focus on Technology 4-1.

A Virtual Life Insurance Company.

General Life Insurance Company may be the first true "virtual insurance company" in North America. Since its inception in 1995, GeneraLife has outsourced almost all of its operations.

The rationale behind a virtual insurer like GeneraLife is as follows: Life insurance companies traditionally employ hundreds or thousands of people to issue and administer policies. The fixed overhead costs (such as employee salaries and facilities expenses) of this method of operating are substantial, up to 80 percent of total costs. The fixed costs remain the same whether the company sells one policy or one million policies. The remaining 20 percent of costs are variable—that is, the costs fluctuate according to sales.

A virtual insurance company reverses that number. At GeneraLife only 20 percent of costs are fixed, and 80 percent are variable. GeneraLife achieves this cost reversal by (1) employing only a few people, (2) using current and emerging technologies to conduct operations, and (3) outsourcing (or subcontracting out) to third party administrators (TPAs) most of the functions typically found in life insurance home offices. These functions include application processing, underwriting, commission accounting, policyowner service, agent appointments, policy illustration design and support, policy filing, state licensing, technology development, and investment management.

GeneraLife incurs most of its expenses only when a policy sale takes place. As sales increase, overall company costs increase, but unit costs—the costs per policy—decrease. Theoretically, the company is able to pass the cost savings on to its policyholders in the form of more affordable products than those sold by competitors.

A key to the success of any virtual company is technology. GeneraLife makes a variety of information available through its Internet site, such as the status of policy applications, daily production reports, changes in existing policies, price quotations, and policy illustration software for agents (primarily agents with brokerage agencies). Also, the company has put in place the technology necessary to allow the TPAs to communicate with each other and with the home office.

Other cost savings are achieved through

- Short (one-page) policy applications, which reduce the time and expense associated with the traditional underwriting process
- Allowing policyowners to access their policies via GeneraLife's Internet site and to make their own changes of beneficiary, premium payment method, and name and address •

Sources: "GeneraLife," http://www.generalife.com (23 September 1999). Ron Panko, "Virtual Possibility," *Best's Review,* Life/Health ed. (May 1998): 56–58.

---

business. These committees, which are discussed in more detail in Figure 4-6, include the executive committee, investment committee, audit committee, and tax committee. By participating on committees, board members keep informed of the company's activities during the intervals between regular board meetings and can report on these activities at board meetings.

Insurance companies also have interdepartmental committees comprised of executives and upper-level managers from different departments. The responsibilities and types of interdepartmental committees vary from insurer to insurer. Examples of interdepartmental committees, which are shown in Figure 4-7, include the product development committee, underwriting committee, asset/liability committee, budget committee, corporate communications committee, research committee, and human resources committee.

FIGURE 4-6. Committees of the Board of Directors.

Executive Committee: Deals with questions of overall company policy, the lines of business that the company sells, the territories in which it operates, policies affecting the company's employees, and items not specifically assigned to other committees of the board of directors

Investment Committee: Determines the broad investment policy of the company

Audit Committee: Sets policy for the company's accounting department, reviews all company policies, oversees internal and external accounting and market conduct audits, and reviews the company's periodic financial statements

Tax Committee: Analyzes and evaluates the tax implications of company policies, programs, and rules, and keeps informed about corporate tax legislation

---

Human Resources Considerations

Keys to any successful organization are hiring the right people, adequately training them, and retaining these valued employees to help the company grow and prosper. Even the most carefully planned operations would be useless without qualified employees to carry them out.

The increasingly competitive and ever-changing business environment requires insurance companies to establish and maintain effective programs for training and developing employees. *Training* is generally defined as an activity directed toward learning, maintaining, and improving the skills necessary for current job performance. The primary purpose of training is to prepare employees to perform specific tasks, such as handling claims or programming a new computer system. *Development* is an activity directed toward learning and improving the skills needed for future job performance. Development tends to focus on strengthening the general business and management abilities of employees. Development usually provides employees with both technical knowledge and insights into the workings of human relationships in the business setting.

Training and development programs can be conducted *on-the-job* (while participants remain in the workplace) or *off-the-job* (while the participants are away from the work area). In traditional on-the-job training and development, an employee's co-worker or supervisor demonstrates procedures and techniques to the employee. For example, in the development technique known as *coaching*, a junior employee or junior manager is assigned to work with an experienced employee or manager and is given some of the work of the experienced person. In the technique known as *job rotation*, also called *cross training*, an employee moves from one position to another at regular intervals in

---

FIGURE 4-7. Interdepartmental Committees.

Product Development Committee: Reviews market research and recommendations from agents, brokers, and various departments within the company to decide whether enough consumer demand exists for the company to develop a new product or revise a current product

Underwriting Committee: Oversees the company's underwriting practices and underwriting research

Asset/Liability Committee: Analyzes the unique asset and liability characteristics of a company's products and asset portfolios; recommends optimal investment and product design strategies to better manage these separate components

Budget Committee: Prepares an annual budget of the company's estimated operating revenues and expenses

Corporate Communications Committee: Reviews and coordinates the company's policies on advertising, sales promotion, publicity, charitable contributions, relationships with the public, and internal communications

Research Committee: Analyzes product development and structure, underwriting practices, operational procedures, and actuarial problems; collects data and participates in intercompany studies; appraises the competitive position of the company; and reports on the actions of other companies

Human Resources Committee: Develops rules and regulations pertaining to the hiring, training, dismissal, and welfare of employees

---

order to develop expertise in a variety of jobs. Off-the-job training and development usually consist of lectures, conferences, seminars, college or university programs, and *programmed instruction*, in which educational devices—such as textbooks, workbooks, and computers—are used to provide trainees with (1) information about a subject, (2) opportunities to apply their knowledge of the subject, and (3) feedback about their progress in gaining knowledge.

Although more and more emphasis is being placed on training and developing employees, employee training and development have certain risks. Companies invest a great deal of time and money to train and develop their employees. However, a company receives no guarantee of a return on this investment because some employees change jobs frequently. A risk of providing employees with training and development opportunities is that the employees will take these new skills to another employer.

Because employers do not want their productive, well-trained people leaving the company, life insurers are focusing on retaining employees. Essentially, employee retention cannot take place if employees do not feel a sense of loyalty to the employer. We can define *employee loyalty* as an employee's commitment of energy and efforts to an organization. The starting point of employee loyalty is adequate

compensation, including salary, bonuses, and employee benefits. Beyond compensation, important factors in employee loyalty are allowing employees to contribute to the company's success and to be recognized and valued for that contribution.[5] Companies enhance employee loyalty by clearly communicating the performance goals of the organization and then establishing incentive programs that link the performance goals of the company with the performance goals of each employee. In this way, employees feel that they are doing worthwhile work that contributes to the organization as a whole, and they are adequately rewarded for their efforts.

Key Terms

coordination
function
responsibility
authority
accountability
delegation
organization chart
chain of command
unity of command
board of directors
inside director
outside director
strategic planning
tactical planning (operational planning)
centralized organization
decentralized organization
line unit (production department, operating department)

staff unit (service department)
line authority
staff authority
functional authority
profit center
cost center
strategic business unit (SBU)
matrix organization
outsourcing
committee
standing committee
training
development
coaching
job rotation (cross training)
programmed instruction
employee loyalty

Endnotes

1. In some insurance companies, a separate tax department determines the insurer's tax liabilities and oversees compliance with applicable tax laws.

2. *Decentralization* can also refer to the fact that a company maintains regional offices in various geographic locations.

3. A few companies have established traditional cost centers also as profit centers. These companies market the services of their cost centers to outside organizations. For example, an insurance company could sell the services of its own in-

formation systems (IS) department (a traditional cost center) to other companies. In this instance, the IS department would operate as a traditional cost center for its own company, but it would also generate revenue, and, in part, be considered a profit center.

4. Bureau of Labor Statistics, "Median Years of Tenure with Current Employer," *Labor Force Statistics from the Current Population Survey,* 24 September 1998, http://www.bls.gov/news.release/tenure.t05.htm (10 January 1999).

5. Debra Bailey Helwig, "From Paternalistic to Performance-Based: Employee Loyalty and the Changing Role of Human Resources," *Resource* (October 1998): 14.

Managing Information

LEARNING OBJECTIVES

After reading this chapter, you should be able to

- List the key elements of a computer-based information system

- Discuss the principal responsibilities of the information systems (IS) department

- Explain the purpose of a transaction processing system and list some transaction processing systems commonly used in life insurance companies

- Describe how decision support systems and expert systems can help insurers solve problems and make business decisions

- Understand the function of a database management system

- List some of the ways insurers engage in business-to-business electronic commerce and business-to-consumer electronic commerce

The life insurance industry is driven by information about customers, products, producers, investments, mortality rates, regulatory requirements, employees, and many other elements. The industry's main product—the insurance policy—is a collection of information (about the policyowner, policy provisions, policy value, premium rates, and promised benefits) rather than a tangible good like a television or a bar of soap.

To be of use to the company's operations, information must be managed effectively. **Information management** is the process of using a combination of systems and technology to ensure that information users get the right information at the right time in the right format. Effective information management also ensures that these users get only the information they need when they need it, and that they are not overwhelmed by information they don't need. Because all areas of an insurer need to manage information effectively, information management is the backbone of an insurance company's operations.

Information systems are at the heart of information management. An **information system** is a set of interrelated components that collects, manipulates, and disseminates information to meet an objective. The system also has a feedback mechanism to monitor the system and indicate when changes or adjustments are needed. The purpose of an information system is to assure that data and information are available, accessible, and understandable to users.

This chapter examines information systems and the ways that insurance companies manage information. We begin by explaining in more detail what information is and why it is important for insurers. We describe the basic elements of an information system. We conclude with a look at the ways life insurers use information systems and conduct business electronically.

Information Management in Company Operations

The term *information* is often confused with the term *data*. Generally, **data** is raw, unprocessed facts. A policyowner's name, address, and policy number are bits of data. **Information** is a collection of data organized so that it can be used. Data, once processed—that is, converted or transformed—can become useful information that a user applies to

solve a problem or take advantage of an opportunity. As a general rule, information can help people make decisions, whereas data alone does not.

For example, to a marketing manager, names of agents, customers, and products sold represent data. Only when this data is combined or organized in a meaningful way—such as number of sales by agent, by region, or by product—does this data become information of value to the marketing manager.

Life insurance companies need information that is accurate, complete, concise, relevant, clear, timely, accessible, presentable, economical, and secure. An important part of information management is taking steps to ensure that the company's information possesses these characteristics, which are described in Figure 5-1. If the information does not have these characteristics, the company may operate below its capabilities. For example, if customer attitude surveys are not well constructed or are administered too infrequently, an insurer's understanding of its customers' needs can be inaccurate or outdated. Similarly, if underwriters do not have up-to-date, accurate information about insurance applicants, they can make poor decisions in evaluating risks.

By managing information effectively, an insurance company improves its operations and provides itself with an advantage over competitors that do not manage information as effectively. For example, a company that uses information effectively can improve its customer service, and, thus, can increase customer loyalty. The company can attract sales agents by providing them with fast, easy access to product and policyowner information and flexible sales presentation tools. By gathering and analyzing accurate customer information, the insurer can identify potential customers and their insurance needs. Then the company can more quickly develop and price products to meet those needs.

Effective information management generally requires considerable use of computer-based technology—computers, networks, communication systems, software, and other equipment. The operating efficien-

FIGURE 5-1. Characteristics of Valuable Information.

Accurate: Free of errors

Clear: Easy to understand

Complete: Contains everything needed

Timely: Current and available when needed

Concise: Contains only the detail needed

Accessible: Available where needed

Relevant: Meets the needs of the information user

Presentable: Available in forms that meet the needs of the user

Economical: Cost is appropriate for its value

Secure: Accessible only to authorized users

cies gained by implementing technology can be substantial because the cost of computing power typically is far less than the cost of human processing power. However, the initial investment to acquire or upgrade the technology required for effective information management can be sizable. In addition to the cost of purchasing new equipment and software or developing new software, costs include training employees to maintain and use the new technology.

The current pace of technological change presents an insurer with difficult choices. If the insurer invests now in technology-related equipment, will the technology change radically in a year or two, leaving the company with an obsolete system? If the company pays for expensive new technology now to get ahead of its competitors, will its competitors be able to pay discount prices for the same technology in a few years and catch up with the company at a much-reduced cost? If the company waits while its competitors invest in new technology, will it fall behind, lose market share, and hinder its chance to compete?

To help evaluate the costs and benefits of new technology, an insurer develops strategic plans for its information systems. These plans describe the company's goals and strategies and then explain how the company's information systems and technology can be used to achieve those goals. Strategic planning for information systems usually includes goals and strategies for the IS department and for company-wide information systems activities.

Elements of an Information System

Insurance companies develop information systems to manage information and make it available on a timely basis to the people who need it. By definition, an information system is a type of *system*—a set of components that interact to accomplish goals. All systems have four elements in common: input, processing, output, and feedback, as shown in Figure 5-2.

- *Input* is an item or element that needs to be worked on by the system in order to achieve the system's objective. For example, in an underwriting system, completed applications are one type of input.

- *Processing* is the work performed by the system on the input. In our example, processing includes all of the steps in evaluating the application for insurance and collecting additional information about the proposed insured.

- *Output* is the result of the work done by the system. The output in our example is an underwriting decision on the application.

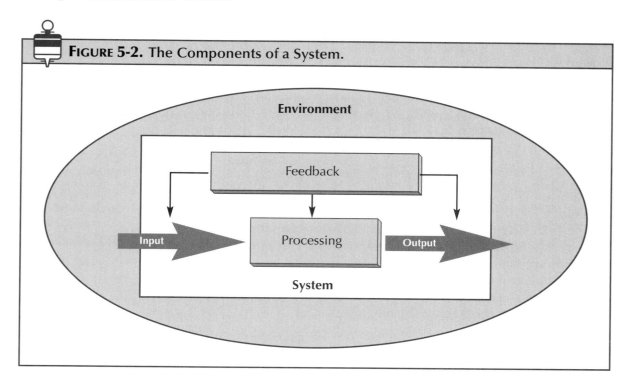

FIGURE 5-2. The Components of a System.

• *Feedback* is the part of the system that watches over and monitors the rest of the system. Feedback detects errors or problems that indicate when the system needs to be adjusted. The feedback mechanism in the underwriting example includes underwriting managers and actuaries who evaluate the underwriting decisions, and other employees, who monitor customers' and agents' satisfaction with the underwriting decisions and the underwriting process. The feedback mechanism alerts system users when adjustments need to be made in response to changes in the system's environment.

Information systems may be manual or computer-based. In a manual information system, people handle all of the steps. Manual systems, especially for routine or repetitive tasks, can be slow, inefficient, and prone to error. For this reason, most information systems today are computer-based information systems that consist of hardware, software, databases, and telecommunications and networks. Figure 5-3 illustrates a computer-based information system.

Hardware

Hardware is the machinery and mechanical devices that make up a computer-based information system. Hardware is used to perform the

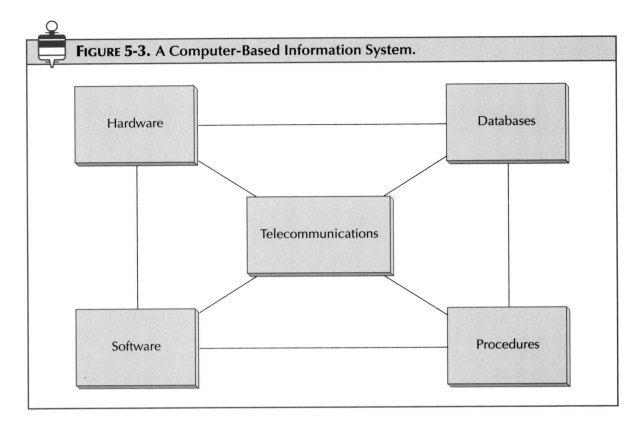

FIGURE 5-3. A Computer-Based Information System.

input, processing, and output activities of a computer-based information system. Examples of input hardware are a computer keyboard, computer mouse, optical scanning device, and voice-recognition device. Processing hardware includes a computer's ***central processing unit (CPU)***—the computer circuitry that performs the processing or data manipulation and that controls all other parts of the computer. Examples of output hardware are computer monitors (screens), printers, and secondary storage devices, such as diskettes and CD-ROMs. The computers used by agents in the field, as well as the computers used in the home office, are part of the hardware for an insurer's information system.

Software

Software consists of programs that provide the sequences of instructions for a computer and that govern its operation. One type of software, known as ***systems software***, coordinates the activities and functions of the hardware components and various programs throughout a computer system. Systems software is like a traffic manager that makes sure the instructions from the computer user are sent accurately

and efficiently to the CPU and other devices. ***Application software*** consists of programs that help users solve particular types of problems. Examples of application software are word processing software that create text documents, spreadsheet software that table data and perform calculations, and browsers that allow users to access and navigate the Internet. Insurers use these and other types of generic, "off-the-shelf" application software, and they also use many specialized application software programs that perform insurance-specific tasks. Figure 5-4 lists the types of application software programs that life insurance companies commonly use.

Databases

A ***database*** is an organized collection of information. Databases are important for virtually any company's success, and they are critical for information-driven companies such as insurers because databases provide a means of storing, organizing, and retrieving vast amounts of

FIGURE 5-4. Application Software in Insurance Companies.

Accounting Software: Maintains the company's essential accounting records and produces standard financial reports

Actuarial Software: Performs actuarial calculations, such as experience studies, profitability projections, surrender values, and statutory reserve valuations

Agency Management Software: Typically includes *database management software* to manage customer records, *policy application software* that contains applications for the company's products, and *illustration software* that generates policy illustrations for customers

Claim Administration Software: Helps staff evaluate claims, calculate correct benefit payments, and print benefit payment checks

Investment Management Software: Tracks individual investments, portfolios of investments, and entire investment markets; also allows users to compare the performance of various investments

Life Insurance Administration Software: Handles underwriting and policy issue processing, commission accounting, policy loan administration, billing and collection, policy value calculations, reinsurance transactions, statement preparation, and variable funds transfer processing

Market Research Software: Connects to databases that contain demographic information about the company's customers and markets, and allows users to perform statistical analyses of the data

Producer Administration Software: Handles agent contracts, licenses, production bonuses, contest qualifications, and commission checks

Production Reporting Software: Tracks and reports sales, premiums, product volumes, and experience

information insurers maintain about applications, policyowners, claimants, employees, producers, products, and competitors, to name a few subjects. The data in databases is used as the input for the company's information systems, including transaction processing systems, decision support systems, and expert systems.

Insurers use databases that vary in size, organization, purpose, and location. Some databases are developed internally and maintained for the insurer's own needs and uses. Insurers also use external databases developed and maintained by information providers. External databases provide information such as market demographics, economic information, actuarial studies, consumer information, and other topics. Figure 5-5 lists a few of the many external databases that life insurance companies use. Insurers access some external databases *online* using telecommunications technology (described in the next section). Other external databases provide their information *offline* in printed formats or on diskettes or CD-ROMs—optical disks that store data. Generally an insurance company pays a fee to the information provider for access to an external database.

FIGURE 5-5. External Databases Commonly Used by Life Insurance Companies.

American Council of Life Insurance (ACLI). Maintains online database of insurance laws, regulations, and insurance department organization.

Best's Database Services. Provides a variety of online- and CD-ROM–based information about insurance companies and insurance markets; available from A.M. Best Co.

Insource. Provides online or CD-ROM database of state insurance laws, regulations, and other insurance regulatory information; available through National Insurance Law Service.

LEXIS-NEXUS. Provides full-text legal research service and news, business, and financial research service. Both services are available via online database, CD-ROM, or books. Available from the LEXIS-NEXUS Group.

LIMRA Online. Contains information about life insurance marketing; available to members of LIMRA International.

MIB, Inc. On request, offers member insurance companies medical information reports on proposed insureds.

National Association of Insurance Commissioners (NAIC). Provides online information about insurance regulators and regulations.

U.S. Securities and Exchange Commission. Maintains an online database of product prospectuses for variable life insurance and annuity products and mutual funds.

WestLaw Service. Provides online databases concerned mainly with insurance law; available through West Publishing Company.

Telecommunications and Networks

Communication between computers is an integral part of most computer-based information systems. *Telecommunications* is the electronic transmission of communication signals that enables organizations to link computer systems into effective networks. A *network* is a group of interconnected computers and computer devices, including the telecommunications hardware and software that connect them. Telecommunications technology allows networks to be established among computers that are within close proximity—such as in the same room—or that are in different places around the world.

- A *local area network (LAN)* connects computer systems and devices located within the same geographical area, usually one building or one complex of several buildings. Each user on the LAN can connect to other users and computer devices on the network. For example, a user in one department can send a document from her computer to be printed on a printer in another location on the network.

- A *wide area network (WAN)* ties together computers and computer devices located across large geographic regions. Microwave or satellite transmission and telephone lines are necessary for a WAN. Two familiar public WANs are the *Internet*—a collection of interconnected networks, all freely exchanging information—and the public telephone system. Some large multinational companies have set up private international WANs so that employees in widely dispersed offices can communicate effectively. Figure 5-6 illustrates a LAN and a WAN.

Telecommunications and networks have numerous business applications for life insurance companies, a few of which are voice mail and electronic mail, electronic data interchange, and teleworking:

- Voice mail and electronic mail have become effective methods of communication. *Voice mail* is a system that ties a company's phone system to its computer system so that verbal messages can be sent, received, stored, and retrieved. *Electronic mail (e-mail)* is a telecommunication system that allows users to type messages or memos into computers and send those messages to other people who are connected to a network. Electronic mail can be sent over a small network within a single office or over huge networks that encompass the entire globe.

- *Electronic data interchange (EDI)* is the computer-to-computer exchange of standardized business transaction data between two

FIGURE 5-6. Local Area Network and Wide Area Network.

Local Area Network

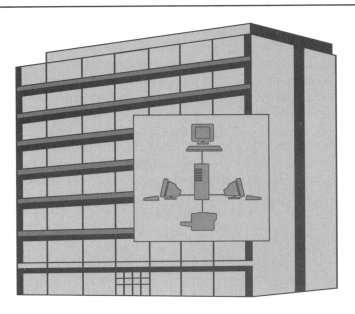

Wide Area Network

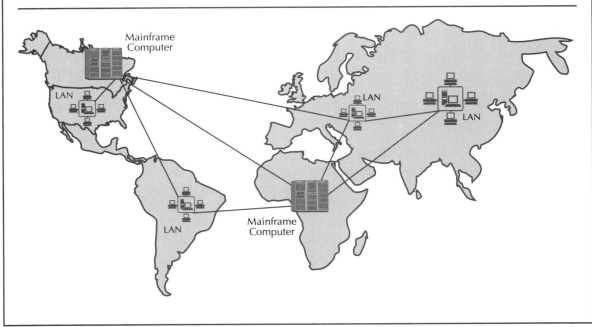

or more organizations. Organizations that agree to exchange information through EDI are said to be part of an EDI network. The primary purpose of an EDI network is to allow an organization to transmit documents directly from its computers to the computers of other organizations on the network. In the life insurance industry, EDI networks are used for many purposes, such as exchanging information with MIB, Inc. (also known as the Medical Information Bureau), transmitting completed insurance applications from agents to underwriting departments, authorizing banks to pay agents' commissions, transferring medical laboratory results to underwriting departments, transmitting policies from policy issue departments to agents, and many others.

- An increasing number of insurance companies are adopting policies regarding *teleworking*, also called *telecommuting*, which is the act of working outside the traditional office or workplace, usually at home, by using electronic means of communication with the office, colleagues, and customers. Teleworking saves employees from having to make a physical commute to the workplace. Insurance company employees likely to be able to telework are underwriters and claim analysts. A properly implemented teleworking program can provide an insurer with competitive advantages in the recruiting and retention of employees, real estate and office overhead expenses, and corporate image.

Security for Information Systems

To provide security for the valuable information in an information system, a company establishes rules and procedures that describe who can use the system (security procedures), how it can be used, what application programs can be run on the system, and disaster/business recovery procedures that will be taken if a fire, flood, earthquake, or other disaster renders the system unusable. For example, access to some information systems and databases is restricted to only certain authorized employees. These employees are given appropriate passwords and other procedures to enter the system or database. Insurers that have established Internet sites limit the public's access to their internal computer systems by installing firewalls on their internal systems. A *firewall* is a device that sits between a company's internal network and the outside Internet and limits access into and out of the internal network. The firewall can be a dedicated computer equipped with security measures or it can be a set of related software programs. For more on security issues and IS, read Insight 5-1.

Insight 5-1. **Security Is Vital to an Insurer's IS Operations.**

Security is one of the most important aspects of information systems management. Even if IS succeeds in all other areas, failure in security can lead to disaster for the IS area and the organization. Unauthorized access to corporate data and information can cause major disruption to business processes and may lead to financial losses. No matter the size of the IS department, security is an important issue.

Periodically, IS organizations perform a security audit or review. This audit will determine how well the organization's information is protected. Such an audit can be performed alone or with the assistance of an outside consulting firm. The end result of the audit is to correct any areas where security and/or confidentiality may be breached.

As companies open their systems to the public and to business partners, security risks increase greatly. IS managers need to research and deploy security software, such as Web server firewalls, to protect corporate data and to deal with growing threats from both internal and external sources.

Many software packages and in-house–developed systems have built-in security and auditing features. These features may allow those in charge of security to set user profiles and authorization levels. Performing regularly scheduled security audits can show where improvements need to be made. •

Source: Adapted from Gregory J. Blatnik, "Coping with New Challenges in Information Systems Management," *Resource* (April 1998): 34–35. Used with permission.

Organization of the Information Systems Department

The department that oversees a life insurance company's information systems and information management is usually called the *information systems (IS) department.* Other names for this department are *information technology (IT), management information systems (MIS), information management (IM),* and *information resources (IR).* The IS department is responsible for developing, operating, maintaining, and modifying computer-based information systems and for helping company employees make the most effective use of these systems.

IS operations may be centralized in a single department, decentralized throughout the company, or established through some combination of the two. In a centralized organization, one department performs all information systems functions for the entire company. This type of organizational structure ensures that (1) IS procedures are standardized throughout the company, (2) hardware and software throughout the company are compatible, and (3) IS initiatives are not duplicated. In a decentralized IS structure, major divisions within the insurance company hire their own information systems specialists and establish their own data processing units. Each division's IS staff can respond to requests for information systems support from within the division. Also, information systems can be tailored to meet the specific needs of the division, rather than the general needs of the entire company.

Today, many insurance companies organize the IS function using an approach that combines elements of centralization and decentralization. In such a system, a central IS department is responsible for setting and enforcing company-wide standards for system development, system security, and data quality. Any changes that affect company-wide systems are the responsibility of the central IS department. In addition, each division or business unit has the authority to buy hardware and software and to develop application programs that are critical to the division, even though they may not be critical to the entire company. By combining aspects of a centralized and decentralized organization, the company can respond effectively to the IS needs of users in various divisions and can assure that company-wide information systems development is directed toward achieving the company's strategic goals.

The head of the IS department is usually an executive known as the *chief information officer* or the *director of information systems.* This person organizes the IS department's equipment and people in a manner that will help the company achieve its goals. The chief information officer has management authority over a diverse group of managers, programmers, operators, administrators, and other technical employees. The range of technical expertise required of IS employees is significant and expanding as new technologies are created and applied by insurance companies.

The basic functions of the IS department are generally the same in most insurance companies. As shown in Figure 5-7, we can divide these functions into systems development, operations, and technical services.

Systems Development

The *systems development group* handles information systems analysis and design—in other words, the planning and creation of the company's information systems. This function is also responsible for maintaining system documentation, including descriptions of the system and user manuals. Key activities in systems development are

- *Systems analysis and design*—The process of examining business processes, suggesting ways to improve the processes, and designing computer systems to enhance the processes

- *Program development*—The process of using programming languages to design, code, test, and implement application software

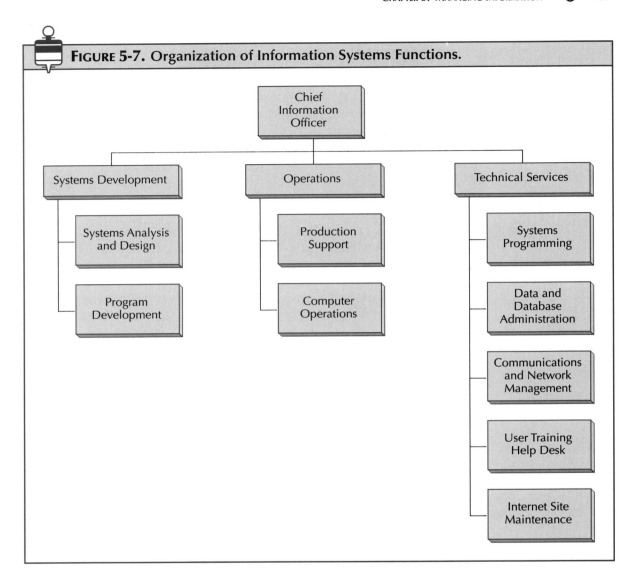

FIGURE 5-7. Organization of Information Systems Functions.

Operations

The *operations group* runs and maintains the company's computer systems, hardware, software, and other IS equipment. Operations activities include operating networks, tape drives, disk devices, and mainframe computer systems, and also preparing system inputs and outputs. A **mainframe computer** is a large central computer shared by hundreds of users connected through terminals. Some insurance companies have moved away from mainframe-based systems to using smaller personal computers that are distributed throughout the company.

These personal computers can accomplish many tasks independently but they are connected to a network using a ***client/server architecture*** in which users (clients) on the network make service requests from other computers (servers) that are dedicated to special functions. For example, network servers can be dedicated to printing, database management, communications, and executing programs. The servers distribute programs and data files as clients request them. Processing can take place at the server or the client. The operations group maintains the servers and other computers on the network.

Technical Services

The *technical services group,* sometimes called the *support group,* assists information users in acquiring and using hardware and software, as well as data administration, network management, and training. Although the duties of the technical services group can vary considerably from company to company, employees in this group typically

- Maintain the company's operating system software, including upgrading and testing the software, fine-tuning the software, implementing system security, and developing software to help the operating system work more effectively

- Establish and maintain the company's electronic databases, including choosing database management software and establishing and enforcing procedures for database use, database security, and data quality

- Establish the company's telecommunication networks, including voice communication (through traditional telephone lines) and computer communication (through computer-based LANs and WANs). The technical services group selects the communications hardware and software, network management software, and network security software. This group oversees, establishes, and enforces policies and procedures for network use.

- Establish, update, and manage the company's Internet site, intranet, and extranet. An ***intranet*** is an organization's internal network that uses Internet technology but is accessible only to people inside the organization. An ***extranet*** is a portion of an organization's internal computer network that uses Internet technology but is accessible only to selected parties outside the organization. (We will discuss intranets and extranets more later in this chapter.) Technical services staff work closely with company employees who provide the content of these sites to make sure that they are functional and appealing to customers and users.

"And this is Charles, our web-master."

- Operate a *help desk* that provides information users with computer assistance and training, application development, equipment selection and setup, technical assistance, and troubleshooting problems

---

Insurance Company Information Systems

Employees throughout an insurance company use computer-based information systems to do their jobs. The most common types of information systems that insurers use are transaction processing systems, decision support systems, expert systems, and database management systems.

Transaction Processing Systems

All insurance companies have **transaction processing systems**, which are organized collections of procedures, software, databases, and devices

used to record high-volume, routine, and repetitive business transactions. A *transaction* is any business-related exchange, such as a policy benefit paid in exchange for a proof of loss received, a policy underwritten in exchange for an application submitted, or wages paid in exchange for hours worked. The first—and still most widely used—computer-based information systems used by insurers were transaction processing systems designed to handle high-volume, routine, and repetitive activities, such as application processing, policy issue and administration, claim administration, salary and commission payment, and premium billing.

Think of the data generated when a person submits an application for insurance. The insurer must capture and process data about the applicant, the insured, the agent, the beneficiary, and the policy. After processing this transaction, the insurer must process additional transactions, such as those related to underwriting, premium billing, commission payments, and so on, that generate even more data. Without transaction processing systems to capture and process all the data, the insurer's operations would become cumbersome.

Like all systems, transaction processing systems have the four elements described earlier: input, a processing mechanism, output, and feedback. The input is some type of data that the transaction processing system captures. During processing, the captured data is used to (1) change the information that is currently in the system and (2) prepare the system to take some sort of action based on the new data it has obtained. For example, when a company receives a change of address request from a customer, that information is processed to change all permanent files affected by the change.

The output produced by a transaction processing system is a paper document or an electronic notice intended for a specific recipient. The output is also used to update the company's databases. Types of output documents include the following:

- Documents that provide a service for the recipient. Examples of this type of document are commission checks, benefit checks, and employee paychecks.

- Documents that request payment or other action from the recipient. A premium due notice and a purchase order are two examples.

- Documents that provide information to the recipient. A newly issued policy, a statement of policy values, a financial report, and a statement of benefits are examples of this type of output. Output documents also provide system operators with feedback about whether or not the transaction processing system is functioning properly. For example, an edit report describes any irregularities that the transaction processing software has found.

Decision Support Systems

In a general sense, a ***decision support system (DSS)*** is an organized collection of procedures, software, databases, and devices used to support decision making. A decision support system typically uses data and information captured and processed by transaction processing systems. The DSS then produces reports that help insurance company employees analyze business situations, make decisions, and solve problems.

One type of decision support system provides information about the company's daily operations and helps employees and managers make day-to-day decisions and control routine activities. This type of DSS is sometimes called a ***management information system (MIS)***. Reports produced by an MIS include sales reports, budget reports, benefit payment reports, lapse reports, commission reports, and balance sheets. An insurer can program its MIS to produce these reports (1) automatically at scheduled times, such as daily or weekly, (2) automatically when certain predetermined conditions or exceptions in operating performance occur, and (3) in special situations when a system user requests a report.

Another type of decision support system—the typical form of DSS—provides non-routine information that is used to support higher-level, problem-specific decision making. This type of DSS is designed to help managers develop alternative solutions to a particular problem, evaluate the possible impact of each solution, and choose the most appropriate solution. The DSS includes a database of information that will be used in decision making, a collection of mathematical models and analytical tools that the decision maker uses to study alternative solutions, and software and procedures that allow the decision maker to interact with the DSS. An example is an investment DSS that screens and compares different bonds and stocks so that an insurer's investment managers can decide which securities to buy and sell.

Expert Systems and Artificial Intelligence

Many insurance companies have developed expert systems that emulate human approaches to decision making. An ***expert system*** is a system of hardware and software that stores knowledge in the form of rules and uses that knowledge to make inferences and solve problems similar to the way a human expert does. We can distinguish expert systems from decision support systems in that decision support systems are designed to provide information that help people make decisions, whereas an expert system is designed to analyze the information and actually recommend or make specific decisions.

The basis for expert systems is ***artificial intelligence (AI)***, a field of technology that involves computer systems modeled on the

characteristics of human intelligence. AI software allows computers to make inferences and judgments as a human does. For example, to solve a problem or make a decision, AI software programs imitate the reasoning of human experts by applying certain rules to the facts of a particular situation and even, as necessary, modifying those rules to produce more effective results.

Two common applications of expert systems are in underwriting and claim administration. Many insurers use automated underwriting and claim administration systems based on "traditional" technology. Such an underwriting system analyzes routine insurance applications and makes an underwriting decision. Similarly, an automated claim administration system analyzes claim forms and claimant statements of routine claims and makes a decision as to the company's liability for each claim, then calculates the correct benefit amount and prints a benefit payment check. Although these systems have been used without artificial intelligence technology, the use of AI improves the capabilities of the systems and the quality of system decisions. Insurers also use AI to detect claim fraud.

Database Management Systems

Life insurers maintain databases in which they store vast amounts of data. But storing data is of little help to a company, unless employees and managers can access and use the data to guide the company's operations. To access databases, employees and managers typically use a ***database management system (DBMS)***, which is a group of programs that manipulates a database and allows users to obtain the information they need. A DBMS controls how databases are structured, accessed, and maintained. As shown in Figure 5-8, a DBMS is the link between a database and its users.

To illustrate a DBMS, consider the following example. An insurance company stores a wealth of data about its policyowners, the products they own, the producers who sold the policies, the claims made on those policies, the benefits paid, and so on. This data is critical for many types of applications, such as marketing, claim administration, accounting, and others. Rather than keeping this data in separate database files for each separate application, the insurer maintains the data in one customer database. Many companies call this database their *customer information file (CIF)*.[2] With the help of a DBMS, different application programs run by users throughout the company can share the data in the CIF. Employees in the agency operations unit can obtain data regarding company agents, the underwriting department can obtain data on policy applications, and the claim administration department can obtain data involving claims and benefits—all at the same time while using different application programs.

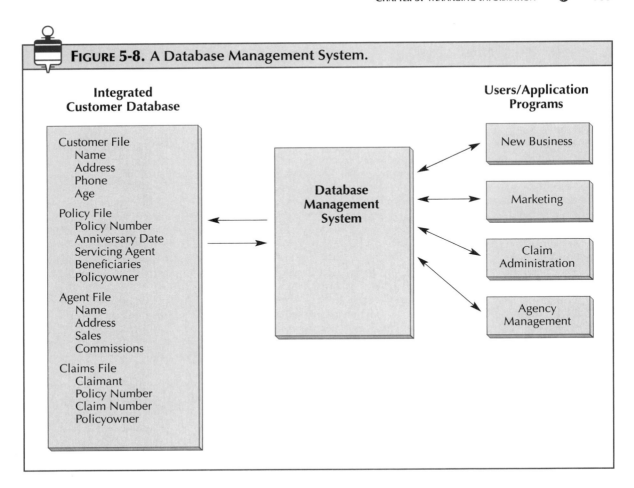

FIGURE 5-8. A Database Management System.

Many insurers use a type of DBMS known as a ***data warehouse***, which is designed specifically to support management decision making. The data warehouse collects data from the company's existing databases and from sources outside the company. The system then "cleans" the data—in other words, screens and edits the data and puts it in a standard format—and channels the data into a decision support database so that managers can use it to make business decisions.

An insurer can analyze the data in its data warehouses through ***data mining***, which is the analyzing of data in a data warehouse to discover trends, patterns, and relationships. Data mining uses advanced data structuring techniques and analysis tools to make discoveries about the patterns in the data. Data mining is often used in marketing to (1) analyze customer retention patterns, (2) identify opportunities to sell multiple products to existing customers, (3) analyze markets, distribution channels, and pricing, and (4) perform customer segmentation analyses. Focus on Technology 5-1 further discusses data mining in life insurance companies.

Focus on Technology 5-1. **Data Mining.**

In late 1996, IBM (White Plains, NY) approached the Farmers Insurance Group of Companies (Los Angeles) with an offer it couldn't refuse. IBM's research division had been working on a software package designed to predict policyholder profitability, and it wanted to test the software against the huge amounts of data being collected by the country's third-largest provider of automobile and homeowners' insurance.

The software, called the Underwriting Profitability Analysis Business Tool, relied on advanced mathematical and statistical algorithms to divide policyholders into categories based on risk. Such algorithms, which can find previously unknown and even unsuspected relationships among data, are fueling a database management function known as data mining.

Thanks to software like IBM's, and ever faster and cheaper hardware, insurers are increasingly able to take advantage of emerging data mining techniques to analyze the enormous amounts of data they are collecting about their customers. In the process, these companies are gaining a better understanding of their customers and are increasingly able to predict their behavior.

Insurance companies will begin seeing their customer databases as a corporate asset, says Harris Gordon, a partner in PriceWaterhouseCoopers' (New York) market and customer management practice. "What we're seeing now is that a lot of the leadership goes to companies that are using their customer information. This is an asset they own—it is a hidden asset because no one else can see the same information very easily. That now becomes a key asset that companies are managing," he says.

Data mining allows companies to rely on facts instead of anecdotal evidence about their customers' identities, the products they own, and their unserved needs. As a result, insurance companies can use data mining to divide customers into logical categories, to figure out what products to cross-sell to existing customers, to identify potential new customers, to identify their most profitable customers, and to improve their customer retention.

In order to begin implementing data mining technology, companies first go through a process of choosing the data they plan to analyze, aggregating it into a single data store, and making sure that the data is free of errors. Once a company has built such a "customer-centric" database, it can use data mining algorithms to compare customers and to find those with similar demographics or product portfolios.

The ultimate goal, according to a report by the Deloitte & Touche Consulting Group (Wilton, CT) entitled "Competing for Your Customers: The Future of Retail Financial Services," is to create customer segments. "The firm that attains this level of knowledge will offer customers only the products they need, when they need them. The results will be lifetime customer loyalty and superior returns," the Deloitte report says. ●

Source: Excerpted and adapted from Michele Rosen, "There's Gold in That There Data," *Insurance & Technology* (December 1998): 28–30. Used with permission.

Electronic Commerce

Many insurance companies use information systems to conduct some of their business electronically. ***Electronic commerce (e-commerce)***, also known as *electronic business (e-business)*, is the use of the Internet and other information technologies to perform or facilitate the performance of business transactions. Most people think of electronic commerce as simply the sales of products over the Internet. E-commerce does include sales and marketing, but it may also include billing and collecting, product delivery, customer service, and maintenance of information. With e-commerce, an insurer can use information systems

technology to allow customers to access and exchange information directly with the company without human intervention. The insurer can use the customer information to develop new products and services that encourage long-term relationships with customers. E-commerce eliminates some of the limitations of traditional commerce, because e-commerce can take place at any time of day and between businesses and people that are on opposite sides of the world.

Electronic commerce can take place between companies (*business-to-business e-commerce*) and between companies and consumers (*business-to-consumer e-commerce*). For insurance companies, business-to-business e-commerce includes electronic business transactions between the insurer and its producers, vendors, reinsurers, medical suppliers, and banks and other financial intermediaries.

Business-to-Business E-Commerce

Business-to-business e-commerce is becoming a favored way for some insurers to do business because transactions and information are captured electronically and are automatically input into the company's information system. As a result, transaction processing takes place automatically and immediately. Such electronic transactions are faster and cost less than comparable manual transactions. Best Case Scenario 5-1 illustrates how business-to-business e-commerce can improve an insurer's operations and reduce costs.

Best Case Scenario 5-1. | **Business-to-Business E-Commerce: Reinsurance Claims.**

The Best Friend Life Insurance Company issued a block of life insurance policies and ceded (transferred) a portion of the risk on these policies to Barrington Reinsurance Company. When claims were submitted under these policies, Best Friend paid the policy proceeds to the beneficiaries. Best Friend then submitted its own claim, using electronic data interchange (EDI) technology, to Barrington Re for the reinsurance benefit. Barrington Re's computer system received the electronic claim and automatically forwarded it into a claim adminis-

tration expert system for evaluation. Because the reinsurance claim met the criteria programmed into the system, the system approved the claim and automatically sent an electronic message to its bank. The message instructed the bank to transfer funds in the amount of the reinsurance proceeds to Best Friend's account at its own bank.

Barrington Re's bank then sent an electronic message to Best Friend's bank notifying it of the payment. After receiving the electronic payment, Best Friend's bank automatically sent an electronic message to

Best Friend confirming that the payment had been received.

This reinsurance claim was submitted, evaluated, processed, and paid quickly and accurately with virtually no human intervention. Information did not have to be re-keyed into a computer system, and thus data entry errors were eliminated. The system reduced the volume of paper moving throughout Best Friend and Barrington Re, and employees in both companies were able to view updated electronic records instantly. •

Business-to-business electronic commerce generally takes place through the Internet, intranets, extranets, and private networks. The Internet is a relatively simple and inexpensive way to transfer data between organizations that are business partners and to allow colleagues in different offices to send and receive electronic mail messages. However, security of Internet-based transactions is a concern for many people and businesses. Any user who is connected to the Internet may be able to gain access to data that is traveling over the Internet or to the proprietary systems of an insurer whose systems are also connected to the Internet. Some observers believe that the Internet presents too many security risks to be used for transmitting sensitive data about insurance companies and their customers.

Intranets, extranets, and private networks are generally considered more secure options than the Internet for conducting business-to-business e-commerce.

- As we defined earlier in this chapter, an *intranet* is an organization's internal network that uses Internet technology but is accessible only to people inside the organization. Intranets use the infrastructure of the Internet, but they are separated from the public Internet by a firewall (see Figure 5-9). Company employees can access the intranet, of course. The company can also use the intranet to communicate and exchange information with its captive agents.

- An extranet is a portion of an organization's internal computer network that uses Internet technology but is accessible to selected parties outside the organization, such as other organizations and business partners, with which the insurer needs to exchange information. In general, people from outside the insurer can access the extranet only if they follow established security procedures. An insurer usually grants access to its extranet to reinsurers, vendors, group insurance plan sponsors, independent agents, broker-dealers, and policyowners.

- Private networks represent a third option for secure business-to-business e-commerce. Some insurers establish private networks and supply their business partners with the appropriate security technology and procedures to transmit data along the network. Insurers may also use private networks, known as *value-added networks (VANs)*, that independent organizations make available for a fee. As with insurer-owned private networks, the insurer's trading partners are granted access to the VAN. Organizations that operate VANs include telephone companies, computer companies, and credit card companies.

FIGURE 5-9. Intranets, Extranets, and Firewalls.

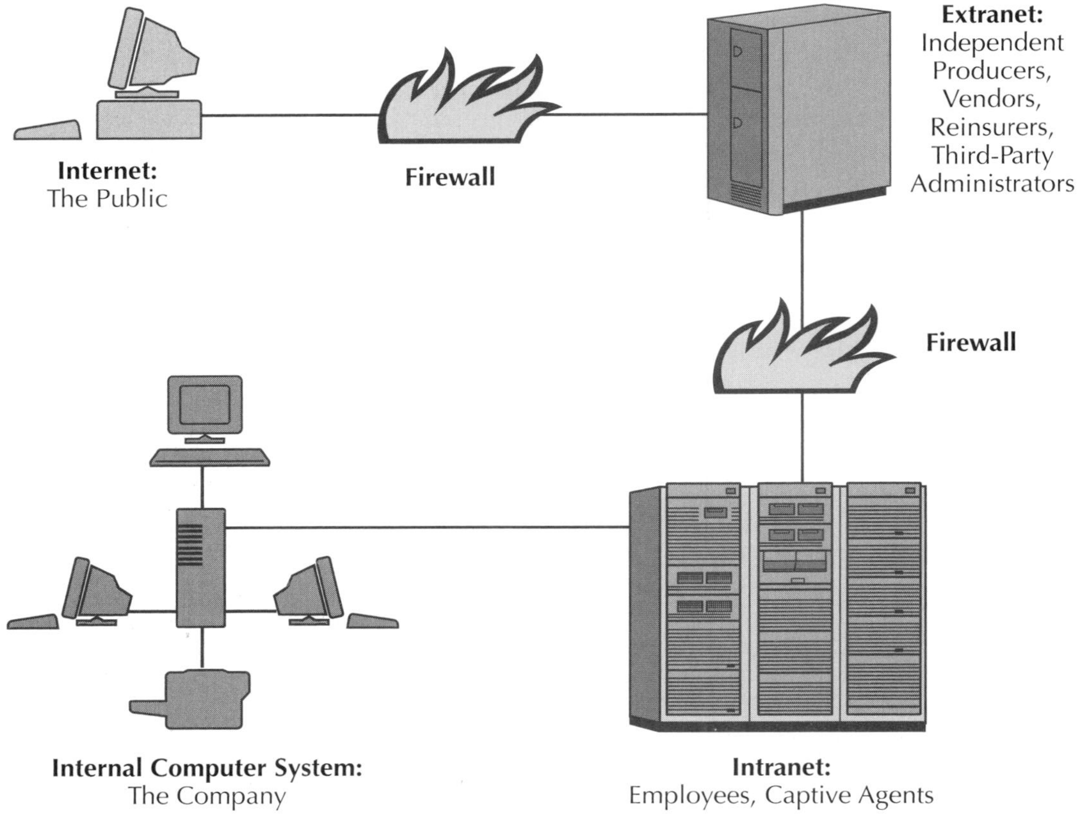

Internet:
The Public

Firewall

Extranet:
Independent
Producers,
Vendors,
Reinsurers,
Third-Party
Administrators

Firewall

Internal Computer System:
The Company

Intranet:
Employees, Captive Agents

Business-to-Consumer E-Commerce

An insurance company has several options for conducting product sales
electronically. One option is to offer products directly to consumers
via the insurer's Internet site. Potential customers visit the site, conduct their own insurance needs assessment, view a list of products,
obtain rate quotes on the products, and apply for products online. Another option is to provide product information on the insurer's site
and instruct customers to contact the company or one of its agents to
initiate a purchase.

A third e-commerce alternative is for an insurer to use an Internet
intermediary that links consumers with several insurance companies
either directly or through the companies' producers. For example, online

insurance marketplaces, also called *insurance aggregators,* list products from different insurers on a single site where consumers can comparison-shop for various forms of coverage. Depending on the site, a consumer may be able to obtain rate quote information and then be directed to the desired company. At other insurance marketplaces, customers can initiate the application process online with the insurer and pay the initial premium online by credit card or bank draft authorization. The insurance marketplace typically receives a fee from an insurer in return for each submitted application or qualified lead.

Some insurance companies allow customers to conduct customer service transactions and submit claims online. These activities are also considered aspects of electronic commerce and are expected to become more widely available in the future. We discuss online customer service in Chapter 13 and online claim administration in Chapter 14.

Key Terms

information management
information system
data
information
system
input
processing
output
feedback
hardware
central processing unit (CPU)
software
systems software
application software
database
telecommunications
network
local area network (LAN)
wide area network (WAN)
Internet
voice mail
electronic mail (e-mail)
electronic data interchange (EDI)

teleworking (telecommuting)
firewall
systems analysis and design
program development
mainframe computer
client-server architecture
intranet
extranet
transaction processing system
transaction
decision support system (DSS)
management information
   system (MIS)
expert system
artificial intelligence (AI)
database management system
   (DBMS)
data warehouse
data mining
electronic commerce
   (e-commerce, electronic
   business, e-business)

Endnotes

1. Rubin Systems, Inc., "Year 2000 Survey Results," *Survey & Reports,* http://www.hrubin.com/survey/financials.html (26 October 1999).

2. Many companies use the terms *file* and *database* interchangeably and not consistently with strict definitions.

Identifying Customers and Their Needs

LEARNING OBJECTIVES

After reading this chapter, you should be able to

- Describe the basic marketing activities of a life insurance company

- List the four variables that comprise the marketing mix

- Compare market segmentation and target marketing

- Discuss factors that insurers consider when identifying the needs of target customers

- Explain the role of marketing research in an insurer's marketing operations

- List the factors from a life insurance company's internal environment and external environment that affect the insurer's marketing operations

- Describe the function and purpose of a marketing plan

As market-driven organizations, life insurance companies respond to the needs of consumers who make up the market for insurance products and services. A ***market*** is a group of individuals or companies within the total population that make up the actual or potential buyers of a product. Life insurers satisfy the needs of their markets by providing financial protection in exchange for money. To create these exchanges, life insurance companies engage in a broad series of activities known collectively as marketing. Formally defined, ***marketing*** is the process of planning and executing the conception, pricing, promotion, and distribution of ideas, goods, and services to create exchanges that satisfy individual and organizational objectives. Effective marketing operations involve (1) determining organizational marketing objectives and customers' needs; (2) designing, developing, and pricing products to meet those needs; and (3) establishing and executing methods of promoting and distributing products to prospective buyers. In its broadest sense, marketing involves the following activities, which are discussed further in Figure 6-1:

- Market identification

- Planning and controlling

- Marketing research

- Product development

- Distribution

- Promotion

- Pricing

- Customer service

Marketing is generally considered to be the starting point for new business in an insurance company. ***New business*** is the general term used to describe all the activities required to market insurance, submit applications for insurance, evaluate the risks associated with those applications, and issue and deliver insurance policies. Along with marketing, other areas involved in new business include underwriting and policy issue. You should note that the term *new business* can also refer to (1) insurance applications submitted to insurers or (2) the area of an insurance company that actually receives the applications.

FIGURE 6-1. Basic Marketing Activities for Life Insurance Companies.

Market Identification. Marketers examine and select potential markets for the company's products. Market identification typically involves segmenting the total market into smaller submarkets and determining which market segments to target.

Planning and Controlling. Important aspects of marketing are (1) developing a marketing plan, (2) measuring and comparing marketing results to the marketing plan, and (3) modifying marketing activities as necessary to meet the plan's objectives.

Marketing Research. Research analysts within the marketing area find and compile information about the company's environment, including its competition, marketing opportunities or threats, and marketing performance. By studying the company's environment, marketers are able to develop sound marketing strategies.

Product Development. Marketers help undertake many of the activities needed to create or revise products to meet the needs of a particular market. The product development process involves many functional areas in a life insurance company, such as marketing, underwriting, claim administration, investments, actuarial, information systems, customer service, legal/compliance, and accounting.

Distribution. Marketers help coordinate the activities and resources involved in making products available to consumers. In some companies, a separate sales unit manages distribution.

Promotion. Marketers manage the various communication activities that the insurer uses to influence consumers to purchase its products.

Pricing. Marketers help determine the appropriate price to charge for an insurance product.

Customer Service. Marketers must help ensure that the company's customers are satisfied so that they will want to continue as clients of the company.

In this chapter, we introduce the concepts of the marketing mix and positioning. We then describe the processes of market segmentation and target marketing by which insurers identify and select potential markets for their products and design marketing strategies to reach these markets. Finally, we describe how insurers use marketing research to gather information and how they use this information to develop marketing plans that will enable them to effectively sell the products and services that consumers want and need.

The Marketing Mix

As you saw in Figure 6-1, marketing in an insurance company involves many aspects of conceiving product ideas, creating and developing those products, and distributing the products to consumers. In order to perform these tasks effectively, marketers develop strategies to manipulate four primary marketing variables—product, price, promotion, and distribution—collectively known as the ***marketing mix***.

- *Product* is the good or service that a seller offers to consumers to satisfy a need. For example, life insurance companies sell life insurance policies to satisfy consumers' need for protection against financial loss in the event of death.

- *Price* is what consumers give in exchange for the product being marketed.

- *Promotion* is the collection of activities that sellers use to communicate with consumers in an attempt to influence them to purchase products. Promotion may include anything from one-to-one conversations with customers to television advertising.

- *Distribution* is the collection of activities and resources involved in making products available to consumers.

Each of these variables in the marketing mix affects and is affected by the other variables. For example, the distribution method an insurer uses for a product affects the price of the product because the cost of the distribution method must be figured into the product's price. The type of product offered also affects the ways in which the company can promote the product. The insurer can promote a relatively simple product through a television or radio advertisement, whereas a more complex product generally requires promotion through sales agents who can explain its features.

Marketers develop specific strategies for planning and controlling each element of the marketing mix so that the company will be in the best position to achieve its marketing goals. These marketing goals should align with the overall strategic (long-term) goals of the company. For example, if a company's strategic goal is to be an industry leader in variable life insurance, then the marketing mix should contain specific product, price, promotion, and distribution strategies that will enable the company to sell variable life insurance policies to consumers who have a need for such insurance.

> **FAST FACT**
>
> During the first 11 months of 1998, Allstate Corporation spent more money on advertising—$74.4 million—than any other U.S. life insurer. The leading advertising spender among all financial services companies during that time was American Express Company with $235 million.[1]

Positioning

Insurance companies develop marketing mix strategies to achieve a desired position in the marketplace. *Positioning* involves defining a certain place or market niche for a product relative to competitors and their products and then using promotion and other elements of the marketing mix to support that position. Through positioning, an insurer attempts to distinguish itself from other insurers by building a company image or product image that contrasts with the images offered by competitors. An insurer may position itself on the basis of

- Company or product attributes

- Types of products offered

- Price and quality of products

- Target markets served

- Distribution characteristics

For instance, an insurer might attempt to position itself as "the most financially stable company," "the company for variable insurance products," or "the credit insurance leader." Other insurers may position themselves as "the company that offers the best value on term insurance products" or "the company for farming families." Still other insurers may position their appeal to consumers who want to purchase insurance products using the Internet or to consumers who want to develop a long-term relationship with an agent. The insurer develops its marketing campaigns and promotional pieces to support its intended position.

Market Identification

No life insurance company can profitably serve the needs of every imaginable consumer. Instead, marketers carefully direct their marketing efforts toward people whose needs the company can feasibly meet and whose business will contribute to the company's earnings, growth, and overall financial strength. Before beginning to develop and market its products, a life insurance company typically (1) identifies and evaluates the total market for the products the company is capable of offering, (2) selects the segment(s) of the total market on which the company will focus its marketing efforts, and (3) develops and implements a marketing mix strategy that will satisfy the needs of the chosen market segment(s). In order to accomplish these tasks, the company's marketers engage in market segmentation and target marketing.

Market Segmentation

Market segmentation is the process of dividing large, heterogeneous (dissimilar) markets into smaller, more homogeneous (similar) submarkets that have relatively similar needs. Each submarket, or group of customers with similar needs, is known as a ***market segment***. This process of identifying various market segments that make up the

total market helps the company determine which market segments to pursue.

If you imagine the entire market for life insurance as being comprised of every potential life insurance customer, a simple segmentation method is to divide the entire market into two broad categories known as consumer markets and organizational markets. **Consumer markets** consist of people who buy products for themselves or their families. **Organizational markets**, also called *business markets*, consist of people, groups, or formal organizations that purchase products and services for business purposes.

Although dividing the entire market into consumer segments and organizational segments is a first step in market segmentation, generally life insurance companies further divide these markets into smaller, more narrowly defined submarkets. These narrow submarkets can be based on a wide variety of characteristics, such as the following:

- The geographic location of market participants

- Variables such as age, gender, marital status, household composition, income, educational level, occupation, and nationality

- Types of consumer response to a particular product, such as benefits sought and the preferred method of purchase. For example, Figure 6-2 shows the preferred methods of purchase for life insurance buyers.

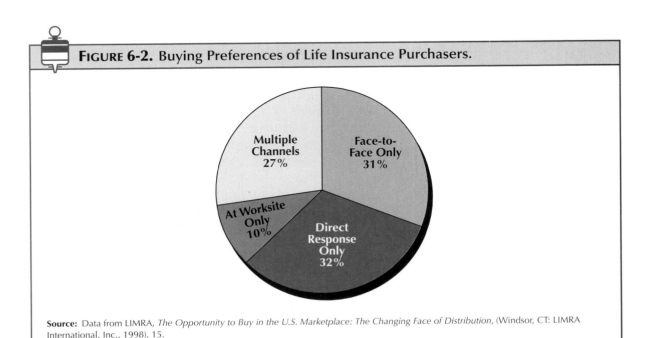

FIGURE 6-2. Buying Preferences of Life Insurance Purchasers.

Multiple Channels 27%

Face-to-Face Only 31%

At Worksite Only 10%

Direct Response Only 32%

Source: Data from LIMRA, *The Opportunity to Buy in the U.S. Marketplace: The Changing Face of Distribution,* (Windsor, CT: LIMRA International, Inc., 1998), 15.

The more narrowly defined each market segment is, the more precisely the insurer can identify the needs of that segment and focus its marketing efforts. For this reason, marketers often use more than one or two characteristics to segment a market. For example, a company typically cannot develop an effective marketing mix for a segment that is defined by sex and age alone. A segment of 35- to 45-year-old women has needs that are too diverse for an insurer to meet with just one marketing mix. Instead, the insurer can develop a more effective, meaningful marketing mix if it segments a market by age, gender, marital status, family status, and income. A marketing mix designed for 35- to 45-year-old divorced single mothers who earn between $50,000 and $75,000 per year is more likely to be successful.

Target Marketing

Once a company has subdivided the total market into clearly defined market segments, the company chooses the specific segments on which to concentrate its marketing efforts. *Target marketing* is the process of evaluating the attractiveness to the company of each market segment, selecting one or more of the segments—the *target markets*—on which to focus the company's marketing efforts, and designing the marketing strategy to reach them. Because each target market requires its own marketing mix, a life insurance company's choice of target markets helps determine the products the company develops, the prices it charges, its methods of distribution, and its advertising and promotional techniques.

Selecting Target Markets

Which market segments should a life insurance company pursue? Young singles or retired couples with grandchildren? Lower-income households in the United States or high-income households in Canada? Preferred risk teachers or substandard risk construction workers? Businesses and groups in urban areas or individuals and families in rural areas? Figure 6-3 shows several basic consumer market segments for life insurance companies. These are only a few of the many market segments that a life insurance company may target. Some factors that an insurer typically considers when selecting its target markets are each segment's growth potential, distribution and service costs, the current and expected competition within each segment, and the segment's fit within the company's overall corporate objectives and position within the industry.

FIGURE 6-3. Consumer Market Segments Targeted by Life Insurance Companies.

Segments Targeted by Life Cycle Stage:

- **Families:** Single parent (male), single parent (female), dual income with dependents, dual income without dependents

- **Singles (no dependents):** Retired, middle-aged, young professionals, college/university students

Segments Targeted by Income:

- High-income households (over $80,000 annually)

- Middle-income households ($25,000 to $80,000 annually)

- Low-income households (under $25,000 annually)

Segments Targeted by Buying Behavior:

- Homeowners

- Other borrowers of money

- Direct-response buyers

- Multiple/repeat purchasers of insurance

Segments Targeted by Affinity Group:

- Workers in certain occupations

- Members of social, religious, and ethnic organizations

- Alumni associations

Segments Targeted by Health:

- Preferred risks

- Standard risks

- Substandard risks

Target Marketing Strategies

The number of target markets an insurer chooses affects its marketing mix decisions. Three ways to categorize target marketing strategies are undifferentiated marketing, concentrated marketing, and differentiated marketing.

- ***Undifferentiated marketing***, also known as *mass marketing*, is a target marketing strategy by which a company defines the total

market for a product as its target market and produces only one product for that market. Henry Ford's strategy of marketing only one type and color of automobile to all customers is an example of undifferentiated marketing. Undifferentiated marketing requires only one marketing mix and may result in cost savings for the company and lower prices charged for the product. However, undifferentiated marketing ignores any differences that exist between various market segments of the total market. Some limited-face-amount term life products are sold through undifferentiated marketing.

- *Concentrated marketing* is a strategy by which a company focuses all of its marketing resources on satisfying the needs of one segment of the total market for a particular type of product. An example of concentrated marketing is offering mortgage protection life insurance policies to new homeowners. The advantage of concentrated marketing is that it allows a smaller insurer with limited resources to enter and compete in a particular market segment. A company can also gain extensive expertise in that market segment through concentrated marketing. The risk of concentrated marketing is that the company's profitability for the chosen product is tied to only one market segment. If conditions in that segment change, sales could suffer and the company may find itself in financial trouble.

- *Differentiated marketing* is a strategy by which a company attempts to satisfy the needs of different segments of the total market by offering a number of products and marketing mixes designed to appeal to the different segments. An example of differentiated marketing is an insurance company that offers traditional whole life insurance, universal life, variable life, and term life to different market segments within the total market for life insurance. Differentiated marketing can satisfy the needs of a greater number of customers than can the other strategies. The disadvantage of differentiated marketing is the relatively high cost of developing separate marketing mix strategies for each market segment.

Matching Products to Target Markets

You have seen that three important steps in life insurance company marketing are to first identify the total market, then divide the total market into narrowly defined segments, and finally select the market

segments that will be the target of the company's marketing efforts. With these steps completed, the insurer determines which products to sell to the consumers in its target market(s). Insurers attempt to market the product or products that its target consumers will be most likely to purchase. Generally speaking, this means marketing the products that best meet the needs of the target consumers. As we will explain, an insurer uses marketing research information to assess the needs of each target market so that it can match products to the consumers in that market.

For example, assume that one of an insurer's target markets is unmarried men aged 50 to 60 with no children or other dependents. For most of the members of this market segment, the need for life insurance is low, because the members have no dependents that would suffer financial distress in the event of the members' death. On the other hand, the members of this segment probably have a significant need for products that assure that they will not outlive their assets. Such products include variable life products and financial planning services. As another example, consumers in a market segment comprised of young, dual-income families with children—the market segment of our hypothetical family, the Carpenters—have a pressing need for affordable life insurance protection, perhaps with features that increase the death benefit (and the premium) over time.

After considering the needs of the consumers in its target markets, the insurer determines whether it already manufactures an appropriate product. If it does not, the company either develops a new product, revises one of its existing products, or purchases that line of business from another insurer. If none of these options is feasible, the insurer may decide not to pursue that target market.

Marketing Research

At the heart of insurance company marketing activities is information—information about market segments, the company itself, the competitors, the economy, the regulatory environment, and many other factors. Indeed, effective marketing would be an impossible task without timely information to guide decision making. ***Marketing research*** is the systematic gathering, recording, and analyzing of specific information that is essential in selling a company's goods and services. Marketing research includes all information gathering and evaluation techniques that insurers use to make effective marketing decisions. Insurers use marketing research information to identify and define opportunities and threats; to determine which consumers to pursue, what products these customers need and are most likely to purchase, and the most effective ways to inform customers about the insurer's

products; to monitor marketing performance; and to improve understanding of the marketing process.

Some insurance companies devote an entire unit of the marketing department to marketing research. In other companies, information gathering is one of several responsibilities assigned to certain marketing employees. Still other companies rely primarily on outside research firms for their marketing research. An insurer needs the answers to questions such as the following:

- What benefits are most important to customers?

- Who or what influences the purchasing decisions of customers?

- What are the general economic and business trends in the industry?

- What differentiates our products and services from those of our competitors?

- What changes should we make in our current distribution channels?

- What impact does our advertising have on sales?

- What changes might we make to our premium rate structure to give ourselves a competitive advantage?

The answers to these questions provide the insurer with information about the marketing environment in which it operates. The *marketing environment* consists of all of the elements in the company's internal and external environments that directly or indirectly affect the company's ability to carry out its marketing activities. A company's *internal environment* consists of those elements within the company that affect the company's business functions and over which the company has control. The *external environment* consists of those elements that are outside the company and over which the company has little or no control.

You should be aware that factors in the internal environment may also be factors in the external environment. For example, marketers normally consider a company's distribution system to be part of the company's internal environment, but the distribution system could be part of the internal environment, the external environment, or both. If the insurer uses only captive agents to sell its products, the distribution system would be part of the internal environment, because captive agents work exclusively for the insurer. If the insurer uses only brokers to sell its products, the distribution system is part of the external environment, because brokers are independent salespeople, not

"Our study concludes that this is the percentage
of our customers who will buy from us
without any effort whatsoever on our part."

© 1998 Ted Goff. Used with permission.

exclusive agents of the company. If an insurer uses both captive agents and brokers, the distribution system is part of both the internal and external marketing environments.

Internal Marketing Environment

A variety of internal factors affect an insurer's internal marketing environment. The primary internal factors are the company's (1) product mix, (2) target markets, (3) distribution systems, (4) corporate form, and (5) size and financial condition. Figure 6-4 graphically illustrates these internal factors.

The elements of a company's internal environment are sometimes strengths that marketers can build on. For example, a company's solid reputation can be a valuable asset. Sometimes, however, internal elements create constraints that limit the company's marketing activities. Only by honestly assessing its internal elements can a marketer create realistic marketing plans.

FIGURE 6-4. Factors Affecting the Internal Marketing Environment.

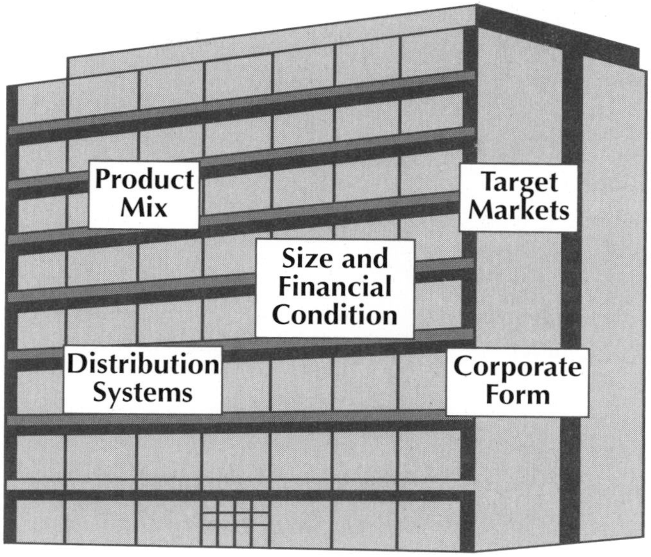

Product Mix

Life insurance companies can sell many types of products: life insurance, health insurance, annuities, mutual funds, and so forth. A ***product mix***, also called a *product portfolio,* is the range of products that a company makes available to consumers. An insurer's product mix and its experience with different types or lines of products have a significant impact on its marketing strategy. For example, an insurer may develop and sell more whole life insurance products than term life products. Thus, even if that insurer's marketing researchers uncover a marketing opportunity for term life, the company may not be prepared to pursue this market without a significant initial investment of money and time. In this case, the company's relative inexperience in term life is a ***constraint***—a factor that limits the marketing activities of the firm—when the company considers changing its product mix.

Target Markets

Companies generally do not attempt to serve every imaginable consumer. As you saw earlier in this chapter, insurers segment, or divide, the total market for their products into narrower markets and focus their marketing efforts on the members of only some of those markets. A company's experience in serving a particular target market can affect

its marketing strategies. For example, a company that concentrates on products for a lower-income market might not have the necessary knowledge or resources to expand into the variable life product line, which usually is directed toward a more affluent market segment.

Distribution System

A *distribution system*, also called a *distribution channel*, is a network of organizations and people that, in combination, performs all the marketing activities required to transfer products from the insurer to the customer. Life insurance companies can use several different distribution systems, such as career agents, insurance brokers, salaried sales staff, worksite marketing, direct mail, the Internet, securities firms, banks, and others. We describe distribution systems in Chapter 9.

Each distribution system requires its own sales techniques and, frequently, its own types of products. As we have noted, a complex product such as universal life insurance may be easiest to sell through an agency system, whereas a simpler product, such as term life insurance, may be sold efficiently through direct mail, the Internet, or banks. As part of its marketing mix strategy, an insurer matches the choice of distribution method with the company's products and target markets.

Corporate Form

The corporate form of an insurer—that is, whether the company is a stock company or a mutual company—affects the ability of the insurer to obtain additional sources of funds to use for growth, expansion, acquisition, or financial stability. Expanding sales activities into new states or provinces typically require a great deal of funds. The ability of a stock life insurance company to issue additional stock to raise funds quickly is an advantage if the company wishes to pursue such an expansion strategy.

Company Size and Financial Condition

The company's size can either limit or enhance the number of marketing opportunities it can pursue. As a general rule, a large company with vast resources (financial, technological, and human) is better able to enter more markets and provide more products than is a smaller company with fewer resources. Smaller companies, however, are not always at a disadvantage. One advantage of a smaller company is that it may be able to react to a change in the environment more quickly and efficiently than a larger company. Regardless of size, a life insurer on stable financial ground is better equipped to accomplish long-range marketing objectives than is an insurer in a weak financial position.

External Marketing Environment

Marketing research must also gather information about factors in a life insurance company's external environment. Figure 6-5 shows five categories of external factors: the (1) economic environment, (2) demographic environment, (3) technological environment, (4) competitive environment, and (5) regulatory environment. Because they are typically beyond the insurer's control, these external factors can be more difficult to predict and to plan for than are internal factors. Complicating the marketing department's job of evaluating the external environment is the fact that the external environment does not stand still. Changes occur continually. As a result, insurers must find ways to anticipate and respond to environmental changes.

Economic Environment

All businesses operate within several different economies, such as a state or provincial economy, a national economy, and a global economy. An *economy* is a system for producing, distributing, and consuming goods and services. Economic factors can significantly affect the way life insurance companies operate and market products and can affect the spending habits of consumers. A few of the many economic factors of concern to insurers are

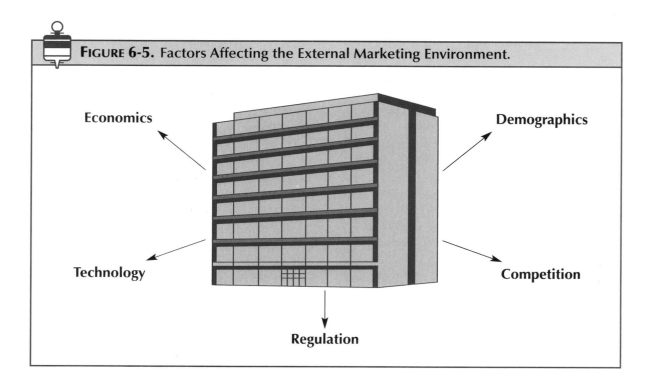

FIGURE 6-5. Factors Affecting the External Marketing Environment.

Economics

Demographics

Technology

Competition

Regulation

- The *business cycle*, which is a process of cumulative change in the total economic activity of a nation over a time span longer than a year. Research has shown that the level of economic activity and consumers' willingness and ability to purchase goods and services tends to progress through several stages.

- The level of interest rates, which reflect the cost of borrowing in an economy. Because many life insurance products contain interest rate guarantees, and because insurers collectively invest billions of premium dollars in interest-sensitive investments (such as bonds and mortgages), insurers are mindful of actual and expected changes in interest rates.

- The rate of *inflation*, which is a rise in the average level of prices in the economy. During periods of high inflation, consumers lose purchasing power and tend to reduce their spending on discretionary goods, such as life insurance products. High inflation also tends to increase the level of interest rates, which, as noted above, is of great concern to insurers.

- The rate of unemployment, which is the percentage of people in an economy's labor force that are not currently working. High levels of unemployment can slow down economic activity, including the sales of new insurance products, and increase the lapse rates of policies in force.

- The value of securities prices. High or rising securities prices tend to increase the public's demand for variable and equity-based insurance products, while low or falling securities prices create more demand for traditional, guaranteed insurance products. The value of securities also affects the performance of insurers' investment portfolios.

Insight 6-1 discusses how recent economic conditions are affecting insurers' marketing operations.

Demographic Environment

Marketing specialists typically study various groups of consumers who comprise a population. The needs of these consumer groups are strongly related to their *demographics*, which are measurable characteristics that define or describe a given population. Commonly used demographic characteristics include age, sex, marital status, household composition, income, stages in the life cycle, race, nationality, education, and occupation. Consumers' insurance needs are based, at least in part, on their demographic characteristics. As a result, changing

Insight 6-1.   Adjusting to the New Economy.

Since the 1990s, many of the world's nations have witnessed the rise of what has been dubbed the New Economy, sometimes called the Digital Economy or the Information Economy. This New Economy is characterized by low inflation, a sustained high growth rate, more productive workers, and moderate-to-low levels of unemployment.

The catalysts for the New Economy are a wave of technological innovation and the resulting globalization of communications and operations. New technologies have made employees and companies more efficient and productive than ever before, and a mass of worldwide computer networks has effectively created a global economy. Global competition has increased and has kept down the prices of goods and services and the rate of inflation. An outcome of the New Economy is that money, technology, information, and goods flow across national borders with unprecedented ease and speed. In many industries, including the insurance industry, companies are marketing products in multiple countries more than ever before, and they are continually searching for new markets abroad to enter.

However, the global economy has also created an environment in which events in virtually any country can almost immediately affect financial conditions around the world. The result is an increased potential for wide, short-term fluctuations in certain economic conditions. For example, in the summer and fall of 1998, stock prices in the United States and Canada fluctuated wildly, in part because of financial crises in Asia, Russia, and Latin America. Many U.S. and Canadian insurers were affected because they had operations in these countries, they held investments that originated in these countries, and/or they sold products whose values were based in part on the values of investments that originated in these countries.

On a broader scale, the entire financial structure supporting the modern global economy is put at risk by continuing, or worsening, financial crises in countries around the world. In consideration of the vital, global new economy, life insurance companies are now aware that, as economic conditions and trends in other parts of the world change, marketing opportunities and constraints both at home and abroad change as well. •

Sources: Dean Foust and Owen Ullmann, "Alan Greenspan's Brave New World," *Business Week,* 14 July 1997, 45–50. Debra Bailey Helwig, "The Digital Economy: Twelve Steps for Navigating the Infobahn," *Resource* (May 1997): 7–15. Catharine M. Johnson, "The Changing Structure of the Life Insurance Industry and the International Financial Crisis," *Resource* (November 1998): 6–15. Michael J. Mandel, "The New Economy: For Better or Worse," *Business Week,* 19 October 1998, 42.

demographic characteristics, such as the following, are important considerations for life insurance marketers:

- The overall populations of most industrialized countries are maturing. Consumers are not only concerned about life insurance protection, but also want to be protected against outliving their assets, and they are preparing to fund most of their retirements themselves. This situation has created many new marketing opportunities and challenges for insurers.

- As shown in Figure 6-6, the percentage of women in the labor force continues to rise. Families are more likely than ever to have two incomes, thereby increasing the need for life insurance because two incomes need to be protected rather than one.

- The populations of most developed nations are achieving higher levels of education than ever before. Contrasted to people with lower levels of education, well-educated people tend to have

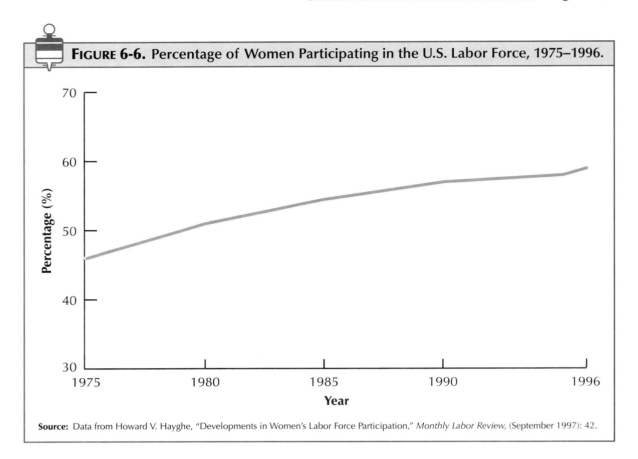

FIGURE 6-6. Percentage of Women Participating in the U.S. Labor Force, 1975–1996.

Source: Data from Howard V. Hayghe, "Developments in Women's Labor Force Participation," *Monthly Labor Review,* (September 1997): 42.

higher-paying jobs and are more likely to recognize their need for financial security and to take the necessary steps to obtain that security.

Technological Environment

One of the most powerful external factors affecting life insurance company marketers is the ongoing revolution in computer, telecommunications, and information technologies. Advances in technology have led to the development of new insurance products, new pricing methods, new promotion methods, and new distribution systems. For example, the rise of the Internet has spurred electronic commerce and has given insurers a new method of promoting, distributing, and servicing products and conducting marketing research. Also, portable computers and CD-ROMs allow sales agents to develop personal policy illustrations almost instantly and virtually anywhere, thereby reducing the amount of time and the number of sales calls needed to inform a customer and generate a sale.

Focus on Technology 6-1 further discusses the impact of technology on marketing.

Competitive Environment

All companies face **competitors**—other companies that can provide a product or service to satisfy the needs of a specific market. As you learned in Chapter 2, competition for the sale of life insurance products comes from other insurance companies as well as other types of financial institutions that are selling similar products to the same markets. An insurer's marketing mix and marketing strategies are influenced by the approaches taken by competitors in products, target markets, prices, and marketing strategies. Marketers must regularly monitor the competitive environment to identify potential threats to the company's market share and opportunities to increase it.

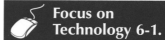

Focus on Technology 6-1.   Technology and Marketing.

Marketing used to be about creative execution—the wittiest commercial, the best copy, the most elegant layout. But that's all changing. As technology becomes more common in the marketing department, marketing becomes both art and science. The creative marketing program is now being supported by stronger and more detailed demographic analysis and customer analysis.

So marketers are growing more reliant on the information systems department to build, buy, or outsource the hardware and software solutions needed to survive in the 21st century. The result is that marketing departments across all industries are changing rapidly on five fronts:

1. *From mass marketing to database marketing.* The marketing executive must use database technology to target advertising much more precisely. This entails gathering more information about customers and exploiting that information by tailoring the message to the needs of the target audience, and so more clearly differentiating products and services.

2. *From mass media to interactive media.* Customers increasingly want to choose when, where, and how they deal with suppliers. This means addressing customer needs individually and providing services the way the customer prefers. Interactive media will play a critical role in this process.

3. *From market share to relationship enrichment.* Because the marketing department may serve rather than sell, the emphasis will be on enrichment of the customer relationship rather than on market share alone.

4. *From sales to customer service.* Marketing no longer means getting one message out to the broadest possible audience. It means taking care of customers. So marketing is beginning to move into production, logistics, customer service centers, and help desks, helping to remove the barriers that stand in the way of sales.

5. *From most creative to most technologically sophisticated.* Today, the Internet is a basic requirement in all marketing strategies. In the past, the best marketers were the most creative. Today, the best marketers are the most technologically sophisticated.

The successful marketing professionals of the future will be those who embrace the changes and implement them as effectively as possible. The successful application of technology to the problems of the marketing department will allow the leveraging of traditional marketing skills to create more efficient and more effective campaigns. Customers are more likely to receive the marketing message they are really interested in, and the corporation is able to spread its resources more effectively. •

Source: Excerpted from Scott Nelson, "Marketing," *Executive Edge* (September 1998): 8. Reprinted by permission of Executive Edge Magazine © 2000 Forbes, Special Interest Publication 1998.

Regulatory Environment

Laws and regulatory requirements specify the permissible and prohibited activities of a life insurer's operations, including its marketing activities. For example, state laws typically modeled after the Unfair Trade Practices Act govern many aspects of an insurer's marketing operation as well as the activities of its sales force. The **Unfair Trade Practices Act** is an NAIC model act that defines certain practices as unfair and prohibits those practices in the business of insurance if they are committed (1) flagrantly in conscious disregard of the Act or (2) so frequently as to indicate a general business practice. Unfair trade practices laws are intended primarily to protect the interests of consumers purchasing insurance and cover such topics as the use of sales materials and advertisements, unfair discrimination, policy replacements, and the handling of consumer complaints.

New laws and regulations can open or close markets for the company's products, can affect distribution plans, and can enhance or limit product development opportunities. Marketing strategy not only incorporates current legal requirements, but also considers the possible consequences of proposed regulatory changes and makes provisions to adapt to such changes if they occur.

Sources of Marketing Information

Insurance companies use a number of sources for gathering information about their internal and external environments. Figure 6-7 lists many of these sources. The vast majority of the information gathered today comes from public sources, such as online computer databases and business and insurance periodicals. Marketing researchers also study their own company's internal reports to determine current sales and profits for various products. Researchers use this information to forecast likely trends within their own company and thus create plans for a variety of future situations. Researchers also keep track of their primary competitors' products, commission schedules, and premium rates. Marketing researchers survey insurance agents and policyowners to determine their feelings about insurance products. Companies that do not distribute their products through agents have become especially adept at using surveys, interviews, and analyses of insurance applications to obtain product development information directly from consumers.

FIGURE 6-7. Sources of Marketing Research Information for Life Insurance Companies.

Business and insurance periodicals, such as *The Wall Street Journal, The Financial Post, Best's Review, National Underwriter, BusinessWeek, Business Insurance, Advertising Age, Marketing News, Sales and Marketing Management, American Demographics,* Deloitte & Touche *Review, Life Association News,* Tillinghast-Towers Perrin's *Emphasis, The Record of the Society of Actuaries, Journal of the American Society of Financial Services Professionals,* LIMRA's *MarketFacts,* and LOMA's *Resource*

Online databases, such as the Internet-based sites of the U.S. Census Bureau, the U.S. Department of Labor, and Statistics Canada

Industry and professional association committees and meetings, such as those of LIMRA International, LOMA, the American Council of Life Insurance (ACLI), and the Canadian Life and Health Insurance Association (CLHIA)

Competitors' advertisements and publications

Insurance industry vendors, such as consultants, advertising agencies, public relations firms, and management service companies

Personal and professional contacts with managers, brokers, and sales agents of other insurance companies

---

The Marketing Plan

Market-driven life insurance companies plan and control their marketing activities with an instrument known as a marketing plan. The ***marketing plan*** is a set of specific, detailed, action-oriented tactics dealing primarily with the product, price, distribution, and promotion strategies that a company will follow in order to reach and satisfy the needs of its target markets. The marketing plan spells out the marketing aspects of an insurance company's strategic plans and provides details about the company's marketing mix. A marketing plan helps an insurer coordinate all of its marketing activities.

Developing the Marketing Plan

Careful development of this plan is critical to a successful marketing operation. Furthermore, the marketing plan affects many of an insurer's other operations. For these reasons, senior company executives and participants from other divisions and departments join in creating the marketing plan. Typically, key members of the distribution system also participate. For example, life insurance companies that

use an agency distribution system usually include members of the agency force in developing the marketing plan.

Development of the marketing plan begins with a careful review of the company's long-range and short-range business objectives. By considering both types of objectives, the marketing staff assures that the marketing plan agrees with overall corporate goals and helps turn these goals into specific, action-oriented strategies. Typically, a marketing plan covers a period of one to five years, with goals and actions for the first year described in more detail than are the goals and actions for subsequent years.

Elements of the Marketing Plan

Marketing plans differ from company to company depending on the size of the company and its marketing objectives. But most marketing plans include the following seven elements:

- *Executive summary*—A summary of the plan's proposed actions, the total costs involved with these actions, and the intended results of the actions

- *Situation analysis*—A list of the environmental factors (both internal and external) that affect the company's marketing operations

- *Marketing objectives*—A list of the goals that the company hopes to achieve as a result of its marketing efforts

- *Marketing strategies*—The broad plans for achieving the company's marketing objectives

- *Tactical/action programs*—Descriptions of the marketing activities that are to be performed, the people who are responsible for performing the activities, and the results (revenue, profit, awareness, attitude change, etc.) that are expected to be produced by the activities

- *Budgets*—Schedules of projected expenses and revenues that (1) show how funds will be allocated to various elements of the marketing mix and (2) divide those funds among the activities associated with each element

- *Evaluation and control methodology*—The controls that the company will use to analyze the progress and success of the marketing plan

Best Case Scenario 6-1 illustrates a life insurer's marketing plan. You should be aware that an actual marketing plan is much longer and much more detailed.

Communicating the Marketing Plan

A marketing plan affects many of an insurer's functional areas in addition to the marketing department. Once a life insurance company prepares its marketing plan, senior managers communicate the goals, strategies, and action programs of the plan to all areas of the company. Each area must be aware of the marketing plan in order to determine the impact of the plan on the area's own operations. For example, the claim administration area needs projections of the expected number of policies issued and claims expected during each of the next five years so that it can develop an adequately trained staff to handle the workload.

Control and the Marketing Plan

After the marketing plan has been in effect for a specified period of time, marketing specialists study the results of the company's efforts to analyze why the company has or has not met its goals. Marketing research techniques can be used to evaluate the effectiveness of the company's customer service and advertising campaigns as well as the overall success of the company's various products. If sales results do not reach the levels projected in the marketing plan, marketing analysts can attempt to determine why and can help marketers choose corrective actions.

Key Terms

market	consumer market
marketing	organizational market (business market)
new business	
marketing mix	target marketing
product	target market
price	undifferentiated marketing (mass marketing)
promotion	
distribution	concentrated marketing
positioning	differentiated marketing
market segmentation	marketing research
market segment	product mix (product portfolio)

Best Case Scenario 6-1. **A Marketing Plan.**

Marketing Plan for the Best Friend Life Insurance Company

Executive Summary
This marketing plan directs the marketing actions of the Best Friend Life Insurance Company in State A and State B. The goal of the plan is to increase life insurance premium income by 15 percent within 12 months. This plan proposes to accomplish this goal by establishing specific increases in premium income for the company's various life insurance products.

Situation Analysis
Significant factors affecting Best Friend's external and internal environment include the following:

1. Two new competitors have entered the life insurance market in State A and State B.

2. State A and State B are undergoing greater-than-average population growth.

3. The current level of national inflation is expected to remain relatively stable for the next 12 months.

4. The U.S. Congress is debating a bill that would make electronic signatures legally binding and would pre-empt state regulations on validating electronic signatures until the states have their own policies in place.

5. Best Friend actively uses an Internet site that provides basic information about the company and its products.

Marketing Objectives
In order to increase overall life insurance premium income by 15 percent, Best Friend must increase premium income for its universal life product line by 20 percent and increase premium income for its term life product line by 10 percent.

Marketing Strategies
To increase universal life premium income by 20 percent and term life premium income by 10 percent, Best Friend proposes to (1) open two new sales offices in State A and two in State B and (2) expand the company's Internet site to enable consumers to obtain term life insurance price quotations, to locate a Best Friend sales agent, and to apply for term life insurance online.

Tactical/Action Programs
Appendix I of this marketing plan includes the activities and schedules for opening the new sales offices in States A and B. The activities and schedules cover staffing the new offices and developing contracts with sales agents. Appendix II of this marketing plan lists the activities and schedules for adding the price quotation, agent locator, and online application capabilities to Best Friend's Internet site.

Budgets
Appendix III of this marketing plan includes cost and revenue projections for each new sales office and the costs of expanding the Internet site. The Appendix also shows the funds necessary to provide for Best Friend's ongoing marketing operations.

Evaluation and Control
Senior managers at Best Friend will compare monthly premium income and cash flow projections to actual experience for the universal life insurance and term life insurance product lines. By comparing projections to actual experience, senior managers will be able to determine if the company is meeting its goals and budgets. Company executives will also use this information to determine the effectiveness of the marketing plan and to suggest modifications to improve the marketing planning process in the future.

Key Terms, continued

constraint

distribution system (distribution channel)

economy

business cycle

inflation

demographics

competitor

Unfair Trade Practices Act

marketing plan

Endnote

1. Lynna Goch, "Name That Brand," *Best's Review,* Life/Health ed. (May 1999): 26.

CHAPTER 7

Developing New Products

LEARNING OBJECTIVES

After reading this chapter, you should be able to

- List the main phases of product development

- Explain how insurance companies generate and screen ideas for new products

- Describe why and how insurers conduct a comprehensive business analysis of product ideas

- List the main activities involved in the technical design phase of product development

- Identify each area of the company that is involved in product implementation and state the role of each area in implementation

- Discuss how insurers monitor early sales of a new product

- State the elements of an effective product development process for life insurance companies

You have learned how life insurance companies select their target markets and identify the insurance needs of the people and businesses in those markets. An insurer develops new products and revises existing products to meet the recognized needs of its target consumers and contribute to the financial well-being of the company. The focus of this chapter is the product development process—that is, all the steps the insurer takes in transforming a product idea into a marketable product.

The development of new insurance products is similar to product development in most industries. For example, all automobile manufacturers develop essentially the same product: a vehicle with wheels, a chassis, an engine, and so forth, to transport people and cargo. However, in an attempt to satisfy various consumer needs and tastes, each manufacturer differentiates its vehicles from the vehicles of its competitors on the basis of styling, size, fuel mileage, comfort, price, and other factors. Insurance companies also attempt to differentiate the same basic products using such factors as price, features, benefits, customer service, and policy values. Because the current environment for life insurance sales is intensely competitive, each insurance provider is under pressure to make its products stand out from its competitors' products. As long as the finished product is actuarially (i.e., financially and mathematically) sound, practical for the insurer to administer, compliant with applicable insurance laws, and consistent with the insurer's strategic objectives, an insurer can develop and design virtually any type of insurance product it wishes.

We begin this chapter by providing an overview of the process of life insurance product development. We then discuss each phase in the product development process, concentrating on the company personnel who typically are involved in each phase and highlighting some of their concerns. You should note that product development refers not only to totally new products, but also to (1) products that have been available in the marketplace but are new to a particular company and (2) revisions of products currently in the insurer's product mix.

The Process of Product Development

Product development usually originates at the top management level of a life insurance company. As part of their strategic plans for the entire organization, senior executives establish the insurer's strategic marketing objectives. A component of these strategic marketing objectives

is a set of broadly described product development plans for the next several years. For example, the strategic marketing objectives may state that

- Within the next two years, the company will expand into the variable life insurance market

- Within the next two years, the company will increase its share of the term insurance market by developing a new line of term products

- Within the next year, the company will enhance the benefit structure of one of its whole life products

These strategic objectives become the basis for the product development decisions the company makes. Typically, if a new product idea is not consistent with the strategic objectives, the idea will ultimately be rejected. Figure 7-1 illustrates the relationship of strategic plans, strategic marketing objectives, and product development plans.

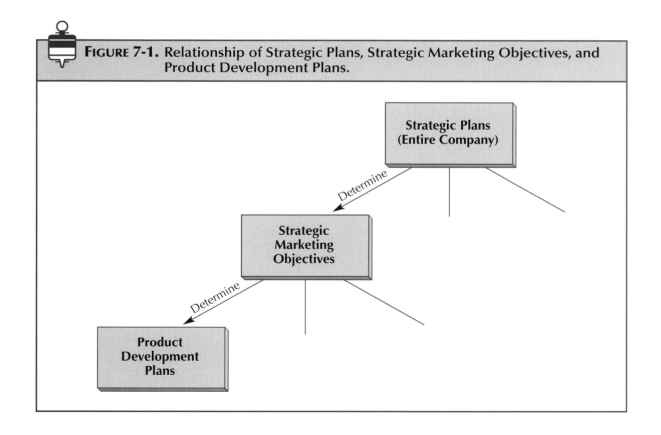

FIGURE 7-1. Relationship of Strategic Plans, Strategic Marketing Objectives, and Product Development Plans.

The current competitive environment requires insurance companies to be flexible enough to respond quickly to new marketing opportunities. If an insurer identifies a product development opportunity that meets the needs of its target market(s) and that is consistent with its strategic goals, the insurer must be able to quickly develop the product. The process of product development generally requires cooperation among more functional areas than does any other insurance company operation. Virtually all areas—including actuarial, legal, compliance, underwriting, investments, information systems, marketing, agency operations, claim administration, customer service, and accounting—have some input in the development of products.

To understand the amount of organization-wide cooperation necessary, let's look at the role of the insurer's actuaries in product development. Actuaries develop the financial aspects and mathematical features of each new product, including the rates that will be charged for the product. To do so, the actuaries need information from many other people. For example, when estimating the level of claims the insurer expects to incur from the product, the actuaries base their calculations on (1) specific underwriting guidelines proposed for the product and (2) industry experience with similar products. From the areas that will be responsible for marketing and servicing the product, the actuaries need projections of the expected volume of sales and the costs these areas expect to incur. The information systems department must estimate the cost to build or modify the technology needed to support the new product.

Staff for Product Development

Many life insurers, particularly larger companies, have formal product development units or departments. These units are staffed by full-time employees with diverse technical backgrounds. The staff may include actuaries, marketers, underwriters, accountants, compliance experts, lawyers, and investment experts.

In other companies, product development is not a full-time job for anyone. Instead, some of these insurers form product development teams with fixed membership. Team members typically are senior or mid-level managers from various areas who meet regularly to conduct business related to product development. Other insurers form *ad hoc* product development committees or task forces to work together temporarily to oversee a product development project. These task forces do not necessarily have fixed membership, but they typically have representatives from all the functional areas that are directly or indirectly affected by product development. In this text, we will use the term *product development team* to refer to any department, unit, team, committee, or task force responsible for managing product development.

Two important members of the product development process are the project sponsor and the project coordinator. The ***project sponsor*** is a senior-level executive who authorizes a product development project and who has ultimate authority over the project. The project sponsor, sometimes called the *project champion,* (1) approves changes to the scope of the project and seeks and/or approves whatever additional funds those changes require, (2) provides problem-solving or decision-making assistance when required, and (3) signs off at (i.e., approves) the completion of each phase of product development. The ***project coordinator****,* also called the *project manager,* is the manager of the product development team and controls the day-to-day aspects of the project. This person manages the project's scope, participants, schedules, costs, quality, risks, contingency plans, and communications. The project coordinator also provides regular status reports to the project sponsor and other management. In some companies, a product line manager, such as the individual life insurance manager or the group life insurance manager, acts as the project coordinator for new products in that product line.

Phases of Product Development

Specific aspects of the product development process vary from company to company. For any company, at each phase of the process, decision makers in upper management decide whether to (1) give the new product idea further consideration, (2) request additional information on, or a revision of, the product idea, or (3) drop the new product idea. As illustrated in Figure 7-2, the product development process typically consists of the following five phases:

- Idea generation and screening

- Comprehensive business analysis

- Technical design

- Implementation

- Introduction and sales monitoring

Some companies establish a product development pipeline. That is, as one new product is being rolled out to the public, the next product idea "enters the pipeline" and undergoes development. Another product development practice is modifying a new product soon after its introduction. After analyzing early sales results and claim experience, the insurer redesigns or modifies the original product to attempt to

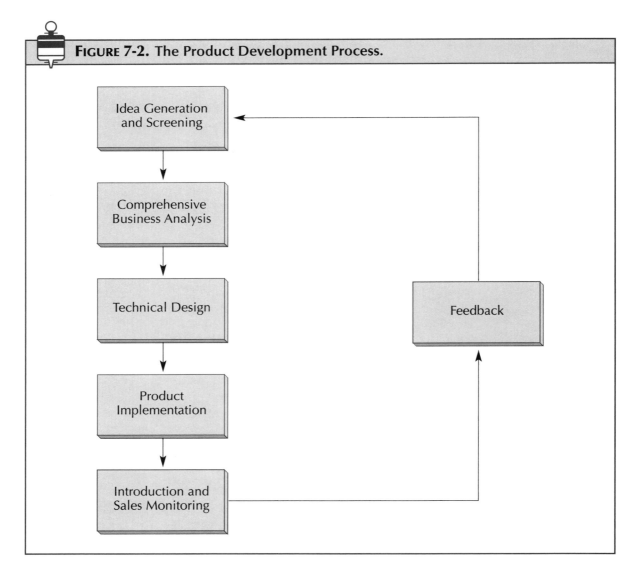

Figure 7-2. The Product Development Process.

improve experience and profitability. This product modification process typically is much shorter than the process for developing the original product.

Idea Generation and Screening

The first phase of the product development process involves the product development team's gathering and generating ideas for product concepts that appear to fill a consumer need. The company then screens—quickly evaluates—the ideas and selects only those ideas

that warrant further investigation. The most promising ideas that pass this initial screen proceed to the next phase of development, during which the development team studies them in much more detail.

Sources of new insurance product ideas are numerous and varied. These sources include

- Policyowners

- Sales agents, brokers, and other product distributors and sales personnel

- Product development team members

- Company management/executives

- Other home office staff

- Marketing research reports of various environmental factors, such as economic, technological, and demographic conditions

- Competitors' products and activities

- Consumer groups

- Consultants

- Business and insurance periodicals

- Changes in insurance laws or regulations

Many insurance companies establish incentive programs to reward employees who submit good ideas for new products.

Screening involves only a limited evaluation of each product idea. It is intended to select promising product ideas and to conserve the insurer's resources by eliminating unfavorable ideas before the insurer invests time and money in developing them. Having a diverse and experienced group of team members is essential for effective screening because, ideally, at least one team member will have enough knowledge and insight to determine quickly whether an idea is worthy of further consideration. To help minimize the chance that the development team will reject a good product idea or accept an inferior idea, many product development teams use screening queries, which are a specified set of questions that must be answered for each new product idea. Figure 7-3 lists some common screening queries for insurance products.

Some insurers also use concept testing during the screening process. *Concept testing* is a marketing research technique designed to measure

> ## Figure 7-3. Typical Screening Queries Used by Life Insurers.
>
> - Is the product idea compatible with the company's corporate goals and strategic objectives?
> - Does the product fulfill a real need in the insurer's target markets?
> - Can any products currently offered by the company be modified, packaged differently, or changed in some other way to meet the needs addressed by the product idea?
> - Will the company's current staff and systems be able to handle the product's technical and service requirements?
> - Will the new product generate additional sales, or will sales of the new product displace sales of an existing product?
> - Will the introduction of the new product lead to internal replacements, and, if so, how will this problem be addressed?
> - Does the market potential for the product appear large enough to generate the insurer's desired level of response, level of growth, return on investment, and contribution to surplus or profit?
> - Can the product be marketed through the company's existing distribution systems? If not, can the company acquire, or quickly develop expertise in, the distribution systems required for the product?
> - Would this product be more attractive or profitable if offered through a separate affiliate or subsidiary company?

the public acceptability of new product ideas, new promotion campaigns, or other new marketing elements before a company incurs the expense of actually producing these items. Concept testing involves describing product ideas to distributors or consumers to determine which product ideas have the greatest appeal. By gathering the opinions of the people who will be selling and buying a potential product, concept testing can provide valuable information about the product idea and its attributes.

Comprehensive Business Analysis

For each product idea that passes the initial screen, the product development team conducts a ***comprehensive business analysis***, during which the team develops initial product specifications and closely examines the product's market potential. Both screening and the comprehensive business analysis involve assessing the merits of a product idea. But unlike the quick evaluation of the screening phase, a comprehensive business analysis is much more detailed.

Conducting a comprehensive business analysis calls for extensive research and requires the work of many people in addition to the

development team. People throughout the organization may become involved in researching certain technical and operational aspects and the product's marketing environment. The amount of research required by a product idea depends on the company's familiarity with the product. A revised product or a new product that is similar to one that the company currently sells generally requires less study than a new product that is unlike any the company has previously developed. The general responsibilities of staff in each functional area during a comprehensive business analysis are as follows:

- *Marketing* conducts a market analysis to learn whether customers want the product and then prepares a preliminary sales forecast. Market research findings include information on competitors' products (such as premiums, cash values, commissions, and riders), and identification of potential target markets. Marketing seeks input from sales agents and evaluates how the new product might affect the insurer's current product mix. Marketing determines the most appropriate distribution methods for the new product, the level of commission rates for the new product, and advertising and prospecting strategies for the product. Marketing also works with the compliance area to determine the best "test" states or provinces—that is, the first states or provinces in which the insurer will offer the new product for sale.

- *Actuarial,* with the help of marketing, underwriting, and compliance, develops the initial product specifications, such as underwriting guidelines and resulting benefit levels, cash values, riders, commissions, and other financial features. The actuaries perform preliminary calculations to determine whether the new product can be priced to be both competitive and profitable. This work involves making initial assumptions as to mortality factors, lapse rates, investment earnings, operating expenses, sales volumes, the amount and timing of claims, distribution expenses, policy reserve methods and requirements, capital requirements, contingencies for unexpected events, and contribution to the company's profit or return on equity.

- *Underwriting,* with the help of actuarial, establishes initial risk classifications and underwriting guidelines for the product, as required.

- *Claim administration* examines the claim assumptions made by actuarial and determines whether the current claim systems and staff can adequately administer the new product's benefit structure.

- *Legal* helps develop the product specifications.

© 1998 *Reinsurance Reporter.* Used with permission.

- *Compliance* reviews the proposed product to ensure that it complies with all legal and regulatory requirements. Compliance determines filing requirements and whether the product will be prohibited in any states or provinces.

- *Information systems (IS)* assesses whether the company's current operating systems can accommodate the new product. The insurer may have to buy or develop new hardware or software to support the distribution, underwriting, customer service, and claim processes required by the new product. IS estimates the costs and time involved to upgrade the equipment and train the staff in its use.

- *Customer service* considers the administrative support and procedures that the new product will require.

- *Agency operations* determines what changes, if any, will be necessary for the current sales force to sell the new product effectively. The agency unit helps determine the proper training materials for agents.

- *Investments,* in collaboration with actuarial, reviews the proposed product to determine what types of investments are needed to provide adequate cash flow and an adequate rate of return to support the expected claims under the product and to add to the company's profit.

- *Accounting* reviews the product proposal to determine financial reporting requirements the insurer must meet in developing and selling this product. Accounting also evaluates how the business will be reflected in the company's financial statements.

If the comprehensive business analysis indicates good market potential, the development team writes a product proposal, also called an *initial business plan,* and presents it to senior management for approval. The ***product proposal*** is an outline of the product's target market and market potential; technical specifications (such as rate structure, policy benefits, and actuarial assumptions); and administrative, systems, and distribution requirements. Figure 7-4 lists the contents of a typical product proposal.

The development team presents each product proposal to the project sponsor and other senior management for review and a "go/revise/kill" decision on the product. The product proposal, therefore, should contain enough information that senior executives and the project sponsor can make an informed decision about whether to proceed with the project. An approved product proposal serves as the overall guide for the development, testing, and introduction of the product.

Figure 7-4. Contents of a Product Proposal.

- Statement of product strategy and product purpose

- Product description

- Cost-benefit analysis

- Market research data

- List of key features

- Preliminary pricing (including profitability targets, preliminary actuarial assumptions, commissions, and benefits and riders)

- Expected sales volume

- Statement of the regulatory and tax environment

- Compliance considerations

- Information system requirements

- Underwriting and claim considerations

- Policy service and other administrative considerations

- Probable distribution channels and selling strategies

- Sales projections

The product proposal may also recommend test marketing a new product before offering it to a broad marketplace. ***Test marketing***, also known as *conducting a pilot program*, is the process of selling a product in a limited number of geographic areas and then measuring its level of success. Test marketing helps the insurer identify and correct any problems with the marketing or operation of the product before the company undertakes a full product rollout. Such a test could be recommended if, for example, there is a high degree of uncertainty about the appeal of the product, there is a high financial risk if the company is wrong about the product, or if the quality of the product design is critical to long-term consumer acceptance.

Technical Design

Product proposals that are approved by senior management proceed to the technical design phase for the drafting of the policy according to applicable laws and regulations. ***Technical design*** is the product development phase of creating the policy form, product provisions, pricing and dividend structures, benefit and commission structures, and underwriting and issue specifications. In this phase, the actual product takes shape, based on the preliminary product specifications developed for the product proposal.

To perform technical design, an insurer may use the original product development team, a separate product design team, or an outside vendor. As with comprehensive business analysis, technical design includes a large number of activities and involves most functional areas of the company. Consequently, collaboration across functional areas is critical to successful technical design. The research and other preliminary work done during comprehensive business analysis are fully developed during technical design.

Figure 7-5 lists the primary roles fulfilled by personnel in each functional area during the technical design phase of product development.

The design team typically drafts a project schedule and budget. Many companies use project management software to create budgets and timetables for each activity in the process. These timetables help the design team allocate the necessary resources (personnel, money, and computer support) needed to complete each activity. In addition, the schedules show the activities that can be undertaken concurrently, thereby reducing the total design time, and the activities that must be done sequentially.

After the product design team completes the technical design, the product development team presents a final design document to the project sponsor for approval. This document is essentially an update

FIGURE 7-5. Technical Design Activities.

Actuarial. Actuarial staff make final assessments of the product's cost and benefit structure, expected experience (mortality, lapse rates, investment performance, and sales volume), tax implications, use of reinsurance, policy wording, and start-up costs. Staff use financial models to determine profit estimates and time to payback (or breakeven point) on the insurer's investment of resources to develop the product and the ability of the product to earn an adequate return on the insurer's investment of capital.

Marketing. Marketing staff resolve issues related to the product's name, consumer appeal, the competitiveness and complexity of the product, the demands of promoting the product and introducing it to the field force, and the consistency of the product's marketing and financial projections with overall corporate objectives for growth and profit.

Sales Force. Field or agency representatives develop and review the best sales approaches for the product and ways to ensure that it meets clients' needs. The representatives also review the competitiveness of the product's pricing and the adequacy of the product's compensation schedule for sales agents and agency managers.

Information Systems. One of the most time-consuming aspects of product development is upgrading, modifying, or enhancing the company's existing information systems in order to support the product. IS staff resolve issues related to (1) determining the hardware and software requirements of the new product, (2) modfiying systems to process transactions for the new product, (3) developing new systems, and (4) developing analysis packages to provide management with information about the new product.

Legal/Compliance. The legal staff drafts the policy form, and compliance ensures that the policy form and policy provisions are in compliance with all applicable laws and regulations.

Investments. Investment staff advise the technical design team on types of investments available to help make the product successful and to provide an adequate investment return. The investment staff consider (1) the investment earnings needed and (2) the timing and amount of cash inflows and cash outflows produced by the product design.

Accounting. If development and introduction are particularly costly, the insurer's comptroller may establish a separate budget for the project. The comptroller also determines whether the new product's financial results will require any special financial reporting procedures.

Administration. Underwriting, customer service, policy issue, and claim administration staffs finalize procedures to accommodate the new product and plan for hiring and training staff to service it.

Source: Portions adapted from Francois Genest, "Product Myopia," *Journal of the American Society of CLU* (July 1986): 67.

of the product proposal but contains the final design of the product, as well as profit and expense figures. The sponsor can approve the design as is, send it back to the design team for further revision or development, or reject the product entirely. When the technical design of a proposed product is approved, the implementation phase of the product development process begins.

Implementation

Implementation is the product development phase that includes establishing all of the administrative structures and processes necessary to take the product to market. Implementing the product involves the following four general tasks:

- ***Policy filing***, which is the process of obtaining all required regulatory approvals for the product from all applicable jurisdictions

- Designing promotional and training materials for the product

- Educating and training staff and sales agents in administrative procedures and forms required to sell, administer, and service the product

- Launching all information systems necessary to market and administer the product

To manage the implementation phase, some companies form a product implementation team, also called a launch team, whose actions are overseen by the product development team. In some companies, the product development team also manages the implementation phase. In either case, the group in charge of implementation develops a written implementation plan, which defines tasks, responsibilities, and schedules for completing each activity. (Best Case Scenario 7-1 illustrates a portion of an implementation plan.)

Policy Filing

Each time it develops an insurance product, an insurer creates a policy form for that product. As you learned in Chapter 2, a policy form is a standardized contract form that shows the terms, conditions, benefits, and ownership rights of a particular type of insurance coverage. The policy form accurately describes the features of the product and the terms on which the insurer will issue the product. All states require that, before an insurer can sell an insurance policy in that jurisdiction, the insurer must file and obtain approval of a copy of the finished policy form and any other legally required forms with the appropriate insurance department of the jurisdiction. In Canada, insurers must file policy forms with provincial insurance regulators in two instances: (1) to obtain a license to sell insurance in the province and (2) to offer a variable life insurance product. Typically, a company self imposes a

Best Case Scenario 7-1.

An Implementation Plan.

Best Friend Life Insurance Company has completed the technical design of a new whole life insurance product—Best Life Plus. Nancy Kirkland, the head of the product implementation team, has written an implementation plan for the new product. In addition to the activities included in the plan, each week the implementation team conducts a marketing meeting and an administration meeting to discuss progress with each area involved in implementation.

Product Implementation Plan for Best Life Plus

Start Date: 16 Weeks prior to product launch

Activity	Start Date (weeks before launch)	Duration of Activity	Responsible Area
Develop "Model Office" to train home office staff	16 weeks	5 weeks	Information systems
Develop training materials for home office administrative staff and sales force	14 weeks	4 weeks	Corporate training
Test new administrative systems and Model Office and reprogram systems as necessary	11 weeks	4 weeks	IS, administrative areas
Begin interviewing candidates to fill additional staffing positions	10 weeks	10 weeks	Human resources
Print marketing materials	9 weeks	1 week	Marketing
File policy form in target states	8 weeks	1 day	Compliance
Re-test administrative systems and Model Office	7 weeks	1 week	IS, administrative areas
Sign marketing agreements with producers	6 weeks	2 weeks	Agency operations
Distribute issue instructions to staff	5 weeks	1 day	Compliance
Conduct informational training classes with home office, focusing on product overview, sales projections, target market segments, and product features that are new to the company staff	5 weeks	1 week	Marketing, corporate training
Conduct training classes with producers, focusing on product overview, product features, sales techniques, and use of sales illustrations	4 weeks	1 week	Marketing, corporate training
Conduct dry runs with home office staff in Model Office, and practice use of new systems technology and administrative procedures	4 weeks	2 weeks	Corporate training
Launch advertising campaign	1 week	6 weeks	Marketing
Conduct new product kickoff luncheon for marketers and announce sales incentive promotion	1 week	1 day	Marketing

condition that a particular policy form must be approved in a minimum number of jurisdictions before the insurer begins selling the policy in any jurisdiction.

In the United States, the specific filing requirements that a company must meet to obtain the approval of the insurance department vary from state to state. For example, many states require that an actuary sign a statement certifying that the policy form complies with applicable nonforfeiture laws.[2] Many states require that a policy form be accompanied by a readability certification, which verifies that the policy is written in clear, easy-to-understand language. Because of variations in requirements, life insurance companies sometimes have to file numerous versions of the same policy form in various jurisdictions. Focus on Technology 7-1 discusses attempts to streamline the process of gaining approval of policy forms.

Variable life insurance products typically require additional filing. In Canada, many variable contracts require approval from provincial securities commissions. The information documents that accompany these variable contracts must be approved by provincial insurance departments. In the United States, variable insurance contracts and the sales materials to be used with them must be filed with and approved by the federal Securities and Exchange Commission (SEC) as well as with state regulatory authorities.

Focus on Technology 7-1.

Expediting Policy Filings.

Until the late 1990s, securing regulatory approval of a policy rate or policy form took an average of two or three months. For new, complex products, the process commonly took a year or more. However, in 1998, a consortium of interested states and insurance companies, backed by the National Association of Insurance Commissioners (NAIC), launched a new system that allows insurance companies to submit regulatory filings electronically over the Internet or a private data network.

The system, known as the System for Electronic Rates & Forms Filing (SERFF), enables insurers to send—and state regulators to receive, comment on, and approve or reject—insurance policy forms and rate filings. In many cases, SERFF reduces the time involved in the policy filing and approval process. SERFF is also expected to reduce the cost of filings by eliminating the cost of mailing policy forms to individual state jurisdictions. By the end of 1999, more than 30 states and 225 insurance companies were using SERFF.

Because SERFF is the result of a partnership between the states and insurance companies, both parties can participate directly in decisions relating to the development and use of the system. The NAIC has taken over the operation of SERFF, but the SERFF board (representing the companies and states) continues to formulate the direction of the program. •

Sources: "SERFF Background and Status," *SERFF Central,* 2 May 1999, http://www.serffcentral.com (19 October 1999). Ara C. Trembly, "NAIC's SERFF Program Launched at IASA Meeting," *National Underwriter,* Life & Health/Financial Services ed. (22 June 1998): 1, 25.

Promotion and Sales Materials

The marketing department is closely involved in several aspects of policy implementation. In particular, marketers

- Decide the name for the new product

- Design sales materials and information kits for sales agents, customer service staff, and customers

- Create product-specific advertisements and policy illustrations

- Place advertising and promotional material about the product in insurance, general business, and consumer publications

Insurance companies that use direct response distribution systems, such as direct mail advertisements, also develop and test the direct market advertising materials during implementation.

Insurers must take great care that their advertisements and policy illustrations conform to applicable laws. In the United States, a variety of state laws, such as unfair trade practices laws, govern the use of advertisements and sales materials and are intended to ensure that consumers understand the insurance products they purchase. An insurer must assure that all of these materials (1) accurately represent the terms of policy forms; (2) are not untrue, deceptive, or misleading; and (3) comply with applicable laws governing insurance advertisements. The company's legal or compliance department reviews advertisements before they are placed to ensure that they comply with applicable regulatory requirements.

To assure that policy illustrations are not misleading to customers, insurance companies must follow state laws, many of which are based on the NAIC *Life Insurance Illustrations Model Regulation*. Adopted in 1995, the Model Regulation contains detailed rules for the use of life insurance policy illustrations and prohibits producers from using any illustration that does not comply with its requirements. The Model Regulation defines an *illustration* as a presentation or depiction that includes nonguaranteed elements of a life insurance policy over a period of years. *Nonguaranteed elements* are the premiums, benefits, values, credits, or charges under a life insurance policy that are not guaranteed or not determined when the policy is issued.

Education and Training

Once an insurer obtains approval of a policy form and the product is available for issue, the company educates its employees and agents

about the product's features and the legal and regulatory requirements that affect the product. For example, compliance specialists typically develop and distribute *issue instructions*, which are guidelines that show the approved policy forms for each jurisdiction, any variations or options in a jurisdiction's forms, and other requirements that various areas, such as underwriting, claim administration, marketing, customer service, and information systems must follow when selling or administering the product. As necessary, the insurer conducts training sessions to teach home office employees the features of the product and any new administrative procedures and special rules regarding it. The customer service staff are likely to receive many calls about the product soon after its introduction, so they must be prepared to answer questions about the product. The actuarial and underwriting departments may also receive appeals from the agency force to make exceptions on underwriting guidelines.

Some insurers conduct training seminars and classes to teach sales agents how to sell a new product. This training helps agents to become familiar with the new product and to be enthusiastic about selling it. Agent-training activities can involve the following:

- Training agents to use policy illustrations and to fill out and submit applications for the policy

- Creating incentive awards for product sales

- Developing a presentation that demonstrates where the new product fits into the company's product portfolio and explains the new product's specific characteristics and provisions

- Designing sample sales presentations and visual aids for agents to use with prospective customers

Information Systems

The systems work associated with product implementation includes (1) installing, programming, and testing the new hardware and software; (2) developing appropriate documentation, internal procedures, and systems maintenance routines; and (3) training the staff to use the new systems. Integrating the new product into the current product mix can require extensive revisions of the current computer systems. For example, if the new product includes five riders, and all of the insurer's other insurance policies have only three riders available, then the main system must be modified to accept five riders. If the insurer intends to market or service the product electronically, the

insurer's Internet site and other computer systems will have to be modified accordingly.

The process of upgrading the information systems for new product compatibility can be lengthy and is typically started as early as possible. Ideally, IS staff are involved at the beginning of the product development process, thus helping to avoid last-minute delays if new systems programming is more complicated than the product development team originally estimated.

Product Introduction and Sales Monitoring

Once the implementation tasks are complete, the insurer is ready to introduce the new product—that is, offer the new product for sale. In this phase of product development, the company advertises the new or revised product and begins to distribute it to the public. During the first few months after introduction, the company monitors results and experience and compares them to expected results. If sales or claims are worse than expected, the company attempts to determine the reasons and implements creative solutions. The managers involved with product development also review the entire process and provide feedback on ways to improve it.

Product Introduction

By the time the introduction phase begins, all necessary marketing and support elements are in place. Additional sales training and educational materials are provided to agents and sales support staff. Press releases and other promotional material are distributed to media outlets. Many companies stage a number of promotional events to coincide with a product's introduction. For example, company executives may visit agencies and regional offices to encourage sales. The company may throw a party, picnic or other celebration to generate awareness of the product. The company may also launch a contest in which sales agents are awarded prizes, trips, or other incentives for the highest sales of the new product.

Sales Monitoring

The profitability of a product is partially a result of the level of sales the product achieves. Therefore, senior managers of the insurance company are keenly interested in the new product's initial sales activity. Typically in the first months after product introduction, the im-

plementation team (or product development team) tracks sales results and compares the results with the projections. These comparisons yield potentially meaningful information to the implementation team as to the product's performance and the effectiveness of the implementation process. The launch team also gathers input from the field force to find out how the product is performing, to learn consumers' impressions of it, and to hear suggestions on enhancing the product.

Early sales results can indicate the effectiveness of the new product's marketing mix strategy—that is, the product's combination of features, price, promotion, and distribution. Marketers also monitor the average premium size, policy face amount, age mix of insureds, and other factors to see how they compare with the assumptions made during technical design. As the company gains more experience with the new product, additional home office and field training sessions may be required to address problems with sales presentations and administration and to suggest additional marketing opportunities. The company can also gather suggestions from the field force for ways to make the product more attractive to consumers.

Usually, sales of a new product do not take off immediately. Agents need time to understand the product and to feel comfortable selling it, particularly if the product is complex or different from the insurer's other products. However, if sales results are far below expectations, investigation is necessary. Figure 7-6 lists reasons that sales might fall below expectations.

When the product is not achieving expected sales results, product researchers and planners assess the situation and recommend corrective actions. These actions can include

- Redesigning the underwriting guidelines, features, and/or price of the product to meet a specific need

- Reintroducing the product to agents

FIGURE 7-6. Possible Reasons for Poor Sales of a New Product.

- A competitor may have introduced a product that offers more competitive premiums and/or benefits.
- A competitor may have brought a similar product to market first.
- A similar product in the company's portfolio is more appealing.
- Customer demographics may have been unclear or inaccurate.
- The agency force is unaware of the product or insufficiently trained in how to sell the product.
- The compensation structure for sales agents and/or agency managers is inadequate.

- Repackaging the sales kit

- Introducing a sales promotion program

If the product's failure is the result of a change in factors outside of the company's control, the company may choose to remove the product from the market. Companies usually choose to remove or discontinue weak products rather than have them reduce the company's profitability and keep the company from channeling resources towards potentially successful products.

Review of Product Development Process

A product development project is not considered complete until the company has critiqued the product development process. The purpose of the review is to determine if the product's objectives were met and to evaluate and document the results of the product development team and team members' performances and contributions. By conducting a detailed review of the process, the company and the product development team can identify strengths and weaknesses of the product development process and suggest modifications to improve future product development projects.

As part of the review, development managers and the project sponsor interview members of the product development team, technical design team, and implementation team to obtain their feedback about all aspects of the process. What went well? How could the process be improved? Did the product come out on schedule and on budget? If not, why not? Were communication and collaboration adequate among the functional areas? These and other questions are answered during this product development critique.

Characteristics of Effective Product Development

Insurers must be flexible enough to respond to an ever-changing environment. This changing environment has increased the pace and frequency of new product development, and this trend is likely to continue. The products that sold well even a few years previously may not continue to appeal to consumers because of changes in economic conditions, demographic conditions, tax laws, and other factors. As a result, insurers are always on the lookout for new product ideas and try to react quickly to environmental opportunities.

An effective product development process can improve the success rate of new products, reduce the costs of developing products, improve the performance of new products, and minimize the time to bring new products to market. Although no evidence exists to indicate that any one product development process works best for all companies, we can generalize about what usually constitutes an effective process.

- **Precise process.** Product development is an established process that includes clearly defined phases and identification of the activities involved in each phase. The insurer defines the roles and authority of people involved with product development. In this way, the company has reliable procedures that can provide guidance for employees, reduce development time, improve communication, and minimize employee frustration. Although the product development process is well defined, it is also flexible enough to allow for modifications when development problems arise. The company should regularly evaluate its product development process to determine how to make it more efficient and effective.

- **Excellent communication.** Because product development involves so many different people and crosses so many functional disciplines within a company, the insurer should establish strong communication lines to ensure that the right resources are available to the right people at the right times. Strong communication lines also ensure that all affected employees and work groups have adequate input into the process and that they are kept informed of progress during the process.

- **Skilled management.** The employees who manage product development should have strong project management skills so that the project is completed according to plan. The product development managers should also have strong working relationships with all areas involved with product development.

- **Successful assessment.** The process should contain a clear definition of how project success is measured. Scheduling timelines, revenue and expense budgets, and sales forecasts and reports are all effective tools for monitoring the success of the project and the performance of the new product.

We should also mention the important role of compromise in product development. As you have seen, a great number of people throughout an insurance company are involved in the process. At times, the interests of certain participants may conflict. For example, if the product contains more than one preferred risk classification, the sales force

may want the product to allow a large number of applicants in generally good health to be assigned to the "super preferred" class so the policy will be attractive to many consumers. However, the staff responsible for underwriting and actuarial projections may conclude that the underwriting guidelines for the product should be strict and should limit the "super preferred" classification to relatively few applicants. To prevent the development process from stalling at potential impasses along the way, development participants should generally be willing to compromise on certain demands or desires for the product. The more realistic team members are during development, the better the final product design will be and the better the chance the product development team will meet the product launch date.[3]

Key Terms

project sponsor (project champion)
project coordinator (project manager)
concept testing
comprehensive business analysis
product proposal (initial business plan)
test marketing (conducting a pilot program)

technical design
implementation
policy filing
Life Insurance Illustrations Model Regulation
illustration
nonguaranteed elements
issue instructions

Endnotes

1. ACLI, *1999 Life Insurance Fact Book* (Washington, D.C.: American Council of Life Insurance, 1999), 15.

2. All states have enacted laws based on the NAIC Standard Nonforfeiture Law for Life Insurance, which specifies how a policy's minimum cash surrender value is calculated. Policies must include a table showing the cash surrender and other nonforfeiture values for each of the first 20 years of coverage. The nonforfeiture values for any policy must be at least equal to those required by law.

3. Janice K. Henderson, "Compromise Critical in Product Development," *National Underwriter*, Life & Health/Financial Services ed. (14 September 1998): 22.

Pricing Aspects of Technical Design

LEARNING OBJECTIVES

After reading this chapter, you should be able to

- Describe the roles and specialties of actuaries in insurance companies

- Discuss factors that insurers consider in planning their pricing strategies

- Distinguish between gross premiums and net premiums

- Describe mortality tables, and explain the purpose of mortality rates in pricing life insurance products

- Describe the assumptions that actuaries make about investment earnings, the loading charge, and policy reserve growth

- Describe the purpose of asset share models in life insurance pricing

- Discuss how actuaries manage the results of the product pricing process

*I*n the last chapter, you learned about the product development process for life insurance companies. In this chapter, we take a closer look at an important aspect of the technical design phase of product development—product pricing, in which the insurer establishes the premium rate structure for a new product. Certain aspects of pricing vary according to the type of product being priced (whole life insurance, term life insurance, group life insurance, and so on). But as shown in Figure 8-1, pricing any insurance product is generally a four-step process: (1) outlining a pricing strategy, (2) making actuarial assumptions, (3) setting and testing rates, and (4) managing pricing results.

The purpose of this chapter is to explain how actuaries formulate life insurance premium rates and benefit structures. This chapter will highlight both the difficulty and the importance of realistic insurance pricing. We begin with a look at the many roles that actuaries play in insurance companies. Then we discuss how actuaries outline a pricing plan. We describe the financial and actuarial assumptions made in order to determine the net premiums and gross premiums to charge for a new product. Lastly, we look at how actuaries manage pricing results.

You should note that actuaries make premium rate calculations according to the age, sex, and risk classification of insureds. After policies are sold, insurers group them into **blocks of policies**, which are groups of policies issued to insureds who are all the same age, the same sex, and in the same risk classification. For example, an insurer may classify into one block all whole life policies issued to females age 30 whose health histories and medical tests are within certain limits.

The Role of the Actuary

An insurance product must be priced competitively, yet still generate enough money for the company to pay all policy benefits as they come due. The task of directing the life insurance pricing process falls to **actuaries**, who are experts in the mathematics of insurance, annuities, and financial instruments. Actuaries calculate the premium rates charged for insurance products, the amounts of their companies' legal reserve liabilities, and any policy dividends. Actuaries also conduct research on long-term and short-term trends in interest rates, inflation, mortality rates, company expenses, policy lapses, and policy loans.

Actuarial work is highly specialized and requires many years of training. Because of their extensive professional training and broad

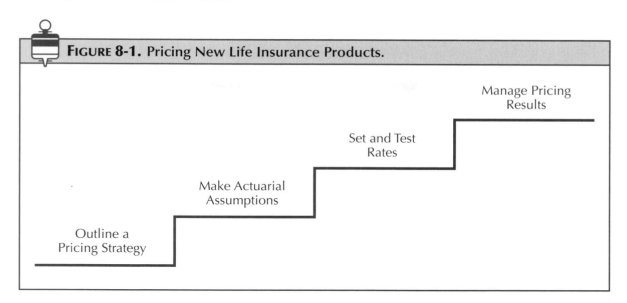

Figure 8-1. Pricing New Life Insurance Products.

Manage Pricing Results

Set and Test Rates

Make Actuarial Assumptions

Outline a Pricing Strategy

knowledge of insurance matters, actuaries typically hold positions of great responsibility in insurance companies and are key members of product development and product design teams. Actuarial positions include a number of different specialties, some of which are listed in Figure 8-2. As shown in this figure, product actuaries specialize in the technical design of new insurance products. One of a product actuary's most important duties is pricing new life insurance products.

The largest life insurance companies may employ dozens of actuaries and actuarial assistants. Small companies may have only one actuary or none at all, choosing instead to hire actuarial consultants on a fee basis. Even companies with large actuarial staffs may occasionally need consulting actuaries for special projects or analyses.

Pricing Strategy

When setting prices for a new product, an insurer attempts to achieve desired goals. *Pricing objectives* are goals that specify what a company wants to achieve as a result of its pricing strategies. Pricing objectives can be expressed in terms of such factors as desired levels of profit earned by a product, desired levels of sales of the product, and desired levels of market share gained by a product. An insurer may have a different pricing objective for each of its products. *Pricing strategies* are the general guidelines that a company follows to achieve its pricing objectives.

Marketing and actuarial staff typically work together to develop the pricing objectives and strategies for a new product. As with all aspects

> **FIGURE 8-2.** Actuarial Specialties in Insurance.
>
> **Illustration Actuary:** Certifies whether an insurer's product sales illustrations conform to applicable regulatory requirements regarding fairness
>
> **Investment Actuary:** Analyzes and makes decisions relating to an insurer's investment strategies
>
> **Marketing Actuary:** Analyzes and makes decisions relating to the marketing of an insurer's product portfolio
>
> **Product Actuary:** Analyzes and makes decisions relating to designing and pricing insurance policies and other financial products
>
> **Valuation Actuary:** Establishes the company's legal reserves and renders opinions as to the adequacy of the insurer's assets and legal reserves to meet the company's financial obligations

of product development, pricing objectives and strategies should be consistent with the company's overall goals and objectives. For example, if an insurer's corporate objective is to be an industry leader in service to customers, then the company may have to establish premium rates that are higher than its competitors' rates in order to cover the greater operating expenses incurred in providing a high level of service. If an insurer's corporate objective is to offer low-cost insurance protection, then offering rates that are lower than competitors' rates takes priority, even if low rates mean that the company will provide customers with fewer services.

Whatever a company's pricing objectives, the price of an insurance product *must* be set so that the insurer generates enough revenue to cover all of the product's claims and other expenses. However, the company also needs to earn a sufficient return on investment for its owners, so the pricing objectives should clearly define the company's desired profit or return on the product. In short, as part of an insurer's pricing strategy, the product actuary must ensure that the premium rates are adequate, equitable, and reasonable.

- *Adequate rates* are premium rates that are high enough to provide the insurer with enough money on hand to pay operating expenses and policy benefits when they come due. Most jurisdictions in the United States and Canada indirectly regulate the adequacy of premium rates by monitoring the policy reserves that insurers must establish for insurance policies. Insurers must charge "adequate" premium rates in order to maintain assets that are at least equal to the amount of their policy reserves.

- *Equitable rates* are premium rates that vary from policy to policy based only on factors affecting the policy's costs. For example,

rates generally are legally permitted to differ among insureds on the basis of such factors as the age, gender, occupation, health, or smoking habits of the insureds, because these factors determine the amount of risk each insured represents to the insurer. Most states prohibit an insurer from charging different premium rates to different buyers of the same product unless the pricing difference is based on factors that affect the insurer's cost of providing the coverage.

- *Reasonable rates* are premium rates that do not exceed those needed to cover an insurer's expenses and provide the insurer with a fair profit. Typically, competitive market factors determine the reasonableness of an insurer's premium rates. An insurer whose rates are excessive relative to what other insurers charge for similar coverage will probably not sell enough policies to make its insurance business profitable.

If actuaries do not price a new product adequately, equitably, and reasonably, several undesirable consequences can result. If premium rates for a product are set too low, the company will lose money on the product. Funds from other profitable products will have to be used to pay the new product's claims and expenses, and the company's overall financial performance may suffer. At worst, inadequate premium rates can jeopardize the solvency and continued existence of the company. Alternatively, if a product's premium rates are set too high, consumers are likely to choose similar, lower-priced products from the insurer's competitors, and the insurer will lose market share and revenue.

A final word about pricing strategies: In setting rates, product actuaries may be subject to several competing influences. Company managers seek to balance the company's profitability with its long-term solvency. Policyowners and regulators, both current and future,

An Actuarial Idea Ahead Of Its Time
· Circa 1912 ·

want policies that are affordable. In stock insurance companies, company stockowners want the company to earn a sufficient return on their investment. Agents and sales staff want competitive compensation for their efforts. The challenge for the product actuary is to establish premium rates that balance the various and sometimes conflicting requirements of the company's managers, owners, policyowners, regulators, and agents, all within the overall constraint of the need to protect the company's solvency.[2]

Actuarial Assumptions

Underlying any premium rate calculation are a number of actuarial assumptions. *Actuarial assumptions* are the values for such elements of product design as mortality rates, investment earnings, expenses, and policy lapses on which an insurer bases its product pricing and policy reserve calculations. These assumptions help ensure that the company charges premium rates that are adequate, equitable, and reasonable. Note, however, that all assumptions are based on *forecasts*, or estimations of possible future scenarios, and forecasts can be wrong. Actuaries make assumptions based on probabilities that are at realistically achievable levels using extensive statistical research and consultation with people in many of the company's functional areas.

Before proceeding, you should understand a few terms that will help you grasp the importance and purpose of the various actuarial assumptions. For ease of use, premium rates usually are expressed in terms of *units of coverage*, which are basic amounts of insurance coverage. The most common unit of coverage is $1,000. A life insurance policy with a face amount of $100,000 has 100 units of coverage ($100,000 face amount ÷ $1,000 per unit of coverage = 100 units of coverage). If the annual premium rate for one unit of coverage under that policy is $3, the annual premium for that policy is $300 ($3 premium per unit of coverage × 100 units = $300 premium).

This $3 premium rate, called the *gross premium*, is the amount the insurer charges for the insurance policy (in other words, the amount the policyowner pays for the policy). The gross premium is composed of two main elements: the net premium and the loading. Formally defined, the *net premium* is the amount per unit of coverage that will cover a product's expected *cost of benefits*, which is the total amount of contractual benefits and cash surrender values the product is expected to pay. The amount of the net premium is based on (1) the potential mortality losses that the insurance company assumes relative to a product and (2) the projected investment earnings on the premium payments the insurer receives. The *loading* is an amount that covers all of the insurer's sales and operating expenses and that provides a profit.

Several factors influence the gross premium. These factors include the pattern of development of the policy's reserves, the growth of the policy's cash value, and policy dividends (for participating policies). We will discuss these various aspects of insurance pricing, and the actuarial assumptions that product actuaries make about them, in the following sections. You should be aware that not all life insurance contracts have an explicit gross premium. A universal life insurance policy, for example, has a scheduled cost of insurance charges, credited interest, and expense loads. These elements represent an "unbundling" of the components of a traditional premium rate scale.

Net Premium Assumptions

As we have said, the net premium is the amount that a product actuary calculates to cover a product's expected cost of benefits. Actuaries base net premium calculations on assumptions as to mortality rates and investment earnings.

Mortality Rates

In order to produce a financially sound life insurance product and to estimate the product's expected cost of benefits, the product actuary predicts as accurately as possible the mortality rates of the people that the product will insure. A *mortality rate* is the rate at which death occurs among a defined group of people. For example, if 1,000 people in a group were alive at the beginning of the year, and 10 people in that group died during the year, the rate of mortality for the group during the year was 10 per 1,000, or 1 percent. Because mortality rates directly affect the level of benefit costs that an insurer will incur, actuaries must carefully consider these rates to calculate sufficient and appropriate premium charges for products.

Actuarial predictions take into account a theory of probability known as the law of large numbers. The *law of large numbers* states that the more times a particular event is observed, the more likely it is that the observed results will approximate the "true" or calculated probability that the event will occur. For example, when you flip a coin, the calculated probability that the coin will land on "heads" is 50 percent, and the calculated probability that it will land on "tails" is 50 percent. If you flip a coin only a few times—say, four times—it is possible that the coin might come up "heads" three times (or 75 percent of the time) and tails once (25 percent of the time). Does this mean that the calculated probability was wrong? No. In a small sample, such as four coin flips, the actual results can vary considerably from expected results. However, if you were to flip the coin a *large number*

of times—such as four million times—the calculated probability of 50 percent "heads" tosses and 50 percent "tails" tosses will be extremely accurate.

Actuaries cannot predict *who* will die in a given period of time. But by using data about a large number of people, actuaries can predict with reasonable accuracy *how many* people in a given population, such as a group of insureds, are likely to die during a certain period. By knowing how many of its insureds are expected to die during a year, the actuary can estimate the amount of policy benefits the insurer will pay each year.

To predict rates of mortality as accurately as possible, actuaries gather and maintain mortality statistics. For example, most insurance companies carefully record their ***mortality experience***, which is the actual number of deaths occurring each year among the company's insureds. Additionally, actuaries use mortality statistics gathered by actuarial organizations such as the Society of Actuaries and the Canadian Institute of Actuaries. These organizations gather data on the mortality experience of many insurance companies to determine the overall mortality experience of the insured populations of the United States and Canada. These mortality statistics are typically presented in ***mortality tables***, which are charts that display the incidence of death by attained age among given groups of people. Most life insurance mortality tables begin at age 0 and end at age 99 or 100 (or age 103 for females), even though some insureds live longer.

A widely used life insurance mortality table is the Commissioners 1980 Standard Ordinary (1980 CSO) table, which was compiled by the Society of Actuaries and is reproduced in Figure 8-3.[3] The 1980 CSO shows the number of males and females living at the beginning of a year, the number dying during that year, and the mortality rate at each age from 0 to 99. See Best Case Scenario 8-1 for more on how to read mortality tables and how to calculate mortality rates.

The mortality tables that actuaries generally use to make assumptions for pricing net premium calculations are known as ***basic mortality tables***, because they have no safety margin built into the mortality rates. Basic mortality tables provide realistic mortality estimates and therefore allow actuaries to set net premium rates that reflect the actual cost of providing life insurance. On the other hand, ***valuation mortality tables*** have a safety margin built into their mortality rates and therefore show higher rates of mortality at each age than do basic mortality tables. Valuation mortality tables are more conservative than basic mortality tables. The safety margins in valuation mortality tables protect the insurance company against adverse mortality experience caused by large numbers of people dying unexpectedly. By assuming that a greater number of deaths will occur than actual mortality statistics would indicate, the insurer helps to assure

FIGURE 8-3. Commissioners 1980 Standard Ordinary (CSO) Table.

	Male			Female			
Age	Number Living	Number Dying	Mortality Rate per 1,000	Number Living	Number Dying	Mortality Rate per 1,000	Age
0	10 000 000	41 800	4.18				
1	9 958 200	10 655	1.07	9 971 100	8 675	.87	1
2	9 947 545	9 848	.99				
3	9 937 697	9 739	.98	9 954 355	7 864	.79	3
4	9 927 958	9 432	.95	9 946 491	7 659	.77	4
5	9 918 526	8 927	.90	9 938 832	7 554	.76	5
6	9 909 599	8 522	.86	9 931 278	7 250	.73	6
7	9 901 077	7 921	.80	9 924 028	7 145	.72	7
8	9 893 156	7 519	.76	9 916 883	6 942	.70	8
9	9 885 637	7 315	.74	9 909 941	6 838	.69	9
10	9 878 322	7 211	.73	9 903 103	6 734	.68	10
11	9 871 111	7 601	.77	9 896 369	6 828	.69	11
12	9 863 510	8 384	.85	9 889 541	7 120	.72	12
13	9 855 126	9 757	.99	9 882 421	7 412	.75	13
14	9 845 369	11 322	1.15	9 875 009	7 900	.80	14
15	9 834 047	13 079	1.33	9 867 109	8 387	.85	15
16	9 820 968	14 830	1.51	9 858 722	8 873	.90	16
17	9 806 138	16 376	1.67	9 849 849	9 357	.95	17
18	9 789 762	17 426	1.78	9 840 492	9 644	.98	18
19	9 772 336	18 177	1.86	9 830 848	10 027	1.02	19
20	9 754 159	18 533	1.90	9 820 821	10 312	1.05	20
21	9 735 626	18 595	1.91	9 810 509	10 497	1.07	21
22	9 717 031	18 365	1.89	9 800 012	10 682	1.09	22
23	9 698 666	18 040	1.86	9 789 330	10 866	1.11	23
24	9 680 626	17 619	1.82	9 778 464	11 147	1.14	24
25	9 663 007	17 104	1.77	9 767 317	11 330	1.16	25
26	9 645 903	16 687	1.73	9 755 987	11 610	1.19	26
27	9 629 216	16 466	1.71	9 744 377	11 888	1.22	27
28	9 612 750	16 342	1.70	9 732 489	12 263	1.26	28
29	9 596 408	16 410	1.71	9 720 226	12 636	1.30	29
31	**9 563 425**	**17 023**	**1.78**	**9 694 485**	**13 572**	**1.40**	**31**
33	9 528 932	18 200	1.91	9 666 876	14 500	1.50	33
34	9 510 732	19 021	2.00	9 652 376	15 251	1.58	34
35	9 491 711	20 028	2.11	9 637 125	15 901	1.65	35
36	9 471 683	21 217	2.24	9 621 224	16 933	1.76	36
37	9 450 466	22 681	2.40	9 604 291	18 152	1.89	37
38	9 427 785	24 324	2.58	9 586 139	19 556	2.04	38
39	9 403 461	26 236	2.79	9 566 583	21 238	2.22	39
40	9 377 225	28 319	3.02	9 545 345	23 100	2.42	40
41	9 348 906	30 758	3.29	9 522 245	25 139	2.64	41
42	9 318 148	33 173	3.56	9 497 106	27 257	2.87	42
43	9 284 975	35 933	3.87	9 469 849	29 262	3.09	43
44	9 249 042	38 753	4.19	9 440 587	31 343	3.32	44
45	9 210 289	41 907	4.55	9 409 244	33 497	3.56	45
46	9 168 382	45 108	4.92	9 375 747	35 628	3.80	46
47	9 123 274	48 536	5.32	9 340 119	37 827	4.05	47
48	9 074 738	52 089	5.74	9 302 292	40 279	4.33	48
49	9 022 649	56 031	6.21	9 262 013	42 883	4.63	49
50	8 966 618	60 166	6.71	9 219 130	45 727	4.96	50
51	8 906 452	65 017	7.30	9 173 403	48 711	5.31	51
52	8 841 435	70 378	7.96	9 124 692	52 011	5.70	52
53	8 771 057	76 396	8.71	9 072 681	55 797	6.15	53
54	8 694 661	83 121	9.56	9 016 884	59 602	6.61	54
55	8 611 540	90 163	10.47	8 957 282	63 507	7.09	55
56	8 521 377	97 655	11.46	8 893 775	67 326	7.57	56
57	8 423 722	105 212	12.49	8 826 449	70 876	8.03	57
58	8 318 510	113 049	13.59	8 755 573	74 160	8.47	58
59	8 205 461	121 195	14.77	8 681 413	77 612	8.94	59
60	8 084 266	129 995	16.08	8 603 801	81 478	9.47	60
61	7 954 271	139 518	17.54	8 522 323	86 331	10.13	61
62	7 814 753	149 965	19.19	8 435 992	92 458	10.96	62
63	7 664 788	161 420	21.06	8 343 534	100 289	12.02	63
64	7 503 368	173 628	23.14	8 243 245	109 223	13.25	64
65	7 329 740	186 322	25.42	8 134 022	118 675	14.59	65
66	7 143 418	198 944	27.85	8 015 347	128 246	16.00	66
67	6 944 474	211 390	30.44	7 887 101	137 472	17.43	67
68	6 733 084	223 471	33.19	7 749 629	146 003	18.84	68
69	6 509 613	235 453	36.17	7 603 626	154 810	20.36	69
70	6 274 160	247 892	39.51	7 448 816	164 693	22.11	70
71	6 026 268	260 937	43.30	7 284 123	176 494	24.23	71
72	5 765 331	274 718	47.65	7 107 629	190 982	26.87	72
73	5 490 613	289 026	52.64	6 916 647	208 260	30.11	73
74	5 201 587	302 680	58.19	6 708 387	227 616	33.93	74
75	4 898 907	314 461	64.19	6 480 771	247 825	38.24	75
76	4 584 446	323 341	70.53	6 232 946	267 830	42.97	76
77	4 261 105	328 616	77.12	5 965 116	286 564	48.04	77
78	3 932 489	329 936	83.90	5 678 552	303 519	53.45	78
79	3 602 553	328 012	91.05	5 375 033	319 008	59.35	79
80	3 274 541	323 656	98.84	5 056 025	333 647	65.99	80
81	2 950 885	317 161	107.48	4 722 378	347 567	73.60	81
82	2 633 724	308 804	117.25	4 374 811	360 484	82.40	82
83	2 324 920	298 194	128.26	4 014 327	371 446	92.53	83
84	2 026 726	284 248	140.25	3 642 881	378 167	103.81	84
85	1 742 478	266 512	152.95	3 264 714	379 033	116.10	85
86	1 475 966	245 143	166.09	2 885 681	373 090	129.29	86
87	1 230 823	220 994	179.55	2 512 591	360 105	143.32	87
88	1 009 829	195 170	193.27	2 152 486	340 480	158.18	88
89	814 659	168 871	207.29	1 812 006	315 180	173.94	89
90	645 788	143 216	221.77	1 496 826	285 520	190.75	90
91	502 572	119 100	236.98	1 211 306	253 005	208.87	91
92	383 472	97 191	253.45	958 301	219 269	228.81	92
93	286 281	77 900	272.11	739 032	185 874	251.51	93
94	208 381	61 660	295.90	553 158	154 503	279.31	94
95	146 721	48 412	329.96	398 655	126 501	317.32	95
96	98 309	37 805	384.55	272 154	102 259	375.74	96
97	60 504	29 054	480.20	169 895	80 695	474.97	97
98	31 450	20 693	657.98	89 200	58 502	655.85	98
99	10 757	10 757	1000.00	30 698	30 698	1000.00	99

A. Males Age 31. Mortality Rate: 1.78 per 1,000

B. Females Age 31. Mortality Rate: 1.40 per 1,000

C. Females Age 1. Mortality Rate: 0.87 per 1,000

Source: Reprinted by permission from "Report of the Special Committee to Recommend New Mortality Tables for Valuation," *Transactions of the Society of Actuaries* XXXIII (1981): 617–54. Copyright 1982 by the Society of Actuaries.

Best Case Scenario 8-1.   Mortality Rates for the Carpenters.

Tom Carpenter is 31 years old; his wife Maria is also 31, and their daughter Christina is 15 months. We can use the 1980 CSO table in Figure 8-3 to calculate the mortality rate for people of the same age and sex as each of the Carpenters.

The magnified segment labeled "A" in Figure 8-3 shows the mortality information for males age 31, which is Tom's age group. This segment indicates that 9,563,425 males (of an original 10 million) were alive at the beginning of the year, and that 17,023 died before reaching age 32. To determine the rate of mortality for males age 31, divide the number dying during the year by the number living at the beginning of the year; then multiply the result by 1,000 to ascertain a rate per thousand:

> No. dying during year ÷ No. living at beginning of year × 1,000 = Mortality rate per thousand people

$17{,}023 \div 9{,}563{,}425 = 0.00178 \times 1{,}000 = 1.78$

In other words, 1.78 of every 1,000 males age 31 died at age 31.

Now look at segment B—females age 31, which is Maria's age group. At the beginning of this age, 9,694,485 women (of an original 10 million) were alive, and 13,572 died before reaching age 32, for a mortality rate of 1.40 ($13{,}572 \div 9{,}694{,}485 = 0.00140 \times 1{,}000 = 1.40$). Thus, 1.40 out of every 1,000 females age 31 can be predicted to die while they're 31. Note that this mortality rate is lower than the mortality rate of 1.78 per 1,000 for 31-year-old males. In fact, you can see by looking at the 1980 CSO table that at all ages the mortality rate for males is higher than the mortality rate for females. Because of this distinction in mortality rates, insurers in most states are legally permitted to charge higher life insurance rates to males than females of the same age, all other risk factors being equal.

Now look at segment "C"—females age 1, which is Christina's age group. Of 9,971,100 females age 1, 8,675 died before reaching age 2, for a mortality rate of 0.87 per 1,000 ($8{,}675 \div 9{,}971{,}100 = 0.00087 \times 1{,}000 = 0.87$). •

that it has enough funds to pay more in death benefits than it will probably have to pay. Valuation mortality tables are used to calculate policy reserves, which we discuss later in this chapter.

Mortality tables can also be sex distinct or unisex. ***Sex-distinct mortality tables***, like the 1980 CSO table in Figure 8-3, show different mortality rates for males and females, reflecting the fact that women as a group experience lower mortality rates at all ages than men. ***Unisex mortality tables*** show a single set of mortality rates that reflect one mortality rate for both males and females at each age. Use of sex-distinct mortality tables to price life insurance products results in lower premium rates for female insureds than for male insureds of the same age. When an insurer uses unisex mortality tables, men and women of the same age and the same risk level are charged the same premium rates for the same types of coverage.

Investment Earnings

You know that actuaries use mortality tables to estimate how many insureds are expected to die each year and therefore to calculate the cost of policy benefits the company can anticipate each year. But for life insurance policies, the entire amount of premiums that policy-

owners remit in any given year is not used to pay current claims and operating expenses. A portion of the premiums will not be needed to pay claims until later. Rather than having these premium amounts sit idle until they are needed, the insurance company puts them to work by investing them in a portfolio of assets—such as bonds, mortgages, and stocks—that generate investment income. If the investments perform satisfactorily, the income earned on the investments will exceed the costs—management fees, transaction fees, and administrative expenses—associated with making the investments. The insurer uses this **net investment income**, which is the excess of investment income over investment expenses, to help pay policy benefits and the cost of company operations. By earning investment income, insurers can charge less for insurance coverage than if they did not invest the premiums.

In pricing a new life insurance product, a product actuary makes assumptions about the rate of investment return on the product's invested premiums. The rate of return can vary depending on the type of investment and changes in investment earnings. During the technical design phase of product development, product actuaries consult with the company's investment staff to determine the appropriate investments to make for a given product and each investment's expected rate of return.

The actuarial assumptions about the product's investment returns affect the amount of the product's net premium. Total investment returns also depend on how long premiums will remain invested. Generally, the longer that the investment earnings can accumulate, the higher will be the total investment returns.[4] For this reason, investment earnings have a much larger impact on long-term products, such as whole life insurance, than on short-term products, such as yearly renewable term insurance.

Loading Assumptions

The gross premiums that a life insurer charges for a product not only pay for the estimated cost of policy benefits, but also cover the commissions and expenses the insurer incurs in issuing and administering the product and in operating the company. As stated earlier, the amount of money added to the net premium to cover the insurer's expenses of doing business and provide a reasonable return on the company's investment in the product is referred to as the *loading*. The loading element of the gross premium

- Pays the company's operating expenses

- Provides for commissions for agents

- Compensates the insurer for the loss of premium income when policies lapse

- Provides money for contingencies in case actual product costs exceed the anticipated levels

- Provides margins for profit and contributions to the insurer's surplus

Operating Expenses

An insurer incurs several different types of expenses in the course of operating the company and selling insurance products. The amount of some expenses varies with the level of sales volume, while other expenses remain the same at all levels of sales. One task of the product actuary is to estimate the company's operating expenses, which include its development expenses, acquisition expenses, distribution expenses, maintenance expenses, termination expenses, general and administrative expenses, and taxes. For more detail on these expense categories, see Figure 8-4.

FIGURE 8-4. Expense Factors Used to Calculate Loading.

Development expenses are the costs of planning and creating insurance products. These costs include the salaries of employees involved in product development, computer resources, and research.

Acquisition expenses include the costs of processing insurance applications and issuing policies. These costs include the salaries of underwriters and the costs of medical examinations, printing, and postage.

Depending on the distribution methods used, **distribution expenses** can include (1) agent compensation (usually commissions); (2) postal, printing, telecommunications, and salary expenses for companies that use direct response marketing; (3) group insurance sales representatives' salaries; and (4) advertising.

Maintenance expenses represent the costs of keeping policies in force and include the salaries of customer service representatives and the cost of customer service systems technology.

Termination expenses are the costs of processing death benefit claims and cash surrenders.

General administrative expenses include the home office and field office costs of rent, building maintenance, supplies, and certain salaries.

Taxes include (1) premium taxes that all state and most provincial governments levy on insurance policy premiums received by insurers and (2) income taxes that state, provincial, and federal governments charge on corporate income.

Policy Lapses

Another component of the loading charge compensates the insurer for policy lapses. A ***policy lapse*** occurs when a policy terminates because of nonpayment of renewal premiums. The ***lapse rate*** is the percentage share of an insurer's business that customers voluntarily terminate over a specified period, such as a year. (The flip side of the lapse rate is the *persistency rate,* which is the share of business that remains in force during the specified period.) Although the relationship between lapse rates and profitability is extremely complex, generally when policies lapse before the insurer receives enough premiums to cover the policies' distribution and acquisition expenses, the insurer loses money on those policies. When pricing a product, a product actuary estimates the lapse rate the company can expect each policy year and adds an amount to the loading to compensate for the lost premium income resulting from these lapses. For simplicity in this discussion, we will assume that the higher the lapse rate, the greater the likely loss in premium income, and therefore the higher the loading charge necessary to compensate the insurer for the lost income.

Being able to accurately predict lapse rates allows an insurance company to manage its finances realistically instead of incorrectly assuming it will receive premium income every year of the premium-paying period for every policy sold. Actuaries obtain lapse information from the insurer's own lapse records and from results of lapse studies of other insurance companies that operate in similar markets and sell similar products.

Numerous factors affect an insurer's lapse rates. Among the factors associated with company operations are product design, marketing, and customer service. In general, an insurance product that requires frequent premium payments—say, monthly or quarterly payments—has a higher lapse rate than will a product on which policyowners make annual premium payments. A product that permits premium payment through an automatic system, such as account debiting or preauthorized checks, typically tends to have a lower lapse rate than a product that requires the policyowner to mail premiums to the company. Lapse rates also tend to be low when (1) an insurer's marketing staff and distribution system maintain close ties with policyowners and are concerned that the insurance appropriately fulfills policyowner needs and (2) an insurer offers high quality customer service that is responsive to policyowners' requests.

Contingencies

Unexpected events can cause mortality experience and claims, investment earnings, operating expenses, and lapse rates to vary significantly from the estimates made when the product was priced. These

unexpected events, known as ***contingencies***, may result in higher-than-expected costs for the company. To make sure that companies have enough money to pay the expenses associated with such contingencies, actuaries add a small charge to the loading. The amount of this charge varies with the characteristics of the policies issued and the amount of insurance involved.

Profit

Because insurance companies have a responsibility to their owners and their policyowners to remain financially healthy and competitive long into the future, the final element of the loading is an allowance for contribution to the company's profit or surplus. Although not a strict accounting term, the word ***profit*** is used in most businesses, including stock insurance companies, to refer to the excess of the company's revenue over its expenses each year before deducting stockholder dividends. Mutual insurers and fraternal benefit societies generally avoid the use of the term *profit* and instead use the term ***contribution to surplus***, which is the excess of the company's revenues over its expenses before payment of policy dividends. A stock insurer distributes a portion of its profits to stockholders in the form of stockholder dividends; a mutual insurer distributes a portion of its surplus to participating policyowners in the form of policy dividends.

Policy Reserve Assumptions

Another actuarial assumption is the pattern of development (in other words, the timing and amount) of the new product's policy reserves. A ***policy reserve***, also called a *policy liability*, is a liability (a future financial obligation) identifying the amount that, together with future premiums and an assumed rate of investment interest, is expected to be needed to pay benefits of the policies then in force. In order to help ensure that the amount of each insurer's policy reserves is adequate, insurance laws in the United States and Canada require insurers to maintain at least a minimum amount of policy reserves for all in-force policies. For example, in the United States, minimum reserve requirements specify that an insurer must maintain reserves that are at least as large as those calculated by using specific mortality tables, interest rates, and other factors. An insurer can maintain policy reserves that are greater, but not smaller, than those calculated using minimum reserve requirements. Because of the legal requirements, policy reserves are also known as *legal reserves* and *statutory reserves.*

When setting gross premiums, product actuaries estimate the pattern by which policy reserves will grow and the effect this growth will have on the timing of a product's earnings. In pricing insurance

products, an insurer must provide for the policy reserve to grow at a rate sufficient to satisfy minimum reserve requirements—that is, to cover all of the claims expected during each policy year. Policy reserves must also be adequate to allow for possible fluctuations in both mortality rates and investment experience—that is, mortality experience that is higher than expected and investment earnings that are less than expected. Therefore, when calculating the amount needed for policy reserves, actuaries use conservative mortality tables. A conservative mortality table allows the company to set aside more assets than it will likely need to pay claims each year.

Cash Value Assumptions

The *cash value* of a permanent life insurance policy is the amount of money before adjustments for factors such as policy loans that the policyowner will receive if the policy does not remain in force until the insured's death. The cash value provided by a policy must be equal to or greater than the cash value required by law.

In the United States, standard nonforfeiture laws require insurers to calculate cash values before issuing a permanent life insurance policy and to include in the policy a table showing the minimum cash values at the end of certain policy years. The policy must also contain a statement about the mortality table and the rate of interest used in calculating the cash values provided by the policy and a description of the method used to calculate the values. During technical design of a new insurance product, the product actuary makes assumptions as to the amount of the cash value that will accumulate between the day a policy is issued and the day it is expected to mature.

Policy Dividend Assumptions

If the product under development is a participating life insurance policy, a final actuarial assumption concerns the amount of policy dividends the company is expected to pay. As you learned in an earlier chapter, policy dividends are the policyowners' shares of an insurer's divisible surplus. Each policy year, actuaries determine how much premium the company can return to policyowners in the form of policy dividends for each type of participating policy and recommend these dividend amounts to the company's board of directors.

The premium rates for a participating life insurance product are usually set at a slightly higher level than for an otherwise identical nonparticipating product. As a result, people who purchase participating policies generally pay slightly higher gross premiums than they would if they had purchased similar nonparticipating policies.

However, if the insurer's actual experience relative to mortality, investment earnings, or expenses is better than anticipated, the company can pay policy dividends to participating policyowners.

Many companies that sell participating policies have long histories of paying regular policy dividends, and they typically strive to maintain this dividend-paying record. To make sure that an allowance for policy dividends is reasonably certain, the product actuary calculates premium rates for participating policies by using conservative mortality, investment, and expense assumptions. In this way, the insurer can pay policy dividends when experience is favorable, yet the established premium rate is sufficient to pay promised benefits when experience is unfavorable.

Setting Gross Premium Rates

After choosing assumptions for mortality rates, investment earnings, and loading factors, and after considering the growth of policy reserves, cash values, and policy dividends, product actuaries can develop tentative gross premiums for various issue ages. Before setting the gross premium scale, the product actuary evaluates a proposed product's profitability by testing the product under a number of different sets of actuarial assumptions. The actuary uses a tool known as an asset share model to test various sets of assumptions regarding mortality, investment returns, expenses, lapse rates, policy dividends, cash values, and taxes. An *asset share model* is a financial simulation model used to indicate how the assets associated with a product can be expected to grow and when the insurer can expect the product to become profitable.

A properly constructed asset share model simulates the amount of money the company will receive each year in premiums and investment earnings as well as the amount of money that will be paid out in claims, cash surrenders, policy dividends, and expenses, based on the set of assumptions used in the model. An assumption set can be very conservative, slightly conservative, or best estimate. Each assumption set produces a different result.

An asset share model also simulates how the policy reserves and *asset shares*—the amount of assets per unit of coverage that an insurance product has accumulated at a given time—increase each policy year. By comparing the amount of the simulated reserves to the amount of simulated asset shares, an actuary can see how the product under development would add to the company's liabilities and assets.

An insurance product does not make a profit for a company or add to surplus until the amount of asset shares are larger than the amount of the policy reserves. The amount of time required for a product to

become profitable or begin adding to surplus is called the **validation period** or the *break-even period.* The **validation point**, also called the *break-even point,* is the point at which the product breaks even and is calculated as the first year that a product's asset share equals or exceeds its policy reserve.

If the validation period is considered to be too long, the actuary can change some of the actuarial assumptions, as long as the changes are actuarially sound. For example, a product design actuary can recommend product design changes that would improve the mortality experience, lapse rate, expense levels, and investment earnings. The actuary may consult with staff from marketing, underwriting, customer service, investments and other members of the product design team to verify the feasibility of such product design changes. Every modification that the actuary makes requires a new asset share calculation. The revision process continues until the product development team agrees on a premium rate structure that it believes will be financially competitive and actuarially sound.

In setting gross premium rates, product actuaries also consider the gross premiums that other companies charge for similar products in similar markets, as we see in Best Case Scenario 8-2.

Asset share calculations for products such as universal life, variable life, and adjustable life pose particular challenges for actuaries. Each of these products grants considerable flexibility to the policyowner with regard to pattern of premium payments—in other words, the timing and amount of submitted premiums—and face amounts. As a result, the actuary must determine the outcome of a much wider variety of scenarios in order to assure a particular product's success over time. Asset share calculations become extremely complex with such products, because the death benefit, premium amount, and cash value can change as many other factors change.

The Role of Technology

While the mechanics of life insurance pricing are essentially the same as they have always been, the job of today's actuary is eased by sophisticated computer programs, the ever-increasing power of personal computers, and networks that connect these computers with other computers. With modern equipment and Internet technology, the actuary can gather and evaluate huge amounts of data and can price a product in a few days, whereas in the past this task could take months. (Focus on Technology 8-1 further discusses technology and actuarial information.) The powerful new equipment and tools allow a much shorter product development time than before and also shorten the life span of products, because product modifications can be made quickly. A shortened product life span is important for

Best Case Scenario 8-2.   **Setting Gross Premiums.**

Claudio Desouza is a product actuary and member of the technical design team at the Best Friend Life Insurance Company. Best Friend is developing a new nonparticipating whole life insurance policy—Best Life Plus—that Best Friend will sell in several states. One of Best Friend's main competitors in these states is the Everyday Life Assurance Company, which already sells a whole life product similar to Best Life Plus.

Claudio has constructed an asset share model and is ready to test gross premium rates for the new Best Friend policy. Because this product will be marketed to the same target consumers as the Everyday whole life product, Claudio wants to make sure that the pricing of Best Life Plus is competitive. Research by Best Friend's marketing department has shown that, for Everyday's product, the gross premium per $1,000 of insurance for men age 35 is $7.70, ignoring any applicable fees. Claudio wants to create a sound and competitive product, so he uses as a starting point a gross premium of $7.55 per $1,000 of insurance. He selects a conservative mortality table and conservative investment return rate

to determine the development of the product's reserves. Then he chooses a realistic mortality table and level of investment return rate to estimate the net premium that will be required to cover the cost of benefits.

To the net premium he adds a loading charge. To determine the amount of the loading charge, he estimates the expenses associated with the product and the anticipated lapse rate for the first year and for all succeeding years. Then he adds an amount for unexpected contingencies and a contribution to profit for the first year and all succeeding years. Finally, he evaluates the results of these assumptions through an asset share model to see how the assets of the policy will grow and to determine the product's validation point.

Based on Claudio's initial assumptions, the validation point for Best Life Plus is in Year 8, which is longer than Best Friend desires. According to the product's pricing objectives, the product should become profitable in Year 5. Claudio could reduce the validation period by increasing the gross premium, but then the product may no longer be competitive with Everyday's simi-

lar product. Instead, Claudio must change some of the other factors in the asset share calculation, but the changes must be actuarially sound.

Claudio understands the importance of making pricing assumptions on an actuarially sound basis. Unrealistic and unsound assumptions can lead to disastrous results. For example, suppose Claudio assumes first-year expenses to be $1.10 per $1,000 of coverage and subsequent year's expenses to be $.30 per $1,000 of coverage. With these expense estimates, the product has a validation period of five years, which meets the company's target. If actual first-year expenses turn out to be $1.50 per $1,000 and subsequent year's expenses are $.50 per $1,000, the product will not reach its validation point until Year 9. Likewise, if actual investment earnings turn out to be slightly below Claudio's assumptions, the validation period could be extended even further. If Claudio's pricing assumptions are inaccurate by a wide enough margin, Best Life Plus may never break even, and Best Friend may lose money on the product and see its surplus decrease as a result. •

an insurance company's competitiveness because rapidly changing environmental conditions can necessitate frequent modifications or even entirely new products.

Setting Gross Premiums for Group Life Insurance

A group life insurance policy insures a number of people under a single contract, called a ***master group insurance contract***. In many ways, establishing gross premiums for master group insurance contracts is similar to setting gross premiums for individual life insurance products.

Focus on Technology 8-1.

Breathing New Life into Mortality Research.

Besides needing to deliver customized analytic solutions to clients as rapidly and effectively as possible, Security Life Reinsurance (a part of the ING Group) launched its Mortality Research Center (MRC) for other reasons. MRC is an in-house virtual information center providing on-line access to digitized and hard copy holdings. These materials represent a comprehensive collection of industry and scientific mortality and medical information to aid clients in establishing competitive risk management programs.

"While we wanted to establish ourselves as the leading mortality experts in the U.S., we felt that our international connections through ING would enable us to do that for several countries throughout the world," says Katherine Anderson, vice president and chief product actuary at Security Life. "In addition to filling our clients' individual needs, we thought we would help the industry as a whole through the publication of quality mortality data."

Although Security Life has always tracked mortality data and produced a new mortality base table every two to five years, the company wanted to update the mortality data quality and analysis. The database repository allows users to perform large-scale manipulation, statistical analysis, and calculations.

Security Life has plans to allow for MRC analysis on its Internet site, making some items publicly available and placing other material in secured areas accessible only by Security Life's clients. ●

Source: Excerpted and adapted from Andy Webb, "Breathing New Life into Mortality Research," *Insurance & Technology* (December 1998): 24. Used with permission.

For example, product actuaries calculate net premiums and gross premiums for group life insurance products. Like individual life insurance premium rates, group life premium rates consider the factors of mortality, investment returns, and expenses. As with individual insurance products, a product actuary developing a group insurance product develops a benefit structure, establishes the premium rate, and tests the actuarial assumptions on which the rate is based.

Product pricing for group life insurance also has unique characteristics that distinguish it from individual insurance pricing. One of the most important differences is that pricing group life insurance depends to a large extent on the claim experience of the group that is seeking insurance. If a group has been covered by another group policy, then the product actuary can use that group's claim experience to help determine the group's initial premium rate for new coverage. ***Experience rating*** is the method of setting group insurance premium rates using a particular group's experience. The size of the group is important in determining the degree to which the company uses experience rating. For a large group, the group's own experience is a very important consideration when setting premium rates.

For a small group, the group's claim experience is not usually a major factor in calculating premium rates. Instead, the product actuary uses ***manual rating***, which is a method of setting group insurance premium rates by using the insurer's own claim experience, and sometimes the experience of other insurers, to estimate the group's expected claims and expense experience. These manual rates are usually ad-

justed according to factors such as age, sex, income, and geographical characteristics of the group seeking insurance. For intermediate-sized groups, the product actuary may use rates that are based partly on manually rated data and partly on the group's experience-rated data. This type of rating is known as *blended rating*.

Another distinguishing characteristic of group insurance is that almost all group life insurance policies are issued as one-year renewable term insurance, and the premiums are intended to cover expected benefits and expenses for only the current policy year. Thus, from an actuarial standpoint, the vast majority of group life insurance products are much simpler than individual life insurance products. Because of the short-term nature of group coverage, the investment return is not as important a factor in the premium rate calculation as it is in the calculation of premium rates for longer-term insurance contracts. In addition, the group actuary generally is not required to determine policy reserves or establish a policy reserve for a one-year term group life policy, because the annual premiums are calculated as sufficient to pay the year's estimated claims. Cash values need not be established, because one-year term insurance has no cash value.

Managing Pricing Results

The final aspect of life insurance pricing that we will discuss is how insurers manage pricing results following the introduction of a new product. Managing pricing results involves comparing the insurer's actual operating experience with the product to the actuarial assumptions—about mortality rates, investment earnings, expenses, lapses, and so on—used to price the product. In other words, the actuarial assumptions serve as performance standards that are used to evaluate how accurately the product was priced. By comparing the actuarial assumptions used to price the product with the insurer's actual experience with the product, an actuary can gauge the success and accuracy of these assumptions.

If the actuary finds that actual experience closely matches the actuarial assumptions, then these assumptions may become the basis for the technical design of the next product under development. In this regard, the process of life insurance pricing is cyclical. If a product's actual performance deviates significantly from the results expected as a result of the asset share calculations, the insurer determines the reasons for these deviations and, if possible, takes corrective action. Corrective pricing actions might range from revising the price or dividend scale to completely revising the rate structure for part or all of the company's product portfolio.[6] Sometimes, the insurer must implement strategies to increase its operating efficiencies and reduce its expenses.

Strategies may include a change in the company's distribution system or a reduction in the amount of first-year commissions paid on certain products.

Key Terms

block of policies
actuary
pricing objective
pricing strategy
adequate rate
equitable rate
reasonable rate
actuarial assumptions
forecast
unit of coverage
gross premium
net premium
cost of benefits
loading
mortality rate
law of large numbers
mortality experience
mortality table
basic mortality table
valuation mortality table
sex-distinct mortality table

unisex mortality table
net investment income
policy lapse
lapse rate
contingencies
profit
contribution to surplus
policy reserve (policy liability, legal reserve, statutory reserve)
cash value
asset share model
asset share
validation period (break-even period)
validation point (break-even point)
master group insurance contract
experience rating
manual rating
blended rating

Endnotes

1. Society of Actuaries, "Actuaries Look to the Millennium," *News Release—Society of Actuaries*, 25 August 1999, http://www.soa.org/newsroom/national.html (25 October 1999).

2. Kenneth Black, Jr. and Harold D. Skipper, Jr., *Life Insurance*, 12th ed. (Englewood Cliffs, NJ: Prentice Hall, 1994), 966.

3. At the time of this writing, the Society of Actuaries was compiling a new standard mortality table to replace the Commissioners 1980 Standard Ordinary.

4. However, total investment earnings will decrease if the rate of return becomes negative.

5. Sally Whitney, "Life's Ups and Downs," *Best's Review*, Life/Health ed. (October 1999): 97.

6. The insurer can change only non-guaranteed pricing elements. Certain elements are guaranteed not to exceed certain levels.

Distributing Products

LEARNING OBJECTIVES

After reading this chapter, you should be able to

- Describe the steps in the life insurance sales process

- Differentiate among personal selling distribution systems, direct response distribution systems, agency-building systems, and nonagency-building systems

- Identify the types of products that insurers distribute through broker-dealers

- Describe the primary types of media used in direct response distribution systems

- Discuss some of the important factors that insurance companies consider when determining what product distribution system or systems to use

You have already seen how insurance companies identify target markets and develop products to meet the needs of consumers in those target markets. But developing superior products is of little value to an insurer if it does not have an effective and efficient way to distribute the products to its target consumers. Insurers can choose from several distribution systems. As you learned in Chapter 6, a *distribution system*, also known as a *distribution channel*, is a network of organizations and people that, in combination, performs all the activities required to deliver products to consumers. An insurer's choice of a distribution system affects and is affected by the insurer's target markets and the products the insurer sells. As you will see in this chapter, certain distribution systems are better suited for certain products and certain target markets than for others.

Selecting a distribution system is not a one-time-only decision. The goal of distribution is to deliver products in a manner that is both efficient for the company and suitable for the consumer. But what is considered efficient and suitable can change as the factors of an insurer's internal and external environment change. Insurance companies periodically modify their distribution systems to remain competitive. In many cases, modification involves adopting some aspects of additional distribution systems rather than completely switching systems.

This chapter and the next discuss the distribution of life insurance products. This chapter will provide you with an overview of the various distribution systems available to insurance companies and will describe some of the factors insurers consider when deciding which systems are best for them. In the next chapter, you will learn about the support services that an insurer's home office provides for its distribution systems.

Distribution Systems

Figure 9-1 lists typical life insurance company distribution systems. Life insurers use one or both of two general types of distribution systems: (1) the personal selling distribution system and (2) the direct response distribution system. A *personal selling distribution system* is an insurance sales system in which commissioned or salaried salespeople sell products through verbal and written presentations made to prospective purchasers. As you can see in Figure 9-1, three types of personal selling

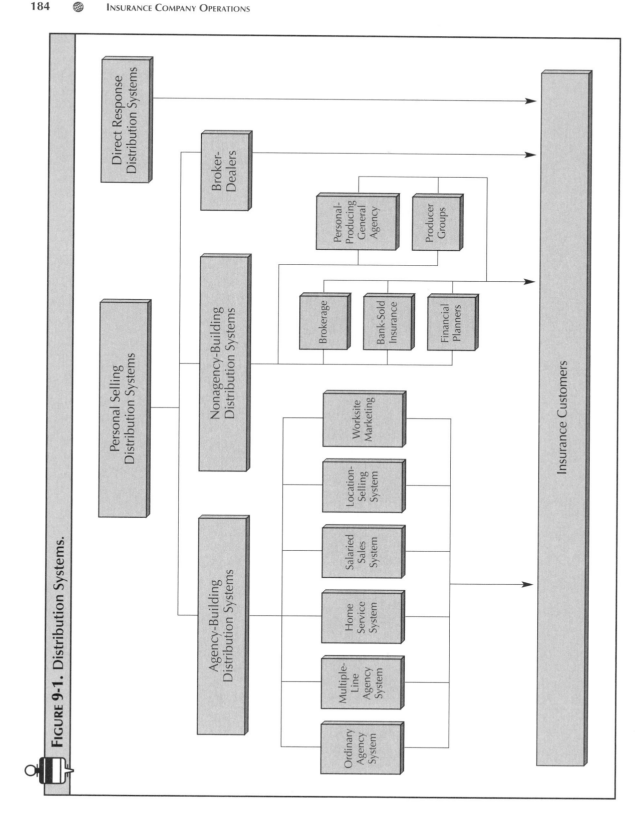

FIGURE 9-1. Distribution Systems.

systems are agency-building systems, nonagency-building systems, and broker-dealer systems. A ***direct response distribution system*** is an insurance sales system in which the consumer purchases products directly from a company by responding to the company's advertisements or telephone solicitations.

Personal Selling Distribution Systems

Because insurance is a complex product that must be fully explained to prospective buyers, insurance companies have traditionally relied on personal selling by people who are knowledgeable about insurance products. Each of the personal selling distribution systems—agency-building systems, nonagency-building systems, and the broker-dealer system—relies on salespeople to act as the link between the insurer and the customer. We will discuss each of these systems in this chapter.

An insurance salesperson typically enters into an agency relationship with at least one insurer. An ***agency relationship*** is a legal relationship by which one party—the ***agent***—is authorized to perform certain acts for another party—the ***principal***. In a personal selling distribution system, the insurer acts as a principal and authorizes its sales agents to act on its behalf in distributing insurance products. In this text, we use the terms *agent* and *producer* to refer in a general sense to any licensed person who sells insurance.

An agent's authority to act for the insurer is typically specified in an ***agency contract***, which is a legal document that defines an agent's role and responsibilities, describes the agent's compensation, and specifically states the agent's right to act for the insurer.[1] An insurance company generally grants a sales agent the authority (1) to act for the company in soliciting applications for insurance policies and annuity contracts and (2) to accept the initial premiums, but not renewal premiums, for those policies.[2] The agency contract also describes other aspects of the agreement between an agent and an insurer, such as the specific terms of the agent's employment. We discuss the provisions of the typical agency contract in more detail in Chapter 10.

The Sales Process

To sell insurance products, agents typically follow a process that consists of five primary tasks:

1. Locate a ***prospect***—a potential buyer of insurance products.

2. Identify the prospect's insurance needs.

3. Develop a proposal of coverage to meet the prospect's needs.

4. Close the sale.

5. Implement the proposal, which includes assisting the applicant in applying for coverage, submitting the application to the insurer for underwriting, and delivering the policy to the customer.

The amount of time spent on each task, and the manner in which the sales agent accomplishes these tasks, varies depending on a number of factors, most importantly the agent's experience level. An experienced agent in the individual market typically spends far less time locating prospects than does a newer agent because the experienced agent can rely on current clients for additional sales and on referrals from those clients for prospects. A newer agent, on the other hand, might need to rely heavily on **cold calling**, which is the process of writing, telephoning, or visiting prospects with whom she has had no prior contact.

After identifying a prospect for insurance and securing an interview, the sales agent meets in person with the prospect and discusses the prospect's insurance needs. During that meeting, the agent performs a **needs analysis**, which is a process by which a salesperson develops a detailed personal and financial picture of a prospect in order to evaluate the prospect's insurance needs. For an example of a needs analysis, see Best Case Scenario 9-1. Using the information gathered during the needs analysis, the agent develops a proposal that recommends one or more insurance products for the prospect. To close the sale, the agent makes a presentation to stimulate the prospect's interest in, and motivation to purchase, the product or products recommended in the proposal. These three tasks—identifying needs, developing a proposal, and closing the sale—can be accomplished during one meeting or can take place over the course of several meetings.

If the prospect agrees to purchase the insurance, the sales agent implements the proposal by helping the prospect complete the application and witnessing the applicant's signature on the application. In many cases, the prospect pays the initial premium at the time of signing. If the insurance company approves the applied-for coverage, the company issues the policy, and the agent completes implementation of the proposal by delivering the policy to the policyowner.

From the standpoint of the agent, the insurer, and the applicant, there are advantages to the applicant's paying the initial premium at the time of application. The advantage to the agent and the insurer is that an applicant is far more likely to accept a policy when the initial premium accompanies the application. If the applicant decides not to accept the policy, the agent will not earn compensation for the sale, and the company will have lost both the applicant's business and the

Best Case Scenario 9-1.

A Needs Analysis.

Louise Chen, an agent representing Best Friend Life Insurance Company, met with Tom and Maria Carpenter to analyze their current financial situation and to determine their life insurance needs. The goal of this needs analysis was to estimate the amount of money necessary to maintain the Carpenter family in its customary lifestyle in the event of either Tom's or Maria's death.

Tom and Maria provided Louise with extensive information about their household income, assets, debts, and existing life insurance. Louise prepared one needs analysis assuming Tom's death and another analysis assuming Maria's death. Using computer software, Louise calculated (1) the amount of money that the surviving spouse would need in the event of the other spouse's death, (2) the amount of money available to meet that need, and (3) the amount of life insurance and types of policies required to cover any shortfall between the amount of money needed and the amount available.

For each needs analysis, Louise divided the needs into five categories:

1. Immediate needs. These needs include expenses associated with the deceased's final medical treatments and burial, estate taxes, and probate costs. Louise estimated this amount as a lump sum payable at death.

2. Continued income for dependent support. This monthly amount is needed to support the family until the youngest child is no longer dependent on the family's financial assistance. Louise es-

timated this monthly amount to be payable until Christina, now age 1, reaches age 22. The total amount of insurance needed decreases each month as the benefit period shortens.

3. Continued income for the surviving spouse. This is a monthly amount needed for the surviving spouse after the youngest child is no longer dependent on the family for financial support. Louise estimated this amount as a monthly sum payable from Christina's 22nd birthday throughout the remainder of the surviving spouse's life.

4. Continued income to cover various expenses. This is the monthly amount needed to pay expenses such as the home mortgage, child care, education expenses, emergency expenses, and miscellaneous expenses.

5. A retirement fund for the surviving spouse.

For needs 2 through 5, Louise estimated the monthly benefit amount to increase each year with the assumed rate of inflation. The calculations also included assumptions about the effects of interest. From the sum of these expenses, Louise subtracted sources of income available to the surviving spouse. For Tom and Maria, these sources of income included the following:

• Salaries
• The estimated monthly Social Security benefit that Tom and Maria would each receive at retirement
• The amount of employer-provided group term life insurance covering Tom and Maria
• The proceeds from a low face amount policy covering Tom's life

that Tom's father had purchased for him 15 years earlier
• The projected monthly benefit from each spouse's 401(k) thrift and savings plan and individual retirement accounts
• Income from investments

The difference between the total amount of funds needed and the total amount of funds available is the amount of life insurance that Tom and Maria could consider purchasing on each of their lives.

After calculating the amount of new insurance needed, Louise used a computer program to determine the types of policies suitable for Tom's and Maria's insurance programs. For example, Louise could offer individual policies covering the lives of Tom and Maria, or she could offer a joint life insurance policy that covers both of their lives and that pays a benefit upon the death of the first spouse. The insurance to provide the monthly income could be met with term insurance. The other insurance needs might be met through a permanent plan of insurance with either fixed or variable cash values and death benefits. Such a policy could also serve as a savings vehicle. The need for retirement funding may also be met with mutual fund products or a deferred annuity.

After Tom and Maria selected plans of insurance that meet their needs, Louise reminded them that they should review their insurance program every few years or whenever a major life event occurs (such as the birth of another child) to verify that the insurance program is still appropriate for their situation. •

expenses associated with underwriting the application. The advantage to the applicant of paying the initial premium at the time of application is that the applicant usually receives a ***premium receipt***, which is a written acknowledgment that the insurer has received the initial premium payment submitted with an application. A premium receipt provides the applicant with insurance coverage for a specified time, usually the time required to underwrite the policy.

In issuing an insurance policy, an insurer typically mails the policy to the sales agent, who is responsible for delivering the policy to the policyowner. Laws in the United States and Canada state that an insurance contract becomes effective once the policy is delivered to the policyowner. For legal purposes, delivery is considered to take place when the insurer relinquishes the policy.

Agency-Building Distribution Systems

Many insurance companies use ***agency-building distribution systems*** in which they recruit and train sales agents, finance those agents, and provide them with office facilities. To establish and maintain an agency-building distribution system usually requires significant investments in money and people, and typically the insurer can exert a great amount of control over the activities involved in product distribution. As a result, insurance companies are considered to "own" their agency-building distribution systems. In this chapter, we describe six agency-building distribution systems—the ordinary agency system, the multiple-line agency system, the home service system, the salaried sales system, the location-selling system, and worksite marketing.

Ordinary Agency System

The ***ordinary agency distribution system***, also called the *career agency system* or the *agency system*, relies on full-time or part-time agents to sell and service insurance products. These agents—who may be called *sales agents, ordinary agents, life underwriters, field underwriters, sales representatives,* or *insurance agents*—are responsible for soliciting applications for new insurance policies, collecting initial premiums, conserving existing business, and providing certain types of policyowner service. The agents in an ordinary agency system are collectively known as the insurer's ***field force***.

The sales agents in an ordinary agency system are usually compensated on a commission basis. A ***commission*** is an amount of money, usually a percentage of the first-year and renewal premiums, that an insurer pays to an insurance agent for selling and servicing an insurance policy. Other forms of agent compensation may include bonuses, group

life and health insurance coverage, and reimbursement allowances for certain business expenses. We discuss agent compensation further in Chapter 10.

Most ordinary agency systems contain one of two types of agents:

- A *career agent* is a full-time salesperson who holds an agency contract with at least one insurance company. Some career agents, called *captive agents* or *exclusive agents*, are under contract to only one insurer and are not permitted to sell the products of other insurers. Career agents are legally considered to be independent contractors rather than employees of an insurance company. An *independent contractor* performs services for another business under a contract between them. The company is a client of the agent rather than an employer, and the insurer can exercise control over only those agent activities that the agency contract specifies.

- An *agent-broker* is a career agent who can place business with her primary company and with other insurance companies. When placing business with her primary company, this agent is functioning as a career agent. When placing business with an insurer other than the primary insurer, a career agent is functioning as an agent-broker. An agent-broker must enter into an agency contract with each insurer with which she places business.

The geographical area in which an insurance company distributes its products is known as the company's *marketing territory*. Located throughout this marketing territory are sales offices known as *field offices*. Career agents and agent-brokers work out of these field offices. Each field office is headed by an agency manager. A field office is considered to be either a branch office or an agency office, depending on whether the insurance company uses the branch office system or the general agency system.

Branch Office System. In a *branch office system*, an insurance company establishes and maintains field offices, known as *branch offices*, in key areas throughout its marketing territory. Branch offices function as extensions of the insurer's home office, and the home office pays all the business and operating expenses that a branch office incurs.

The head of a branch office is a *general manager*, also called a *branch manager*, who is an employee of the company. A general manager's responsibilities include (1) increasing the sales of products that the company wishes to market and (2) recruiting, selecting, and developing career agents to help the company achieve its corporate growth and profit objectives. In most situations, insurers compensate

general managers with a base salary and **overriding commissions**, or *overrides*, which are payments based on the amount of sales produced by the agents in a field office. The support staff in a branch office typically are employees of the insurance company.

General Agency System. Unlike a branch office that is established and maintained by an insurance company, an **agency office** is a field office that is established and maintained by a general agent. A **general agent (GA)** is an independent businessperson who heads a field office and is under contract to an insurance company. A GA's primary function is to build and manage an office of full-time career agents focused on distributing the products of a single company within a defined territory. The insurance company compensates a general agent with overriding commissions based on the amount of all of the agency office's sales. The general agent pays the salaries of the support staff and most or all of the operating expenses of the agency office.

The insurance company grants each general agent certain powers to represent the company and to develop new business. The insurance company's control over its general agents is limited by the terms of the general agents' contracts. In most cases, an insurance company

cannot transfer a GA or redefine the GA's sales territory, except as permitted under the GA's contract.

Multiple-Line Agency (MLA) System

The *multiple-line agency (MLA) system* is a personal selling distribution system that uses full-time, commissioned career agents and agent-brokers to distribute (1) life and health insurance and (2) property/casualty insurance products for groups of financially interrelated or commonly managed insurance companies. Career agents in the MLA system typically establish and maintain their own offices and hire the necessary support staff. Most MLA claim and customer service functions are handled at the insurer's regional offices or home office.

One emphasis of the MLA system is for agents to engage in *cross-selling*, which is the process of offering a variety of insurance and financial services products to a customer. (You should note that cross-selling is not exclusive to the MLA system.) This approach to selling reflects the insurance industry's movement from a product-driven orientation to a market-driven orientation. An important benefit of cross-selling is the reduction in the amount of prospecting necessary to generate new business. Also, cross-selling is believed to improve *persistency*, which is the retention of business that occurs when a policy remains in force as a result of the continued payment of the policy's renewal premiums. The more business one customer generates, and the more satisfied the customer is with the products and service, the more likely the customer is to keep all of the insurance in force. The risk to an insurer of cross-selling is if that same customer becomes dissatisfied with any of the products, he may replace all of the products with those of another insurer.

Home Service System

The *home service distribution system* relies on the use of commissioned sales agents to sell specified products and to provide policyowner service within a specified geographic area or territory. This system primarily targets lower-income households. *Home service agents*, also called *debit agents,* are exclusive agents who work for insurance companies that use the home service distribution system. The policyowner service that home service agents provide includes collecting initial premiums and renewal premiums. The home service system is the exception to the general rule that agency contracts typically do not provide the authority to collect renewal premiums.

Most insurers that use the home service system divide their marketing region into districts. A district manager, who is a company employee, manages each district office and fills a role similar to the role of a branch manager in an ordinary agency system. The size of

the area served by a district office depends on the geographical characteristics of the district. A large city may be divided into numerous districts, but in rural areas, a single district may encompass several towns. The area served by a district office is subdivided into territories, and each agent is assigned a territory.

Salaried Sales System

The *salaried sales distribution system* relies on the use of salaried sales representatives to sell and service insurance products. Like career agents, salaried sales representatives are legally considered agents of the company. Unlike career agents, salaried sales representatives are salaried company employees who may also receive bonuses and commissions based on their job performance.

Although the salaried sales distribution system may be used to distribute all types of insurance products, insurance companies use this system primarily for group insurance products sold by group representatives. A *group representative* is a salaried insurance company employee who is specifically trained in the techniques of marketing and servicing group insurance products. A group representative

- Solicits business from agents, brokers, and consultants

- Finds group insurance prospects

- Designs proposals for group insurance plans

- Installs (implements) group insurance contracts

- Renegotiates the policies at renewal

Group representatives usually work out of group field offices. In some cases, a group representative is the only direct contact between the prospect (the business or organization) and the insurer.

Location-Selling System

A *location-selling distribution system* is designed to generate consumer-initiated sales at an insurance facility—such as an office or information kiosk—located in a store or other establishment at which consumers conduct personal business or shop for other products. The location-selling system offers product information and insurance applications through businesses such as department stores, grocery stores, and funeral homes. The insurer may be affiliated in some way with the store or office or may have entered into a distribution agreement with the facility. The insurance offices are staffed with commissioned sales agents or salaried sales personnel.

Worksite Marketing

Worksite marketing is the process of distributing individual or group insurance products to people at their place of work on a voluntary, payroll-deduction basis. Under a worksite marketing arrangement, an insurer approaches an employer about offering its employees the opportunity to buy insurance coverage at work. If the employer agrees to the offering, the insurer's sales representative then markets the products directly to the employees at the worksite. The employer implements a payroll deduction plan to withhold employees' premium payments from their paychecks and then submits the premium payments to the insurance company.

Worksite marketing insurance plans differ from traditional group insurance. An employee insured under a worksite marketing plan can terminate employment and continue the original coverage under the original terms. Under most traditional group insurance plans, a covered employee who leaves the group must convert the coverage to an individual plan of insurance in order to continue coverage.

As shown in Figure 9-2, worksite marketing has advantages for insurers, employers, and employees, including its cost effectiveness, its value as a gateway to future sales, and its meeting of consumers' needs.

Nonagency-Building Distribution Systems

In an agency-building distribution system, the insurer recruits and trains its sales agents, finances those agents, and provides them with office facilities. Some insurers use **nonagency-building distribution systems**, also called *third-party distribution systems*, in which the insurer does not train, finance, or house the salespeople. Salespeople who work in nonagency-building distribution systems are generally referred to as *independent agents* or *independent producers,* because they do not have exclusive contracts with one insurance company. Insurance companies are not considered to "own" their nonagency-building distribution systems, and insurers cannot exert as much control over the activities involved in nonagency-building distribution as they can with agency-building distribution systems. Five types of nonagency-building systems are (1) the brokerage distribution system, (2) the personal-producing general agent (PPGA) system, (3) the bank-sold insurance distribution system, (4) financial planners, and (5) producer groups.

Brokerage Distribution System

The **brokerage distribution system** is a nonagency-building system that relies on the use of agent-brokers, licensed life insurance brokers, and independent property/casualty agents and brokers to distribute an insurance company's products. Recall that an agent-broker is a

Figure 9-2. Advantages of Worksite Marketing.

Advantages to Insurers

- **Is cost effective**—Insurance distribution and administration can be performed at a lower cost than for individual plans of insurance
- **Serves as door opener**—Plan can be used as a gateway to sell other products offered by the insurer
- **Meets consumer needs**—Is particularly appropriate for middle- and lower-income markets
- **Offers branding of insurer name**—Increased recognition and value achieved through group/benefit plan platform

Advantages to Employers

- **Is cost effective**—Few direct costs or fees to employers
- **Is complementary**—Adds to employer-provided group insurance coverage
- **Enhances goodwill**—Allows employer to offer a benefit that is valued by employees
- **Is nonintrusive**—Does not interfere with existing employee benefit program
- **Avoids nondiscrimination issues**—Exempt from discrimination requirements that apply to employer-provided benefits
- **Offers wide range of products**—Generally no restrictions on the types of products that may be offered

Advantages to Employees

- **Offers buying opportunity**—For some employees, may be the only time they are "pushed" to buy an insurance product
- **Is affordable**—Participation and amount of coverage left to the consumer
- **Is convenient**—Payments made via payroll deduction
- **Provides easy qualification**—Typically, no medical examination needed to apply
- **Offers portability**—Coverage can be continued if employee leaves the company
- **Is flexible**—Coverage can be tailored to meet changing insurance needs

Source: Adapted from Conning & Company, *Life Insurers' Distribution Strategies: Testing the Waters* (Hartford, CT: Conning & Company, 1999), 37. Used with permission.

career agent who has agency contracts with a primary insurance company and with companies other than the primary company. A *licensed broker*, also called a *pure broker*, is a broker who is licensed to sell insurance and is not under an agency contract with any insurance company. A licensed broker enters into a contract—although not an agency contract—with an insurer before submitting insurance applications to that insurer. Because the insurer does not have an agency

contract or an employer-employee relationship with a licensed broker, the insurer cannot exercise control over a licensed broker's activities. Like most ordinary agents, agent-brokers and licensed brokers are compensated primarily on a commission basis.

The use of brokerage distribution by life insurance companies varies widely. Some life insurers actively seek brokerage business; other life insurers accept but do not encourage brokerage business; other life insurers do not accept brokerage business; still others use brokers exclusively. Insurance companies that use the brokerage system exclusively and do not establish a career agency force are usually referred to as **brokerage companies**.

Competition among insurance companies that use the brokerage distribution system is intense because a broker can sell policies for any number of companies. In order to attract and retain brokerage business, an insurer's products, underwriting guidelines, customer service quality, and commission levels must consistently be competitive.

Personal-Producing General Agent (PPGA) System

The **personal-producing general agent (PPGA) system** uses personal-producing general agents to distribute insurance products. A **personal-producing general agent (PPGA)** is a commissioned salesperson who generally works alone, is not housed in an insurer's field offices, and engages primarily in personal production (i.e., sales of new policies). Each PPGA typically holds agency contracts with several insurance companies. PPGAs spend most of their time selling insurance rather than building and managing an agency, although typically PPGAs can appoint **subagents**, who are full-time soliciting agents recruited by PPGAs. PPGAs earn commissions on their own sales and overrides on the sales of their subagents.

PPGAs and brokers are similar in that typically they are under contract to more than one insurance company. The primary difference between the PPGA system and the brokerage system is the agents' contracts. Whereas a broker's contract usually resembles a soliciting agent's contract, a PPGA's contract typically resembles a general agent's contract. In addition, most companies have no minimum production requirements for brokers, but insurers generally set minimum production requirements that PPGAs must meet in order to maintain their agency contracts.

Bank-Sold Insurance Distribution System

Bank-sold insurance is a type of location-selling system that has grown considerably since the mid-1990s and is expected to continue to grow. *Bank-sold insurance* is insurance that is developed and underwritten by an insurance company and distributed through a bank.[5] Banks that

have chosen to sell insurance products offer or plan to offer a wide variety of insurance products, such as term life insurance, whole life insurance, group life and health insurance, long-term care insurance, and disability income insurance, as well as annuities. Banks usually sell insurance through licensed agents, kiosks, telemarketing, and direct mail (telemarketing and direct mail are discussed later in this chapter). An agent who sells insurance through a bank must be appropriately licensed to sell insurance. Banks are not permitted to make the purchase of insurance a condition for a customer's obtaining a loan from the bank. Also, in the United States, the Federal Deposit Insurance Corporation (FDIC), which insures customer deposits in banks, does not insure bank-sold insurance.

Financial Planners

A *financial planner* is a professional who analyzes a client's personal financial circumstances and goals and prepares a program, usually in writing, to meet the client's financial goals. Financial planners assist clients with some or all of the following activities: insurance planning, investment management, asset accumulation, estate planning, tax planning, and retirement planning. Some financial planners charge clients on the basis of service and time and do not sell products. Other financial planners are compensated by the commissions they receive for selling such products as insurance, mutual funds, stocks, and bonds. Financial planners licensed to sell insurance typically enter into sales agreements with insurance companies to sell their products. In some cases, the sales agreement specifies that the planner will receive a fee for selling the insurer's products. Other agreements specify that the planner will receive the usual agent's commission for each sale.

Producer Groups

A *producer group* is an organization of independent producers or firms that negotiates compensation, product, and service arrangements with insurance companies. Producer groups generally focus on a specific segment of the insurance market, such as high-income individuals, small businesses, employee benefits, or worksite marketing. The impact of producer groups in the development of customized products and specialized services has been significant in some companies. For example, a producer group may consult with an insurer in developing products to be sold exclusively by the producer group, and the insurer may have customer service staff dedicated exclusively to supporting the producer group.

Many producer groups own a reinsurance company. Under the agreement between an insurer and the producer group, the insurer cedes—transfers—a portion of the producer group's business to the reinsurance company. Producers in the group are compensated in part

by the profits of the reinsurance company. Although the reinsurance arrangement provides an opportunity to share in the profits, the results are not assured.

Broker-Dealers

Typically, variable life insurance products are bought by different customers and sold by different salespeople than those who buy and sell traditional life insurance products. Variable life insurance products are considered to be equity-based products because they expose the policyowner or contractholder to investment risk, that is, the risk that the amount of the cash value or death benefit may fluctuate because of changes in investment performance of the underlying assets. In the United States, equity-based insurance products are considered to be securities, and variable life products are subject not only to state insurance laws but also to federal securities laws. For example, in order to sell variable life insurance, a person must be registered with the Securities and Exchange Commission (SEC) as a broker-dealer. A ***broker-dealer*** is a firm that (1) provides information or advice to its customers regarding the sale and/or purchase of securities, (2) serves as a financial intermediary between buyers and sellers by underwriting or acquiring securities in order to market them to its customers, and (3) supervises the sales process to make sure that salespeople comply with applicable securities regulations. Broker-dealer firms ensure that people who sell equity-based products meet certain requirements with respect to training, experience, and character. In order to market variable insurance, an insurer must do one of the following:

- Register the company as a broker-dealer

- Establish a subsidiary company that registers as a broker-dealer

- Market its products through an affiliated firm that is a registered broker-dealer

In the United States, the federal Securities Exchange Act of 1934 requires that broker-dealers—including insurance companies that are registered as broker-dealers—be members of the National Association of Securities Dealers (NASD). The NASD is a nonprofit organization of securities dealers responsible for regulating certain types of securities sales, including the sale of variable life insurance. Agents selling variable life insurance products through a broker-dealer must pass a series of examinations sponsored by the NASD. These sales agents and the people who train them to sell variable insurance products are required to obtain an NASD certification as registered representatives. A ***registered representative*** is any person who is a business associate

of an NASD member, engages in the securities business on behalf of the member by soliciting the sale of securities or training securities salespeople, and has passed a specified examination administered by the NASD.

In Canada, variable life insurance is considered to be an insurance product only. Therefore, agents selling variable life insurance in Canada do not need to meet any special securities requirements, and the products can be distributed through any personal selling distribution system.

Direct Response Distribution System

Although most life insurance sales take place through the personal selling distribution systems we have discussed, insurance companies also use a direct response distribution system for some sales. In a direct response distribution system, no face-to-face contact occurs between consumers and sellers or their sales representatives. Instead, the consumer purchases products directly from the insurance company by responding to the company's advertisements or solicitations. The direct response distribution system generally fulfills only the first task and the last task of the traditional sales process—that is, locating a prospect and implementing the proposal.

A direct response distribution system can use various forms of advertising media, such as television, radio, newspapers, magazines, and the Internet. Some companies also mail product advertisements directly to potential customers and solicit sales via the telephone. Figure 9-3 describes forms of direct response distribution media.

Because agents are typically not involved in the direct response distribution system, the products sold through it must be uncomplicated and easy to understand. They also must be relatively simple to underwrite, simple to administer, and simple to pay for. Term life insurance and a few forms of traditional whole life insurance are the products most commonly offered through direct response channels.[6] For example, many companies that sell mortgage-protection term life insurance use a direct response system.

Many direct response products are issued on a *guaranteed-issue basis*, under which no individual underwriting takes place, except for a review of the applicant's responses to questions on the application. Every eligible member of a particular group of proposed insureds who applies for insurance and who meets specified conditions (usually concerning the insured's age and other coverage already in force with the insurer) is automatically approved for coverage. Guaranteed-issue products allow insurance companies a quick, simple way to provide a moderate amount of coverage for a large number of people.

FIGURE 9-3. Media Used in Direct Response Distribution.

 Direct mail is an advertising medium that uses a mail service to distribute a marketer's printed sales offer or advertising message. These printed materials usually consist of an introduction letter, a brochure that describes a particular product, an insurance application or an inquiry form the consumer can use to request further information, and a return envelope.

Print media include printed publications, such as magazines or newspapers. To include an advertisement in a newspaper or magazine, an insurance company buys space and designs an ad for the space.

 Broadcast media include radio and television. Insurance companies use broadcast media to disseminate an advertisement message over a wide area to a large, generally undifferentiated audience. The advertisement directs the consumer to contact the insurance company or one of its agents for more information about a specific product or product line.

Telemarketing is the use of the telephone to produce sales. Telemarketing can be used to initiate sales contact with prospective customers, and it can support other direct response media. For example, an advertisement or mailing may encourage the consumer to call a toll-free number or to check the insurer's Internet site for information.

Internet sales involve the use of online technology to distribute products. Internet sales include (1) direct sales of insurance products via an insurer's Internet site or (2) sales of insurance through an online insurance marketplace.

The use of direct response distribution within the life insurance industry is widespread. A few insurance companies rely completely on the direct response system to distribute their products. Most insurers use direct response systems in conjunction with various personal selling distribution systems. Nearly all insurance companies have established an Internet site that contains information about the company. Many insurers also include product information on the Internet site and enable consumers to obtain a rate quote. Some insurers allow the consumer to initiate the sales process online. For more on Internet distribution of insurance, see Focus on Technology 9-1.

Determining the Appropriate Distribution System

As you have seen in this chapter, insurance companies can use many different systems to distribute their products. Changes in consumer

Focus on Technology 9-1. Cornering the Online Market.

The Internet has great potential for life insurance companies, but it will not be realized without a focused marketing strategy. Basic concepts such as market segmentation, product differentiation, and determining the right mix of product, price, place, and promotion strategies will be key to using it effectively.

Like any advertising medium, the Internet will generate far more indirect sales than direct sales. The Internet offers a raft of new marketing tools—hyperlinks, banner ads, click-through measurements, and search engines. As insurance marketers better understand these tools, they can build in greater sophistication based on experience and customer feedback.

While it's tempting to characterize all Internet users as alike, they're not. Insurers still must identify customer needs and perceptions. With this type of information, we can properly segment markets, focusing on targets of opportunity in each. In cyberspace, the traditional "sales push" model—in which customers react to information and proposals provided by agents—is replaced by a "market pull" model, where a customer can electronically assess product features and compare prices without personal contact with the insurer.

Internet users still must be offered compelling reasons to buy. Basics like market potential research, customer needs analysis, distinct product design, and, most important,

customer communication will still be requisites to success. The Internet's effectiveness will be diluted if it is perceived as a venue for selling any product anywhere, anytime.

The most promising Internet market segments are characterized by relatively simple, low-cost products, a short sales process, and high customer product awareness and understanding. By placing the right product information in cyberlocations most frequented by target audiences, and by taking advantage of bannering and search engines, independent agencies and insurers can attract Internet surfers. Targeting markets that best fit the right cybertemplate will result in the best return on investment. •

Source: Excerpted from Edward F. Ryan, "Cornering the Online Market," *Best's Review,* Life/Health ed. (December 1998): 97. © A.M. Best Company. Used with permission.

buying preferences, consumer demographics, economic conditions, the regulatory environment, and many other factors affect the distribution systems that insurers use. The predominant method of distribution for life insurance sales has changed over time to match these changing conditions. At one time, most life insurance was distributed through the home service system. Then the ordinary agency system became dominant. In recent years, new environmental changes have caused nonagency-building systems to become more widely used than ordinary agencies, as shown in Figure 9-4.

An insurer's choice of distribution system is critical because the distribution system affects the design and pricing of a product and the way the company promotes the product. For example, a term life policy that will be distributed through direct mail must be relatively simple to understand and underwrite, but a universal life policy that will be sold by a career agency force can be much more complex. Additionally, the costs associated with a product can vary according to the distribution system used. The premium for a policy sold by a career agent will contain a higher expense charge than will a policy sold by direct mail, in part because the commissions associated with agent distribution are generally higher than the expenses associated with direct mail.

FIGURE 9-4. U.S. Market Share of New Individual Life Premiums by Distribution System.

	1983	1986	1989	1993	1997
Ordinary Agency	42%	38%	40%	43%	39%
Home Service	15	13	5	5	2
Multiple-Line Agency	5	5	11	7	6
Independent Agents	36	43	43	43	50
Direct Response	2	1	1	2	2
Banks	NC	NC	NC	+	1
Other	NC	NC	NC	+	+

NC Data not collected

  + Less than one-half of 1 percent

Source: Adapted from Cheryl Dake and Bette Mayo, "Market Share by Distribution Channel in the United States," *LIMRA International, Inc.,* 1 April 1999, <http://www.limra.com/> (5 November 1999). Used with permission.

With so many distribution options, how does an insurer choose which distribution systems are most appropriate? A starting point is evaluating the advantages and disadvantages of each distribution system, such as those summarized in Figure 9-5. In addition, an insurer studies several factors associated with distribution, such as the

- Costs associated with each system

- Degree of control the insurer intends to exercise over distribution

- Characteristics of the buyers in the insurer's target markets

- Characteristics of the products the insurer sells

- Insurer's business environment

- Characteristics of the insurer

Costs Associated with Each System

Some distribution systems are more expensive than others for insurance companies to establish and maintain. Typically, the company-owned personal selling distribution systems, such as the ordinary

FIGURE 9-5. Comparison of Insurance Distribution Systems.

System	Salespeople	Products	Compensation	Key Characteristics	Advantages	Disadvantages
Ordinary Agency (divided into Branch Office System and General Agency System)	• Career agents • Agent-brokers	All types of life insurance	• Commissions • Group life and health insurance • Bonuses	Field offices managed by a branch manager (branch office system) or general agent (general agency system)	High degree of control over distribution activities	• High cost of financing and managing distributors' activities • High fixed costs
Multiple-Line Agency (MLA)	• Career agents • Agent-brokers	• Life • Health • Property/casualty	• Commissions • Group life and health insurance • Bonuses	• Agents sell all types of insurance for groups of financially interrelated insurers • Agents establish their own offices	Improved persistency because policyowners own more than one policy	Unhappy policyowners may cancel all policies
Home Service	Home service agents	• Monthly debit ordinary • Premium notice ordinary	• Commissions • Bonuses • Conservation awards • Other fees	• Agents collect renewal premiums and provide policyowner service in customers' homes • District managers oversee district offices (agencies)	High degree of control over agents' activities	High cost to establish and maintain
Salaried Sales	Group representatives	Group insurance	Salary plus bonuses	• Group reps work out of group field offices • Regions are supervised by regional manager	Very high degree of control over agent activities	High fixed costs because agent salaries are paid regardless of sales activity
Location-Selling	• Career agents • Salaried salespeople	All types of life insurance	Commissions or salary plus incentives	Insurance offices established in noninsurance locations (e.g., retail stores, funeral homes)	Offices are relatively easy and inexpensive to establish and maintain	• The actual sale may not take place at the office location • Some locations used only for promotion
Brokerage	• Agent-brokers • Licensed brokers • Independent agents	All types of life insurance	• Commissions	Producers can sell the products of many companies	• Inexpensive to establish and maintain • Can be used in conjunction with a career field force	Low degree of control over agents' activities
Personal-Producing General Agent (PPGA)	Personal-producing general agents	All types of life insurance	• Commissions • Overriding commissions	• PPGA's primary goal is to make sales • PPGA usually works with regional office or home office • PPGA usually must meet minimum production requirements	• PPGAs are already trained and experienced • Relatively inexpensive to establish and maintain	Low degree of control over PPGA activities
Broker-Dealers	Registered representatives	• Variable life insurance	• Commissions	Producers must be licensed as registered representatives with the NASD	Provide a means for insurers to sell variable products	Additional training and licensing requirements
Direct Response	None or telephone sales representatives	• Graded-premium whole life • Term life	Salary plus sales incentives	• Sales made without face-to-face selling • Several media used	Can reach a wide, yet targeted, audience	• Not effective for selling complex products • Packaged products may not meet customers' actual needs

agency system, the home service system, the multiple-line agency, and the salaried sales system, carry the highest cost. The insurer is responsible for paying virtually all of the expenses associated with product distribution, such as agent commissions, agent training, salaries of field office managers and support staff, and the rent, utilities, and other expenses associated with maintaining field offices.

Less expensive personal selling distribution systems are the brokerage distribution system and the personal-producing general agent distribution system. In these two systems, insurers incur few costs until sales are made and commissions are due. Moreover, the agent-brokers and PPGAs are experienced salespeople who do not require the training that an insurer's own new captive agents do.

Over the long run, direct response techniques, such as direct mail, broadcast media, and the Internet, present several relatively inexpensive ways to distribute certain products. Two important cost considerations with direct response distribution are that (1) the start-up costs associated with a direct response system—such as postage and advertising—can be substantial, and (2) the insurer must absorb most of the costs of distribution *before* any sale is made and income is received. In contrast, with many personal selling distribution systems, the insurer does not incur expenses—usually commissions and overrides—until *after* the sales are made. The Internet holds much promise as a low-cost distribution channel because it can be used to reach consumers in virtually any geographic location. A large portion of the up-front costs associated with Internet distribution is for adequate technology and employee training.

Degree of Control the Insurer Intends to Exercise over Distribution

An insurer that wishes to exercise a great deal of control over the activities involved in distributing its products typically develops its own distribution systems. An insurer that is willing to pay for company-owned systems can control these systems fully, including being able to transfer branch office staff from one field office to another. Insurance companies can also fully control their direct response distribution systems.

Instead of owning its own system, an insurer can form contractual agreements with brokers and PPGAs. An insurance company has no authority to transfer staff from one brokerage office or PPGA office to another. Also, because brokers and PPGAs may be under contract to several different insurance companies, they may recommend that customers purchase the products of more than one insurer. As a result, a particular insurer has no assurances that a broker will recommend its products over the products of other companies.

Characteristics of the Buyers in Target Markets

The distribution system by which a product is sold should meet the distribution needs of consumers in the insurer's target markets. For example, some consumers may want to buy all of their insurance products from one sales agent and one company. Such a consumer may feel comfortable dealing with a multiple-line agent or a captive agent of one insurer who can sell many or all of the company's products. Other consumers may prefer to contact several agents from several companies and comparison-shop for the best deal. A consumer in this group may also prefer to buy products from an insurance broker or a PPGA. An insurer that has targeted technologically skilled people may choose to market some of its products through its Internet site. An insurance company that has targeted people who have a particular credit card may choose to distribute some of its life insurance products through the bank that issues that credit card. And an insurer that wishes to sell coverage to lower-income consumers may choose a home service distribution system or direct mail that offers limited amounts of term life insurance.

Characteristics of the Products the Company Sells

Some products are more effectively and efficiently sold through one distribution system than another. A complex product, such as whole life insurance, typically requires a personal selling distribution system rather than a direct response system. Insurance companies that sell universal life products generally use ordinary agents, agent-brokers, PPGAs, or multiple-line agents. Simpler products, such as term insurance, can be distributed either through direct response systems or personal selling systems. U.S. insurers that want to sell variable life insurance must distribute the product through licensed broker-dealers. Insurers who sell group life insurance typically use group representatives in a salaried sales system.

The Insurer's Business Environment

Changing conditions in the insurer's business environment can make one distribution method relatively more appealing than others to certain insurers. As these environmental factors change, the choices regarding how best to distribute products may also change. For example, the escalating use of the Internet created a new distribution opportunity for insurance companies. As laws and regulations change regarding Internet distribution of insurance products, insurance companies will change the way they use the Internet as a distribution channel.

Characteristics of the Insurer

Many company characteristics can affect an insurer's choice of distribution method. These factors include the company's resources, its business goals and objectives, its experience with various distribution channels, and its current relationships with various channel participants. For example, a relatively new company with fewer financial resources than an older, more established insurer may not be able to afford a company-owned distribution system and may instead have to contract with brokers or PPGAs. An insurance company with a large, established career agency force may use the field force to sell all the products that the company develops, or the company may decide to use multiple distribution channels. For example, the company's career agents would sell its current portfolio of products and PPGAs would sell a specific new product the company is introducing. And some insurers use multiple distribution channels to sell the same products in order to expand their market reach to potential customers.

Key Terms

personal selling distribution system
direct response distribution system
agency relationship
agent
principal
agency contract
prospect
cold calling
needs analysis
premium receipt
agency-building distribution system
ordinary agency distribution system (career agency system, agency system)
field force
commission
career agent
captive agent (exclusive agent)
independent contractor
agent-broker
marketing territory

field office
branch office system
branch office
general manager (branch manager)
overriding commission (override)
agency office
general agent (GA)
multiple-line agency (MLA) system
cross-selling
persistency
home service distribution system
home service agent (debit agent)
salaried sales distribution system
group representative
location-selling distribution system
worksite marketing
nonagency-building distribution system (third-party distribution system)
brokerage distribution system
licensed broker (pure broker)

Key Terms, continued

brokerage company
personal-producing general agent
   (PPGA) system
personal-producing general agent
   (PPGA)
subagent

financial planner
producer group
broker-dealer
registered representative
guaranteed-issue basis

Endnotes

1. As we describe later, a licensed broker enters into a contract with an insurer, but this contract typically is not an agency contract.

2. One exception is home service agents, who are granted the authority to accept renewal premiums for in-force policies.

3. LIMRA, *The Opportunity to Buy in the U.S. Marketplace: The Changing Face of Distribution* (Windsor, CT: LIMRA International, Inc., 1998), 8.

4. Terence O'Donnell, *History of Life Insurance in Its Formative Years* (Chicago: American Conservation Company, 1936), 682–683.

5. Many banks in the United States are permitted to form agreements with insurance companies to distribute the insurers' products. In Canada, the sales of most insurance products (with the exception of credit and travel insurance) through retail bank branches are currently not permitted.

6. The most common form of whole life insurance sold through direct response is graded-benefit whole life. Under this type of policy, the death benefit payable in the first few policy years is usually limited to a return of premiums paid or a percentage of the policy's face value. Following this initial period, the full face amount is payable upon the insured's death.

Supporting the Insurer's Distribution Systems

The previous chapter described the methods that life insurance companies use to distribute their products to customers. As you recall, these distribution systems can generally be divided into personal selling systems, in which salespeople sell products through presentations to prospective purchasers, and direct response systems, in which consumers purchase products directly from the insurer. Recall further that personal selling systems can also be divided into agency-building systems, nonagency-building systems, and broker-dealers.

In this chapter, you will learn how an insurance company's home office supports these distribution systems. Typically, the marketing area of an insurance company is responsible for establishing and maintaining distribution systems for the company's products. Thus, home office support of product distribution activities generally flows through the insurer's marketing department. Although insurers can organize their home office support of product distribution in many ways, Figure 10-1 shows one typical organizational structure. In this figure, you can see that the person who has direct authority over all product distribution is sometimes called the *sales manager*.

We begin this chapter by examining the home office support services that are specific to agency-building distribution systems. Then we describe the way the home office supports nonagency-building systems, broker-dealers, and direct response distribution systems. As you will see, many aspects of support are similar for agency-building systems, nonagency-building systems, and broker-dealers.

Home Office Support of Agency-Building Distribution Systems

Life insurance companies provide several supervisory and support functions for their agency-building distribution systems, which include the ordinary agency system, the multiple-line agency system, the home service system, the salaried sales system, the location selling system, and worksite marketing. Some insurers have a single agency unit that handles all supervisory and support activities and reports to the company's sales manager. In other insurers, supervisory and support functions are divided between an agency operations unit and an agency services unit.

The agency operations unit assumes the supervisory functions and is headed by the *manager of agency operations*, also known as the

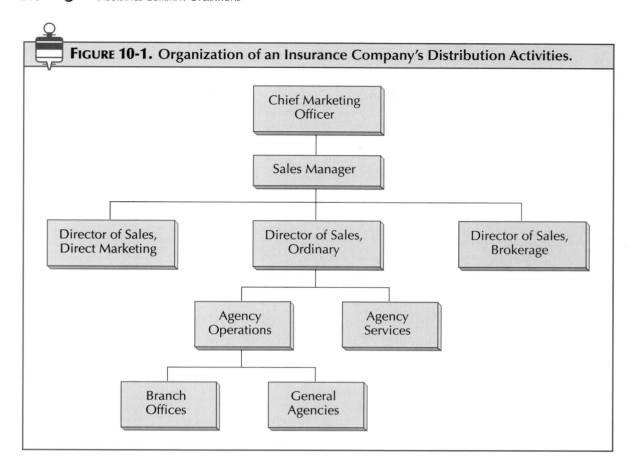

FIGURE 10-1. Organization of an Insurance Company's Distribution Activities.

superintendent (or director) of agencies. This person is the primary link between the insurer's home office and its agency offices. The manager of agency operations is typically a vice president-level executive who has the following responsibilities:

- Supervising agency operations through the insurer's regional managers and agency managers

- Establishing strategic goals and objectives for agency offices that are consistent with the home office's goals and objectives

- Establishing policies and procedures for the operation of field offices and the sale of life insurance products to ensure (1) that company objectives are met and (2) that the sales force complies with all applicable regulatory requirements

- Developing goals for sales production and persistency

- Evaluating the performance and profitability of the agency offices

Whereas the agency operations unit has management authority over the company's field offices, other areas of the company provide support services for the agencies. These services include agent recruiting, training, contracts and licenses, compensation and benefits, technical support, and sales promotion. In some insurance companies, one department, known as the *agency services unit* or *agency administration unit*, handles many of these support functions. Other insurers divide these services among several different departments, including agency services, marketing, accounting, finance, and compliance.

In order to guide the operations of the insurer's agency-building distribution systems, the agency operations unit develops an agency distribution plan based on the insurance company's broad marketing plan. The agency distribution plan describes the company's goals and objectives for product distribution and serves as a guide for each agency office's own operating plan. The agency distribution plan ensures that the company's distribution goals are communicated to the agencies and that each agency's plans and objectives are consistent with the plans and objectives of the entire company. Included in the agency distribution plan are forecasts of sales revenues and expenses, and a forecast of the number of agents needed to produce the desired level of sales.

We will divide the remainder of our discussion of home office involvement in agency-building distribution into four broad categories: recruiting and licensing, compensation and performance evaluation, sales support, and technology support.

Recruiting and Licensing

An insurer's home office assists in recruiting new agents, writing agent contracts, and training and licensing agents.

Agent Recruitment

The success of an insurance company's product distribution activities depends on the achievement of its salespeople, so insurers and agency managers are continually on the lookout for promising new agents. Agent recruitment carries a significant financial risk to the insurer. One study estimated that the home office investment in one new agent is about $40,000 in the first three years of the agent's career.[1] This investment includes the initial financing and subsidy of the new agent, a share of the costs borne by the recruit's agency manager, and the costs of training and licensing the new agent. If a new agent leaves the company within the first few years of employment, the insurer receives little or no return on its investment in the agent. In addition, selecting unqualified or unethical agents can damage an insurer's relations with its customers, damage its image in the marketplace, adversely affect

company morale, and hamper the achievement of an agency's sales and profit objectives.

Agent recruitment is primarily the responsibility of agency managers. However, because finding new agents is such an important and expensive aspect of the agency distribution system, the home office typically helps agency managers with recruiting by establishing formal guidelines for recruitment. The home office also helps agency managers locate prospective agents and screen and evaluate agent recruits. The home office can also develop a profile or model of an ideal agent recruit. Some desired characteristics of an agent recruit may include ambition, self-motivation, enthusiasm, strong communication ability, and congeniality.

Screening is a process by which an agency manager attempts to identify candidates qualified to be successful insurance agents. Screening can include administering tests to and conducting personal interviews with prospective candidates. Figure 10-2 lists three general questions that an agency manager should be able to answer after screening a particular candidate. Insurance companies use a variety of tests to help them determine whether a job candidate has the necessary traits to be a successful insurance agent. A screening test that is widely administered in the United States and Canada is the *Career Profile System* developed by LIMRA International. This test gathers information about a candidate's work history and personal background and uses that information to predict the candidate's likely success as an insurance agent or financial services consultant. The Career Profile System is not designed to indicate whether a candidate should be hired, but instead to indicate whether a candidate should not be hired.

Candidates that successfully complete the screening phase are then eligible for **pre-contract training**, a trial program that permits an agent candidate to prepare to become an agent while continuing to work at his or her current job. During pre-contract training, an agent candidate learns (1) the principles of life insurance, (2) the products

FIGURE 10-2. Questions to Answer After Screening an Agent Candidate.

1. Does this person have a reasonable chance of succeeding as an insurance salesperson?

2. Can this individual master the concepts and procedures needed to pass required insurance examinations and licensing requirements?

3. Will he or she approach dealings with customers and company management with the required level of business integrity?

Source: Excerpted and adapted from Steven H. Brown and Richard W. Schmidt, "The Job of Selling—Some Things Don't Change," *LIMRA's MarketFacts* (November/December 1996): 46. Used with permission.

and practices of the hiring agency and insurance company, and (3) insurance sales techniques. Typically, the home office develops pre-contract training programs for agency managers to use. Candidates who perform well during pre-contract training are offered agency contracts by the insurance company.

Agency Contracts

In order to begin selling insurance on behalf of an insurance company, an agent—a new agent or an experienced agent—must sign an agency contract with the insurer or an agent's contract with a general agent in some general agency systems. If the agent's contract is with an insurance company, the home office's marketing department collaborates with the legal department to develop the contract. If the agent's contract is with a general agent, the general agent usually develops the agent's contract, although the contract may contain the insurer's standard contract language.

The contract between an agent and an insurance company describes all aspects of the agreement between the agent and the insurer. The exact terms of the agency contract vary widely depending on the company and the type of personal selling distribution system being used. Typically, however, an agency contract contains the following provisions:

- A statement of the existence of the contract

- The statement that the agent is or is not an employee of the company, whichever is the case

- A description of the agent's authority to represent the company, including the authority to solicit and submit applications, collect initial premiums, and issue premium receipts

- A description of the limitations placed on the agent's authority, such as prohibiting the agent from changing premium rates, altering contracts, incurring debts on the company's behalf, or otherwise acting outside the scope of the authority the insurer has given the agent

- A listing of the agent's performance requirements, particularly with respect to adherence to company rules and the prompt remittance of initial premium payments

- Minimum production requirements and persistency rate required for the agent to earn compensation and remain associated with the company

- Termination provisions, stating (1) justifiable causes for termination of the agency contract and (2) the length of time required for notice of termination by either the agent or the company

- The agent's compensation schedule, stating the rate of commissions, the amounts of service fees, and any bonuses that the agent will earn

- A statement of the insurer's right to revise the commission schedule or to reduce commission rates on policies that replace existing insurance coverage

- Vesting provisions, if any, stating the circumstances under which the agent is entitled to receive renewal commissions after the agent's contract has been terminated

- Expense provisions covering the types of expenses, if any, that an agent may incur and be reimbursed for by the company

- A list of the circumstances under which the agent is permitted to submit insurance applications to another insurance company

The contract between a soliciting agent and an insurance company typically does not grant the agent the authority to enter into an insurance contract on behalf of the insurer. Instead, only certain specified people in the company's home office have authority to bind the company to any insurance contract.[3]

Agent Licenses

All insurance agents in the United States and Canada must be licensed by each state or province in which they sell life insurance. As you learned in Chapter 2, the Financial Services Modernization Act of 1999 calls for the establishment of uniform agent licensing laws from state to state. In most jurisdictions, a person may qualify for an agent's license only after being appointed by an insurer to solicit insurance on its behalf. An *appointment* is a written statement made by an officer of the insurer indicating that the insurer designates a specific person as an insurance agent for the line(s) of insurance the agent is authorized to write for the insurer. In order to obtain an agent's license, an agent/applicant must submit to the state insurance department an application for a license, a copy of the agent's appointment with the insurer, and a licensing fee. The agent/applicant must also pass a written examination in each line of insurance the agent plans to sell.

Licensing specialists in the insurer's home office follow a system to oversee agent licensing. These specialists ensure that the com-

pany's agents (1) have been properly appointed by the company to sell insurance on its behalf, (2) are qualified to sell insurance, (3) are appropriately licensed to sell insurance, and (4) are conducting business only in jurisdictions in which they are licensed to do so. Licensing specialists maintain databases to ensure that agent licenses are renewed on a timely basis and that correct licensing forms are filed and licensing fees are paid in each jurisdiction. Some jurisdictions require licensed agents to continue their formal education in order to renew their licenses, and licensing specialists keep agents informed about their continuing education status in each jurisdiction.

Whenever an insurance company terminates an agent's appointment, the home office is responsible for notifying the state or provincial insurance regulator. Typically, the insurer files with the insurance commissioner a **termination report** that specifies the date of and reason for the termination. For more on agent licensing and termination, see Insight 10-1.

Agent Training

Agencies need to train newly appointed agents, and the home office usually provides some of the necessary training programs to ensure that all agents receive a standard level of training. Agent training is conducted through self-study and through formal classes at the home office, at regional offices, or in the field or branch office. Within each

---

 Insight 10-1.   Tracking Agent Licenses.

Through its Insurance Regulatory Information Network (IRIN), the National Association of Insurance Commissioners (NAIC) has taken two steps to help insurance companies and state insurance regulators track agent licenses. IRIN is an NAIC affiliate that was established (1) to develop and operate a national repository for producer license information and (2) to establish a network to facilitate the electronic exchange of producer information.

IRIN's Producer Database (PDB) is an Internet-accessible database of information relating to insurance agents and brokers. Information available for each producer includes demographic information, a license summary, continuing education status, and any regulatory actions taken against the producer. The PDB's development is based, in part, on the belief that the widespread availability of such information will make it more difficult for a producer with significant disciplinary history to continue illegal or unethical prac-

tices. As of 1999, the PDB contained information on more than 2 million producers.

IRIN's Producer Information Network (PIN) is an electronic communication network that links state insurance regulators with insurance companies to facilitate the electronic exchange of producer information, including license applications, appointments, and terminations. All data flowing over PIN conforms to specific data standards. •

Sources: *Insurance Regulatory Information Network: Insurance Industry Frequently Asked Questions,* http://www.irin.org/products_services/irin_faqs.htm (19 October 1999). Meg Green, "NAIC Effort to Standardize Agent Licensing Advances," *BestWeek,* Life/Health ed. (28 September 1998): 8.

**"I have a confession. I skipped Sales Training
the day they taught us how to make cold calls."**

© 1998 Randy Glasbergen. Used with permission.

field office, the agency manager or an agency supervisor typically supplements these training programs with on-the-job training.

A comprehensive training program for new agents is an extension of the pre-contract training and generally consists of the following parts:

- **Life insurance basics**—Principles of life insurance, types of insurance products, industry terminology, and laws and regulations affecting insurance sales

- **Product knowledge**—Awareness of and knowledge of all the products offered by the insurance company

- **Sales techniques**—Target marketing, locating prospective customers, needs analysis, making sales presentations, closing sales, and communicating effectively with customers

- **Company procedures**—Filling out company forms, maintaining required records, using product brochures and computer sales illustrations, operating computer equipment, and performing field underwriting

- **Company goals, plans, and policies**—Understanding the company, including its industry ratings, investment strategies, and position in the marketplace

- **A code of ethics and compliance issues**—The ethics of selling and an awareness of all market conduct laws that apply to the sale of insurance products

In addition to training new agents, insurance companies also provide regular training for their experienced agents. Certain types of training for experienced agents include training for (1) new products that the company develops, (2) new market conduct regulations, (3) new company policies and procedures, and (4) new computer equipment, systems, and software.

Compensation and Performance Evaluation

An insurer's home office sets the compensation and benefit levels for agents and agency managers and administers their compensation and benefits. In a few jurisdictions, these compensation and benefit levels are limited by insurance laws. The home office provides its agents and agency offices with regular reports of compensation earned and paid. More and more insurers are enabling field personnel to access up-to-date compensation data via a computerized system. We discuss these and other technologies in detail later in this chapter.

Agent Compensation

Insurance companies typically compensate their agents according to a commission system that is designed to motivate agents to produce business that is likely to remain in force for many years. Traditionally, insurance companies have operated under a *heaped commission system*, which is an approach that features relatively high first-year commissions and lower renewal commissions. A *first-year commission* is a commission paid to an agent who sells a policy and is equal to a stated percentage of the amount of the premium the insurer receives during the first policy year. Generally speaking, first-year commission rates fall in the range from 40 to 90 percent. For example, if the premium collected on a policy during the first policy year is $1,000, and the first-year commission rate is 50 percent (or 0.50), the first-year commission for that policy is $500 ($1,000 × 0.50 = $500). *Renewal commissions* are commissions paid to an agent (1) only for policies he sold and (2) for a number of years after the first policy year. Renewal commission rates are generally lower than the first-year commission rate—usually between 2 and 5 percent of premiums received—and they are paid only on policies that remain in force. First-year commissions are designed to give an agent incentive to make new sales. Renewal commissions encourage agents to sell quality business and provide service to policyowners while the policies are in force.

In recent years, some companies have established alternatives to the heaped commission system. These alternative compensation plans place additional emphasis on persistency of business. One such alternative is a *level commission schedule* that provides the same commission rate for the first policy year and renewal policy years, thereby encouraging agents not only to make the initial sale but also to conserve the business. Another alternative to the heaped commission system is a *levelized commission schedule*, in which first-year commissions are higher than renewal commissions, but the gap between first-year and renewal commissions is much smaller than the gap in the traditional heaped commission system. For example, Figure 10-3 compares the maximum first-year and renewal commission rates that insurers operating in the state of New York were permitted to pay before and after a change to New York insurance law in 1998. Regardless of the compensation plan used, insurance companies try to set commission rates that are competitive with those offered by other insurers and, where necessary, within the limits set by law.

In addition to commissions, insurance companies may provide their agents with the following types of compensation:

- Security benefits, such as group life insurance, group health insurance, group disability income insurance, and pension plans

- Bonuses to reward production, persistency, or both. Bonuses can be in the form of cash, trips, or merchandise.

- *Service fees*, which are a small percentage of premiums payable on life insurance policies after renewal commissions have ceased.

FIGURE 10-3. New Commission Rates for Life Insurance.

Policy Year	Maximum Old Rate	Maximum New Rate
1	55.0%	55%
2	6.5	22
3	6.5	20
4	6.5	18
5–10	6.5	no limit
11–15	4.5	no limit
16+	2.0	no limit

Source: Excerpted from Paul D. Laporte, "Compensation Breaks Loose—The Modernization of New York's Section 4228," *LIMRA's MarketFacts* (September/October 1997): 30. Used with permission.

Service fees reward persistency. They differ from renewal commissions in that renewal commissions are generally paid to the agent who sold the policy, whereas services fees are paid to the agent who is currently servicing the policy, even if that agent did not originally sell the policy. Also, renewal commissions are often vested, whereas service fees generally are not vested. A ***vested commission*** is guaranteed payable to an agent even if the agent no longer represents the company when the commission comes due.

- Expense allowances to reimburse agents for certain business expenses they incur

Many insurance companies also provide financing for new agents during their first years in the insurance business when they generally have difficulty earning enough commissions to maintain an adequate standard of living. This financing may be an advance against future commissions, a higher-than-normal commission rate for new sales, or an additional monthly payment to supplement the agents' regular commission. The company may require that a new agent who receives additional financing attend training classes or sell at least a minimum number of policies. Typically, insurers stop providing any additional financing by the end of an agent's third or fourth year of appointment.

Minimum Production Requirements

Insurance companies incur considerable costs to provide office space and benefits for agents. To control the cost of carrying agents who are unproductive, many insurance companies impose minimum production requirements on their agents. Insurers commonly impose two minimum production requirements: one minimum requirement to maintain a full-time agency contract and another minimum requirement to qualify for security benefits. The amount of first-year commissions earned is typically used as the production measure. For example, a 1996 survey showed that, on average, insurers required agents to earn a minimum of $19,738 per year in first-year commissions in order to maintain an agency contract, and they required agents to earn a minimum of $20,383 in first-year commissions to qualify for security benefits.[4]

Evaluating Agency Performance

The manager of agency operations is ultimately responsible for the profitability of the company's agency-building distribution systems. In order for distribution to be profitable, agencies must generate enough revenue to

- Cover the insurer's cost of recruiting, training, and licensing and financing new agents

- Cover the cost of maintaining experienced agents (including licensing and security benefits)

- Cover the distribution system's overhead expenses (including salaries of home office personnel who support agency distribution, salaries of administrative personnel in the agencies, and agency office expenses such as rent, utilities, and office equipment)

To monitor profitability of the agency system, the manager of agency operations regularly evaluates the sales and expense performance of the distribution system as a whole and the performance of each field office. Figure 10-4 lists some typical measures of agency sales performance.

Evaluating the performance of individual agencies is handled by regional managers who report to the manager of agency operations. Each regional manager compares each agency's sales and expense results against projections established at the beginning of the evaluation period. A regional manager may compare an agency's current sales results with its sales results from the previous period and also with the sales results of other agencies operating under similar conditions. The regional manager and the manager of agency operations plan corrective action when an agency's performance falls below expectations.

Sales Support

A life insurer's home office can take several steps to support the selling efforts of its agents. This support includes prospecting support,

FIGURE 10-4. Agency Sales Performance Measures.

- First-year or renewal premium income generated
- Total commissions earned
- Total face amount of life insurance coverage sold
- Average annual premium per sale
- Number of policies sold
- Average face amount of coverage sold
- Number of sales per interview with prospective customers
- Persistency rate achieved

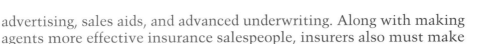

advertising, sales aids, and advanced underwriting. Along with making agents more effective insurance salespeople, insurers also must make sure that their agents comply with market conduct laws.

Prospecting Support

One of the most difficult tasks for agents, particularly new agents, is locating qualified prospects for insurance. New agents typically have few personal leads and must resort to cold calling to find prospects. The home office assists in the prospect search by giving referrals to their agents. For example, many insurance companies use their Internet sites to refer prospects to specific agents. Prospects who visit the insurer's Internet site can view a list of agents, usually organized by geographic locations. The address and telephone number of each agent is provided. In some cases, the prospect can contact the agent online. For example, the insurer's site allows the prospect to send an electronic mail message directly to the agent, or the prospect can access the agent's own Internet site via a link from the insurer's Internet site.

Many insurers also provide agents with tools to help them organize and manage their prospecting activities. Insight 10-2 discusses one insurance company's system to help its agents organize their prospecting efforts.

Advertising and Sales Aids

Advertising can be an effective tool to promote the sale of life insurance products. Insurance companies place advertisements in a variety of media, such as newspapers, television, magazines, radio, and the Internet. Much of this advertising is ***institutional advertising*** that promotes an idea, a philosophy, or a company, rather than a specific product or service. By contrast, ***product advertising*** is advertising used to promote a specific good or service. Institutional advertisements are designed to build an awareness of the insurance company so that when an agent calls on a prospect, that prospect is more receptive to the agent. Insurers also place advertisements that promote the quality of their sales agents. The insurer's marketing management generally establishes the company's advertising budgets and selects the media, the timing of the advertising, and the content and design of the advertisements, sometimes with the assistance of an advertising agency.

Explaining how insurance products can work to meet a prospect's needs can be difficult for an agent. To help agents with this task, insurance companies have developed several types of sales promotion materials designed to be used during or after a sales presentation. Such sales aids include sales literature that explains various products or policy benefits, visual sales kits that help agents "walk a prospect through the sale," and policy illustrations—typically computer

Insight 10-2. Working in Concert.

Mutual of Omaha and its career agents are making beautiful music together. The goal? Not only to improve the bottom line in the short term but to provide a permanent fix: to fundamentally change our way of doing business. Our initial charge was to design and implement a co-ordinated, measurable prospecting process, consistent from agency to agency. The changing business climate made it clear that prospecting must be a shared responsibility of money, resources, and effort.

Our challenge was to quickly move agents to a higher degree of efficiency, in which they learn to prospect using more personal sources such as existing clients, centers of influence, and referrals. These sources are more efficient because fewer contacts are required to secure appointments and sales. We've made progress in this area by providing our agents with the right instruments—the Mutual Card System, an Initial Prospecting Plan, the Client Action Report (CAR), and Symphony.

• **Mutual Card System.** Recognizing that new agents' success largely depends on their ability to locate and track many prospects, we developed an effective tracking tool. The Mutual Card System helps agents manually organize, record, and manage daily prospecting activities. Early on, they gain a sense of control and organization over the prospecting process.

• **Initial Prospecting Plan (IPP).** The plan, developed by each agent, serves as a road map, pointing new agents in the right direction and keeping them on course toward their ultimate goal: finding enough prospects to see. The plan provides agents with a clear sense of what markets they will target and how they will locate enough prospects to consistently generate at least 15 appointments per week.

• **Client Action Report (CAR).** Each month, the home office generates about 61,000 Client Action Reports, an average of 26 per agent. Each CAR contains information about upcoming policy events that signal an opportunity or a need for the agent to contact the client. This might include information on dependents in need of individual coverage or information on business insurance opportunities. Roughly 10 percent of CARs involve multiple events, giving agents multiple reasons for customer contact, all in a single report. I consider the CAR to be the single best tool in the prospecting process. In 1996 it helped us triple our closure rate and write approximately $40 million in new premiums. It represents a much improved way of communicating policy and life events.

• **Symphony.** This program helps agents maintain regular contact with prospects and clients. It combines direct mail with telephone follow-up to help agents get appointments and build client relationships. Symphony is managed at the home office, using a third-party mailing firm. It automates our direct-mail process, relieving agents of the time-consuming tasks of developing lists, writing letters, ordering materials, negotiating with printers, and dealing with postal regulations. Last year, this program generated more than $5 million in annualized new-business premiums.

For new agents, the processes bring order into what otherwise could be a somewhat unstructured environment. Communication is constant, expectations are clear, and managerial involvement and support are extensive (especially in the early stages). •

Source: Excerpted from Dwane C. McFerrin, "Working in Concert," *LIMRA's MarketFacts* (May/June 1997): 28–32. Used with permission.

generated—giving year-to-year descriptions of a policy's premiums, cash values, and other features.

Life insurance companies must take great care to ensure that all of their advertisements and policy illustrations comply with applicable unfair trade practices laws, life insurance illustration laws, and other regulatory requirements governing the use of advertisements and sales materials. These laws apply not only to advertisements and sales materials produced by the home office, but also to any sales materials used by the company's producers in presentations to customers. Insurers typically prohibit agents from using any sales materials that

have not been approved for use by the home office. Some insurers prohibit agents from using any sales materials that were not developed by the home office.

Advanced Underwriting Department

Insurance agents often are involved in helping their clients develop estate plans and financial plans. **Estate planning** is a type of planning to help a client conserve, as much as possible, the personal assets that the person wants to pass on to his heirs at his death. An agent working with a complex estate plan must be familiar with the laws governing the taxation and distribution of the estate and must be able to work well with the client's other legal and financial advisors. In contrast to estate planning, **financial planning** is a process in which a client's lifetime financial goals are reviewed and a plan is developed to help the client attain those goals. These financial goals generally involve building and protecting assets of the client. Recommendations are usually made regarding retirement planning, protecting the client's lifestyle with products that protect her income in case of disability or death, educational funding for children, and providing for long-term care, if necessary.

To assist agents with estate planning and financial planning, some insurers establish an **advanced underwriting department**. The advanced underwriting department, which typically is staffed with lawyers and financial planning specialists,

- Prepares proposals based on the information the agent has collected

- Provides staff to accompany the agent, if requested, to make sales presentations

- Provides computer support services

- Conducts seminars and counsels agents regarding tax laws and methods of using insurance products in estate planning and financial planning

Monitoring Agents' Market Conduct

In order to protect consumers, insurance regulators have placed increased emphasis on regulating the market conduct of the people who sell insurance. For example, agents must truthfully represent the features of the products they sell, and they must not engage in certain prohibited sales practices, such as churning, twisting, and rebating, which are described in Figure 10-5. Agents also must conduct their businesses in an honest and ethical manner.

> ### FIGURE 10-5. Prohibited Sales Practices.
>
> Sales practices that are prohibited in most jurisdictions include the following:
>
> - *Churning:* A practice in which a producer induces a customer to replace one insurance policy after another so that the producer can earn a series of first-year commissions on the replacements.
>
> - *Twisting:* A producer's act of misrepresenting the features of a policy in order to induce the client to replace the policy.
>
> - *Rebating:* A practice in which a producer offers a prospect an inducement, such as a cash payment, to purchase an insurance policy from that producer.

Insurance companies are required to adequately train all of their agents and producers (regardless of the producers' relationship to the insurer) in market conduct laws and acceptable sales practices. Insurers must regularly monitor the sales activities of their producers in order to evaluate their compliance with market conduct requirements. Also, whenever regulatory requirements change, the insurance company must communicate these changes accurately and promptly to the agency force. Figure 10-6 lists other actions an insurer can take to ensure that agents comply with market conduct laws.

The monitoring system that an insurer establishes to supervise its agents' activities should contain a method of identifying and reporting agents who are found to be unsuitable to sell life insurance. The system should also explain the penalties that the insurer will impose on producers who do not comply with the terms of the compliance program. Some producer infractions are unintentional and indicate a need for additional training. However, if a serious infraction occurs, the insurer is responsible for taking appropriate disciplinary action, which generally ranges from a written warning to temporary suspension from the company's field force or termination of the agent's appointment with the insurer.

Technology Support

Recent advances in technology have greatly changed how insurance companies can support their agency-building distribution efforts. The range of technologies available are numerous and varied—powerful computers, networks, software, storage media, and many others. The purposes of implementing new technology into an agency-building distribution system are to make agencies and producers more productive, speed the flow of information between the home office and the field, and reduce expenses.

FIGURE 10-6. Insurance Company Actions to Enforce Market Conduct Compliance.

- Develop and communicate clear, specific compliance standards, ethical guidelines, or codes of ethics

- Appoint a compliance officer and establish a compliance team

- Improve field selection to avoid hiring producers who have questionable backgrounds

- Enhance compliance training

- Conduct field audits, such as (1) reviewing an agent's case files to ensure that all the proper documentation is present and (2) going on joint calls with the agent to see that the sales approach is compliant

- Examine complaint files to identify any patterns that might suggest market conduct problems

- Increase database monitoring of policy replacement activity

- Require that the prospect sign the policy illustration and include the signed illustration with the application in order to have the application underwritten

Source: Excerpted and adapted from Albert J. Sheridan and D. Layne Rich, "Are Your Compliance Efforts Working?" *LIMRA's MarketFacts* (May/June 1995): 26. Used with permission.

Equipment and Software

New equipment and software that many insurance companies use to support agency distribution include computers (desktop and portable), CD-ROMs, diskettes, various software programs, pagers, and cellular telephones. Innovations in these technologies have made agents and agency offices more productive and have allowed agents to spend less time on paperwork and more time on sales and policyowner service. Some companies provide their agents with portable computers equipped with integrated software that supports virtually every sales activity: managing client contacts, tracking finances, word processing, sales presentations, and training. A comprehensive sales software package ensures that agents gather all necessary information from clients and make informed presentations and recommendations about products. Some companies also provide their agents with portable printers, so that the agents can print policy applications or sales illustrations for a client during a sales call. Insurers may also distribute product-related updates, agent training manuals, compliance manuals, and company procedures manuals on CD-ROM or software. (Focus on Technology 10-1 illustrates one insurer's creative use of new equipment to assist its field force.)

Many insurers also provide each agency with an agency management system. Such a computer-based system typically includes word processing software, prospect contact software, client contact software,

Focus on Technology 10-1.

High-Tech with a Twist: Barcoding Technology Satisfies Home Service Need for Mobile Computing.

Almost every insurance company is investigating different ways to improve the flow of information between agents and the home office. It's a matter of competitive advantage. The Continental Life Insurance Company, a small home service company, wanted to give its agents a mobile computing solution. "We wanted them to be able to process premiums more accurately than ever before," says Brian Lenherd, vice president of Wistar Management Corporation, the organization that manages Continental Life.

Their solution? Barcodes.

"With our system, the agent only has to swipe a (handheld) scanner over a barcode in the policy-owner's premium book and press 'enter,'" Lenherd says. "We built it ourselves, using our experience in home service, to provide all the functionality a home service agent needs to accurately maintain a book of business."

When an agent has an application approved, the agent is given the policy and a new premium receipt book with a barcode in it. The barcode contains all the client information. Policyowners keep their premium receipt books at home, and the agent swipes the barcode of each policyowner every time premiums are collected.

To transmit data to the home office, agents use an acoustic coupler—a speaker on the back of the unit that allows the agent to transmit from any phone. Even from a pay telephone, an agent can call the home office, put the unit up to the speaker, push "send," and transmit data.

"When we built the system, we were looking at improving accuracy of premium collection," Lenherd says. "But the collateral gains we've made in increasing productivity, reducing shortages, and increasing agent retention would have made the system worthwhile on its own." •

Source: Adapted from Debra Bailey Helwig, "High-Tech with a Twist: Barcoding Technology Satisfies Home Service Need for Mobile Computing," *Resource* (March 1998): 32–34. Used with permission.

a training management system, a recruiting system, a commission tracking system, and an expense tracking system.

Computer Networks

Computer networks provide a means for electronic communications between the home office and the field. A computer network enables an insurer to communicate quickly and inexpensively with agents and give agents and agency managers convenient and timely access to information and databases that are maintained by the home office.

Computer network communications in the insurance industry take the form of private networks, Internet-based networks, or some combination of the two. In a private network setup, an agent uses a computer modem to make a direct connection from his computer into the insurer's network. The agent can send and receive information through the private network.

Internets, intranets, and extranets eliminate the need for insurers to distribute information (forms, product updates, rate changes, and other data) to producers via paper, diskette, or CD-ROM. Instead, the insurer makes the information available through the intranet or extranet, and agents can view or access the information at their convenience. Some companies support their network sites with telephone

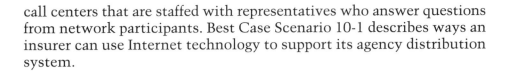

call centers that are staffed with representatives who answer questions from network participants. Best Case Scenario 10-1 describes ways an insurer can use Internet technology to support its agency distribution system.

Home Office Support of Nonagency-Building Distribution Systems

Nonagency-building distribution systems include brokerage systems, personal-producing general agent (PPGA) systems, bank-sold insurance systems, financial planners, and producer groups. (Unless otherwise specified, for simplicity we will use the term *independent producers* to refer to any type of nonagency-building distribution system.) Insurance companies typically provide less support for their independent producers than they do for their agency-building distribution systems. For example, insurance companies do not provide independent producers with training in principles of insurance or basic sales

Best Case Scenario 10-1. Using Internet Technology to Communicate with Agents.

Best Friend Life Insurance Company uses its intranet to communicate with and exchange information with its agents. This capability helps agents to perform their jobs more efficiently and to provide better service to their customers.

For example, Best Friend agent Louise Chen submitted the insurance applications for her clients Tom and Maria Carpenter. A few weeks later, Louise received a call from Tom wondering why they had not yet received the policies. Louise was able to use Best Friend's intranet to check on the status of her clients' applications and see any outstanding requirements.

Through her personal computer, Louise accessed Best Friend's Internet site, then supplied the appro-

priate passwords to gain entrance into Best Friend's intranet, which is accessible only by Best Friend's employees and captive agents. Once on the intranet, she was able to track the status of all of the policy applications she had submitted, including the Carpenters' applications. Louise discovered that the underwriting decisions on their applications were pending because the bank that owns the Carpenters' mortgage loan had not yet given Best Friend a requested document showing the balance of the loan. Insurance companies need personal financial information such as this to help establish an applicant's need for insurance.

Once Louise uncovered the cause for the underwriting delay, she in-

structed the Carpenters to contact their bank, ask for the missing financial statement, and forward it to the insurance company. They did so, and within a few days, underwriting decisions were made on the two policies.

In addition to viewing the status of policy applications, Louise can use the Best Friend intranet to view her clients' in-force policies and her own commission earnings statements; access product brochures and forms necessary for policy submission, policy changes, and policy service-related functions; obtain up-to-date policy illustrations for all of the company's products; and order office supplies from the home office. •

techniques. An insurer does train its independent producers in (1) the features and operation of the specific products they will be selling for the company, (2) regulatory requirements governing insurance sales practices, and (3) the company's compliance procedures.

Although independent producers receive fewer services from the home office than do career agents and other agency-building systems, an insurer must work hard to establish and maintain close relationships with its independent producers. The quality of service the independent producers receive should at least equal the quality of the services that the company's agency-building systems receive. In many respects, an insurer's independent producers—and not just the purchasers of insurance—are the insurer's true customers. Insurers compete with each other to entice independent producers to offer their products. Because independent producers can place business with more than one insurance company, they are likely to place business most often with the companies that communicate efficiently, provide them with the highest quality of service, and have competitive compensation.

The following aspects of home office support for independent producers are similar to home office support for agency-building distribution systems:

- **Agency contracts.** Insurance companies enter into agency contracts with most independent producers just as they do with career agents. These contracts specify the producers' duties, responsibilities, limits of authority, performance requirements, and compensation.

- **Agent licenses.** The home office licensing specialists who maintain records of career agents' licenses also ensure that the company's independent producers are appropriately licensed in each applicable jurisdiction.

- **Compensation.** Agent-brokers typically receive first-year and renewal commissions, and they may qualify for service fees, expense reimbursement allowances, and incentive bonuses. Compensation for PPGAs typically resembles compensation for general agents—first-year and renewal commissions and overriding commissions. PPGAs also may be reimbursed for some of their overhead expenses.

- **Sales support and advertising.** The home office generally does not provide independent producers with prospecting plans, but some companies' Internet sites enable consumers to locate independent producers who sell the companies' products. Insurers also use institutional advertising to promote the independent producers with whom they do business.

- **Compliance monitoring.** Because an insurer has fewer contacts with its independent producers than with its own agents, monitoring the independent producers' market conduct compliance can be a challenge. An insurer typically performs an extensive background check on independent producers before offering them appointments with the company. Independent producers must also be informed of and trained in the company's overall producer monitoring program.

- **Technology.** Many insurers use diskettes, CD-ROMs, and Internet technology to supply independent producers with sales brochures, policy illustrations, policy forms, other sales materials, and company data. Insurers that maintain both an intranet and an extranet typically grant independent producers access to the extranet.

One type of nonagency-building distribution system—banks—deserves additional mention. As you learned in Chapter 2, banks in the United States and Canada are able to market insurance in accordance with applicable regulatory requirements. Banks have devised several strategies to distribute insurance products manufactured by insurance companies. Some banks follow only one strategy, and some use a mix of strategies. The amount and type of support that an insurance company provides for its bank distribution channel can vary considerably depending on the strategy or strategies chosen by the bank. The following are typical marketing strategies banks use to market insurance:

- A ***third-party marketer*** is an independent general agency that sells insurance products for one or more banks. Typically, the bank provides the TPM with office space and access to the bank's customers. In such a case, the insurance company's relationship is with the TPM, rather than with the bank. The home office provides the same support functions—contracting, compensation, licensing, compliance monitoring, product training, sales literature, and technological support—for a TPM as it would for other independent producers. TPMs may be under contract to more than one insurance carrier, so insurers must provide a high quality of service in order to attract the TPM's business.

- ***Platform employees*** are a bank's own employees who are trained and licensed to sell insurance products of an insurance company. Platform employees include the bank's customer service representatives, branch managers, and assistant branch managers. A bank that uses platform employees generally enters into a distribution agreement with an insurer to distribute the insurer's

products to the bank's customers. The types of support that the insurer's home office provides to the bank include contracting with the platform employees, product training, compliance monitoring, technological support, and licensing. In a platform employee arrangement, the insurer compensates the bank—not the soliciting platform employees—by paying commissions on product sales and service fees for persistency. The bank then compensates the platform employees for their insurance sales.

- A bank may buy an existing insurance agency or establish its own agency by hiring and training sales agents. Banks' agencies operate like independent insurance agencies, but they are located in the bank or in an office near the bank. The insurance company's home office contracts with these agencies as they would with other independent agencies.

- A bank may enter into a distribution agreement with an insurer under which the bank provides the insurer with qualified leads and promotes the insurer's products to the bank's customers. In this situation, bank employees are not licensed to sell insurance. Instead, interested customers are directed to contact the insurance company's home office. The insurance company provides the bank with marketing materials only, and the bank receives a fee for the leads that result in sales of insurance. All sales are completed by the insurer's own licensed employees.

Home Office Support of Broker-Dealers

Because variable life insurance products are considered to be securities in the United States, a life insurance company that sells variable life insurance must register as a broker-dealer or distribute these products through broker-dealer firms. The sale of variable life insurance through broker-dealers presents special challenges for a life insurer's home office. For example, the insurer must ensure that the salespeople who market variable products on behalf of a broker-dealer are appropriately licensed and adequately trained both as insurance salespeople and as registered representatives legally permitted to sell securities. The insurer must make sure registered representatives and broker-dealers conduct business according to statutory requirements and that they comply with all applicable rules of the Securities and Exchange Commission (SEC) and National Association of Securities Dealers (NASD) with respect to the marketing and sale of variable insurance products. Many of the provisions that insurers include in their contracts with broker-dealers are tied to securities regulations. Insurers

typically make on-site visits of broker-dealer offices to review completed forms, review their record-keeping, and outline any pending changes in regulation or procedures.

A security cannot be made available for sale until the security is registered with the SEC. Prospective purchasers of a variable insurance product must be given a *prospectus* of the product, which is a written communication that offers a security for sale. The home office's legal department, or a law firm specializing in sales of securities, drafts the prospectus and files a copy with the SEC for approval. Once a prospectus is approved, the insurer distributes the prospectus and other sales materials to the broker-dealers who will be selling the product.

Home Office Support of Direct Response Distribution

Many life insurance companies distribute products through one or more direct response distribution channels. Most of the activities involved in direct response distribution are carried out by a direct response marketing unit of an insurance company's home office. Typically, the direct response marketing staff decide

- **Which prospects to target through direct response distribution.** Target consumers can range from groups of people, such as the readers of a particular publication, to specific individuals.

- **Which direct response media to use.** Types of media include direct mail, print publications, radio and television, the Internet and other online services, information kiosks, and interactive television broadcasts (also known as "infomercials").

- **What content to include in the direct response media.** The direct response marketing department, with assistance from the legal department, may be responsible for designing the text and format of a direct mail letter, the advertisement to place in a magazine or a newspaper, or the information to include on the insurer's Internet site. Alternatively, the direct response marketing department may outsource this creative work to an advertising company.

- **Which products to make available via direct response distribution.** The company can use its Internet home page, a telemarketing campaign, or information kiosks to promote several different types of life insurance products. The company could also distribute one product through direct mail.

The specific activities required for direct response distribution vary depending on whether the direct response distribution system is intended to solicit and close a sale or whether it is intended to generate sales leads. The most common type of direct response communication that is intended to solicit and close a sale is direct mail. With a direct mail campaign, the consumer bases the buying decision on the information provided in the advertisement or mailed sales literature. The advertisement or mailing must include all the information—such as benefit levels, terms, conditions, and an application for insurance—that a consumer needs to make a purchase decision and to apply for insurance coverage. The insurance company's marketing department designs a fulfillment kit to send to people who submit applications for insurance. A ***fulfillment kit*** is a package of materials designed to address or "fulfill" the respondent's request. A fulfillment kit may include such items as the insurance policy, insurance identification and service materials (such as claim forms and policy change forms), and billing for the first premium. Fulfillment kits must comply with all applicable regulations involving policy forms and sales materials.

If the direct response distribution system is intended simply to generate sales leads for the insurance company, the direct response communication includes all materials to (1) generate interest in a product or service, and (2) provide prospective buyers with a means to request and receive additional information. Common direct response distribution media used to generate sales leads include print media, broadcast media, and the Internet. When a prospect responds to the direct response insurer's advertisement, a customer service representative or salaried sales agent contacts the prospect, or the insurer sends the prospect a fulfillment kit containing product information and an application for coverage.

Key Terms

sales manager
manager of agency operations (superintendent [director] of agencies)
pre-contract training
appointment
termination report
heaped commission system
first-year commissions
renewal commissions
level commission schedule
levelized commission schedule

service fees
vested commission
institutional advertising
product advertising
estate planning
financial planning
advanced underwriting department
third-party marketer
platform employee
prospectus
fulfillment kit

Endnotes

1. Richard K. Berry, "So What Does an Agent Cost?" *Best's Review*, Life/Health ed. (September 1998): 79.

2. "LIMRA's Reluctant Applicant Recruiting Study," *LIMRA International, Inc.*, 1997, http://members.limra.com (17 April 1999).

3. An agent may have the authority to issue a premium receipt that is a temporary insurance agreement. This receipt binds the insurer to the temporary contract.

4. Cheri L. Collins and Kathleen E. Krozel, *Career-Building Agent Contract and Benefit Requirements* (Windsor, CT: LIMRA International, Inc., 1996): 2.

5. Al Sheridan, *Independent Producer Clearinghouse (IPC)* (Windsor, CT: LIMRA International, Inc., 1999): 1–2.

Underwriting Basics

Buying life insurance is not like buying groceries. Except for certain guaranteed-issue products, a customer does not simply select an insurance policy from a shelf, pay the ticketed price, and take the policy home. Each potential insurance customer is unique, and each proposed insured represents certain risks to a life insurance company. To be financially healthy and able to pay contractual benefits, every insurer must have a way of measuring the level of risk each proposed insured presents so it can charge a premium rate that is adequate to pay policy benefits and that reflects the level of risk the insurer assumes in providing the coverage.

Underwriting, also called *risk selection* or *selection of risks*, is the insurance function that is responsible for assessing and classifying the degree of risk a proposed insured or group represents and making a decision concerning coverage of that risk. An insurer's employee who evaluates risks, accepts or declines applications, and determines the appropriate premium amount to charge acceptable risks is known as an *underwriter*. Generally, an insured who presents a higher degree of risk pays a higher premium for the insurance coverage. The decision an underwriter makes regarding the classification of a risk and the premium amount to charge for insurance coverage is commonly referred to as the *underwriting decision*. Underwriting decisions greatly affect the success or failure of an insurance company.

This chapter and the next explore the important activity of underwriting and continue our discussion of new business in life insurance companies. Recall from Chapter 6 that *new business* is the term used to describe all the activities required to market insurance, submit applications for insurance, evaluate the risks associated with those applications, and issue and deliver insurance policies. In this chapter, we'll explain the fundamental principles of underwriting. The next chapter discusses the underwriting process—the steps involved in processing applications, classifying risks, and issuing policies—and the ways that insurance companies use reinsurance to transfer to other insurance companies a portion of the risks they underwrite.

In these chapters, you frequently will see the terms *proposed insured* and *applicant*. The proposed insured is the person whose life is to be covered by the applied-for insurance policy. The applicant is the person who submits the application for insurance and seeks to purchase the coverage. When a person applies for an insurance policy on his own life, the applicant and the proposed insured are the same person. You should also be familiar with the difference between the terms *premium rate* (the charge per thousand dollars of coverage) and *premium amount* (the dollar amount of each premium). We will use the term *premium amount* to represent the result of the premium calculation, which includes the *premium rate*.

The Importance of Sound Underwriting

Underwriting is considered to be sound if each risk is evaluated accurately, classified properly, approved for an appropriate premium amount, or denied accurately. Sound underwriting has important benefits for insurance companies and their owners, insureds, and insurance salespeople.

Sound underwriting helps insurance companies remain competitive and strong financially. An insurer's profits are primarily determined by controlling expenses, accurately pricing products, and exercising sound judgment in underwriting. Sound underwriting enables insurance companies to charge premium amounts that correspond to the risk that each proposed insured represents. An insurer's good reputation and ability to compete successfully in the insurance industry depend largely on how well the insurer is prepared to fulfill the contractual obligations it has with its insureds.

An insurer has to underwrite wisely to remain strong. If an insurer's underwriting standards are too high, it will discourage marketers from submitting applications and will, therefore, lose potential premium income. If an insurer charges excessive premiums, it will become uncompetitive in the industry. And if an insurer accepts too many poor risks or charges premium amounts that are too low in relation to the level of the risks accepted, the insurer may not have sufficient funds to pay claims submitted under the coverage. Eventually, the insurer could face disciplinary action from insurance regulators, and the company's good name would be tarnished. In the worst case, the insurer would become insolvent and would no longer be able to operate as an insurance company.

For insureds, sound underwriting ensures that each person pays his or her fair share for the insurance coverage. Sound underwriting prevents unfair situations, such as a person with a high mortality risk and a person with a low mortality risk being charged the same premium amount for the same type and amount of coverage.

Sound underwriting benefits sales agents because they can use an insurer's sound underwriting practices as a selling point to demonstrate the company's focus on fairness to policyowners and its commitment to financial strength.

Antiselection and Persistency

Two concepts that are important to sound life insurance underwriting are antiselection and persistency. ***Antiselection***, also known as *adverse selection* or *selection against the insurer*, is the tendency of people who believe they have a greater-than-average likelihood of loss

to seek insurance protection to a greater extent than do those who believe they have an average or less-than-average likelihood of loss. For example, a woman who is terminally ill is more likely to be interested in insuring her life than is a woman in excellent health. The possibility of antiselection makes the underwriter's role particularly important in the risk assessment process. The underwriter must analyze available information about each applicant to determine whether the company has an accurate picture of the applicant's insurability and whether antiselection, and even possible fraud, are a threat.

Underwriters must also approve amounts of coverage that consumers can afford. As you know, persistency is the retention of business that occurs when a policy remains in force as a result of the continued payment of the policy's renewal premiums. The longer a policy or group of policies remains in force, the better its persistency. When a large number of policies lapse or are surrendered, the insurance company can suffer financially from the loss of premium income. Insurers strive to write policies that will remain in force for a long time. Generally, policyowners will keep policies in force as long as they have a need for insurance and an ability to pay for the coverage. In order to improve persistency, an underwriter must be able to assess each applicant's ability to pay for coverage.

Organization of Underwriting

Many people in an insurance company are involved in underwriting individual and group life insurance policies. Most of the employees involved are located at the insurer's home office. In some large companies, underwriters may work in regional offices as well. Also, life insurance agents are important participants in the underwriting process. In fact, life insurance agents have traditionally been known as *life underwriters* or *field underwriters*. In this text, the term *underwriter* means a home office or regional office underwriter unless otherwise noted.

Figure 11-1 shows one way to organize the underwriting function in a life insurance company. Following are brief summaries of the duties of key underwriting participants.

- **Chief underwriter.** The highest-ranking underwriter in an insurance company is usually called the *chief underwriter, chief underwriting officer*, or *vice president in charge of underwriting*. Some insurers have one chief underwriter in charge of both individual underwriting and group underwriting, while other insurers assign separate chief underwriters for individual insurance and group insurance. The chief underwriter directs all of the insurer's

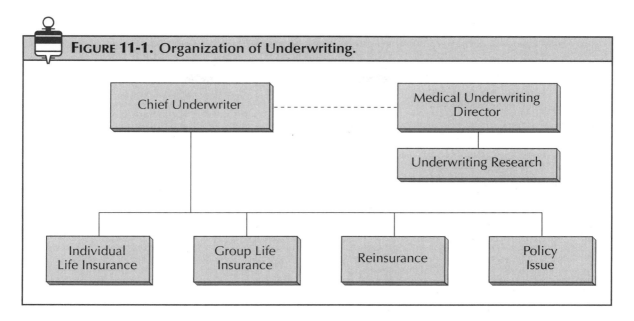

Figure 11-1. Organization of Underwriting.

underwriting activities, including the establishment of the company's underwriting philosophy, guidelines, and procedures. The chief underwriter monitors the cost and quality of underwriting and assists in underwriting large or difficult cases.

- **Medical underwriting director.** Many insurance companies employ physicians who serve as medical experts to advise the underwriting staff and provide them with medical information and guidance. The medical underwriting director is the person in charge of these medical experts. Along with the medical underwriting director, the medical staff prepares and updates the company's medical underwriting standards and consults with underwriters about proposed insureds who have unusual or difficult medical histories.

- **Individual and group underwriting executives and supervisors.** These executives oversee all of the insurer's individual underwriting and group underwriting activities and report to the chief underwriter. Reporting to the individual and group underwriting executives are underwriting supervisors, each of whom is responsible for one or more individual or group insurance products the company sells.

- **Underwriters.** These technical professionals assess the risks presented in the life insurance applications submitted to the company. Typically, the more experience and training an underwriter

has, the greater the amount of coverage the underwriter can approve without review by a more experienced underwriter or underwriting supervisor. An underwriter's authorization to approve an application without a second signature by a more senior underwriter usually increases with the underwriter's experience.

- **Agents.** In personal selling distribution systems, life insurance agents are the starting points of the risk selection process. Agents are involved in gathering initial information about a proposed insured (either a person or a group) and in screening applicants. This process, called *field underwriting*, helps ensure that qualified applicants apply for an appropriate type and amount of coverage. We discuss field underwriting in detail in the next chapter.

FAST FACT

The term *underwriter* comes from the practice of signing one's name under the signature of a responsible party to an action. Specifically, this practice originated with ship captains in the 15th century. When a captain agreed to deliver cargo to a certain place at a certain time, an underwriter signed below the captain's signature to assure that, if the agreed performance was not met (in other words, the cargo was not delivered), then monetary compensation would be paid.

Underwriting Objectives

Effective underwriting enables insurers to issue policies that are (1) equitable to policyowners, (2) deliverable by agents, and (3) profitable to the insurance company.

Equitable to the Policyowner

In Chapter 8, you learned that a concept underlying life insurance pricing is to ensure that the premium amounts charged to policyowners are *equitable*—that is, that the premium amount charged for a policy is based only on factors affecting the policy's costs. This notion that an insurance policy must be equitable to the policyowner is also a basic principle of insurance underwriting. As the underwriter receives each application for insurance, she evaluates the degree of risk presented by the proposed insured and charges a fair premium to insure the risk.

Deliverable by the Agent

The consumer makes the ultimate decision as to whether a particular insurance policy is acceptable to him. If the consumer chooses not to accept the policy when the agent attempts to deliver it, that policy is said to be **undeliverable**, or *not taken*. One of the many reasons a policy may be undeliverable is that the underwriting decision has resulted in a premium or coverage that is different from what the buyer expected. To be acceptable to the buyer, a policy must satisfy three basic requirements.

1. The policy must provide benefits that meet the buyer's needs.

2. The coverage provided by the policy must be affordable to the buyer.

3. The premium charged for the coverage must be competitive in the marketplace.

The third requirement is particularly important because of the intense competition in the life insurance industry. When an agent presents information about an individual life insurance product to an applicant, the agent usually quotes a premium that is based on the rate charged to the company's standard or preferred risks. If the underwriter's assessment results in the proposed insured's being evaluated as a greater risk than standard or preferred, the application is said to be rated. **Rating** is the process of increasing the premium rate or modifying the type or amount of coverage in order to approve a risk.

As an example, Susan Ramsey, an experienced life underwriter, received an application for $350,000 of whole life coverage on the life of Robert Upchurch, age 62. Medical information on Mr. Upchurch indicated that he had suffered a moderately severe heart attack at age 58, and at the time of application his blood pressure was elevated. On the application, he admitted to using tobacco. After evaluating the risk presented by Mr. Upchurch, Ms. Ramsey rated him as substandard and noted that the insurer would offer to cover Mr. Upchurch's life for $100,000 at a premium rate that was established for a substandard risk, which was higher than the rate for the same amount of coverage issued to a standard risk.

Profitable to the Insurance Company

Insurers are in business to provide coverage for a reasonable price. Just as insureds should be charged premium amounts that are appropriate for the level of risk they present, insurance companies should be compensated for the level of risk they accept on each policy. All insurance companies, whether stock, mutual, or fraternal benefit societies, require sound underwriting to help assure favorable financial results. Although underwriters are only indirectly involved in establishing a company's premium structure, underwriters' decisions are crucial in producing actual mortality results that correspond to the actuaries' mortality projections, and, thus, produce profitable business. Focus on Technology 11-1 discusses the effect that electronic commerce will have on underwriting and insurance company profitability.

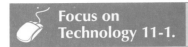

Focus on Technology 11-1.

Electronic Commerce and Underwriting.

Electronic commerce via the Internet will continue to transform the insurance industry in several ways. The organizational structure of the industry will change, away from its traditional geographic basis (the Internet has no boundaries), and the balance of power will shift from sellers to buyers. Full knowledge of prices by the buyer will force lower prices and lower profit margins.

Comparative pricing by customers will require skillful underwriting, as price reductions put pressure on margins. Innovative companies will target the customers most likely to be profitable policyowners by warehousing and successfully mining the extensive information companies are able to gather on consumer behavior and attributes.

Underwriting as a profession will evolve along two paths. Life risk managers will be marketers, deeply involved in the insurer's sales strategies. Direct customer interaction will be their norm. Technical underwriters will be knowledge engineers providing continuous research and analytical support to the expert systems of the insurer.

Electronic commerce is forcing insurance companies to rethink their way of doing business and to redefine customer relationships. The challenge for underwriters is to make sure they are helping to facilitate those changes within their organizations. •

Source: Excerpted and adapted from Maureen C. Zupan, "Technology Watching: The Underwriter's Job," *John Krinik's Underwriter Alert* (August 1999): 1–2. Used with permission.

Underwriting Philosophy and Underwriting Guidelines

When evaluating proposed insureds and making underwriting decisions, underwriters follow their companies' underwriting philosophies and underwriting guidelines. An ***underwriting philosophy***, also called *underwriting objectives*, is a set of objectives that generally reflect the insurer's strategic business goals and include pricing assumptions for products. An insurer's underwriting philosophy describes in general terms the types of risks that the company will and will not accept. For example, some insurance companies decline coverage to extremely high-risk applicants, while other insurance companies will insure high-risk applicants. The underwriting philosophy also describes in general terms how the underwriter will use reinsurance, which is a method of sharing risk in order to decrease the amount of risk assumed by any one insurance company. We discuss reinsurance in detail in Chapter 12.

An insurer's underwriting philosophy, in turn, shapes its ***underwriting guidelines***, the general standards that specify which applicants are to be assigned to the risk classes established for each insurance product (we'll explain risk classes in the next section). For individual life insurance, underwriting guidelines focus on such characteristics as the proposed insured's age, sex, build, blood pressure,

medical history, tobacco use, occupations or hobbies, and ability to pay for the amount of insurance requested. Underwriting guidelines for group life insurance consider such factors as the type of industry in which the group operates, the relative ages of group members, and the type and amount of insurance requested.

Individual Life Insurance Underwriting

Life insurance underwriting is mainly concerned with **mortality**, which is the relative incidence of death occurring among a given group of people.[1] **Mortality risk** is the likelihood that a person will die sooner than statistically expected. To evaluate the degree of mortality risk, the underwriter looks at information about possible impairments associated with each person or group that applies for coverage. An **impairment** is any aspect of a proposed insured's present health, medical history, health habits, family history, occupation, or other activities that could increase that person's expected mortality risk.

Risk Classes

One purpose of individual life insurance underwriting is to place each proposed insured in the correct risk class according to the level of risk that the proposed insured represents. A **risk class** is a group of insureds that represent a similar level of risk to an insurance company. The insurer charges the people in each risk class premium amounts that are consistent with the amount of risk that class of insureds represents.

Accurately classifying risks helps achieve the underwriting objectives—ensuring that each underwriting decision is equitable to the policyowner, deliverable by the agent, and profitable to the insurance company. Properly classifying risks also helps ensure that the company has sufficient funds to pay claims as they are received.

Although the specific criteria for each risk class vary from insurer to insurer, most insurance companies use the following four general risk classes:

- The **preferred class** designates proposed insureds whose anticipated mortality is significantly lower than average and who represent a lower-than-average degree of risk. Life insurers typically assign their healthiest proposed insureds to the preferred class. Those who are assigned to the preferred class are charged lower-than-average premiums to reflect their low level of risk. Many companies subdivide the preferred class into specific preferred

© 1998 *Reinsurance Reporter*. Used with permission.

sub-classes based on such factors as the proposed insureds' use of tobacco products.

- The *standard class* designates proposed insureds whose anticipated mortality is average. The mortality of people in this class is higher than the mortality for people in the preferred class but lower than the mortality for people in the substandard class. Consequently, proposed insureds in the standard class are charged standard premium rates that are higher than the premium rates charged to people of the same age and sex in the preferred class but lower than the rates charged to people of the same age and sex in the substandard class. Most insureds are standard risks.

- The *substandard class*, also called *special* or *impaired risk*, designates proposed insureds whose anticipated mortality is higher than average. Insurance companies typically establish this risk class for proposed insureds who (1) have permanent medical impairments or conditions, (2) are recovering from serious illnesses or accidents, or (3) have occupations or avocations that significantly increase their degree of risk. For example, a proposed insured who has recently had a heart bypass operation would probably be placed in the substandard class. The premiums

> **FAST FACT**
>
> At the beginning of 1999, 83.1 percent of the ordinary life insurance policies in force in the United States were issued to people in the standard risk class.[2]

charged to people in the substandard risk class are higher (sometimes significantly higher) than the premiums charged to people in the standard class. Like the preferred class, the substandard class can have several subclasses.

- The *declined class* designates proposed insureds whose impairments and anticipated extra mortality are so great that the insurer cannot provide coverage at an affordable cost. For example, a person with a terminal illness would typically be declined for insurance coverage. Only about 1 to 4 percent of all applicants are assigned to the declined class. Insurers typically attempt to offer some level of affordable coverage to as many proposed insureds as possible.

Risk Assessment Factors

Various types of risk factors and impairments affect a proposed insured's level of mortality risk and, consequently, determine the risk class to which the person is assigned. Some factors increase the insured's level of mortality risk, while other factors decrease the mortality risk. An underwriter's task is to determine the extent to which risk factors and impairments affect the proposed insured's mortality risk.

Insurers typically divide risk factors into three categories: medical risk factors, personal risk factors, and financial risk factors.

Medical Risk Factors

Medical risk factors for underwriting life insurance include the person's build, personal medical history, and family medical history.

Build. A person's *build* is the shape or form of the person's body, including the relationships among height, weight, and the distribution of weight. A person who is significantly overweight relative to height represents a greater mortality risk than does a person of average weight relative to height. A proposed insured who is underweight generally causes less concern about mortality risk. However, significant and rapid weight change may indicate medical impairments.

Personal Medical History. A proposed insured's medical history can be an important indicator of mortality risk. For example, a 55-year-old woman who suffered a heart attack at age 52 is more likely to live a shorter life—all other factors being equal—than a 55-year-old woman with no previous heart condition. Many medical conditions, such as high blood pressure, kidney disease, heart or lung disorders, cancer,

diabetes, and human immunodeficiency virus (HIV), can increase mortality risk.

Insurance companies maintain statistics on various causes of death in order to improve the accuracy of their underwriting decisions. Underwriters also keep informed about recent mortality and public health trends, because the relative risk presented by a particular medical condition can change over time as a result of advances through medical or scientific research.

An emerging issue related to personal medical history concerns insurers' use of information about a proposed insured's genetic characteristics. Genetic testing permits researchers to identify human genes that are strong indicators of a person's likelihood of developing specific physical and mental conditions. Some states have passed laws that prohibit an insurer from basing an underwriting decision solely on the proposed insured's possession of a specific gene, unless claim experience or actuarial projections establish that substantial differences in claims are likely to result from a person's possession of that gene compared to absence of the gene in a person. For more on genetic testing and underwriting, see Insight 11-1.

Family Medical History. The death of a proposed insured's family member from any disorder of the heart, a hereditary disease, or certain other disorders can be important in identifying a current or potential impairment in the proposed insured. However, family medical history is considered important only if it reflects a characteristic that also appears in some form in the proposed insured. For example, even if both parents of a proposed insured died of heart attacks before age 60, family history would probably be significant *only if* the proposed insured has high blood pressure or some other condition that, taken in isolation, increases the probability of heart attack.

Personal Risk Factors

A proposed insured can represent many types of risks that are not related to the person's age, sex, or medical condition. In this section, we identify and describe the personal risk factors that most frequently influence life insurance underwriting decisions.

Occupation. A proposed insured's occupation can have a strong influence on the mortality risk the person presents. Generally speaking, the workplace has become increasingly safe, but occupational hazards in certain industries still exist. Examples of hazardous occupations include (1) those in which accidents are possible, such as professional auto racing and jobs involving demolition, and (2) those that present health hazards, such as asbestos handling and mining.

Insight 11-1. Genetic Testing Questions That Remain.

Many consumers and lawmakers fear that genetic testing will result in genetic discrimination. Meanwhile, insurers realize that limited access to genetic test results could hinder the underwriting process, promote antiselection, and ultimately put insurers at an unfair disadvantage. Here we present some consumer arguments against genetic testing and the insurance industry's responses.

Consumers' Fears

Guarding public health—Allowing insurers access to genetic test information will have a "chilling effect" on research in genetics. Mark Rothstein, an attorney from the University of Houston, questions whether people will decide to forego genetic tests out of fear that the results may affect their insurability.

Autonomy—An individual's right to autonomy—that is, being free to make his own choices—will be violated if he is coerced into testing by the insurance company.

Stigma—An individual or his blood relatives could be stigmatized by an adverse genetic test result.

Discrimination—Since it is too early to know what a genetic test result means, those with abnormal genetic test results will be subject to "irrational discrimination" by insurance companies.

Insurance Industry's Response

Guarding public health—This issue addresses access to existing information. We are not aware that the insurance industry has had a chilling effect on any other aspect of medical research. The fact is that most research is done under the auspices of an institutional review board, and insurers don't see the research data. Concern about insurability—primarily with respect to medical expense insurance—may be an issue for those who have moderate to severe genetic conditions. Fortunately, these conditions are rare, and it is unlikely that they will be screened for in the general population. Furthermore, as the molecular basis of disorders becomes better understood, treatments and monitoring programs will be developed to modify risk and will be considered in the underwriting process.

Autonomy—This issue addresses testing by an insurer. We predict that even if screening tests are developed for common genetic disorders,

many companies will not require them. This means that the consumer will have to shop around for the company and product that best fits their needs, similar to the way other purchasing decisions are made.

Stigma—This concern arises out of the unfounded fears that insurers may not respect the confidentiality of genetic information. However, the truth is that insurers have an admirable record of handling medical and other information in a responsible and confidential manner.

Discrimination—Genetic information is no different from any other type of medical information. Just as medical research is being done constantly, insurers continually update their risk classification guidelines to reflect the most current and accurate understanding of the mortality risks associated with medical impairments. As professionals, we have a responsibility to stay abreast of the latest developments, make timely and accurate projections of the risks involved, and translate this information into accurate and appropriate underwriting actions. •

Tobacco Use. Extensive research has proven that the use of tobacco products significantly increases mortality risk. Most life insurance companies have separate actuarial tables and premium rates for tobacco users and tobacco nonusers, and some insurance products are issued to nonusers only.

Alcohol and Substance Abuse. A proposed insured's abuse or excessive use of alcohol or drugs can increase the person's risk of death. Abuse of alcohol or drugs can lead to health problems or be the cause of a fatal accident. Underwriters attempt to obtain sufficient information

about an insured's abuse of alcohol or other substances. If the underwriter verifies the presence of alcohol or drug abuse, standard practice is to decline the application.

Moral Hazard. *Moral hazard* is the likelihood that a person involved in an insurance transaction may be dishonest in that transaction. Moral hazard exists when a proposed insured makes a deliberate attempt to conceal or misrepresent information that might result in an unfavorable underwriting decision. For example, moral hazard exists when, on the application for insurance, an applicant lies about the proposed insured's criminal record, financial position, or use of tobacco. Dishonesty or fraud associated with moral hazard can lead to significant and unexpected losses for the insurer, so underwriters must check for the appearance of moral hazard in the insurance application. The risk of antiselection is typically high in cases involving moral hazard.

Avocations and Hobbies. An applicant's hobbies or avocations can have an effect on the person's mortality risk. People who take part in potentially dangerous activities such as skydiving, hang gliding, and amateur motorcycle racing have a greater mortality risk than people whose hobbies are playing computer video games and collecting stamps.

Aviation Activities. Proposed insureds who are pilots may present an increased risk to an insurance company. Insurance companies typically distinguish between civilian and military aviation. A proposed insured's total hours of flying experience, the number of hours that the person plans to fly annually, the type of aviation certificate the proposed insured holds, and the type of aircraft flown are important pieces of information in determining the likelihood that a pilot or flight crew member will be involved in an aviation accident. For military aviation, the underwriter also looks at the age, duty area, and type of aircraft flown by proposed insureds. Generally, commercial airline pilots who fly regularly scheduled routes do not present an increased risk to an insurer.

International Residence. Some insurance companies in the United States and Canada do not approve coverage for proposed insureds whose permanent residence is in another country. The reason is that obtaining accurate underwriting information on these cases and investigating claims in other countries can be difficult. Insurance companies that do issue policies to insureds in other countries may charge higher rates for this coverage than for similar coverage approved for people not living abroad. Some factors that underwriters consider when assessing this type of risk are the country of residence, the insured's proximity to medical facilities, and whether the policy premiums will be paid in domestic or foreign currency.

Driving History. Motor vehicles are involved in many accidental deaths. Although anyone who drives faces some level of risk, drivers with risky driving habits or who drive as their occupation are more likely to be involved in accidents. Higher-risk drivers include those who (1) have a large number of traffic violations, (2) have habitually abused alcohol or controlled substances, and (3) suffer from certain disorders, such as epilepsy, that may affect their ability to operate a vehicle effectively.

Military Status. An insurer typically approves applications on the lives of military personnel when they are not involved in a military conflict. Many insurers decline applications for insurance on the lives of military personnel while the proposed insureds are engaged in a military conflict. Other insurers insert "war clauses" in life insurance policies to exclude coverage if the insured's death results from a military conflict.

Financial Risk Factors

You have learned that an underwriter determines whether the amount of insurance for which a person applies is in line with his financial needs. For example, the underwriter makes sure that the face amount of insurance applied for and the amount of insurance already in force are consistent with the financial loss that would result from the insured's death. An amount that seems excessive could indicate the presence of antiselection. In addition, the underwriter determines whether the applicant will be able to afford the insurance coverage. If not, the policy will probably lapse.

Insurable Interest. Life insurance is intended to compensate for financial losses that result from an insured person's death. As a rule, beneficiaries should not gain from the insured's death. To verify the existence of a genuine financial loss, underwriters require that the proposed beneficiary has an insurable interest in the proposed insured's life. ***Insurable interest*** is the likelihood that a beneficiary of an insurance policy will suffer a genuine loss or detriment if the event insured against occurs. In almost all states, if the underwriter finds no insurable interest, then the application must be declined.[3] Note that insurable interest is required only at the time of policy issue, but not after the policy is in force.

A person applying for insurance on her own life is considered to have an insurable interest. In most jurisdictions, an applicant who is also the proposed insured can apply for as much insurance on her own life as the insurer is willing to issue and can name anyone as beneficiary. In other words, the underwriter does not question whether or

not an insurable interest exists, but the underwriter may question the level of financial need of the beneficiary.

An underwriter has a more difficult time assessing insurable interest in a ***third-party application***, which is an insurance application submitted by a person or party other than the proposed insured. Insurable interest involving a third-party application is assumed to exist when the applicant is

- A close relative of the proposed insured by blood or marriage—for example, a proposed insured's spouse, parent, child, grandparent, grandchild, or sibling. However, a proposed insured's aunt and uncle do not automatically have insurable interest.

- A relative of the proposed insured who is financially dependent on the proposed insured

- A business partner or employer of the proposed insured

- A creditor of the proposed insured

An underwriter inquires fully about the reasons for naming a beneficiary who appears to have little insurable interest in the life of the proposed insured.

For more on how underwriters consider various risk factors when evaluating applications, read Best Case Scenario 11-1.

Group Life Insurance Underwriting

Underwriting for group life insurance follows essentially the same principles and procedures that are used in individual life insurance underwriting. The key difference between individual underwriting and group underwriting is that the group underwriter evaluates information about the composition of and the risk presented by the group as a whole, rather than evaluating information about individual members of the group (except for extremely small groups). The goals of group underwriting are the same as the goals of individual underwriting—to determine the level of risk presented by a group of people and to charge a premium for group coverage that is adequate and equitable to the insureds and the insurance company.

A large group normally includes people with medical impairments that would make them substandard or declined risks if the underwriter evaluated them using individual underwriting guidelines. However, the group underwriter is not concerned with the high risks presented

Best Case Scenario 11-1.

Risk Factors and the Underwriting Decision.

Tom and Maria Carpenter have submitted applications for life insurance policies on their own lives. Listed below are three pieces of information from each of their applications. For each person, Best Friend's underwriters need to decide which of the three factors presents the greatest potential risk to the company. Note that the family's total net worth (total assets – total liabilities) is $130,000 and that Tom and Maria's combined annual income is $93,000 before taxes.

Tom: Underwriting Information	Maria: Underwriting Information
Occupation: Airline mechanic Smoker/nonsmoker: Nonsmoker Driving history: Seven moving violations in the last 24 months	Amount of insurance applied for: $4.5 million Height/weight: 5' 6", 130 Diabetes: Yes (Onset at age 30. Controlled well by change in diet. No family history of diabetes.)
Tom's driving history is the factor that probably presents the greatest potential risk to the insurance company. The large number of moving violations increases the likelihood that he will be involved in a serious traffic accident. Certainly, before making an underwriting decision, the underwriter would investigate further why Tom had had so many violations in such a short period of time and what, if anything, he has done to alter his driving habits. As for the other two factors, the fact that Tom is a nonsmoker obviously does not increase his mortality risk, but the underwriter may want to find out more about the potential physical risks associated with Tom's occupation as an airline mechanic. For example, is the workplace potentially dangerous? Does Tom frequently fly to test repaired aircraft? These or other potential physical risks might affect Tom's mortality risk.	The most significant potential risk factor for Maria is the amount of insurance she has applied for. The underwriter would probably consider $4.5 million of insurance coverage to be excessive in relation to the Carpenters' financial situation and the financial loss that would result from Maria's death. The underwriter would also question the Carpenters' ability to pay for that amount of insurance. Maria's height and weight present no abnormal risk. Maria's diabetes may present a risk, but the fact that the disease is under control through diet alone will likely have a more favorable impact on risk assessment.

by a few group members but rather is interested in whether the group as a whole is an acceptable risk.

Risk Assessment Factors

Each insurer establishes its own underwriting guidelines that define the types of group insurance coverage it will provide and the types of groups it will insure. The risk assessment factors that most insurers include are the type of proposed coverage, the reason for the group's existence, the size of the group, the nature of the group's business, the geographic location of the group, the stability of the group, the age and sex distribution of group members, the level of participation,

classes of employees, the group's expected persistency, and the group's prior experience.

Proposed Coverage

In examining the risk associated with the proposed plan of group insurance coverage, the underwriter evaluates the requested plan's eligibility requirements, benefit levels, method of plan administration, and mode of commission payment.

Eligibility Requirements. Insurers normally allow only full-time, permanent employees and their dependents to enroll in a group plan of insurance. Allowing part-time employees to be eligible for coverage would increase the possibility of antiselection because some high-risk people might seek part-time employment specifically to obtain insurance.

Benefit Levels. The level of benefits requested by the group applicant can have a significant effect on the success of the plan for the insurer and the group. The group underwriter must determine whether the plan includes excessive benefits, which could result in higher-than-average claim costs for the insurer and higher-than-average premiums later for the group policyholder. On the other hand, an insurance plan with unusually low benefits will probably not be well received by the employees.

Administration Method. Effective administration of the group life insurance plan is essential for keeping plan costs low and keeping the group policyholder and group insureds satisfied. Underwriters evaluate the willingness and ability of a group policyholder to support the administration of the plan, such as promoting the plan to eligible employees, maintaining accurate records of the plan and plan participants, and assisting with the submission of claims.

Mode of Commission Payment. When an underwriter has doubts about the persistency of a proposed group, the underwriter may recommend that the agent's commission be spread out over a number of years. In this way, if the policy lapses after the first year, the agent and the insurer share in the loss. Also, the agent has an incentive to help keep the policy in force, and to submit applications for groups that will have good persistency.

Reason for the Group's Existence

Traditionally, group underwriting guidelines in the United States and Canada have prohibited the issuance of group life insurance to any group that was formed for the sole purpose of obtaining group insurance. This requirement is designed to prevent antiselection, which is

likely to occur if high-risk individuals join together to purchase group insurance coverage. The primary factor underwriters consider in determining the reason for a group's existence is the type of group. The majority of groups are *employer-employee groups*, and each group consists of the employees of a single employer. Other types of groups include members of labor unions, professional associations, and credit unions, as well as borrowers of money from a bank or other lending institutions.

Some insurers now can issue group insurance coverage to groups that were formed solely for the purpose of obtaining group insurance. These groups are known for regulatory purposes in the United States as *discretionary groups*. If a discretionary group presents a risk that is similar to the risk presented by an employer-employee group, the insurer can issue coverage. Some insurers individually underwrite each member of a discretionary group, rather than underwriting the group as a whole. Insurers that use group underwriting techniques to underwrite discretionary groups generally consider such factors as whether the group members are actively at work on a regular, full-time basis, have a reasonably steady income, and work in a job or industry that presents a low level of risk.

Size of the Group

In order to establish the premium to charge for a given group, the underwriter must predict the amount of loss the group is likely to experience. The size of a group affects the underwriter's ability to predict the group's losses. As a general rule, in comparison to a small group, a large group tends to

- More closely follow actuarial predictions regarding mortality rates

- Have fewer and smaller fluctuations in claims

- Generate less administrative expense as a percentage of the total premium amount the group pays

Nature of the Group's Business

The nature of the industry in which the group operates can affect the degree of risk the group presents. Group underwriters also consider potential hazards and the economic prospects of the industry in which the group operates, as well as the strength and financial condition of the group's employer. Insurers are wary of underwriting groups in industries that are subject to the risk of major layoffs or large fluctuations in income.

Geographic Location of the Group

Mortality rates vary in various regions of the world and even in various regions of a particular country. For example, one region can differ from other regions in its susceptibility to natural disasters, the quality of economic and living conditions, and the quality and accessibility of health care. These factors can affect the rate of mortality in the region, which in turn affects the premium required for group insurance coverage on insureds who live in that region. Also, some groups, such as the employees of large multinational corporations, have members scattered throughout many regions. The group underwriter must be aware of the risks in each location.

Stability of the Group

To underwriters, the stability of a group refers to how the general composition of the group—for example, the distribution of ages and sexes of group members and the size of the group—changes over time. From an underwriter's perspective, the ideal situation is for a steady flow of new, younger members to enter the group as current insureds age and eventually leave the group. A group whose membership remains static for a long period of time presents an increased risk because the ages of the group members increase, and impairments generally increase with age. However, groups that exhibit frequent turnover or whose composition otherwise changes dramatically can represent considerable risk and produce additional administrative expenses, such as the cost of enrolling new members in the group plan.

Age and Sex Distribution of Group Members

Underwriters do not consider the age and sex of each group member (except for very small groups), but they do examine the age and sex distribution of the entire group. Groups with a majority of older members tend to experience higher rates of mortality than groups with a majority of younger members. Also, women as a group exhibit lower mortality than men, and so a group with a large proportion of women represents a statistically lower risk for life insurance coverage than does a group with a large proportion of men.

Level of Participation

Group insurance plans can be either noncontributory plans or contributory plans. In a **noncontributory plan**, insured group members are not required to contribute any part of the premium required for their coverage. In most noncontributory plans, all eligible group members must participate in the plan. In a **contributory plan**, insured

group members must contribute some or all of the premiums required for their coverage. Insurers usually require that between 75 and 100 percent of eligible group members participate in a contributory plan. This minimum participation requirement helps prevent antiselection, because people other than those who have the greatest impairments—and the greatest need for insurance—are participating in the group policy and helping to maintain a desirable distribution of risks.

Classes of Employees

One way to prevent antiselection under an employer-employee group insurance plan is for each group member to be assigned to an employee class and for the amount and type of benefits available to each group member to be based on the member's employee class. This system prevents low-paid employees from receiving amounts of life insurance coverage that are higher than their financial situation reasonably allows. The insurer can classify employee group members in many different and objective ways, such as by occupation, by salary amount, and by length of service with the employer. Federal laws in the United States and Canada prohibit the classification of employees in discriminatory ways, such as by marital status, sex, or age.

Expected Persistency

Marketing, underwriting, and administering a group insurance policy are expensive for an insurer, and usually a group policy must be in force for several years in order for the insurer to recover all of the initial costs of setting up the policy. Ideally, the underwriter looks for groups that are likely to keep the group policy in force for many years. Indications of a particular group's expected persistency can be found by examining the group's prior coverage with other insurers. For example, if the group has changed insurance carriers every year, an underwriter has reason to suspect that the group's persistency on the applied-for policy will be poor. In this case, the underwriter can either deny the coverage or approve coverage at an increased premium rate to recover the insurer's initial costs more quickly.

Prior Experience

If the group has been covered by group insurance in the past, the group's previous experience can be an important indicator of the degree of risk it presents to a new insurance company. Underwriters usually require such groups applying for coverage to provide information about previous benefit changes and their effective dates, premi-

ums paid, claims incurred, and claims paid for the previous three years. By considering a group's previous experience with insurance coverage, the underwriter can develop a picture of what her company's own experience might be and can charge premiums accordingly.

Underwriting Factors Considered in Renewal Business

When an insurance company issues a group life insurance policy, it typically guarantees the premium rate for one year. At the end of the initial period, and usually each year thereafter, the underwriter reevaluates the group contract because the nature of the risk insured can change each year—for example, old employees leave the group and new employees enter. The reevaluation typically focuses on the group's claim experience and, for contributory plans, the current level of participation.

Claim Experience

If the group's claim experience for the previous year was better than expected, the premium rates for the coming year may be reduced. If the experience was as expected, and if the underwriter anticipates that the company's operating expenses will remain the same, the premium rate for the coming year may remain the same. If the claim experience was worse than expected, the underwriter can raise the premium rate for the coming year. If the group's experience was extremely adverse, the group's coverage could be cancelled.

The degree of importance that an underwriter assigns to a group's claim experience varies with the size of the group. For a very large group, such as one with 1,000 or more members, the group's own experience is the most important factor in determining the amount of the next annual premium. For a smaller group, the underwriter places less emphasis on the group's experience. For groups with only a few members, the underwriter can pool the experience statistics from many small groups in order to calculate accurate premiums.

Level of Participation

For contributory plans, the underwriter verifies at the time of policy renewal that the level of employee participation meets the required minimum for that plan of insurance. If the level of participation has dropped below the minimum, the underwriter can require increased participation before approving the contract for renewal.

Regulatory Requirements and Underwriting

An insurer's underwriting activities are constrained by certain laws regarding unfair discrimination and the protection of consumer privacy.

Unfair Discrimination

Most states have enacted laws that are designed to protect consumers against unfair discrimination in underwriting. In these states, insurers are prohibited from basing underwriting decisions on factors such as the proposed insureds' sex, race, marital status, national origin, or religion. For example, an insurer is allowed to decline or rate the applications of all proposed insureds who present a certain health impairment, but is generally prohibited from declining or rating only those proposed insureds who present that health impairment *and* are of one national origin. Some states also prohibit insurers from unfairly discriminating against proposed insureds on the basis of certain mental or physical impairments.

Unfair discrimination laws protect proposed insureds only from discrimination that is *unfair*. If an insurer bases an underwriting decision on sound actuarial reasoning, and if this underwriting decision discriminates against a particular group of proposed insureds, then the discrimination is not considered to be unfair.

Consumer Privacy

As part of its underwriting processes, an insurer collects a large amount of personal information about proposed insureds. Many people have become increasingly concerned about the accuracy, confidentiality, and sensitivity of this information; how insurers handle the information; and with whom they share the information. Insurers must comply with federal, state, and provincial privacy laws that regulate the way insurance companies collect, use, and disclose personal information.

In the United States, an important federal privacy law affecting life insurance underwriting is the **Fair Credit Reporting Act (FCRA)**, which regulates the reporting and use of consumer credit information and seeks to ensure that reports from consumer reporting agencies contain only accurate, relevant, and recent information. A **consumer reporting agency** is a person or organization that regularly prepares consumer reports and furnishes them to other people and organizations. If an underwriter decides to use a report generated by a consumer reporting

agency, the insurer is required by the FCRA to give three types of notice to the applicant.

- The first notice, given before a consumer report is obtained, discloses to the applicant that a consumer report will be used.

- The second notice specifies the nature and scope of the investigation that produced the information.

- The third notice notifies the applicant if the insurer makes an adverse decision based wholly or partially on information contained in the report from the consumer reporting agency. Examples of adverse decisions are a denial of insurance, issuance of a policy with a substandard risk classification, and reduction in the amount of coverage applied for.

Insurance companies must also comply with state privacy laws that many states have patterned after the **NAIC Insurance Information and Privacy Protection Act**, commonly known as the **NAIC Model Privacy Act**. This act established standards for the collection, use, and disclosure of information gathered in connection with insurance transactions, such as underwriting. State laws based on the NAIC Model Privacy Act apply only to personal insurance, not insurance purchased for business or professional needs. The Act has the following stated purposes:

- To minimize intrusions on a person's privacy

- To establish a mechanism that allows a person to determine what information about him relevant to insurance transactions is currently being collected or has already been collected

- To enable such a person to have access to information collected in order to verify or dispute its accuracy

- To limit the disclosure of protected information

- To enable applicants, policyowners, and claimants to obtain a justification for adverse underwriting or claim decisions

Key Terms

underwriting (risk selection, selection of risks)
underwriter
underwriting decision
antiselection (adverse selection, selection against the insurer)
field underwriting
undeliverable (not taken)
rating
underwriting philosophy (underwriting objectives)
underwriting guidelines
mortality
mortality risk
impairment
risk class
preferred class
standard class

substandard class (special risk, impaired risk)
declined class
build
moral hazard
insurable interest
third-party application
employer-employee group
discretionary group
noncontributory plan
contributory plan
Fair Credit Reporting Act (FCRA)
consumer reporting agency
NAIC Insurance Information and Privacy Protection Act (NAIC Model Privacy Act)

Endnotes

1. In companies that sell health insurance, underwriters are also concerned with *morbidity*, which is the relative incidence of sickness and injury occurring among a given group of people. As the focus of this book is life insurance, we will concentrate on mortality.

2. ACLI, *1999 Life Insurance Fact Book* (Washington, D.C.: American Council of Life Insurance, 1999), 17.

3. At least one state—California—does not require insurable interest to be present at the time of policy issue.

The Process of Underwriting

You have already learned some of the basic principles of risk assessment for life insurance companies. The focus of this chapter is the process of underwriting—the activities in which an insurance company engages when evaluating insurance applications. As with most insurance company operations, the specific activities involved in underwriting vary from company to company. The activities also vary depending on the type of insurance product.

For example, some products, such as some of those sold through direct response distribution, require little or no underwriting. In these *guaranteed-issue products*, the underwriting is "built in" to the product and its pricing, and the applicant satisfies the underwriting guidelines by meeting the product's broad eligibility requirements. For most types of insurance products, however, the underwriting process involves four steps: (1) performing field underwriting, (2) reviewing the application in the home office, (3) gathering additional information, if necessary, to make a sound underwriting decision, and (4) making an underwriting decision. Generally, the information developed during underwriting is conveyed to the policyowner (through the agent, if an agent was used) as an offer. If the applicant accepts the offer, the insurer issues the policy. Figure 12-1 provides a graphic overview of the underwriting process.

We begin this chapter by discussing how insurers distribute their underwriting cases among underwriting employees. Then we examine each step in the individual underwriting process and the group underwriting process. We also discuss the role of technology in the underwriting process. Finally, we describe reinsurance, which is a method insurers use to transfer some of their risk to other insurance companies.

Distributing Underwriting Cases

Life insurers develop systems to assign underwriting cases to employees. Two commonly used systems are the case assignment system and the work division system. Some insurers use a combination of the two systems.

Case Assignment System

In a *case assignment system*, underwriting cases are distributed to an appropriate person or a group for underwriting according to certain

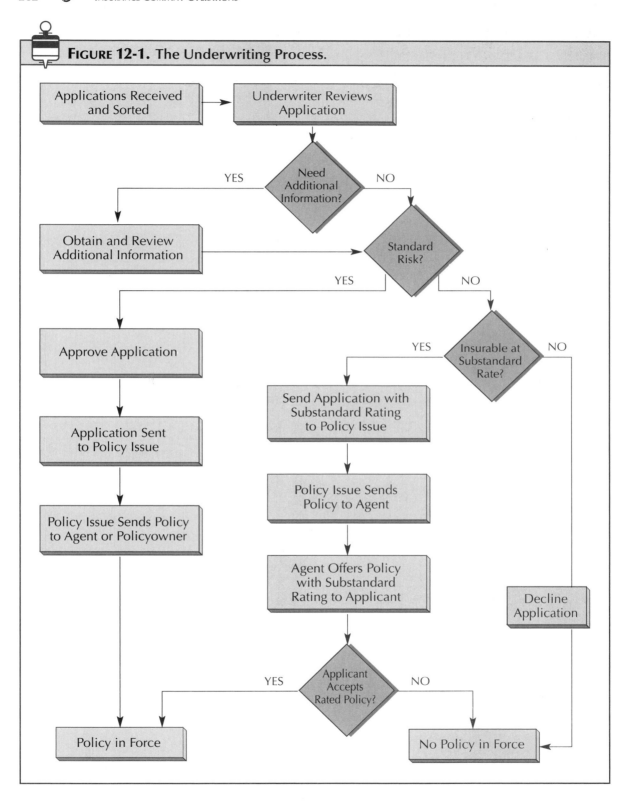

FIGURE 12-1. The Underwriting Process.

characteristics of the case. For example, a case assignment system can distribute underwriting case files according to the

- Face amount of insurance requested

- Type of application

- Geographic origin of the application

- Last name of the applicant

The case assignment system allows underwriters to specialize in certain types of cases.

Work Division Systems

A *work division system* is a method an insurer uses to divide underwriting cases according to the person or group that underwrites them. In some insurance companies, most cases are assigned to groups, and only cases involving large face amounts of coverage or requiring extensive research are assigned to underwriters working independently. Three group approaches used for assigning the remaining cases are team underwriting, jet unit underwriting, and committee underwriting.

Team Underwriting

Team underwriting is a risk selection approach in which underwriters form small groups to evaluate applications. The team usually consists of one or more senior-level underwriters to handle larger cases and one or more junior-level underwriters to evaluate simpler cases. Team members usually have considerable autonomy to make underwriting decisions, set work assignments, and establish priorities for the team. Compared with other underwriting methods, team underwriting can reduce the cost and time involved in underwriting applications.

Jet Unit Underwriting

Jet unit underwriting is a risk selection approach in which employees screen applications that meet specific criteria. The jet unit is authorized to approve certain types of applications for immediate policy issue. If the application does not meet the criteria for immediate issue, then the application is passed to an independent underwriter or underwriting team for evaluation. Jet unit underwriting is designed to evaluate simple cases quickly and inexpensively. Figure 12-2 lists

some criteria that insurance companies typically use to select applications for jet unit underwriting.

A jet unit typically is not authorized to decline or rate an application except when certain specified impairments are present. The speed of jet unit underwriting can be further increased with the use of computers and electronic systems.

Committee Underwriting

Committee underwriting is a risk selection approach in which a group of highly qualified people from inside and outside the underwriting area is formed to assess difficult cases. Committees typically consult on cases involving extremely large amounts of coverage or special underwriting concerns, such as combinations of impairments or unusual occupations. A committee may be comprised of the chief underwriter, the medical underwriting director, and senior members of the legal, compliance, actuarial, and agency operations areas.

Combination Systems

Some insurers combine a case assignment system with a work division system. For example, one underwriting team may handle only whole life insurance applications for face amounts up to $500,000, while another team handles whole life applications for face amounts above $500,000.

Field Underwriting

As you learned in the previous chapter, the underwriting process begins with *field underwriting*, which is the process of gathering initial information about a proposed insured and screening applicants

FIGURE 12-2. Criteria Used to Select Applications for Jet Unit Underwriting.

- Proposed insured's age, height, and weight are within specified ranges
- Proposed insured has no significant health problems and has an acceptable occupation
- Application is made for an amount of insurance below a specified limit (such as $50,000 or $100,000), depending on the proposed insured's age and the insurer's requirements
- Applicant's beneficiary designation conforms to specific standards
- Applicant has answered all questions on the application

who have requested coverage. The key person involved in field underwriting is the agent who solicits the insurance business. An agent's responsibility in the selection of risks is important because, in most cases, the agent is the only person who has firsthand knowledge of the applicant.

Agents perform field underwriting by determining a proposed insured's suitability for the requested insurance coverage and making preliminary assessments of his likely insurability. An agent initiates field underwriting by helping the applicant complete the application for insurance. Agents are trained to make sure that the applicant answers all questions on the application and that descriptions of any health problems are complete and exact. Also, agents are urged to report any information they know or suspect about a proposed insured that could influence the underwriter's decision, but which the applicant may not have mentioned. The agent reports this information in the ***agent's statement***, which is a portion of the insurance application in which an agent can comment at length on any factors relevant to the case and the risk it involves. Figure 12-3 lists the facts about a proposed insured's health problems that an agent includes in the application.

Comprehensive field underwriting benefits the agent, the insurance company, and the applicant by reducing the likelihood that the underwriter will have to take time to request additional medical evidence or other information about the proposed insured. Effective field underwriting reduces the overall time and cost of processing applications. Also, field underwriting helps ensure full disclosure of information about proposed insureds and makes claim information easier for insurers to verify.

To assist the agent during field underwriting, most insurance companies develop a ***field underwriting manual*** that (1) presents specific guidance for an agent's assessment of the risks represented by proposed insureds and (2) guides the agent in assembling and submitting the evidence of insurability needed for the underwriter to evaluate

FIGURE 12-3. Facts About Proposed Insured's Health Included in the Application.

- The precise name of each medical problem
- The date, duration, and frequency of any attacks or episodes
- Any complications of the problem, such as any loss of time from work
- The dates and types of any treatment or medication
- The names and addresses of physicians visited and the dates of those visits
- The names of hospitals and dates of hospitalization

the risks. *Evidence of insurability* is documented proof that the applicant is an insurable risk. The field underwriting manual typically contains instructions for filling out applications for various types of coverage, information about common medical conditions and other impairments, definitions of medical terms, and the insurer's underwriting philosophy.

Teleunderwriting

An alternative to field underwriting is *teleunderwriting*, which is a method by which a home office employee or a third-party administrator (TPA), rather than the agent, gathers most of the medical, personal, and financial information needed for underwriting. The agent and the applicant complete an abbreviated application, which includes only basic information about the proposed insured.

As the name suggests, teleunderwriting usually takes place in a telephone interview. Teleunderwriting relieves agents from having to complete detailed applications and allows them to spend more time acquiring new customers and servicing current customers. Teleunderwriting also speeds the underwriting processes. The interviewer can obtain all the detailed information necessary to make an underwriting decision. If the interviewer is also the underwriter, she may be able to make the underwriting decision soon after the telephone conversation.

Reviewing the Application for Insurance

When an application is reviewed in the underwriting department, an underwriter verifies that (1) the application form is the proper one for the proposed insured's state or province of residence and (2) the agent is licensed to sell the requested type of policy in that jurisdiction. The underwriter then searches the insurer's records to determine whether the proposed insured is covered by another of the company's policies. Any information regarding previous policies applied for or claims submitted by the applicant or proposed insured is attached to the application. Then, depending on the insurer and the type and amount of insurance applied for, the case is assigned to an independent underwriter, an underwriting team, a jet unit, or an underwriting committee.

The Application for Insurance

Traditionally, an insurance application has contained two parts: Part I and Part II. Some insurers no longer divide the application into

two parts, but essentially the same information is still required on all applications. For simplicity, we discuss the traditional two-part application.

Part I Information

Part I of the life insurance application identifies the proposed insured and the applicant (if different from the proposed insured), specifies the amount and type of coverage requested, and provides basic insurability information, including the following:

- Identification of the proposed insured by name, Social Security number (or social insurance number in Canada), birth date, birthplace, age, sex, address, telephone number, length of time at residence, occupation, current employer, and length of time with current employer

- Identification of the applicant, if different from the proposed insured

- Mode of premium payment requested

- Dividend options and special features or riders requested

- Beneficiary designation and the beneficiary's relationship to the insured

- Information concerning the proposed insured's hobbies, aviation activities, use of tobacco, and insurance history (such as the amount of life insurance the proposed insured already has in force)

The applicant, proposed insured, and agent all sign Part I of the application, which becomes part of the insurance contract.

Part II Information

Part II of the insurance application provides the insurer with medical information about the proposed insured. Part II generally takes one of three forms: (1) a medical report, (2) a nonmedical supplement, or (3) a paramedical report.

The most extensive Part II information form is a ***medical report***, which is a report on the proposed insured's health that is designed to be completed by both the proposed insured and a physician. The physician records the results of a medical examination of the proposed insured and completes a medical questionnaire to record the proposed insured's answers to health questions. The proposed insured signs

this section of the medical report, and this section becomes part of the insurance contract.

A ***nonmedical supplement*** contains health history questions that an agent or a teleunderwriting specialist asks a proposed insured. The proposed insured provides names and addresses of her personal physician, and the dates of, locations of, and reasons for any hospital stays in the previous five or 10 years. In a nonmedical supplement, the proposed insured answers the same health questions that appear in the medical questionnaire portion of a medical report. The nonmedical supplement becomes part of the insurance contract.

A ***paramedical report*** contains (1) the proposed insured's answers to medical history questions and (2) the results of certain physical measurements taken by a paramedical examiner. The proposed insured's answers to the medical history questions become part of the insurance contract. The paramedical report is less extensive, less expensive, and faster to obtain than a medical report, and in many cases provides all the medical information necessary for an underwriter to make an underwriting decision. For these reasons, a paramedical report is the most commonly used Part II application. The underwriter can request a medical examination if a paramedical examination reveals the need for one.

The insurer's choice of which of these three forms to use generally depends on (1) the insurer's ***nonmedical limits***—the total amounts of life insurance that will be issued to an applicant at one time without requiring a medical examination—and (2) the cost of a medical or paramedical examination in relation to the amount of insurance applied for. An insurer's nonmedical limits generally vary according to the age category of the proposed insured. For example, an insurer's nonmedical limit may be $250,000 for proposed insureds aged 36–40 and $50,000 for proposed insureds age 46–50. In this case, a 37-year-old proposed insured with no significant impairments could purchase up to $250,000 of insurance on his life without undergoing a medical examination, while a 49-year-old proposed insured could purchase a maximum of $50,000 without undergoing a medical examination. In some insurance companies, nonmedical limits apply to the sum of the insurance being applied for and the insurance already in force with the insurer. Other insurers consider only the amount being applied for.

Gathering Additional Information

In most cases, the application for insurance (or the teleunderwriting interview) and medical or paramedical examination provide an underwriter with all the information needed to make an underwriting deci-

sion. However, for some cases, the underwriter needs more information about the proposed insured's various risk factors—medical, personal, and financial.

Sources of Additional Medical Information

Underwriters obtain additional medical information about proposed insureds from a number of sources, such as attending physician's statements (APSs), specialized medical questionnaires, MIB reports, and laboratory tests.

Attending Physician's Statement (APS)

An *attending physician's statement (APS)* is a report by a physician who has treated, or who is currently treating, the proposed insured. For example, if an application for insurance states that the proposed insured has a history of a heart murmur but does not indicate the seriousness of the disorder, the underwriter may find it helpful to contact the insured's physician for a clarification. Although an APS can be a valuable source of information to an underwriter, doctors can be slow to respond to requests for APSs, and many doctors charge fees to complete them. As a result, insurers are relying less and less on APSs for medical information.

Specialized Medical Questionnaire

A *specialized medical questionnaire* is a document that requests from a proposed insured's attending physician detailed information about a specific illness or condition. The specialized medical questionnaire is less open-ended than an APS and asks specific questions about the proposed insured's condition. Many insurance companies develop specialized medical questionnaires for certain serious impairments such as epilepsy, respiratory impairments, mental or nervous disorders, high blood pressure, severe gastrointestinal disorders, immunodeficiency, and cancer.

MIB Report

Underwriters often request information about proposed insureds from *MIB, Inc.*, a nonprofit organization established to provide information to insurers concerning impairments that applicants have disclosed or that other insurance companies have found in connection with previous applications for insurance. MIB maintains information about people applying for coverage in the United States with MIB-

member life insurers. MIB members may request information to find out whether proposed insureds have significant impairments or other risks that they did not disclose on their current applications for insurance. Insurers report impairment information to the MIB as well as obtain information from it.

The use of MIB information for underwriting purposes is strictly defined. MIB prohibits its member companies from using MIB information as the sole basis of an unfavorable underwriting action or investigation, except under limited conditions. Any information an insurance company receives from MIB must be kept strictly confidential. MIB rules require that when an insurer uses MIB information to consider the insurability of a proposed insured, the insurer must obtain the person's written consent to obtain and use the information in connection with the evaluation of the application. Typically, a notice of consent becomes part of the insurance application. For more on the flow of information between MIB and insurance companies, see Best Case Scenario 12-1.

Laboratory Tests

Insurance agents may order laboratory tests on a proposed insured in accordance with the insurer's published underwriting requirements. Underwriters may also order such tests if they are deemed necessary to make a sound underwriting decision. Figure 12-4 lists four laboratory tests commonly ordered for underwriting.

Best Case Scenario 12-1. **The Flow of Information to and from MIB.**

The Best Friend Life Insurance Company, a member of MIB, Inc., received separate applications for life insurance on the lives of Maria Carpenter and Wesley Hardwick. Janie Grabowski, a Best Friend underwriter, requested information about Maria and Wesley from MIB, but MIB had no information on either person.

The paramedical report submitted with Maria's application noted that she was a diabetic and that her condition was being controlled successfully by a change in diet. Janie reviewed Maria's application and supporting information and approved her for coverage. Janie also reported Maria's diabetic condition to MIB.

Wesley underwent a medical examination as part of the underwriting process for his application. The examination revealed that Wesley had a life-threatening heart condition. Janie reviewed Wesley's application and supporting information and declined his applica-tion. Janie then reported Wesley's heart condition to MIB.

A short time later, Wesley submitted an application for life insurance coverage to the Evergreen Insurance Company. On the application, Wesley did not include the information about his heart condition. During the course of underwriting, Evergreen requested information about Wesley from MIB. Evergreen was alerted to Wesley's heart condition and conducted its own investigation into his health. ●

FIGURE 12-4. Four Tests Commonly Ordered for Underwriting.

Electrocardiogram (EKG): A graphic record of the electrical forces produced by the heart to screen for a disease or an abnormality of the heart.

Urinalysis: Analysis of urine specimen to screen for the presence of protein, sugar, blood cells, and certain medications and drugs, including nicotine.

Blood chemistry profile: A group of laboratory tests that screen a blood sample for possible chronic and acute disease.

Oral specimen (saliva) test: Analysis of saliva to screen for the presence of HIV antibodies and the use of cocaine; can also detect use of nicotine.

Sources of Additional Personal Information

Underwriters sometimes consult three additional sources of personal information about proposed insureds: motor vehicle records, inspection reports, and personal questionnaires.

Motor Vehicle Record

A *motor vehicle record* is a record of information about a person's driving history, including traffic violations and arrests and convictions for driving-related incidents. Motor vehicle records are available from public records and from consumer reporting agencies.

Inspection Report

An *inspection report* is a type of investigative report that is prepared by a consumer reporting agency and that contains information about a proposed insured. The information collected for an inspection report can include virtually anything about a proposed insured's personal life, occupation, hobbies, health, and financial status. To prepare an inspection report, the investigative agency collects publicly available information and conducts interviews with the proposed insured and his family, friends, neighbors, and business associates.

An underwriter uses an inspection report to clarify information received from the application or other sources. Before an underwriter can order an inspection report, the proposed insured must sign a release form that becomes part of the application and that authorizes various people and organizations to release information for the inspection

---

FAST FACT

In 1997, the leading cause of injury-related deaths in the United States was motor vehicle accidents, which accounted for 29 percent of all injury-related deaths. Fatalities from firearms were the second leading cause of deaths from injuries and accounted for 22 percent of deaths.[1]

report. The proposed insured has the right to see a copy of the finished report and must be informed if information contained in the report is the reason for an unfavorable underwriting decision.

Although inspection reports can supply valuable information to the underwriter, they can be expensive and time-consuming to complete. Typically, insurers do not use inspection reports for applications that request less than $500,000 of insurance coverage.

Personal Questionnaires

Insurers have developed specialized questionnaires to gather additional personal information from proposed insureds. A personal questionnaire is designed to tell the underwriter the extent of a proposed insured's involvement in a specified activity that is known to increase mortality risk. An insurer usually develops a separate personal questionnaire for each of a number of different activities, such as driving, aviation, scuba diving, and skydiving. For example, if a proposed insured notes on the application for insurance that she is a scuba diving instructor, the underwriter may ask the proposed insured to fill out a scuba diving questionnaire.

Sources of Additional Financial Information

If an underwriter needs additional financial information, it can be found in inspection reports, which, in addition to including the per-

**"I have a copy of your credit report.
On February 5th, 1992 you borrowed five dollars
from your wife's purse and never paid it back."**

© 1998 Randy Glasbergen. Used with permission.

sonal information mentioned above, may contain information about a person's investments, income, assets, and liabilities. The underwriter can also ask the investigative agency compiling the inspection report to check the proposed insured's credit history. For some inspection reports, the investigators interview the proposed insured's banker, securities broker, and accountant.

Table of Underwriting Requirements

For each insurance product that it sells, a life insurance company typically develops a *table of underwriting requirements* that specifies the kinds of information the underwriter must consider in assessing the insurability of a person who is proposed for coverage under that policy. Figure 12-5 shows a portion of a table of life insurance underwriting requirements for one insurance product. As the figure shows, the greater the risk being evaluated—such as large amounts of insurance or older proposed insureds—the more information the underwriter must gather in order to make an underwriting decision. For example, if a proposed insured is age 35 and applies for $100,000 of insurance, only a nonmedical supplement is usually required to make an underwriting decision. If that same person applies for $800,000 of coverage, the underwriter must obtain from the proposed insured a paramedical examination, blood chemistry profile, urinalysis, and personal questionnaire. For any underwriting case, an underwriter can gather more information than is required by the insurer's table of underwriting requirements.

Making an Underwriting Decision

After gathering and reviewing all relevant information about a proposed insured, the underwriter makes an underwriting decision, generally one of three choices:

1. **Approve the coverage as applied for.** In the majority of cases, underwriters approve policies as applied for.

2. **Rate the application.** If the proposed insured has certain medical, personal, and/or financial impairments but is nonetheless an insurable risk, the underwriter rates the application either by modifying the coverage or charging a higher premium rate before approving the case. For example, if an otherwise standard-risk proposed insured is a student pilot, the underwriter can approve the application at a standard rate but exclude coverage in the

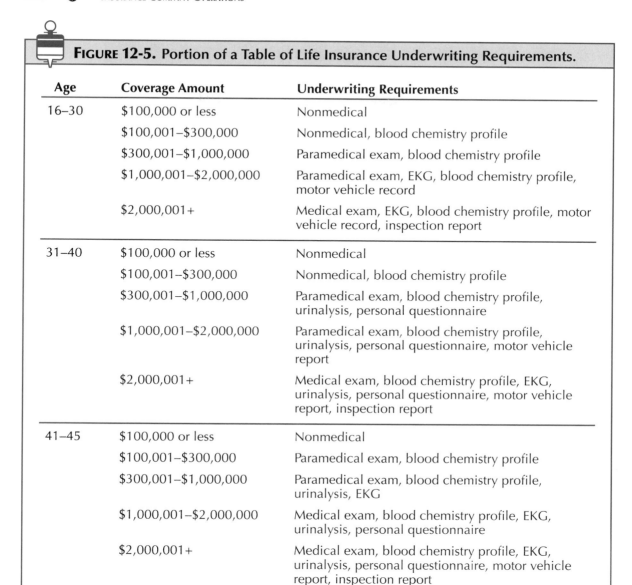

FIGURE 12-5. Portion of a Table of Life Insurance Underwriting Requirements.

Age	Coverage Amount	Underwriting Requirements
16–30	$100,000 or less	Nonmedical
	$100,001–$300,000	Nonmedical, blood chemistry profile
	$300,001–$1,000,000	Paramedical exam, blood chemistry profile
	$1,000,001–$2,000,000	Paramedical exam, EKG, blood chemistry profile, motor vehicle record
	$2,000,001+	Medical exam, EKG, blood chemistry profile, motor vehicle record, inspection report
31–40	$100,000 or less	Nonmedical
	$100,001–$300,000	Nonmedical, blood chemistry profile
	$300,001–$1,000,000	Paramedical exam, blood chemistry profile, urinalysis, personal questionnaire
	$1,000,001–$2,000,000	Paramedical exam, blood chemistry profile, urinalysis, personal questionnaire, motor vehicle report
	$2,000,001+	Medical exam, blood chemistry profile, EKG, urinalysis, personal questionnaire, motor vehicle report, inspection report
41–45	$100,000 or less	Nonmedical
	$100,001–$300,000	Paramedical exam, blood chemistry profile
	$300,001–$1,000,000	Paramedical exam, blood chemistry profile, urinalysis, EKG
	$1,000,001–$2,000,000	Medical exam, blood chemistry profile, EKG, urinalysis, personal questionnaire
	$2,000,001+	Medical exam, blood chemistry profile, EKG, urinalysis, personal questionnaire, motor vehicle report, inspection report

event of death relating to an aviation accident. As another example, a proposed insured with a history of a heart murmur could be approved for the requested coverage but at a higher-than-standard premium rate because of the increased mortality risk associated with the heart condition.

3. **Decline the application.** If the proposed insured presents greater mortality risk than the insurance company is willing to cover, the underwriter declines the application.

Depending on the type and amount of coverage applied for and the underwriter's level of experience, a more senior-level underwriter or underwriting manager may review the initial underwriting decision.

For several reasons, underwriters must make objective decisions. Objectivity helps ensure that underwriting decisions are consistent from application to application throughout an insurance company. For example, if two different underwriters in the same insurance company receive same-amount applications for a certain type of whole life insurance from 45-year-old women with similar medical, personal, and financial risk factors, the premium rates charged on those policies should be similar. Objectivity in underwriting also helps ensure that each insured is charged an equitable premium for the insurance coverage provided.

To help underwriters make objective, consistent underwriting decisions, life insurance companies develop **underwriting manuals**, which are documents that contain descriptive information on impairments and serve as guides to underwriting decision making. The underwriting manual provides the underwriter with guidance about how to rate a large number of medical risks, including impairments and diseases associated with each organ and system of the body. The underwriting manual also contains medical reference material and a list of medical and insurance abbreviations and definitions to help the underwriter interpret information in the applicant's file. Finally, the underwriting manual may include suggested ratings for nonmedical impairments, such as a dangerous hobby or a poor driving record.

The ratings for an impairment can vary from one insurer to the next because each insurer's underwriting manual and guidelines generally reflect the insurer's experience insuring risks under its coverages. Insight 12-1 discusses how insurers update their underwriting manuals in response to medical advancements.

No underwriting manual can completely suffice as an underwriting guide, however, and so the experience of the underwriter is crucial to the accurate underwriting of insurance applications. Insurers emphasize that the suggested actions and ratings listed in an underwriting manual are intended to be guidelines, not rules, and may be modified by the underwriter as characteristics and circumstances warrant.

The Numerical Rating System

You already know that underwriters evaluate risk factors so that they can assign proposed insureds to risk classes. But how do underwriters make risk classification and premium rate decisions? Life underwriters typically use a **numerical rating system**, which is a risk classification method in which each medical and nonmedical factor is assigned a numeric value based on its expected impact on a person's mortality. The numerical rating system assigns *positive* numbers to

Insight 12-1. Tracking Medical Advances.

Given today's highly competitive marketplace, most life insurers continually seek appropriate opportunities to extend their range of coverage and to make their pricing as favorable as possible. Accordingly, the guidelines provided by underwriting manuals have changed frequently—and often dramatically—over the years in response to medical advances that affect mortality.

One of the best examples of this phenomenon is the classification of diabetes. Around the middle of the 20th century, nearly all diabetics were considered to be uninsurable. With improved treatments and new maintenance-of-control techniques, the approval of proposed insureds with diabetes is now commonplace.

Similarly, recent medical advances mean that the prognosis for certain cancers has improved greatly and this also is reflected in revised underwriting guidelines. Along the same lines, in view of the promising results achieved by the so-called "AIDS cocktail," a few insurers are beginning to consider coverage for certain HIV-positive people. All HIV patients were considered uninsurable just a few years ago.

As a final example of revised guidelines, some companies have taken a new look at how they classify applicants who suffer from coronary artery disease. In the past, it was common practice to place all applicants with this disease in the same risk class, regardless of their age. Recent clinical studies, however, indicate that the mortality experience for individuals at older ages who have had successful coronary artery bypass grafting and have modified their lifestyles to help reduce risk factors may actually approach standard mortality.

Based on this information, more favorable pricing is now available from some insurers for applicants who fall into that category. Conversely, consistent with clinical research, guidelines have become stricter for people in their 40s and early 50s with coronary artery disease. •

Source: Excerpted from Robert F. Haran, "Tracking Medical Advances," *Best's Review*, Life/Health ed. (July 1998): 83. © A.M. Best Company. Used with permission.

factors that have been determined statistically to *increase* a person's mortality risk; the system assigns *negative* numbers to factors that have been determined statistically to *decrease* a person's mortality risk.

Standard mortality is represented by a base value of 100. To this base value, the underwriter adds positive and negative values to arrive at a sum that represents the numerical value of the proposed insured's risk and determines the proposed insured's risk classification. The higher the numerical rating for a proposed insured, the higher the degree of risk the proposed insured represents.

For example, assume that the sum of the standard mortality (100) and the various positive and negative values for a proposed insured is 150. This proposed insured represents 150 percent of standard mortality and thus is a greater-than-standard risk. Similarly, a proposed insured whose risk is represented numerically as 80 represents 80 percent of standard mortality and is considered a lower-than-standard risk.

The positive and negative numbers assigned to the risk factors are based on extensive statistical studies that generally compare the mortality experience of people affected by various medical and nonmedical factors with the mortality of unimpaired people. For example, people with heart disease have been shown statistically to have higher mortality risk than people without heart disease. Similarly, people who rock climb have been shown statistically to have higher mortality risk than people who do not rock climb.

After determining a proposed insured's numerical rating, the underwriter calculates a premium rate for the coverage. If the numerical rating system indicates that a proposed insured is a standard or preferred risk, the underwriter charges the standard or preferred premium rate, based on the proposed insured's age and sex. If the numerical rating system indicates that a proposed insured is classified as a substandard risk, the underwriter determines an appropriate premium rate to charge. Insurers use different methods to charge for substandard risks depending on whether the mortality pattern of a given characteristic or impairment is expected to remain constant, increase with age, or decrease with age. These methods include (1) consulting tables that show the percentage of extra premium to charge based on the proposed insured's numerical rating, (2) adding a flat dollar amount per $1,000 of insurance, or (3) using some combination of methods. In either case, the extra premium charged to a substandard risk compensates the insurer for the extra mortality risk.

Policy Issue

After reaching an underwriting decision, the underwriter notifies the soliciting agent of the decision, and the agent communicates the decision to the applicant. If the underwriting decision is to approve the coverage, the underwriter releases the applicant's file to the policy issue department. *Policy issue* is the insurance company functional area that prepares the insurance contract and facilitates the delivery of the policy to the customer, usually by way of the agent who sold the insurance. In some companies, underwriting and policy issue are separate, but closely related, departments. In other companies, underwriting and policy issue activities are combined into one unit.

Insurance companies generally use automated systems to produce the policy documents. These systems (1) create a computerized client record that contains the customer's name, contact information, and policy number, (2) verify receipt of the initial premium payment, and (3) verify that all underwriting requirements have been met.

Denial or Rating

If the application is denied or rated because of a condition that was disclosed on the application, the underwriter usually tells the agent the specific reason for the denial or rating. If the application is denied or rated because of an impairment that was not disclosed on the application—such as for a medical condition that was discovered during a medical examination—then, to protect the proposed insured's privacy, the underwriter does not tell the agent the reason for the underwriting decision. Instead, the underwriter typically refers

the applicant to the physician or other source of the unfavorable information. In some jurisdictions, the insurer must explain to the applicant in writing the reasons for a policy rating or a declined application. Even if not required to do so by law, insurance companies usually write to applicants to explain underwriting decisions.

Group Life Insurance Underwriting Procedures

The process of underwriting group life insurance differs considerably from the process of underwriting individual life insurance. After a group wishing to obtain insurance contacts a sales agent or group representative, the agent completes a *Request for Proposal*, a document that provides detailed information about requested insurance coverage and that requests a bid from an insurer for providing the coverage. The agent attaches to the RFP proposed rates for the requested coverage and an agent's statement commenting about the feasibility of providing the requested coverage to a proposed group. The agent sends the RFP and the attachments to the insurance company.

A group underwriter at the insurance company evaluates the information and determines whether the group is an acceptable risk. If the risk is acceptable, the underwriter develops a *proposal for insurance*, which is a document that provides a number of specifications for the insurance coverage approved by the insurer for the proposed group. The proposal includes

- A schedule of benefits

- A list of premium rates and the periods for which they are guaranteed

- The underwriting principles and assumptions used in developing the proposal

- Details about administration of the plan

The specifications in this proposal may or may not coincide with the requested coverage.

The proposed policyholder can accept, decline, or negotiate changes in the insurer's proposal for insurance. After reaching an agreement, the proposed policyholder fills out a *master application* that contains the specific provisions of the plan of insurance being applied for and is signed by an authorized officer of the proposed policyholder. The

proposed policyholder sends the insurer the master application, the required premium deposit, and a sample of the enrollment cards that will be completed by each employee covered by the plan. The insurer uses information from the master application to develop the master group insurance contract, which certifies the relationship between the insurer and the group policyholder.

Policy issue for group insurance involves the agent or group representative presenting the master contract to the group policyholder. The agent or representative collects the enrollment cards from covered employees and distributes certificates of coverage to each person covered under the group insurance plan.

Technology in Underwriting

Technology has greatly increased the speed, efficiency, and effectiveness of the underwriting process. Virtually all insurance companies use computers and other automated systems to facilitate underwriting, as you can see in the following examples:

- For some underwriting cases, many insurers automate the entire underwriting process through expert systems and other specialized computer systems.

- Underwriters can use integrated image processing to manage the many paper documents associated with each case. **Integrated image processing** is a computer-based approach to capture, index, store, retrieve, and distribute documents in electronic form. With image technology, a paper document is transformed into a digitized image that can be stored on a computer where it can be easily and quickly accessed.

- Underwriters use electronic data interchange (EDI) to send and receive insurance applications, inspection reports, paramedical exams, laboratory results, motor vehicle reports, MIB reports, and other information.

- Networked computers working in conjunction with EDI and integrated image processing can establish an **automated workflow**, which is an information management system that both enhances the flow of work within an organization and generates data about the procedures used to accomplish work. For example, an agent uses EDI to submit an electronic application to an insurer. The underwriter electronically gathers laboratory test results, medical information results, and other information. If the case

meets established requirements and criteria, the computer system underwrites the case and automatically produces a printed policy. Applications that do not meet the criteria for electronic underwriting are automatically forwarded to underwriters.[2]

- Underwriters use the Internet to locate information about virtually every aspect of risk assessment. Underwriters also use the company's intranet and extranet to communicate and exchange information with producers and information providers.

Although new technologies have a significant impact on underwriting, computers and other technology will never completely replace underwriters, as discussed in Focus on Technology 12-1.

Reinsuring Excess Risk

Insurance companies cannot accept all the risks presented to them without jeopardizing their financial condition. Although an insurer may issue enough policies to be able to predict—with a good deal of accuracy—the number of claims it will receive each year, the dollar amount of the claims can fluctuate significantly, especially if the company issues policies for large amounts of coverage. A series of large claims can severely damage a company's financial position. To

Focus on Technology 12-1. | **The Underwriter's Place in a High-Tech World.**

Today's competitive environment has called for changes. The realities of our dynamic industry have demanded that distribution systems be streamlined, unnecessary steps be eliminated, and products be simplified. Many companies have improved their new business workflow by installing technology able to order, collect, and present underwriting information. Technology has advanced to the point where it can even make underwriting decisions for the large number of cases that can be issued automatically.

But technology still can't underwrite the complex, high face amount cases that we see increasingly more of today. Technology hasn't advanced to the point where it can take the place of people skilled in applying both the science of probability and the art of informed judgment to a given set of facts.

Productivity gains achieved through technology have had more to do with the front end of the new business process than the back end. Small, uncomplicated cases can be issued automatically, but the decision process for large, complicated cases can be extraordinarily complex and far removed from the capabilities of existing technology. Systems installed piecemeal can wind up slowing down the process, fueling underwriters' frustrations over having to deal with both technology and paper as opposed to just paper.

In short, insurance companies still need people who understand the art and the science of underwriting. •

Source: Excerpted and adapted from Daniel M. Farrimond, "Where Have All the Underwriters Gone?" *Reinsurance Reporter* (Third Quarter 1999): 18. © 1999 Lincoln National Reassurance Company. All rights reserved.

safeguard their financial stability and still maximize the amount of risk they can safely accept, insurers use reinsurance.

Essentially, reinsurance is risk sharing for insurance companies. *Reinsurance* is a form of insurance that enables an insurer to be indemnified or reimbursed in the event of covered losses claimed under insurance policies the insurer has issued. Reinsurance is a method of sharing risks in order to decrease the severity of risks assumed by any one entity.

Basic Concepts of Reinsurance

In a reinsurance relationship, an insurance company that transfers all or part of an insurance risk is called a **ceding company**. An insurance company that transfers risk to another company is said to *cede* the risk to the other company. The company that assumes the risk from the ceding company—in other words, provides the reinsurance to the ceding company—is known as the **reinsurer** or the *assuming company*.

Reinsurance functions according to agreements between ceding companies and reinsurers. The terms of a reinsurance agreement are specified in a **reinsurance treaty**, which is a statement of the agreement between a ceding company and a reinsurer.

Insurers have many plans of reinsurance available to them, but most reinsurance coverage is yearly renewable term (YRT) insurance. For individual policies, the amount of the premium is typically based on the age and sex of the insured person and is expressed as a rate per $1,000 of risk reinsured.

The policyowners whose risks are transferred from a ceding company to a reinsurer have a contractual relationship only with the ceding company that originally wrote the business, and not with the reinsurer. An individual or a group whose risk has been transferred is usually unaware of the transfer. When a claim is submitted under the insurance policy, the reinsurer pays to the ceding company its share of any insured claims for which it has received a premium. However, the ceding company remains *legally* responsible for paying the entire benefit to the policy beneficiary.

Retention Limits

To help an underwriter determine how much financial risk the insurance company can assume on a person or group, an insurer establishes retention limits. A **retention limit** is the maximum amount of insurance that an insurer will carry at its own risk. The retention limit may be stated as the amount of loss per insured person, the amount of loss per accident or event, or total loss amounts per class

FAST FACT

The earliest recorded reinsurance contract was entered into on July 12, 1370, in the city-state of Genoa in what is now Italy. To protect the cargo of his ship from loss during a voyage from Genoa to Flanders (now Belgium), Giovanni Sacco purchased insurance from Guiliano Grillo. Using an insurance broker, Grillo then purchased reinsurance from Goffredi di Benavia and Martino Morruffo for the most hazardous part of the voyage—from Spain to Flanders. The reinsurance contract was written in Latin. There is no record of whether or not the voyage was successful.[3]

of business. Sometimes an underwriter is presented with a case that is insurable by the insurer's underwriting guidelines, but the amount of insurance coverage requested exceeds the insurer's retention limit. Rather than modify the amount of insurance approved, the underwriter sends the excess risk to a reinsurer. For instance, if an insurer's retention limit on a type of whole life coverage is $200,000 per life, a requested policy of $350,000 face amount would probably be reinsured for $150,000 ($350,000 – $200,000).

Retention limits can vary widely from insurer to insurer, ranging from as little as $10,000 per policy in small, new insurers to several million dollars per policy in large companies. Companies typically set retention limits that are lower for substandard risks and older insureds (who represent greater risk) than for standard risks and younger insureds.

Reinsurance companies also establish retention limits. When the total amount of reinsurance in force and applied for on any one life exceeds the reinsurer's limits, the reinsurer transfers the excess amount of insurance to another reinsurer. A reinsurer that assumes risks transferred from another reinsurer is known as a **retrocessionaire**. The act of transferring a risk from a reinsurer to a retrocessionaire is called **retrocession**. In such a risk transfer, the reinsurer is the ceding company and the retrocessionaire is the assuming company. A retrocessionaire pays to the reinsurer a share of any claims submitted under the retroceded coverage. Best Case Scenario 12-2 illustrates the mechanics of a reinsurance agreement and a retrocession.

Reinsurance Treaties

Each reinsurance treaty is customized to suit the business needs and objectives of the parties to the treaty. However, certain provisions are common to almost all reinsurance treaties. Every treaty contains provisions that identify the parties to the agreement, the type of reinsurance used in the treaty, the risk classes that may be ceded under the treaty, and the premium rates the reinsurer will charge for each risk class.

Certain types of reinsurance agreements have proven to be successful and have become standardized in the insurance industry. Although our discussion will concentrate on two standardized agreements—facultative reinsurance and automatic reinsurance—keep in mind that insurers and reinsurers can develop any form of reinsurance that is acceptable to both parties.

Facultative Reinsurance

Facultative reinsurance is a reinsurance agreement in which a ceding company may choose whether to submit a case or a block of cases to

Best Case Scenario 12-2.

A Reinsurance Agreement and a Retrocession.

Tom Carpenter submitted to the Best Friend Life Insurance Company an application for a $500,000 life insurance policy on his life. Best Friend underwriter Janie Grabowski found Tom to be an acceptable risk, but Best Friend's retention limit for this type of risk was $200,000. Best Friend issued the $500,000 policy to Tom, and according to the terms of its reinsurance treaty with Barrington Reinsurance Company, Best Friend ceded $300,000 of the risk to Barrington Re. However, Barring-ton Re's retention limit for this type of risk was $200,000. Barrington Re therefore ceded $100,000 of the risk to Castle Rock Reinsurance Company.

In this case, Best Friend is the ceding company, Barrington Re is the reinsurance company, and Castle Rock Re is the retrocession-aire. In exchange for ceding the $300,000 risk to Barrington Re, Best Friend paid Barrington Re a reinsurance premium. In exchange for ceding the $100,000 risk to Castle Rock Re, Barrington Re paid Castle Rock Re a reinsurance premium.

If Tom dies while the policy is in force, Best Friend is liable for paying the full $500,000 to Tom's beneficiary. Barrington Re is liable for reimbursing Best Friend for $300,000 of the death benefit. And Castle Rock Re is liable for reim-bursing Barrington Re for $100,000 of the death benefit. •

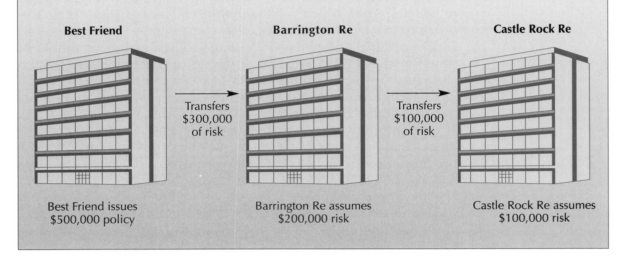

Best Friend	**Barrington Re**	**Castle Rock Re**
Best Friend issues $500,000 policy	Transfers $300,000 of risk → Barrington Re assumes $200,000 risk	Transfers $100,000 of risk → Castle Rock Re assumes $100,000 risk

a reinsurer, and the reinsurer may choose whether to accept each case or block of cases. In other words, individual risks are offered and considered on a case-by-case basis. Generally, if the ceding company offers to transfer a risk to a reinsurer, the reinsurer can conduct its own underwriting of the risk. If the reinsurer declines to assume the risk, the ceding company may submit the case to another reinsurer. Typically, risks ceded under facultative arrangements are either substandard risks or standard risks with unusual characteristics, such as extremely high face amounts.

Most ceding insurers have facultative agreements with several reinsurance companies. Once a ceding company decides to apply for facultative reinsurance on a case, the case is simultaneously submit-

ted to the reinsurers. The reinsurer offering the lowest premium is usually awarded the case.

Automatic Reinsurance

In contrast to the case-by-case underwriting of facultative reinsurance, **automatic reinsurance** is an agreement in which an insurer *must* cede specified types of cases or blocks of business to a reinsurer, and the reinsurer *must* accept the risk for those cases up to a predetermined maximum amount. An automatic reinsurance agreement generally specifies that the ceding company insures at its own risk all coverage up to its retention limit and then passes excess risks to the reinsurer.

For example, an automatic reinsurance agreement may specify that a ceding company will insure standard whole life policies up to a retention limit of $100,000 and will cede every risk over $100,000. The reinsurer must accept every ceded risk that meets the standards established in the reinsurance agreement. The ceding company can issue policies without delay, knowing that it has a guaranteed source to which to transfer excess risks.

Under an automatic reinsurance treaty, the reinsurer establishes a binding limit for each product that the ceding company can cede. A **binding limit** is the dollar amount of risk that the reinsurer obligates itself to accept under an automatic agreement without making its own underwriting assessment of the risk. In other words, the binding limit is the amount of insurance that the reinsurer *must* accept on a ceded case. For example, if the reinsurer's binding limit for a particular product is $800,000, and the ceding company submits $1 million of risk to the reinsurer, the reinsurer is obligated to accept only $800,000 of the risk. The reinsurer can choose to conduct its own underwriting of the case, and if the risk is satisfactory, the reinsurer can accept the remaining $200,000.

Key Terms

case assignment system
work division system
team underwriting
jet unit underwriting
committee underwriting
agent's statement
field underwriting manual
evidence of insurability
teleunderwriting
Part I

Part II
medical report
nonmedical supplement
paramedical report
nonmedical limits
attending physician's statement (APS)
specialized medical questionnaire
MIB, Inc.

Key Terms, continued

motor vehicle record
inspection report
table of underwriting
  requirements
underwriting manual
numerical rating system
policy issue
Request for Proposal
proposal for insurance
master application
integrated image processing

automated workflow
reinsurance
ceding company
reinsurer (assuming company)
reinsurance treaty
retention limit
retrocessionaire
retrocession
facultative reinsurance
automatic reinsurance
binding limit

Endnotes

1. Judith Yavarkovsky, "Statistical Information, Please," *Statistical Bulletin* (October–December 1999): 19.

2. Nazir Damji, "Handling Applications Electronically," in *Life and Health Insurance Underwriting* (Atlanta: LOMA, 1998), 103.

3. ICA, *Understanding Reinsurance,* Reinsurance Sub-Committee of the Individual Life Insurance Committee, International Claim Association, 1998, 1.

Customer Service

Insurance consumers can choose from many insurance companies, each offering relatively similar products. So how can an insurer stand out from the crowd and attract and retain customers? One way is by providing high quality service to its customers. *Customer service* is the broad range of activities that a company and its employees undertake to keep customers satisfied so they will continue doing business with the company and will speak positively about the company to other potential customers. Providing customer service involves learning what customers want and taking whatever reasonable steps are required to make sure they receive it.

Customer service is not only a sound business practice, but a way to fulfill certain promises in the insurance policy. For example, insurance policies typically describe the policyowner's rights with respect to making changes in the policy. An insurance company must be able to fulfill such contractual promises to policyowners.

Any employee who has contact with a customer is responsible for serving that customer. Any interaction that a customer has with the company helps shape the customer's view of the company's customer service. Thus, virtually all company employees are responsible for customer service, as illustrated in Insight 13-1.

We focus in this chapter on the services provided by the functional area within the insurance company whose primary responsibility is performing customer service activities. This department can go by many different names, such as *customer service, policyowner service, client services, member services*, and *policy administration*. The employees who perform these services are usually known as *representatives* (customer service representatives, policyowner service representatives, client services representatives, and so on). For simplicity, we will use the terms *customer service department* and *customer service representative (CSR)* to refer to any unit and employee, respectively, whose primary responsibility is to provide services to policyowners, beneficiaries, agents, and other customers.

We begin this chapter by identifying the various customers of an insurance company. Then we describe the importance of customer service and the general properties of effective customer service. Next we describe typical customer service transactions that insurance companies handle. Finally, we look at the way insurance companies evaluate their customer service and the way that technology is changing customer service delivery.

Insight 13-1. Making a Difference with Customer Service.

More than 30 years ago, a woman in Arizona wrote to my insurance company and said that, because she was a widow and was living on a fixed income, she could no longer pay the premium on her late husband's life insurance policy. It seems he had once told her that when the bill for the insurance premium comes each month, it was very important to pay it right away. So she did ... and she kept on paying for 25 years *after* he died. She did not understand the exact purpose of the bill, so she continued to pay it.

As soon as my boss, who was an actuary, heard about the letter he immediately called the woman. She told him the story of her husband's passing. He then called the local coroner's office and verified the date of her husband's death. We calculated the policy proceeds due (including interest) and the return of the excess premiums paid (also with interest). The original policy had a face amount of only $10,000, but with all the additions, the proceeds amounted to $23,900. My boss authorized that funds be wired to a bank in her area. We called an agent nearby and had him hand-deliver a check the next morning.

A short time later we received a thank-you letter from the woman along with a homemade cake. The woman was 79 years old, and that money let her live the rest of her life in relative comfort. •

Source: John F. Brancato, Assistant Vice President, New York Life Insurance Company.

The Customers of an Insurance Company

At first glance, it may appear that a life insurance company's only customers are its policyowners. After all, without policyowners, the company would not exist. But many other people who have business dealings with the insurer are customers and must be provided with quality service. Figure 13-1 shows many groups of customers and how they relate to the customer service department.

Most of an insurance company's customers can be characterized as either external customers or internal customers. As you will see, one group of customers has characteristics of both internal and external customers.

External Customers

An ***external customer*** is any person or business who (1) has purchased or is using the insurance company's products, (2) is in a position to buy or use the company's products, or (3) is in a position to advise others to buy or use the company's products. The most visible external customers are individual policyowners, group policyholders, insureds (individual and group), beneficiaries, and applicants for insurance. Later in this chapter, we will discuss some of the customer service interactions between an insurance company's customer service department and these external customers.

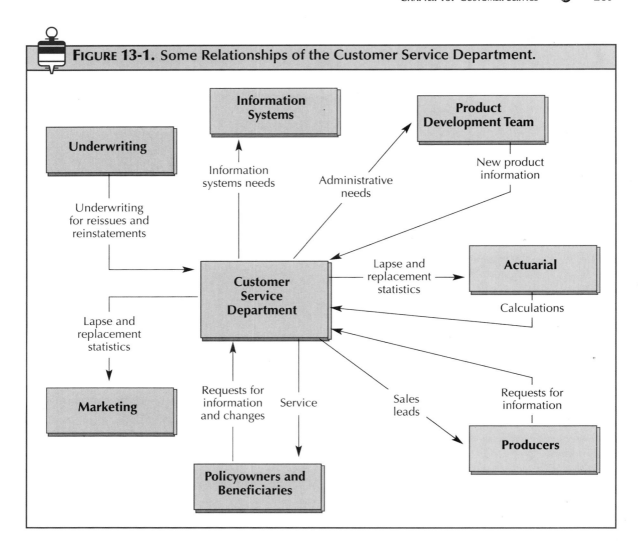

FIGURE 13-1. Some Relationships of the Customer Service Department.

Other external customers of insurance companies include the following:

- Employee-benefits advisers and other consultants who help in-surance consumers make purchase decisions

- Third-party administrators

- Stockholders of the insurance company

- State and provincial insurance regulators, with whom insurers file numerous forms and reports and who regularly examine insurance companies

Internal Customers

Internal customers are insurance company employees who receive service from other employees of the company. At any time, one employee of an insurer may be a customer of another employee in the same company. For example, when a product actuary asks the underwriting department for information regarding mortality, the actuary becomes a customer of the underwriters. Ultimately, all customer service provided by one employee to another reaches and has an effect on external customers, such as policyowners and beneficiaries.

Producers

Agents, brokers, financial planners, and other insurance salespeople have characteristics of both internal and external customers of an insurance company. Producers are external customers because they are in a position to advise consumers regarding the purchase of insurance products. Many producers, particularly brokers and general agents, are largely independent of insurer control and are free to take their business elsewhere if they are not satisfied with the service they receive from the insurer. However, producers are also considered internal customers because they are paid by the company and receive services from company employees.

Insurance companies serve producers so that producers can serve policyowners. Providing producers with prompt, accurate information is one of the most important functions of the customer service department, because the producer's relationship with the policyowner depends on the speed and quality of this service. If a producer's response to a customer is slow or incomplete, the policyowner may become dissatisfied with the company and the producer. If the producer's slow or incomplete response was the result of poor service from the company, the producer will also be dissatisfied with the company's service and in the future may place business with another insurer that provides better service. Customer service representatives also provide producers with sales leads and can help producers conserve policies that have already been sold. The customer service area can enhance the service that producers provide to policyowners and potentially bring new business to the company.

Why Is Customer Service So Important?

All businesses provide customer service; some just do a better job than others. The companies that do the best job reap the benefits. In a highly competitive environment like life insurance, many of the prod-

ucts have become similar, so price and service are the two compelling reasons for a customer to select a particular company. However, an insurer cannot reduce its prices very much without threatening its solvency, so service becomes the most distinguishing factor among insurers.

Some of the major benefits an insurance company can receive by providing quality customer service include the following:

- **Building long-term customer loyalty.** Satisfied customers generally want to continue to do business with the company. Insurance companies have found that the cost of keeping an existing customer is five to six times less than the cost of acquiring a new customer.[1]

- **Attracting new customers.** A company that has a reputation for good service can more easily attract new customers. Today's insurance customers are better educated, better informed, and more financially sophisticated than ever before, and they expect high-quality customer service. Many consumers have come to view customer service as a product unto itself, and they compare the customer service "products" of different companies before making purchase decisions.

- **Attracting and retaining producers.** Producers are more likely to do business with a company that has a reputation for good service.

- **Attracting and retaining high-quality employees.** People are more likely to want to be employed by a company that has a reputation for excellent customer service.

- **Increasing productivity.** As the quality of a company's customer service improves, employees become more productive because they spend less time dealing with problems caused by poor service.

- **Improving the company's profitability.** By attracting and retaining satisfied customers, producers, and quality employees, an insurance company can improve its profitability.

An insurance company can achieve these benefits only if it takes steps to promote a culture in which the company and all its employees make customer service a primary business goal. Among the steps that insurers have taken to promote a customer service culture are delegating more authority and accountability to front-line employees, creating systems that are customer-oriented, focusing more efforts on measuring customer satisfaction, and providing their employees with tools—such as technology, training, and education—needed to provide high-quality customer service.

Effective Customer Service

Effective customer service may have different meanings to different people, but, generally speaking, customer service is considered to be effective if it is prompt, complete, accurate, courteous, confidential, and convenient.

- Customer service is *prompt* if it is delivered in a timely manner and without undue delay. Customers expect insurers to handle their problems and inquiries promptly.

- Customer service is *complete* when the whole of the customer's problem or inquiry is resolved to the customer's satisfaction. Customers typically will not be satisfied until all facets of their requests are completed.

- Customer service employees must be careful to provide customers with *accurate* information so that customers can make educated decisions about their insurance coverage. Accurate information also helps to avoid future problems.

- Customer service is *courteous* if the employees delivering the service are polite, tactful, and attentive to the customers' feelings and situations. Courtesy is important for making customers want to continue to do business with the company.

- Insurance companies go to great lengths to ensure *confidentiality* in customer service delivery. For example, customer service representatives must verify that the people making customer service requests have the right to do so and that only authorized personnel can retrieve and view customer information and perform transactions. Confidentiality in customer service helps the insurer earn the customer's trust and strengthens the bond between the customer and the company.

- *Convenience* in customer service means that customers have relatively easy access to the services they need. Virtually all insurance companies have toll-free telephone numbers to the customer service department. Many insurers provide customer service operators from early in the morning until late at night, and some insurers have automated phone systems that allow customers to perform certain transactions any time. Some insurance companies use their Internet sites for customer service transactions.

The Changing Role of Customer Service Representatives

Performing administrative tasks has been and will continue to be an important part of a customer service representative's job. However, a growing number of insurance companies have given their customer service representatives additional responsibilities. CSRs in these companies are asked not only to fill specific customer requests but also to recognize marketing opportunities and match customer needs to the company's products and services. Figure 13-2 lists the skills and knowledge that customer service representatives should possess or develop to meet their expanding role.

Customer Service Transactions for Individual Life Insurance

The customer service department typically has both an administrative and a customer service function. In order for an insurer to administer

---

FIGURE 13-2. Skills and Knowledge for Customer Service Representatives.

- **Communication skills.** A CSR must be able to communicate effectively in writing (letters and electronic mail), on the telephone, and in person.

- **Broad interpersonal skills.** Interpersonal skills help CSRs listen effectively, negotiate solutions that are satisfactory to the customer and the insurance company, gauge the effectiveness of their service to customers, and manage numerous and varied situations.

- **Understanding customers' motivations.** CSRs must be able to understand their customers' wants and needs and to elicit enough information to satisfy customers' requests. CSRs should also understand the type of service that customers expect.

- **Computer skills.** CSRs routinely use computers to retrieve and update customer information, to process customer requests and transactions, to find information about the insurer's services and products, and to maintain records of customer transactions.

- **Knowledge of company products.** CSRs need a solid and continually updated understanding of the products the company sells in order to be able to recommend products that fill customers' needs and answer customers' questions about these products. This knowledge is especially important for nontraditional or complex products, because customers typically require more information about them.

- **Knowledge of the company's position relative to the industry.** Knowing products offered by competitors and how these products compare with those of their own company is important for customer service staff. Some customers want information about the company's financial stability, its ratings, and whether the company is involved in a merger, an acquisition, or demutualization.

---

a policy, the policy must have its own record or file. This policy record indicates the payment of premiums, the designated beneficiary, the various options the policyowner has selected, current address, and any other information necessary to provide effective service to the policyowner and beneficiary.

Departmental employees are responsible for maintaining and correcting policy records. They are also responsible for administering financial transactions that relate to policy values, informing policyowners of developments that affect their policies, and processing simple policy changes. When a customer contacts an insurer in response to a written communication from the insurer, the CSR must be aware of what was sent to the policyowner. The focus of this section is on customer service transactions between CSRs and policyowners and beneficiaries, but you should keep in mind that CSRs also provide numerous services for producers and other customers.

Customers initiate many customer service transactions. For example, a policyowner contacts the insurer to change a beneficiary designation, to add or delete coverage, or to request information about the policy. From the insurer's perspective, this type of customer service

transaction is *reactive* because the company is reacting to a policyowner inquiry.

In other cases, the company initiates the customer service transaction. These transactions are *proactive* from the company's point of view. For example, contacting a policyowner whose agent has retired and assigning the policyowner to a new agent is a proactive transaction. Because customers generally do not expect to receive proactive service, such service helps demonstrate the company's commitment to its customers' satisfaction.

Certain aspects of customer service are the same for virtually all transactions. Typically the CSR verifies that the person requesting a transaction has the authority to do so. For example, the CSR verifies the identity of the policyowner and searches the insurer's policy records to determine whether the policy has been assigned or specifies an irrevocable beneficiary. An **assignment** is an agreement under which one party transfers some or all of his ownership rights in a particular policy to another party. An **irrevocable beneficiary** is a life insurance policy beneficiary whose designation as beneficiary may not be cancelled by the policyowner unless the beneficiary consents. Some customer service transactions cannot be made without the consent of the irrevocable beneficiary.

Determining Policy Values, Policy Loans, and Policy Dividends

Life insurance policyowners often have questions about the amounts of various policy values, such as cash values, policy loan values, and the value of paid-up additions. CSRs must be able to supply information about policy values and understand the degree to which policy values are subject to taxation.

A **policy loan** is a loan made by a life insurance company to the owner of a life insurance policy that has a cash value. If the policy includes an automatic premium loan provision, under which the insurer automatically pays any unpaid premium by making a loan against the policy's cash value for as long as the cash value is sufficient to cover the amount of the premium due plus interest, a CSR notifies the policyowner when the provision takes effect.

Owners of participating policies receive policy dividends when the insurance company's claim experience is favorable. CSRs answer questions about dividends declared and dividends paid, resolve problems that policyowners have in receiving their dividend payments, and fulfill policyowners' requests to switch from one dividend option to another. Typical policy dividend options offered by life insurance companies are listed in Figure 13-3.

FIGURE 13-3. Policy Dividend Options.

- Receive the dividends in cash
- Apply the dividends to pay some or all of the premiums on the policy
- Apply the dividends to pay off some or all of the loan on the policy
- Use the dividends to buy paid-up additional insurance
- Leave the dividends on deposit with the insurer to accumulate at interest and add to the policy's cash value

---

Policy Surrenders

A policyowner may decide to discontinue paying premiums on a permanent life insurance policy and request that the insurer send the policyowner the cash value of the policy. Before processing a surrender, a CSR usually attempts to conserve the policy by suggesting an alternative to surrender, such as one or more of the following:

- The policyowner can avoid future premium payments and still continue insurance coverage by using the policy's net cash value to purchase either reduced paid-up insurance or extended term insurance.

- The policyowner can obtain funds and continue the insurance coverage by taking out a policy loan.

- The owner of a universal life insurance policy can reduce the amount of future premium payments by reducing the policy's face amount.

- The owner of a universal life policy that provides a policy withdrawal feature may withdraw part of the policy's cash value in cash.

If the policyowner still wishes to surrender the policy for its cash surrender value, the CSR calculates the cash surrender value of the policy and orders a check for that amount sent to the policyowner.[3]

Coverage Changes

Major life events such as the birth of a child, a marriage or divorce, a promotion or retirement, or a dependent child's marriage can prompt

a policyowner to change the coverage provided by a life insurance policy. CSRs administer policy coverage change requests to increase coverage and decrease coverage. For example, two ways to accomplish an increase in coverage provided under a life insurance policy are to increase the dollar amount of coverage or to add a *policy rider*, which is an amendment to an insurance policy that either expands or limits the benefits payable under the policy. Best Case Scenario 13-1 describes one way that an insurance company could handle a request for an increase in the dollar amount of coverage. Notice that the CSR sometimes collaborates with the policyowner's agent.

Noncoverage Changes

Policyowners sometimes submit requests for policy changes that do not affect the type or amount of insurance coverage, such as changing the name or address of the policyowner, changing the beneficiary designation, and transferring policy ownership rights. Some insurance companies require these requests to be in writing, but other insurance companies handle certain noncoverage requests over the telephone.

Best Case Scenario 13-1.

Increasing the Dollar Amount of Coverage.

Six months after Tom and Maria Carpenter received the Best Friend Life Insurance Company policies covering each of their lives, Maria gave birth to the couple's second child, Michael. Tom called the Best Friend customer service department to have the new baby added as a contingent beneficiary on both policies. Customer service representative Arlene Merriweather said that she would send Tom the appropriate beneficiary designation change form to complete and return to the company.

Arlene also asked Tom if he and Maria had reconsidered the face amounts of their policies in light of Michael's birth. The Carpenters discussed Arlene's suggestion and decided to increase the death benefit of both policies by $50,000. Tom asked Arlene to send him two copies of a change-of-coverage request form. Arlene also contacted Louise Chen, the Best Friend agent who had sold the original policies, and apprised her of the increase requests. Louise helped the Carpenters complete the required forms.

Because increasing the amount of coverage can increase the risk to the insurance company, Arlene had to determine whether additional underwriting would be required. To make this determination, she considered the following factors:

• The type and amount of current coverage
• The amount of additional coverage requested
• Tom's and Maria's risk classifications, impairments, ages, and occupations
• Length of time the original policies were in force

• The length of time since the Carpenters last submitted evidence of insurability
• Best Friend's underwriting guidelines

Arlene assessed the case and determined that no formal underwriting would need to be done on the case. However, the company would need confirmation that the health of the insureds had not changed since policy issue.

The additional insurance coverage resulted in premium increases for both policies. Louise advised the Carpenters of the new premium amounts. Arlene printed new policy face pages showing the coverage changes and sent these face pages and new premium payment schedules to the Carpenters. •

- When a policyowner undergoes a name change as a result of a marriage, divorce, adoption, or court order, most life insurers require that policyowners who request a name change supply proof of the change, such as a copy of the divorce decree, marriage license, or court order that effected the name change.

- An address change can signal that other customer service action should be taken. For example, if the policyowner has moved out of the selling territory of the agent who sold the policy, the insurer may attempt to assign the policyowner to a new agent.

- A CSR examines a written beneficiary change request to verify that it meets all required conditions that are designed to avoid delays and confusion in the event of a claim and to ensure that the policy proceeds are distributed according to the policyowner's wishes.

- Most insurers require that the policyowner notify the insurer in writing of an ownership change. Some insurers require such an ownership change to be added to the policy by a policy *endorsement*, which is a document that is attached to a policy and becomes part of the policy. A transfer of ownership by endorsement has no effect on the policy's beneficiary designation, although the written consent of an irrevocable beneficiary is necessary for the transfer to take place. As noted earlier in the chapter, policy ownership also may be transferred by means of an assignment.

Policy Reinstatements

After a policy has lapsed, the policyowner may ask to have the original policy reinstated. CSRs calculate the amount of back premiums due and the amount of outstanding premium loans payable, if applicable. Underwriters usually review the application for reinstatement and the evidence of insurability and determine whether or not to approve the reinstatement. In cases in which the lapse period is relatively short, the amount of insurance coverage is relatively small, and the health of the insured is unchanged, the CSR may be authorized to approve the reinstatement without assistance from the underwriting department.

Policy Replacement

Policyowners sometimes decide to replace one life insurance policy with another. *Replacement* is the act of surrendering an insurance policy or part of the coverage provided by an insurance policy in order

to buy another policy. Most states and provinces permit replacements, but they have imposed requirements that insurers and agents must meet for replacements. The customer service department helps to ensure that the replacement is carried out ethically and legally, and with full disclosure to the policyowner.

When a policyowner decides to replace one company's policy with a policy from another company, a CSR at the *replacing* company obtains from the soliciting agent a copy of the "Notice Regarding Replacement," a form that must be signed by the agent and the applicant when a replacement takes place. The CSR also notifies the *original* insurer about the replacement and provides detailed information about the applied-for policy. When the original insurer receives notification about the replacement, a CSR for that company typically contacts the policyowner and the original soliciting agent to attempt to conserve the existing policy or to offer a competitive replacement product. If the policyowner still decides to replace the original policy with one from another insurer, the CSR updates the insurer's policy records to reflect the termination of the policy. If the policy provided a cash value, the CSR calculates the net cash surrender value and sends a check in that amount to the policyowner.

Section 1035 Exchanges

A policy replacement can result in unfavorable tax consequences to the policyowner. For federal income tax purposes in the United States, a policy replacement is treated as if the original policy were surrendered. The policyowner of a policy that builds a cash value may either receive the net cash surrender value in cash or use that net cash surrender value to purchase the new policy. In either case, if the net cash surrender value is greater than the cost basis of the original policy, then the difference is considered a gain and generally is taxable as ordinary income. The **cost basis** of a life insurance policy is generally the sum of the premiums paid for the policy plus accumulated dividends less any withdrawals.

Section 1035 of the U.S. Internal Revenue Code permits the tax-free exchange of specified types of insurance policies. Such a tax-free exchange is known as a **Section 1035 exchange**. Two types of exchanges that qualify as permissible Section 1035 exchanges and, thus, are not taxable events are (1) the exchange of one life insurance policy for another life insurance policy where both policies insure the same person and (2) the exchange of a life insurance policy for an annuity. A CSR determines whether the requested replacement qualifies as a permissible Section 1035 exchange and calculates the original policy's cost basis and net cash surrender value. If the exchange is internal, the CSR also handles the administrative details of terminating the original policy and issuing the new policy. If the exchange is external,

the replacing company's CSR issues the new policy and requests the cost basis information from the original insurer's CSR.

Managing Orphan Policies

Policyowners and their agents sometimes lose contact with each other. For example, a policyowner might have moved to a location not served by the original agent, or the agent might have moved, stopped marketing the insurer's products, retired, or died. The customer service unit provides service for **orphan policies**—policies for which the original agent is no longer available to provide service. Orphan policies present a special challenge to insurers because they are more likely to be lapsed or surrendered than policies that are not orphaned. In some companies, the customer service unit attempts to assign orphan policies to new agents. Other insurers manage orphan policies from the home office. Insight 13-2 discusses one insurer's efforts to conserve the business on orphan policies.

Premium Payments

CSRs usually process policyowners' requests to increase or decrease the frequency of premium payments, to increase or decrease the amount of premium payments on flexible premium products, and to change the mode of premium payment. CSRs also send producers

Insight 13-2. Orphan Policy Management.

In the beginning of 1997, Pacific Guardian Life created a Client Relations Department to improve and enable direct client servicing to the company's orphan clients. The unit typically does not assign orphaned clients to new agents; instead it manages those clients directly from the home office. The unit is staffed with people whose backgrounds include sales, administration, customer service, and orphan management. These employees are responsible for the management, retention, relationship building, and financial-need fulfillment of the company's orphan clients. Staff members are licensed to sell insurance and so are able to market to the orphan client base in addition to performing conservation activities.

The Client Relations Department receives a daily report of newly orphaned clients. These clients are sent a letter to introduce them to their personal contact in the Client Relations Department. The mailing includes a survey card to assess each client's immediate concerns and need for additional life insurance. The Client Relations staff follows up these letters with telephone calls. Pacific Guardian also gathers extensive data about orphaned clients through surveys, telephone calls, face-to-face interviews, and the purchase of data from research firms. This detailed demographic information allows the company to precisely segment its clients and market to targeted orphaned clients. •

Sources: Judith A. Reyes, "Orphan Management," an Activity Report of the Individual Insurance Services Committee II, LOMA (September 1997); subsequent interview with Wendy P. Hanna, Manager—Client Relations Department, Pacific Guardian Life Insurance Company.

periodic lists of policyowners whose policies have lapsed because of nonpayment of premiums. Producers can then contact the policyowners and attempt to encourage them to reinstate the coverage. The premium amount that a policyowner pays for coverage sometimes changes, or premium payments cease altogether. For example, a policy may provide for a change in premium amount when the insured reaches a specified age. The insurer notifies a policyowner of a pending premium change and updates the company's records so that the amount of renewal commissions can be adjusted to reflect the new premium amount.

Allocating Funds in Variable Insurance Products

A variable life insurance product allows the policyowner to choose the investment funds in which the policy's premium payments will be invested. The performance of these investment funds determines the amounts of the policy's cash value and death benefit. CSRs carry out variable insurance policyowners' requests to (1) reallocate currently invested money from one investment fund to another and (2) allocate future premium payments.

Customer Service Transactions for Group Life Insurance

The principles of customer service for group life insurance are similar to the principles of effective customer service for individual life insurance. That is, customer service should be prompt, complete, accurate, courteous, confidential, and convenient. However, some customer service transactions for group insurance differ from the usual customer service transactions for individual life insurance. For this reason, some insurance companies devote a certain segment of the customer service unit exclusively to group insurance.

Group insurance CSRs have important duties during the installation of a new group insurance plan, including

- Providing information to and answering questions from the group contractholder and eligible group members about the plan's eligibility requirements, benefits, provisions, and premium payment schedule

- Establishing the policy's records, including the number of covered group members, the benefits stated in the contract, the date

that coverage begins for each member, and the premium rate for the policy

- Processing enrollment cards completed by group members

- Issuing certificates of coverage to the policyholder for delivery to covered group members

Once installed, a group insurance plan may be administered by the insurance company that sold the coverage, by a third-party administrator, or by the group itself. If the insurance company administers the insurance plan, the customer service unit maintains the enrollment cards and records of dates and amounts of premiums received, claims filed and paid, commissions paid, and other payments that affect the group policy. CSRs update the insurer's records as group members and their dependents are enrolled in or terminated from the plan. CSRs also handle complaints and answer inquiries from the group policyholder, the plan administrator, and covered group members.

When a group life insurance policyholder does not renew its group coverage, the group plan terminates. The customer service unit closes the files for that contract and informs the group members of their right, if any, to convert their group coverage to an individual plan of life insurance. CSRs also handle conversion requests from covered group members whose coverage terminates because they are no longer eligible for coverage under the group policy. A group member loses eligibility for coverage if he terminates his employment or is no longer a member of an eligible class of employees. When the insurer receives a completed conversion form from a covered group member who is eligible to convert to an individual insurance policy, a CSR issues an individual policy.

Evaluating Customer Service

Because keeping customers satisfied is critical to the success of an insurance company, most insurers regularly evaluate the customer service they deliver. Generally, customer service evaluations focus on the speed and the quality of customer service.

Evaluating the Speed of Customer Service

Customers today expect that when they have a problem with or question about an insurance product, the insurer will solve the problem

or answer the question quickly. This expectation puts great pressure on the insurer's customer service unit. Customers who are dissatisfied with the speed of the insurer's customer service are likely to take their business elsewhere or file a complaint with the state or provincial insurance department.

To determine whether they are delivering rapid customer service, most insurers establish benchmarks for various aspects of customer service and regularly compare their actual performance to the benchmarks. A *benchmark* for a specific process is a performance standard that has been achieved by a recognized leader in that process and that represents the company's goal for its own performance of the process. For example, an insurer may establish benchmarks for components of customer service such as

- *Wait time*, the average length of time that customers must stay on the telephone before they receive assistance

- *Call abandonment rate*, the rate at which customers who telephone the company and are put on hold to wait for assistance hang up before receiving assistance. Generally, companies can reduce their call abandonment rate by reducing the wait time.

- *Turnaround time*, the amount of time necessary to complete a particular customer-initiated transaction. Figure 13-4 summarizes a LOMA study of industry turnaround times for individual life insurance customer service transactions.

- Number of transactions completed in a defined period, such as the number of policy changes made each day, each week, or each month

- *Error rate*, a measure of the accuracy of the work done by either an individual or a team. Error rate is also a measure of the quality of work performed by the customer service unit. Typically, evaluators examine error rates in conjunction with measures of customer service speed to determine whether or not accuracy is being sacrificed in order to reduce the turnaround time.

Wherever significant deviations from a benchmark occur, management can investigate the cause and take steps to improve performance. Management should take care not to misinterpret the results. Evaluators should look at each performance measure in context, and, sometimes, in association with other measures. For example, if a particular department shows a decrease in the number of calls answered, then management should also check that department's call abandonment

FIGURE 13-4. Sample Individual Life Insurance Turnaround Times

Customer service transaction	Average Days to Complete
Cash loans	3
Cash dividends	3
Cash surrenders	7
Changes to dividend option	4
Address changes	3
Premium mode changes	3
Assignments	5
Beneficiary changes	5
Full term conversions (with or without underwriting)	9
Reinstatements (with or without underwriting)	12
Policyowner correspondence—responses to information requests	5

Source: LOMA, *Individual Life Insurance Service Turnaround Times Survey* (Atlanta: LOMA, 1999), 4–5. Used with permission.

rate. If the call abandonment rate has increased, then the decrease in calls answered is likely the result of more customers giving up on receiving service.

Evaluating the Quality of Customer Service

Customers of an insurance company expect that the services they receive are not only timely, but also effective. However, evaluating the quality of customer service is more difficult than evaluating the speed of customer service, because quality can be difficult to associate with numbers or statistics. Error rates can provide a sense of customer service accuracy, but they do not indicate the courtesy, completeness, confidentiality, and convenience of the customer service.

One way that insurance companies measure the overall quality of their customer service is to ask the customers themselves. Many insurers poll their customers by using one or more types of customer satisfaction surveys, which are designed to measure whether the company is delivering a specific type of customer service in a manner that meets the expectations of customers. Some companies (1) send out surveys

to randomly selected customers, (2) include satisfaction surveys with letters, disbursement checks, premium notices, and other communications to customers, or (3) invite customers to respond to telephone surveys at the conclusion of a customer service call. Typically these surveys are designed to elicit customers' opinions regarding the

- Friendliness and professionalism of the customer service staff

- Timeliness of the service

- Accuracy in completing the customer service request

- Overall level of service

Another way that insurers measure the quality of service is to have managers monitor customer service transactions. For example, a manager may review written correspondences between CSRs and policyowners, or the manager may listen to live or recorded telephone conversations between customers and CSRs. Insurers must follow federal and state or provincial laws and regulations regarding notification to callers about the company's call-monitoring practices. Monitoring written and telephone communications enables managers to hear or see CSRs "in action" and to rate each transaction according to the level of the CSR's listening skills, communication skills, ability to solve problems, and empathy with customers. In addition, monitoring is also a useful teaching device in that the manager can later review the conversation or letter with the CSR and point out the strengths and weaknesses of the CSR's techniques.

Some insurers use mystery shoppers, who are trained evaluators that approach or call CSRs and pretend to be customers. The mystery shopper conducts a transaction with the CSR and evaluates the way the CSR handles the transaction. In addition to being able to monitor the CSR's performance, a mystery shopper has the advantage of being able to manipulate the encounter to see how the CSR responds to various customer situations.

Another method of evaluating quality is monitoring customers' complaint letters and telephone calls. A study of the source, number, frequency, and nature of complaint letters may indicate trends in customer concerns or ongoing customer service problems. By categorizing complaints, an insurer may be able to identify and eliminate or improve the problems that are causing the complaints.

Insurers also monitor their persistency rates as a way to gauge the quality of customer service. Theoretically, a high or rising persistency rate signifies that customers are satisfied with the company's products and the quality of its customer service. Conversely, a low or declining

FAST FACT

During one year, the Pennsylvania Department of Insurance received 30,000 written complaints, 3,000 walk-in complaints, and approximately 5,000 telephone complaints.[4]

persistency rate could signify that customers are dissatisfied with the company and its products.

Technology and Customer Service Delivery

Several technologies substantially enhance the speed and quality of customer service. Computer networks and database management systems allow an insurer to capture a customer's data only once and then share it throughout the company by using a number of integrated databases (policy database, marketing database, premium billing database, claim database, and others). When information about a policy or policyowner is changed in one database, the same information is automatically updated in other company databases.

Also, some insurance companies use the Internet to provide customer service. Through the insurer's extranet, for example, policyowners can conduct certain customer service transactions for themselves. Typically, the policyowner must type in the policy number and a secret password in order to view current policy information and conduct customer service transactions, such as updating the policyowner's name or address or changing the beneficiary designation. Other insurers allow policyowners to make customer service requests via electronic mail, as an alternative to telephone or regular mail requests.

Call Centers

Many life insurance companies have established call centers to handle customer service calls. A **call center** is a customer service unit composed of telephone representatives trained to handle questions about the insurer's product lines. Some call center representatives respond only to general customer inquiries, and they direct specific inquiries to more experienced CSRs or subject matter experts. Other call center representatives are experienced problem solvers who have the training and authority to handle almost all aspects of each customer service call.

Insurers enhance their call centers with forms of **computer/telephony integration (CTI)**, which is technology that unites computer systems with telephone systems so that the two can work together as one system. One form of CTI is **automatic call distribution (ACD)**, a technology that automatically routes incoming calls to available telephone representatives. Typically, the ACD distributes a call to a specific unit or operator based on preset criteria such as the caller's area code or some other code that the caller is asked to enter to identify the type of inquiry. Another form of CTI is an **interactive voice response (IVR) system**, which answers a telephone call, greets the caller with a recorded or digitized message, and prompts the caller to respond to

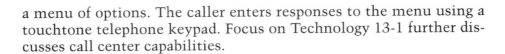

a menu of options. The caller enters responses to the menu using a touchtone telephone keypad. Focus on Technology 13-1 further discusses call center capabilities.

Customer Relationship Management (CRM)

Some insurance companies are trying to improve their customer service by implementing customer relationship management programs. *Customer relationship management (CRM)* is a combination of strategies and technology that allows an organization to manage all aspects

---

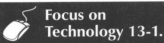 **Focus on Technology 13-1.** | **Measuring Call Center Capabilities.**

Today's call centers make it easy for consumers to do business with insurers. If your systems aren't easy to use, you're going to lose customers (and employees) to competitors with state-of-the-art systems. The following are some of the most important call center features for insurers to implement.

A Seamless, Integrated System. Advanced call center systems use an all-in-one desktop. All of the processing systems necessary to sell or service an insurance policy are accessible on one desktop, making the entire business process seamless to both the service representative and the caller. Consumer needs can be met quickly while providing the highest levels of customer service.

Insurance Call Flow Scripting. Dialogues designed for selling and servicing insurance products will reduce the time required to design your call center—most insurers will require only simple revisions. Scripts will prompt your call center representatives to ask all the questions necessary to provide once-and-done service. Scripts also can prompt representatives to make cross-selling inquiries and automatically notify the sales agent if a customer expresses an interest.

Capture Customer Feedback. Customer feedback is the most valuable resource you have. Not only do you need to know what products and services are most valuable to your customer; you should also capture complaints. Most customers don't bother to complain; they just buy from another company at the first opportunity. So when one customer does complain, you know that customer speaks for many others. To show you value their feedback, reward the customers who do call. Listen to what they say, and act on it.

Marketing Management Tools. A marketing management reporting system supplies powerful views on sales leads or cross-selling opportunities. These can be e-mailed daily to agents. When producers respond promptly to a prospect that expresses an interest, they are more likely to close the sale. Sophisticated data mining tools also are available for pinpointing the prospects and customers most likely to buy specific products and services. They can be used to identify hidden patterns in customer data that agents and brokers can use for cross-selling or up-selling.

Workflow Systems. An intelligent workflow system creates and manages daily work items for processing. With scanning and imaging capabilities, paperwork of any type can become a work item to be viewed on the call center desktop. Work items are automatically prioritized and queued to the appropriate staff resources to be processed. Workflow management reduces the time and cost of processing and improves the consistency and quality of work—benefits that are sure to satisfy your customers' desires for quality service.

Automated Access to Valuable Data Providers. Gaining online access to obtain authorization for credit card payments, motor vehicle registration verification, vehicle identification numbers, or laboratory reports to fulfill life insurance underwriting requirements will speed application processing and significantly increase the efficiency of your call center staff. •

Source: Excerpted from LaDonna Hansen, "Measuring Call Center Capabilities," *Best's Review—Technology Supplement* (May 1999): S-28. © A.M. Best Company. Used with permission.

of its relationship with a customer. The aim of CRM programs is to assist in building lasting customer relationships and in turning customer satisfaction into customer loyalty.

Insurers use CRM programs to effectively serve prospective and existing customers by getting to know who the customers are and what they need. This knowledge goes beyond basic customer identification—name, address, policy numbers, and so on—to a more comprehensive system that documents the client's complete relationship with the company. The insurer gains an understanding of all of the customer's purchases from the company, demographic information about the customer, and the customer's profitability to the company. A CRM program can become the basis for customer identification, market segmentation, target marketing, and sales forecasting.

The ability to store, access, and analyze this information enables an insurer to develop a complete profile of each customer, make informed decisions about the products and services the customer needs, and develop a service strategy that focuses on servicing customers according to their identified needs. (Figure 13-5 lists 10 essential elements of a complete customer profile.) For example, a customer who has purchased several investment products might be interested in the insurer's new variable annuity product. CRM programs also extend to producers, who are important insurance company customers. For example, a producer may have a preferred method of communicating with the company (traditional mail, electronic mail, or telephone), and a preferred method of receiving commission payments (check or direct deposit). Being aware of these preferences and acting on them helps improve the service provided to producers.

The technology involved in CRM goes by many names, such as *customer relationship management (CRM) systems, enterprise relationship management (ERM) tools, customer asset management (CAM) systems,* or *customer value management (CVM) programs.* These systems focus on the ability to access valuable client interaction information from more than one functional area. Typical components of a CRM system include the following:

- Database management tools—such as data warehouses and data mining technology—for gathering, storing, and analyzing information about customers

- Data-sharing technology that allows users throughout the organization to share customer information

- Internet technologies that capture information about customers and that allow customers to service themselves

- Call centers with computer/telephony integration (CTI)

FIGURE 13-5. Ten Essential Elements of a Comprehensive Customer Profile.

1. **Customer Relationships**—A list of the financial services and products that a customer has with the organization, including the products of other companies in a family of affiliated financial services companies.

2. **Customer Behaviors**—The types of transaction activities the customer has, such as payment patterns and preferences and past customer service inquiries made.

3. **Customer Demographics**—The demographic and other marketing-related attributes of each customer.

4. **Household Relationships**—The customer's immediate family members and relationships they have with the insurer.

5. **Customer Risk**—The risk tolerance of the customer, and the types of claims the customer has made.

6. **Distribution Preferences**—The distribution channels the customer prefers to use in transacting business. For example, does the customer prefer to use direct response, an agent, or the Internet?

7. **Propensity to Buy**—The specific products that the customer is most likely to purchase next.

8. **Customer Profitability**—The value or profitability of the customer to the company.

9. **Life Events**—Major life events occurring in the household include births, marriages, retirement, and college graduation.

10. **Satisfaction Level**—The level of satisfaction that the customer has with the insurer and its service, and anything about the service the customer would like to change.

Source: Catharine Johnson, "Customer Relationship Management: The Time Is Now," *Resource* (June 1999): 8.

Key Terms

customer service	wait time
external customer	call abandonment rate
internal customer	turnaround time
assignment	error rate
irrevocable beneficiary	call center
policy loan	computer/telephony integration
policy rider	(CTI)
endorsement	automatic call distribution
replacement	(ACD)
cost basis	interactive voice response (IVR)
Section 1035 exchange	system
orphan policy	customer relationship
benchmark	management (CRM)

Endnotes

1. Kathryn N. Holt and Mary L. Kelly, "Superior Customer Service: A Race Without a Finish Line," *LIMRA International, Inc.*, January 1997, http://members.limra.com (7 April 1999).

2. LOMA, *Individual Life Insurance Service Turnaround Times Survey* (Atlanta: LOMA, 1999), 13.

3. The amount of the cash value paid to the policyowner is found by adding the cash value of paid-up additions to the cash value amount listed in the policy, then subtracting the amount of policy loan outstanding.

4. Hedy and Les Abromovitz, "The Importance and Handling of Customer Complaints," *Resource* (June 1998): 22.

5. LIMRA, "24-Hour Customer Service Center," *LIMRA's MarketFacts* (July/August 1998): 17.

CHAPTER 14

Administering Claims

LEARNING OBJECTIVES

After reading this chapter, you should be able to

- Describe the people involved in claim administration

- Discuss the purpose and importance of an insurer's claim philosophy

- List the basic steps in the claim decision process

- Explain how coverage exclusions in an insurance policy can affect a claim decision

- Define and explain how an insurer handles a material misrepresentation

- Discuss the actions that a claim analyst takes when approving and denying claims

- Describe the purpose and procedures for a claim investigation

- Explain the duties of both the ceding company and the reinsurer when a claim is filed under an insurance policy that has been reinsured

*I*n issuing a life insurance policy, a life insurance company promises to pay a specified amount if the insured person dies while the policy is in force. The insurer carries out that promise by paying the policy proceeds following the insured's death. The functional area of an insurance company responsible for evaluating and paying claims for policy proceeds is known as the *claim department* or the *claim administration department.* The claim department reviews all relevant information about each claim, determines whether policy proceeds are payable, and, if so, the amount of the benefit payable and the correct recipient of the proceeds. This process of determining the company's liability for each claim is usually referred to as *claim administration, claim adjudication, claim handling, claim processing,* or *claim servicing.*

Managing the insurer's claim liability is an important insurance company operation because the company is legally and morally obligated to fulfill its contractual promises, but not every claim is valid. A small number of claims are submitted (1) under erroneous interpretations of policy provisions or (2) with fraudulent intent. Effective claim administration enables an insurer to meet its contractual obligations to pay valid claims promptly and accurately and helps to assure that the insurer does not pay fraudulent or improper claims. By denying invalid claims, the claim department protects the company, its policyowners, and the insurance industry from abuses of the insurance contract and helps control the cost of insurance.

The speed, courtesy, and fairness with which an insurer administers claims reflect the level of service the company provides to its customers and significantly affect customer satisfaction. An insurance company can develop a reputation—good or bad—for the manner in which it services claims.

We begin this chapter by presenting an overview of the claim function. Then we discuss the process by which life insurers review claims and make decisions as to the company's liability for each claim. We examine why and how insurers investigate some claims. Finally, we discuss the roles of the ceding company and the reinsurer in handling claims under policies that have been reinsured.

Overview of the Claim Function

To begin our discussion of claims, we will look at the staff that handle claims and the ways insurance companies typically organize their claim

operations. We also discuss the importance of establishing and abiding by a claim philosophy.

Claim Staff

Most insurance companies have vice president–level executives that oversee the claim operations for each line of the company's business. Each chief claim executive has ultimate responsibility for the administration of all claims that the company receives for that line of business. A few companies have a single chief claim officer that oversees all claims for all lines of business, and line-of-business executives report to this senior officer. Insurers typically have various levels of claim managers and supervisors within each product line.

The bulk of claim administration is handled by *claim analysts*, also known as *claim examiners, claim specialists,* or *claim approvers.* A claim analyst is trained to review each claim and determine the company's liability. Most claims are routine and are paid relatively quickly. In other cases, the claim analyst must obtain additional information in order to make a claim decision. For each claim, the claim analyst maintains a file that contains all documents relevant to the claim. The claim analyst also maintains a complete record of the progress and disposition of each claim.

Life insurance claim analysts interact directly with *claimants*, who are the people who submit claims to the insurance company. A claimant may be the beneficiary, the policyowner (if also the beneficiary), or a person acting on behalf of the policyowner or beneficiary. Because interactions between claim analysts and claimants generally occur at times when claimants have experienced a loss—personal, financial, or both—claim analysts must be sensitive in interacting with each claimant. In addition, claim analysts undergo extensive training in contract provisions and medical terminology and develop a comprehensive understanding of the legal issues that affect claims. Claim analysts are also trained to maintain complete, accurate records and to be courteous in all conversations and correspondence with claimants.

A claim analyst's experience and training determine the size and types of claims he can approve—his claim approval authority. The dollar amount of claim approval authority and the difficulty of claims reviewed generally increase as staff enhance their experience and training and are promoted from analyst trainees through the job levels to senior analyst and claim manager. Figure 14-1 lists the claim approval authority for each job level in a typical claim area. Some insurers also allow less experienced claim analysts to make initial claim decisions, and then require more senior claim analysts to review and approve those decisions. In cases involving possible fraud or unusual legal

FIGURE 14-1. Sample Levels of Claim Authority in a Claim Department.

Type of Claim	Amount of Claim Approval Authority	
Routine claims that do not involve the contestability provision	Analyst trainee	$25,000
	Analyst.	$100,000
	Sr. Claim Analyst	$200,000
	Asst. Claim Manager.	No restrictions
	Claim Manager.	No restrictions
Claims that involve the contestability provision or the accidental death benefit provision	Analyst trainee.	No authority
	Analyst.	$50,000
	Sr. Claim Analyst	$100,000
	Asst. Claim Manager.	No restrictions
	Claim Manager.	No restrictions
Claims that involve suspicion of fraud or unusual legal complications	Analyst trainee.	No authority
	Analyst	No authority
	Sr. Claim Analyst	No authority
	Asst. Claim Manager	$100,000
	Claim Manager	$1,000,000

complications, the claim decisions are reviewed by an officer of the company or a company attorney.

Claim analysts work closely with many other functional areas in the insurance company. Claim analysts are frequently in contact with the insurer's underwriters to check information submitted with an application or used to make an underwriting decision. Claim handling can also involve consulting with the insurer's medical, legal, and marketing departments and with outside investigators hired to gather or verify information related to a claim. The insurer's product development staff may use claim information to develop new insurance products, and actuaries use statistical information generated by the claim department in setting premium rates for existing and new products. The insurer's auditors use claim statistics to check the accuracy of underwriting decisions by examining the claims submitted under various products.

Many insurers assign claims to individual claim analysts or teams of claim analysts according to some specific factor such as (1) type of

product, (2) geographic region from which the claim was received, or (3) claim amount. Some insurers that allocate claims by geographic region establish regional claim offices that have the authority to handle certain types of claims up to a specified dollar amount. Claims for larger amounts are sent to a central claim department in the insurer's home office.

Electronic information systems are frequently used to evaluate and pay routine claims. An electronic system receives all relevant claim information and performs the claim handling process: making claim decisions, authorizing payment of benefits, generating benefit checks and form letters, and sending proceeds to beneficiaries and policy-owners. Insurers that install electronic claim handling systems establish limits regarding face amount and type of coverage. Claims that do not fall within these limits or that require additional information are handled manually by claim analysts or teams.

Claim Philosophy

In order to guide the decision making of claim analysts, the senior executives of an insurance company develop a *claim philosophy*, which is a precise statement of the principles the insurer will follow in conducting claim administration. Generally, a company's claim philosophy is designed to ensure that claims are handled promptly, fairly, and courteously. In developing a claim philosophy, some insurers adopt part or all of the "Statement of Principles" of the International Claim Association (ICA), an association of life and health insurance companies whose purpose is to promote efficiency, effectiveness, and high standards of performance in claim administration.

In addition to establishing a claim philosophy, insurers must comply with laws in many jurisdictions requiring insurance companies to investigate and settle claims promptly. In many states, these laws are based on the NAIC's *Unfair Claims Settlement Practices Act*, which specifies a number of actions that are unfair claim practices if committed by an insurer transacting business in the state (1) in conscious disregard of the law or (2) so frequently as to indicate a general business practice. Figure 14-2 shows the practices or acts that the NAIC Act deems to be unfair or deceptive.

In Canada, a claim must be paid within 30 days after an investigation of the claim is complete. In the United States, a majority of states require insurers to add interest to the proceeds payable if they do not pay a claim within a certain number of days after receiving sufficient proof of loss. However, the claim examination process should not be so hurried that invalid claims are approved and paid. Claim analysts should proceed in a manner that balances the conflicting objectives of swiftness and accuracy in claim handling.

FIGURE 14-2. Unfair Claims Practices Defined Under the NAIC Unfair Claims Settlement Practices Act.

The following activities constitute unfair claims settlement practices:

- Knowingly misrepresenting to claimants and insureds relevant facts or policy provisions relating to coverages at issue

- Failing to acknowledge with reasonable promptness pertinent communications with respect to claims arising under policies

- Failing to adopt reasonable standards for the prompt investigation and settlement of claims arising under policies

- Not attempting in good faith to arrive at prompt, fair, and equitable settlement of submitted claims in which liability has become reasonably clear

- Compelling insureds or beneficiaries to institute suits to recover amounts due under policies by offering substantially less than the amounts ultimately recovered in suits brought by insureds or beneficiaries

- Refusing to pay claims without conducting a reasonable investigation

- Failing to affirm or deny coverage of claims within a reasonable time after having completed an investigation related to such claims

- Attempting to settle or settling claims for less than the amount to which a reasonable person would believe the insured or beneficiary was entitled by reference to written or printed advertising material accompanying or made part of an application

- Attempting to settle or settling claims on the basis of an application that was materially altered without notice to, or knowledge or consent of, the insured

- Making claim payments to an insured or a beneficiary without indicating the coverage under which each payment is being made

- Unreasonably delaying the investigation or payment of claims by requiring both a formal proof of loss form and subsequent verification that would result in duplication of information and verification appearing in the formal proof of loss form

- Failing in the case of claim denials or offers of compromise settlement to promptly provide a reasonable, accurate explanation of the basis for such actions

- Failing to provide forms necessary to present claims within 15 calendar days of a request with reasonable explanation regarding their use

Source: NAIC, Unfair Claims Settlement Practices Act, Section 4, 1990. Reprinted with permission from the National Association of Insurance Commissioners.

The Claim Decision Process

Life insurance companies receive different types of claims, depending on the types of insurance products they sell. Handling any type of claim involves certain procedures that are unique to the underlying product. However, many aspects of the claim decision process are the

same for all types of insurance products. Generally speaking, deciding whether a claim is valid and payable involves verifying the following facts:

- Whether the policy was in force when the loss was incurred

- Whether the insured was covered by the policy at the time of the loss

- Whether the loss insured against has occurred

- Whether the loss is covered by the policy

- Whether the claim is contestable and, if so, whether the application for insurance contained any material misrepresentations

As each of the foregoing facts is verified, the claim analyst moves on to verifying the next fact. At any point in the evaluation of a claim, the claim analyst may discover a fact that invalidates the claim. In such a case, the claim evaluation process ends and the claim analyst denies the claim. Later in the chapter we describe the procedures followed when a claim is denied. If the claim analyst verifies all of the foregoing facts, then she approves the claim and follows specified procedures in paying the claim.

The process of life insurance claim handling typically begins when the claimant or the sales agent who sold the policy informs the insurance company of the insured's death. The insurer then provides the claimant with a ***claimant's statement***, also called a *claim form*, in which the claimant provides information concerning the deceased insured, including the date, place, cause, and circumstances of death. (Focus on Technology 14-1 describes the filing of claims online.) The claimant's statement typically requires the claimant to provide the following types of information:

- The names of all physicians who were consulted for any condition related to the cause of death

- Information about the deceased insured's hospital confinements within the previous five years

- The signature of the claimant or an authorized representative of the claimant on a section of the claimant's statement—known as an ***authorization to release information***—that authorizes the insurer to obtain claim-specific information from medical caregivers and institutions, government agencies, other insurers, consumer reporting agencies, and other sources

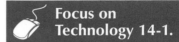

Focus on Technology 14-1.

Online Claim Filing.

Because claim processing is often a significant expense for insurers, many insurers are seeking ways to manage claim costs while providing a timely, efficient service experience for claimants. A number of insurers are using electronic claim submission programs and Internet-based tools to achieve this kind of service.

Two companies that have made significant inroads in using technology to streamline the claim process are Northwestern Mutual Life (NML) and MONY. At NML's Internet site, a person who wants to file a claim can quickly reach the life insurance claim section from the site's main page. The person is instructed to open a form called "report of the insured's death." This form requests the insured's name, address, date of birth, policy number, cause of death, date of death, place of death, other policies owned by the insured, and the filer's name, telephone number, and relationship to the in-

sured. The filer can submit the claim online and read descriptions of alternative benefit payment options.

For assistance, the filer can view a completed sample report-of-death form. The filer can also read frequently asked questions (FAQs) that help claimants complete the claim filing process without having to contact an agent or a representative of the company.

MONY's Internet site also provides access to online claim forms and assistance. The site offers lengthy responses to frequently asked death claim questions, such as the following:

• How do I file a death claim with MONY?
• What do I need to do right away?
• What documents will I need?
• What should I do within the first two weeks?
• What should I do within the first month?

• What should I do within the first six months?
• How will I receive the insurance proceeds?

The answers to these and other questions provide useful information, some of which is extraneous to the claim itself, that a survivor might not have readily available from other sources. For example, the answer to the question about what needs to be done right away includes advice on locating the deceased's will, making funeral arrangements, ordering multiple copies of death certificates, contacting the Social Security Administration, clipping obituary notices, contacting the deceased's bank, consulting an attorney, and arranging for someone to watch the house during the funeral service. Claimants can also provide death claim information and file the claim form online. •

Source: Adapted from Jean C. Gora, "Life Companies Expand Online Service Functions," *Resource* (April 1999): 46–48. Used with permission.

Laws in many jurisdictions require that claimant's statements request only information that the insurer reasonably needs to make a claim decision, and the forms should be simple enough for claimants to complete without undue hardship.

Verification of Policy Status

Upon receipt of a claimant's statement, the claim analyst verifies that the policy under which the claim was filed was in force when the insured died. If the coverage was not in force at the time of the loss, the claim analyst denies the claim. Verification of policy status is usually a problem only when the death occurred near the date that the insurance coverage began or near the date that the insurance policy lapsed or was surrendered. Claim analysts must carefully determine the exact date that the coverage began or ended.

Verification of Coverage of the Insured

The claim analyst verifies that the deceased person was covered under the policy. If the deceased was not insured, then the claim analyst denies the claim. This step is necessary to protect the insurance company from paying invalid claims that have been filed by mistake or for fraudulent reasons. Policies that cover more than one person, such as family insurance policies and group insurance policies, account for the majority of mistakenly filed claims. For example, a beneficiary who honestly—but mistakenly—believed that the deceased person was covered under a family life insurance policy may mistakenly file a claim for the policy proceeds.

Verification of the Loss

For a life insurance claim, the claimant must supply proof of loss—that is, evidence that the loss insured against has occurred—and information about the insured's death. One form of proof of loss is a ***death certificate***, which is a document that attests to the death of a person and that bears the signature—and sometimes the seal—of an official authorized to issue such a certificate.

Life insurers in the United States generally accept an official death certificate—either the original or a certified copy—as proof of loss. Life insurers in Canada generally accept as proof of loss an official death certificate, an attending physician's statement, a coroner's certificate of death, a hospital's certificate of death, or, for lower face amount policies, a funeral director's certificate. (Insight 14-1 further discusses proof of loss documents.) In verifying the proof of loss, claim analysts remain mindful of fraud. For example, in an attempt to collect policy benefits while an insured person is still alive, a policy beneficiary may

 Insight 14-1. **Liberalized Proof of Loss.**

As a result of consumer demand for speedier claim service, a few life insurance companies have liberalized their proof of loss requirements. For example, some insurers accept non-original death certificates as proof of an insured's death. These companies release policy proceeds upon receipt of a faxed death certificate on condition that the original certificate is provided later. Some insurers allow claim analysts to contact the newspaper in which the deceased insured's obituary was placed. The claim analyst verifies certain identifying information and, upon receipt of a faxed or mailed claimant's statement, releases all or part of the policy proceeds to the beneficiary before receiving a death certificate. •

Source: Kimberley A. Jones, "Slippery Slope or Just Reality in the 21st Century?" *Life Insurance Workshop Reports,* International Claim Association, 1997, 29–31.

submit a false claimant's statement along with a fictitious death certificate.

Although verifying proof of loss is routine in most cases, a small percentage of claims require the claim analyst to conduct further investigation. Two such situations arise when the insured (1) dies outside of the United States or Canada or (2) disappears.

The Insured Dies Outside of the United States or Canada

When the insured dies abroad, documents offered as proof of death may be difficult to obtain or to authenticate, or they may be written in a language other than English. The claim analyst may need to hire an independent translator to translate the proof of loss documents. Additional investigation and care are usually required in order to verify the validity of the claim. Because formalities and procedures for registration of death in other countries are not always as rigorous as those in the United States and Canada, situations in which the insured dies abroad increase the likelihood of fraud, as seen in Insight 14-2.

The Insured Disappears

When an insured disappears, the claimant is unable to present proof of the insured's death. The circumstances of the insured's disappearance—whether or not the disappearance can be explained—generally determine how the claim analyst proceeds.

Explainable Disappearance. If the insured disappeared as a result of a specific peril that can reasonably account for the disappearance, the insured may be presumed dead. An example of this circumstance is that the insured was on board an airplane that crashed in the ocean, and the insured's body was not recovered. In such a case, the claim analyst would probably accept the claimant's statement and attached reports of the accident as proof of the disappeared insured's death and would then continue to evaluate the remaining aspects of the claim.

Unexplainable Disappearance. If the insured disappeared under unverifiable circumstances, the insurance company usually denies a life insurance claim that is filed immediately after the disappearance. Before the insured can be presumed dead, a certain number of years must pass, such as five or seven years, depending on the jurisdiction. At the end of the required waiting period, if there is no evidence of the insured's reappearance, the claimant can petition the court for an order presuming the insured's death. A court order stating that the insured is presumed dead establishes proof of the insured's death. If all premiums had been paid to keep the policy in force during the entire

Insight 14-2. Making a Killing by Dying Abroad.

An African Gold Coast citizen arrived in Washington, D.C., and was hired as an interpreter for his native country's embassy. After a couple of years, he became a United States citizen and invited his father to join him and live in Washington.

Soon after the elder's arrival, the son and the father purchased a large life insurance policy on the father. About three years later, the father died of a heart attack while back in his homeland. The son filed for death claim proceeds and provided documents certifying the death.

Because of the circumstances, the insurance company hired a claim investigator with experience in Africa. Adapting his style to the country's culture, the investigator skillfully gleaned information from the chieftain of the village where the insured had allegedly died. The investigator learned that the insured had indeed died in his homeland—two years before the policy was issued.

Developing a claim file for deaths that occur on foreign soil differs from domestic claim inquiries in the amount of documentation gathered, the level of expertise needed, and the expenses involved. The proofs of death needed for substantiation are more extensive, and the claim analyst usually needs to be more proactive and creative.

Hiring a competent investigator adds to the cost, but limiting the scope of an investigation in order to save money is not prudent in today's environment. An investigator goes on-site to conduct interviews and confirm burial sites or cremation arrangements. A reputable, experienced investigator will be aware of cultural distinctions that can go undetected by a claim analyst. Weekly and sometimes daily follow-up with the investigator is vital to ensure that investigations don't prevent legitimate claims from being paid in a timely manner.

Some signs indicate that a claim might be fictitious. One is that the claim is for a newly issued policy or a policy that just passed the threshold of contestability. Another sign is an unusual circumstance surrounding the death. Other clues that should arouse suspicion include

• The insured's body is not found (indicating a possible disappearance)
• The insured dies in an obscure country
• Proof of loss documents are questionable

• Multiple small policies were issued on the insured around the same time
• There is evidence of over-insurance
• The notice of claim is late
• The insured resided within North America only briefly
• The beneficiary pressures for payment of the proceeds
• The claimant knows the exact documents to provide to the claim analyst
• The claimant fails to produce documents that should be readily accessible
• The insured was cremated
• The insured was buried in a foreign country that is neither the place of birth nor the residence of the family

As you build the case file, develop the story. Talk to the claimant about why the deceased was outside the country. With whom was the deceased traveling? What happened in the days prior to the death? And, most importantly, who identified the body? Regardless of what you hear, don't believe any statements without corresponding documentation—after all, anyone who defrauds is prepared to lie. •

disappearance, the claim analyst will accept this proof of loss and will proceed with the claim evaluation process.

Verification of Policy Coverage of the Loss

The claim analyst next determines whether the loss was covered by the policy. This step may take place before the claim analyst verifies that the loss occurred. For example, if the claim analyst receives a

claimant's statement showing a loss that is clearly excluded from the policy, the claim analyst would probably deny the claim before verifying whether the loss actually took place.

Verifying policy coverage of the loss requires an examination of the policy and any coverage exclusions contained within it. If the insured's death occurred as a result of an excluded activity or condition, the claim analyst denies the claim. Many insurance companies exclude deaths that result from acts of war, both declared and undeclared. Insurers generally exclude deaths that result from specific high-risk occupations or hobbies in which the insured is engaged that are specifically named in the policy.

Most life insurance contracts also contain a suicide exclusion. This exclusion generally states that if the insured dies as a result of suicide within a certain period—usually one or two years from the date the policy was issued—the insurance company is not liable for paying the policy proceeds. If death occurs by suicide after the exclusion period expires, the insurer is liable for the proceeds. The suicide exclusion protects the insurance company from people who, at the time they purchase insurance, intend to commit suicide.

When a claim analyst receives a claim showing that the insured person died during the suicide exclusion period, the claim analyst investigates to determine whether the cause of death was a suicide. Courts have maintained that the burden is on the insurance company to prove that an insured committed suicide. If the insurer proves that the insured died by suicide, the insurer returns the amount of the premiums paid for the insurance coverage, less the amount of any outstanding policy loans.

Investigation of Contestable Claims

For each claim, the claim analyst considers whether the claim is a **contestable claim**, also known as a *resisted claim*—that is, a claim that arises when an insured dies during the policy's contestable period. Life insurance policies in the United States and Canada typically provide a period of two years following policy issuance, known as the **contestable period**, during which the insurer has the right to cancel or rescind the policy if the application for insurance contained a material misrepresentation. A material misrepresentation occurs when a proposed insured partially or fully withholds important information relevant to the initial underwriting decision to approve or decline coverage. A **material misrepresentation** is a misrepresentation of fact such that, had the insurer known the truth at the time of application, it would have made a different underwriting decision. In most U.S. states, once the contestable period has expired, the insurer cannot contest the validity of the policy for a material misrepresentation. In Canada and in some

states, an insurer may *at any time* contest the validity of an insurance policy if it can demonstrate that the material misrepresentation was made for the purpose of defrauding the insurance company. Figure 14-3 lists examples of misrepresentations that are material to a life insurer's acceptance of a risk.

Upon receipt of a contestable claim, a claim analyst investigates the possibility that the application for the policy contains a material misrepresentation. If a material misrepresentation is discovered, the law allows the insurer to rescind the policy under certain circumstances. A *rescission* is the legal process under which an insurer seeks to have the insurance contract declared void from the beginning on the basis of a material misrepresentation. The effect of a rescission is to restore the insurer and the policyowner to their precontract positions, so the insurer returns the premiums paid for the policy minus any unpaid policy loans. In many jurisdictions, the cause of the insured's death does not have to be related to the misrepresented information in order for the policy to be rescinded. Rescinding a policy requires considerable cooperation among the claim, underwriting, and legal areas (1) to verify that the insurer followed correct procedures at the time of issue and the time of claim, and (2) to make a fair and justifiable evaluation of the underwriting action that would have taken place originally had information not been misrepresented.

Making a Claim Decision

After reviewing the claimant's statement, proof of loss, and other relevant documents, a claim analyst is prepared to make a decision as to

FIGURE 14-3. Misrepresentations About an Insured That Can Be Material to the Insurer's Acceptance of the Risk.

Category of Misrepresentation	Example
Health	Failure to disclose a known medical impairment
Occupation or avocation	Failure to disclose a dangerous job or hobby
Habits	Failure to disclose past abuse of alcohol or controlled substances
Number of traffic violations	Misstatements of the number or severity of moving violations or collisions
Other insurance applications denied or rated	Concealing information about insurance applications that have been denied, assigned to a high risk class, or charged an additional premium

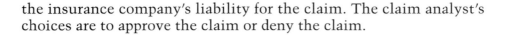

the insurance company's liability for the claim. The claim analyst's choices are to approve the claim or deny the claim.

Approving the Claim

If the claim analyst finds no basis on which to deny the claim, the decision is to approve the claim. Once this decision is made, three steps in the claim handling process remain:

- Calculating the amount of the policy benefit payable

- Determining the person or persons entitled to receive the benefit

- Determining how to distribute the proceeds

The insurer has both a legal and an ethical responsibility to ensure that the policy proceeds are paid appropriately and promptly.

Calculating the Benefit Amount. Usually, the amount of the benefit payable under a life insurance policy is easily determined. For most claims, the amount of the benefit payable is equal to the basic death benefit, which usually is the face amount of the policy. In some cases, however, the basic death benefit is not the policy's face amount. For example, if the policy was in force under a reduced paid-up insurance nonforfeiture benefit, then the basic death benefit is less than the policy's face amount. The basic death benefit of some universal life insurance policies is equal to the policy's face amount plus the accumulated cash value. The death benefit available under a variable life insurance policy fluctuates according to the performance of a separate account fund.

The claim analyst also has to consider factors in addition to the basic death benefit. Some of these factors increase the amount of the benefit payable, while other factors decrease the amount of the benefit payable. The following amounts are added to the basic death benefit:

- Premiums paid in advance

- Accumulated policy dividends

- Policy dividends declared but unpaid

- Paid-up additional coverage

- Accidental death benefits

The following amounts are deducted from the amount of the death benefit payable:

- Outstanding policy loans

- Accrued policy loan interest

- Premiums due and unpaid

To illustrate the calculation of the benefit amount payable, assume that a policy's face amount is $50,000. The policy has a $1,000 policy loan outstanding, along with $50 of accumulated policy loan interest and $500 in accumulated policy dividends. The correct benefit amount payable would be $49,450, calculated as follows: $50,000 – $1,000 – $50 + $500 = $49,450.

Claims for *accidental death benefits*, which are paid in addition to the basic death benefit if the insured dies as a result of an accident, can be challenging for a claim analyst to administer. Evidence supporting a claim for accidental death benefits may not always be clear; for example, what initially appears to be an accidental death may in fact not be accidental. Suppose an insured person is hiking in the mountains along a high ledge and falls to his death. If the insured slipped and fell, the death would be accidental. But the death could also be a suicide (if the insured jumped) or a homicide (if the insured was pushed or otherwise made to fall).[1] Claim analysts examine all facts of the case, autopsy reports, medical records, and police reports in order to gather enough information to determine whether accidental death benefits are payable.

Most life insurance policies limit accidental death benefit coverage to accidents that directly cause the insured's death. However, sometimes it is difficult to determine whether the accident caused the death or whether some natural factor caused the death, which then produced the accident. For example, if a person skiing near the edge of a trail is involved in a fatal collision with a tree, it may seem that the collision—an apparent accident—caused the death. However, an autopsy could reveal that, shortly before the accident, the skier suffered a heart attack, which caused his death and sent him hurtling into the tree. In this situation, the insured's death was a natural event, not accidental, and the accidental death benefit is not payable.

The claim analyst also must adjust the amount of the benefit payable if the insured's age or sex was misstated on the policy application. Most life insurance policies include a misstatement of age or sex provision that specifies how the insurance company handles such a misstatement. Typically, if the insurer does not discover the misstatement of age or sex until after the insured's death, the amount of

benefit payable is adjusted to the amount the premiums actually paid would have purchased at the correct age or sex according to the company's published premium rates on the date the policy was issued. For example, if an insurance application shows the insured person to be age 40 at the time of policy issue, but the claim analyst discovers that the insured was actually age 45 at policy issue, the death benefit would be reduced to the amount that the premiums paid would have purchased for a 45-year-old insured.

Determining the Proper Recipient of the Benefits. After calculating the correct benefit amount, the claim analyst determines the recipient of the proceeds. In most cases, the company is able to distribute the policy proceeds in exactly the way specified by the policyowner. That is, the proceeds are payable to the primary beneficiary or beneficiaries named in the policy. If the primary beneficiary(ies) predeceased the insured, the proceeds are payable to the contingent beneficiary or beneficiaries. If no beneficiaries are alive at the time of the insured's death, the policy proceeds are generally payable to the estate of the policyowner.

Some claims arise in which simple distribution of the proceeds is not possible. For example, the beneficiary may be a minor or may be otherwise disqualified by law from receiving the proceeds. Another difficult situation occurs when the insurer receives multiple claims for the policy, and the insurer cannot determine from its records the identity of the proper payee because the beneficiary designation is ambiguous. This situation of conflicting claimants is particularly troubling because, if the insurer pays the proceeds to one claimant, and if another claimant later proves to have a superior claim, the insurer may be forced to pay the proceeds a second time.

When conflicting claimants exist, the claim analyst consults with the insurer's legal department and conducts a thorough investigation according to the company's procedures for handling conflicting claimants. The claim analyst notifies each claimant of the investigation and the facts of the case. Sometimes, conflicting claimants can reach a written agreement among themselves, and the insurer pays the proceeds according to the terms of this agreement.

If the claimants cannot reach an agreement and the insurer is unable to identify the proper payee, the claim analyst initiates the legal process known in the United States as interpleader. **Interpleader** is a procedure by which the insurer pays the policy proceeds to a court, advises the court that the insurer cannot determine the correct recipient of the proceeds, and asks the court to determine the proper recipient or recipients. In Canada, interpleader may be used (1) when there are disputing beneficiaries, (2) when the named beneficiary is a minor, and (3) when the beneficiary cannot be found. Interpleader eliminates the

risk that the insurer may have to pay proceeds more than once for the same policy. However, the legal expenses associated with interpleader can be high.

Determining the Manner in Which to Distribute the Policy Proceeds. Insurance companies usually distribute the proceeds of a life insurance policy in a lump sum by sending the beneficiary a check for the total amount of proceeds payable. Alternatively, the claim analyst can arrange to have the funds deposited into a ***retained asset account (RAA)***, an interest-bearing money market checking account that is fully guaranteed and is managed by the insurer through a bank intermediary. The beneficiary can draw on the proceeds immediately by writing a check for any amount up to the balance of the account. The RAA provides the beneficiary with convenient access to the policy proceeds, competitive interest rates, and safety of principal. In some jurisdictions, the beneficiary's consent must be obtained before an RAA can be set up.

Insurers also provide several settlement options that allow the policyowner or the beneficiary to specify alternative ways of receiving the policy proceeds. Figure 14-4 describes common settlement options: the interest option, the fixed-period option, the fixed-amount option, the life income option, and other options.

If the proceeds are to be distributed through the fixed-period or fixed-amount option, the claim analyst sends the beneficiary an ***installment certificate*** that specifies the amount of each payment and/or the period during which payments will be made. If the policy proceeds are to be left on deposit with the insurer, the claim analyst sends the beneficiary a ***statement of indebtedness***, which specifies a minimum interest rate that the insurer will pay on the proceeds and the frequency with which the insurer will make interest payments to the beneficiary.

FIGURE 14-4. Life Insurance Policy Settlement Options.

- **Interest Option:** The insurer pays interest on these proceeds to the payee, and the entire proceeds are eventually payable after an agreed-upon period or at the death of the payee, if sooner.

- **Fixed-Period Option:** The insurer pays the policy proceeds and interest in a series of equal installments for a period of time specified by the policyowner.

- **Fixed-Amount Option:** The insurer pays the policy proceeds and interest in a series of equal payments specified by the policyowner for as long as the proceeds last.

- **Life Income Option:** The insurer pays the policy proceeds and interest in a series of periodic installments over the payee's lifetime.

- **Other Options:** The policy proceeds may be payable in any other method to which the payee and the insurer agree.

Denying the Claim

Although insurers approve almost all life insurance claims, they deny claims in the following situations:

- The policy was not in force when the insured died.

- The deceased person was not covered under the policy.

- The claimant could not furnish an acceptable proof of loss.

- The cause of death was excluded from coverage.

If the claim analyst decides to deny a claim, he typically asks a member of the legal department to review and approve the denial. If the legal department agrees with the claim decision, the claim analyst notifies the claimant in writing of the reasons for the decision. The claimant also is informed that the insurer will re-examine the claim if the claimant can provide additional facts that might refute the information on which the denial was based.

A claimant who disputes a claim denial may sue the company. If the dispute goes to court, the claim area works with the insurer's attorneys to provide information needed to defend the case. If the court finds that the insurer improperly denied the claim, the insurer will be required to pay the policy proceeds to the claimant. The insurer may also be required to pay the claimant's legal expenses and sometimes payments for damages.

Life insurance companies try to prevent the improper denial of claims by

- Requiring ongoing education and training of all claim staff regarding changes to laws that affect claim administration

- Communicating claim decisions promptly and clearly to claimants

- Adhering to relevant laws affecting unfair claim settlement practices

Claim Investigation

Most life insurance claims require only routine handling. However, unusual claim situations can arise. An insurer's liability for a claim may not be determinable solely from the claimant's statement and proof of loss document, the appropriate payee may not be readily apparent, or the claim analyst may have reason to doubt some aspect of

the claim. In situations such as these, the claim analyst needs additional information in order to make a claim decision. The process of obtaining the additional information necessary to make a claim decision is known as *claim investigation*. The information can come from a variety of sources, such as medical records, motor vehicle records, criminal court records, autopsy reports, and investigative consumer reports.

Claim investigation does not itself determine the merit of a claim but rather supplies the information necessary for the claim analyst to reach a claim decision. Most claim investigations involve short, simple searches such as checking a medical record or interviewing a medical provider. Claim analysts usually perform these brief investigations.

When a claim requires more extensive investigation, the claim analyst may be able to perform the investigation from the company office. In some cases, however, a field investigation is conducted in the insured's place of residence or the place where the death occurred. To handle extensive investigations, some insurance companies have their own Special Investigative Units (SIUs) comprised of representatives of the claim, legal, and internal audit areas of the company, as well as internal investigators and outside investigators with whom the insurer has contracted. Insurers may also seek investigative assistance from reinsurance companies that have covered the policies under investigation. Because reinsurers have a financial interest in the outcome of a claim investigation, they are generally willing to share their expertise and to participate in the investigation. We discuss reinsurance aspects of claims later in this chapter.

The extent of a claim investigation depends on a number of factors, including the following:

- **The circumstances of the death.** Unusual or mysterious deaths can warrant extensive investigation.

- **The amount and type of information already available.** The less information the claim analyst has about a case, the more investigation is necessary.

- **The age of the insured.** Causes of death that are unusual in relation to the insured's age warrant more investigation. For example, a 30-year-old insured dying of an apparent heart attack typically requires more investigation than a 60-year-old insured dying of a heart attack.

- **The place where the loss occurred.** Deaths that occur abroad generally require more investigation than deaths that occur domestically.

- **The length of time the policy was in force.** When the deceased dies during the policy's suicide exclusion period or contestable period, investigation is more likely than when death occurs after these periods have expired.

- **Policy provisions.** Investigation is more likely when a policy contains supplemental coverages or certain exclusions.

- **The face amount of the policy.** Policies with higher face amounts are subject to more detailed investigation than policies with lower face amounts.

Claim investigations can be expensive. In addition to the salaries of staff members involved in the investigation, costs can include travel expenses and the use of independent investigators. Generally, the more complex the investigation, the higher the cost involved. Insurance companies must continually balance the cost of claim investigations with the benefits these investigations can provide.

Best Case Scenario 14-1 illustrates the use of a claim investigation to resolve a death claim.

Claim Fraud

Claim investigation is typically necessary when a claim analyst suspects *claim fraud*, an action by which a person intentionally uses false information in an unfair or unlawful attempt to collect benefits under an insurance policy. Any person who is in a position to influence a claim decision and benefit from an approved claim can commit claim fraud. Such a person can be an insured, a beneficiary, a medical provider, an insurance agent, or an employee of the insurance company. Fraudulent claims cost the insurance industry billions of dollars each year, increasing insurers' costs of doing business and thereby increasing the cost of insurance for all people. Insurance companies always investigate claims in which fraud is suspected.

Some states require insurers to form Special Investigative Units to investigate suspected cases of fraud. SIU staff members receive training in detecting and investigating insurance claim fraud and in applying the provisions of unfair claim practices statutes. Some state insurance departments have established their own fraud investigation units. States typically require insurers to report cases of alleged fraud to the state insurance department for further investigation and prosecution.

Best Case Scenario 14-1.   **Resolving a Death Claim.**

Tom and Maria Carpenter were the owners and beneficiaries of Best Friend life insurance policies on each other's lives. Each policy contained a two-year suicide exclusion period and a two-year contestable period. Attached to each policy was an accidental death benefit rider containing a drug exclusion provision. This provision stated that accidental death coverage for death caused by drugs would be excluded unless such drugs were taken as prescribed for the insured by a physician.

A year and a half after the policies were issued, Tom fell off a ladder while cleaning the gutters of his house. He suffered a compound fracture to his left leg, requiring surgery and a short hospital stay. He was released from the hospital to continue recovering at home. Tom's attending physician prescribed the drug Lortab, with instructions to take one or two tablets every four to six hours as needed for pain. Tom was further instructed to take the tablets with food but not to take them with alcohol or other medication, as the combination of alcohol and the drug could potentially result in loss of life. These instructions and warnings were also contained on the written product information provided by the pharmacy that filled the prescription.

Three days after his release from the hospital, Tom spent the day alone at home while Maria went to work and their children were in child care. Upon her return home that evening, Maria found Tom on the couch, unconscious and not breathing. The prescription bottle of Lortab and three empty beer bottles

were on the coffee table in front of the couch.

Maria immediately called for an ambulance and then the police. The ambulance arrived in moments and took Tom to the hospital where an emergency room physician pronounced Tom dead. The physician ordered an autopsy and toxicology report to determine the cause of death. The medical examiner's toxicology report revealed evidence of Lortab and alcohol in Tom's bloodstream. According to the report, the effect of either substance acting independently would not have been fatal to Tom. However, the alcohol and Lortab in combination created a synergistic reaction that caused Tom's death. The medical examiner classified the cause of death as "undetermined"; in other words, the autopsy alone was inconclusive as to whether the death was an accident or a suicide. A police inspection of the death scene ruled out the possibility of homicide.

The Claim Investigation
Two weeks later, Maria submitted a claimant's statement and death certificate to Best Friend for the basic death benefit and the accidental death benefit. She maintained that the accidental death benefit was payable because Tom's death was accidental—he had not intended to kill himself.

Best Friend claim analyst Marjorie Passodelis received the case and reviewed the claimant's statement and death certificate. Because she could not determine Best Friend's liability for the claim from these two documents, and because the loss occurred within the policy's suicide exclusion period and the

contestable period, Marjorie ordered a claim investigation.

The investigation was to consider four possible scenarios:
1. The insured died as a result of a suicide during the policy's suicide exclusion period. Result: No benefits would be payable, and the premiums paid would be refunded to the claimant.
2. The death occurred during the policy's contestable period, and the application for insurance contained a material misrepresentation. Result: The policy would be rescinded and the premiums paid would be refunded to the claimant.
3. The death was accidental, but the prescription drugs were not taken in the manner prescribed by the physician, and therefore the death was excluded from accidental death coverage. Result: The company would be liable to pay the basic death benefit but not the accidental death benefit.
4. The death was accidental, and the death was not excluded from the accidental death coverage. Result: The company would be liable to pay both the basic death benefit and the accidental death benefit.

Marjorie informed Maria by telephone and follow-up letter that Best Friend would immediately begin an investigation to determine its liability for the claim. Marjorie also said that she would provide Maria with regular status letters updating the progress in the investigation. Marjorie then notified Best Friend's Special Investigative Unit (SIU) of this case, and the SIU assigned Craig Powell to investigate. Craig's investigation focused on gathering enough information to resolve two related issues: Was the death a

---

Best Case Scenario 14-1. Resolving a Death Claim (continued).

suicide? If not, did the death met the company's definition of accidental?

Death as Suicide?

Craig obtained the autopsy and toxicology reports from the medical examiner and the police department's report of its findings. Craig's initial investigation into the possibility of suicide focused on certain questions: Was a suicide note found? Was there any evidence that Tom had been depressed? Were there other documents or evidence to indicate that Tom might be putting his personal affairs in order or making arrangements for his family after his death? Had he recently drawn up or revised a will?

To gauge Tom's recent state of mind, Craig conducted numerous interviews with the people closest to Tom, such as Maria, Tom's co-workers, his close friends, and the physician who treated his broken leg. Craig performed a database search of public records to learn additional personal and financial information about Tom, such as possible bankruptcy information, sales of property, civil litigation, and criminal records. Craig also ran a credit report on Tom to determine whether he had any un-usually large debts or other financial problems.

Death as Accident?

In investigating the accidental death aspect of the claim, Craig followed Best Friend's guidelines for investigating accidental drug cases. Craig obtained answers for a checklist of questions about the insured, the drug, and the circumstances of the death.

• What was Tom's general physical condition?

• What is the name of the drug and the physician who prescribed it?

• Why and when was the drug prescribed?

• How long had Tom been using the drug in question and in what quantities?

• Did Tom use any other drugs?

• Were there any previous episodes of overdose?

• Had the prescription been re-filled and, if so, in what quantity?

• Does the pharmacy where the prescription was filled have proof that drug manufacturer's written warnings—including potential loss of life if the drug is combined with alcohol—were given to Tom?

• What were the results of the toxicology report?

• What was the position of Tom's body?

• Was there any evidence of attempts to call for help?

The Claim Decision

Craig forwarded his findings to Marjorie. She analyzed the information and compared it with the information contained in Tom's application for insurance. She reached the following claim decision:

• No misrepresentations were evident on the application.

• Tom had not intended to take his own life when he combined the alcohol and the prescription drug. Therefore, the death was not a suicide, and the basic death benefit was payable.

• Tom had ingested the Lortab with alcohol; thus, he had not taken the prescription in accordance with the verbal instructions of the physician and the written instructions of the pharmacy. Therefore, accidental death coverage was excluded by the drug exclusion provision contained in the accidental death benefit rider. Best Friend had no liability for paying the accidental death benefit.

Marjorie notified Maria in writing of the claim decision. •

Confidentiality

Although insurers go to great lengths to protect themselves, the public, and the insurance industry from fraudulent or mistaken claims, they must take care to follow all laws governing a person's right to privacy. Insurers may use only lawful, reasonable, and ethical means of obtaining information when investigating claims. In most cases, conducting an investigation under a false pretext is prohibited in many jurisdictions. Claim analysts must also protect the confidentiality of information gathered during a claim investigation.

Claims on Reinsured Policies

As you know, insurance companies can transfer a portion of their life insurance risks to reinsurance companies. Like a ceding company, a reinsurer must carefully manage its claim liability. When a ceding company approves a life insurance claim, the company pays the full amount of the policy proceeds to the beneficiary and then requests reimbursement from the reinsurer for the amount of the risk that was reinsured. Because reinsurers have a keen interest in which claims are approved and the amount of the proceeds payable, a reinsurer's claim staff maintains close contact with claim analysts of the ceding companies whose risks they assume.

Notification of Claims

Most reinsurance treaties require that the ceding company notify the reinsurer promptly when the ceding company receives a claim. Timely notification is beneficial to both the ceding company and the reinsurer.

- Prompt notification gives the reinsurer ample time to verify its liability and resolve any administrative questions. Later, when the ceding company requests reimbursement for the claim under the terms of the reinsurance treaty, the reinsurer is in a position to rapidly fulfill the reimbursement request.

- Reinsurers' claim staff are experienced in the medical, legal, and investigative aspects of claim handling and can greatly assist the ceding company's claim analysts in deciding the validity of claims.

- The reinsurer may be alerted to situations involving multiple claims submitted by the same insured to different ceding companies. The reinsurer can advise its ceding company clients of this fact, which is particularly important when some or all of the claims are contestable, the claims involve large face amounts, or fraud is suspected.

Claim Decisions

The reinsurer is not a party to the underlying insurance contract and therefore has no authority to approve or deny a claim. The final decision about a claim rests solely with the ceding company. However, the reinsurer can make a claim decision recommendation to the ceding company. In addition, the reinsurance treaty may outline situations

in which the ceding company is obligated to consult the reinsurer prior to making a final claim decision. The ceding company considers the reinsurer's recommendation but is not obligated to follow it. Most reinsurance treaties also contain a provision requiring the ceding company to notify the reinsurer of any potential claim denial, lawsuit, or claim settlement.

Dispute Resolution

Sometimes the ceding company and the reinsurer disagree about the settlement of a claim. Resolving some disagreements may be specifically covered by provisions of the reinsurance treaty. However, a reinsurance treaty cannot address all subjects that may result in future disagreements. In anticipation of an unresolved disagreement between the reinsurer and the ceding company, reinsurance treaties typically contain a provision that calls for the arbitration of disputes; arbitration generally is effective in resolving insurer-reinsurer differences.

Key Terms

claim analyst (claim examiner, claim specialist, claim approver)
claimant
claim philosophy
Unfair Claims Settlement Practices Act
claimant's statement (claim form)
authorization to release information
death certificate

contestable claim (resisted claim)
contestable period
material misrepresentation
rescission
accidental death benefit
interpleader
retained asset account (RAA)
installment certificate
statement of indebtedness
claim investigation
claim fraud

Endnotes

1. In most policies, a homicide in which the insured is not a willing participant is eligible for accidental death benefit coverage.

2. L. Lee Colquitt and Robert E. Hoyt, "An Empirical Analysis of the Nature and Cost of Fraudulent Life Insurance Claims: Evidence from Resisted Claims," *Journal of Insurance Regulation* (Summer 1997): 451–479.

An Overview of Financial Management

very life insurance company has two basic business objectives. First, as a fiduciary charged with protecting its policyowners' trust, an insurer must be able to meet all of its financial obligations as they come due. In Chapter 2 you learned that this ability to meet financial obligations is known as *solvency*. Second, as a business entity, the insurer attempts to maximize the value of the company for the benefit of its owners—stockholders in a stock insurance company and policyowners in a mutual insurance company. The degree of success a business has in generating returns to its owners—including its ability to generate profit and increase the value of the company—is known as **profitability**. A **return** is the reward or compensation that an investor receives for taking a risk.

Risk—the probability of a financial loss—is an important consideration in setting solvency and profitability goals. Protecting solvency and enhancing profitability require an insurer to maintain a careful balance between taking appropriate risks and avoiding undue risk. A tremendous challenge for each life insurance company is to maintain this balance while offering affordable insurance coverage, remaining competitive in the insurance industry, and being a responsible corporate citizen.

This chapter and the next two chapters discuss how insurance companies manage their financial resources to meet their solvency and profitability goals, a process known as **financial management**. Financial management incorporates several professional disciplines, including investments, actuarial mathematics, and accounting and financial reporting. Financial managers must respond to the demands of the company's internal management and board of directors, as well as consumers, investors, regulators, rating agencies, securities analysts, investment bankers, and the general business community.

In this chapter, we begin by laying the groundwork for our discussion of financial management. We examine the organization and responsibilities of financial management and discuss some principles of accounting and finance that are important for an understanding of financial management. Then we examine the financial goals and strategies that financial managers establish. Finally, we discuss how financial managers manage an insurance company's capital and its cash flows. In Chapter 16, we examine the investment operations of insurance companies. Chapter 17 completes our discussion of financial management with a look at accounting and financial reporting.

The Responsibilities and Organization of Financial Management

The financial managers of a life insurance company manage the insurer's finances and assist the company's president in developing, executing, and fulfilling corporate strategies intended to maximize the value of the company while managing the insurer's financial risks. Specific responsibilities of financial management include the following:

- **Planning the company's financial strategy.** This process includes establishing the corporation's solvency and profitability goals and strategies.

- **Managing capital and surplus.** Capital and surplus is the amount by which a life insurance company's assets exceed the amount of its liabilities. Financial managers manage the company's capital and surplus to increase the probability that the company remains financially healthy and also puts its capital and surplus to good use to earn a favorable rate of return.

- **Managing cash flows.** Financial managers track the flows of cash into and out of the organization so that sufficient cash is available to meet obligations under foreseeable economic conditions.

- **Managing investments.** Investment managers buy and sell bonds, stocks, mortgages, real estate, and other assets to help the company achieve its solvency and profitability goals.

- **Reporting the company's finances.** The accounting area regularly generates reports of the company's financial results for internal users (such as company management) and external users (such as regulators, rating agencies, consumers, and potential investors).

- **Performing other accounting responsibilities.** These responsibilities include budgeting, expense analysis, and recording all of the company's financial transactions.

- **Auditing and internal control.** Financial managers establish processes to help ensure that corporate policies and procedures are followed, financial records are maintained correctly, and the firm's assets are properly protected.

- **Performing financial analyses.** Financial management includes analyzing finances to understand the sources of profits and losses, and to identify emerging trends in financial results and deviations from expected results.

Many people in a life insurance company contribute to financial management, although only a few companies have a particular unit or department called *financial management.* Three departments that have financial management responsibilities are investments, accounting, and actuarial. Each of these departments has its own responsibilities, but they also work closely together to manage the company's finances and to help ensure that solvency and profitability goals are achieved.

The president of an insurance company is ultimately responsible for directing the company's financial strategies and objectives. The president delegates most of these responsibilities to senior financial officers. In some life insurance companies, the person who oversees all of the company's finances and its financial policies is known as the chief financial officer (CFO). Figure 15-1 lists some of the duties of the CFO.

The CFO reports to the president and generally has authority over the company's controller, who is the head of the accounting area. The controller is responsible for the timely and accurate accumulation and reporting of all of the company's financial data. (In some companies, the CFO is also the controller). The CFO may also have reporting authority over the chief investment officer, who oversees the company's investment activities. The chief investment officer helps formulate recommendations about the investment policies of the company and ensures that investment decisions comply with the company's investment policies and with regulatory investment limitations.

You already know that the actuarial area, under direction of the chief actuary, has important responsibilities for designing, monitoring, and maintaining profitable products. Actuaries project the future amounts of the company's expected cash flows and resulting assets and liabilities. Accountants and actuaries depend on the investment area to report the current and expected rates of return of the company's investments. Accountants oversee budgeting and expense management

FIGURE 15-1. Duties of a Chief Financial Officer (CFO).

- Coordinate all of the financial aspects of the company on an ongoing basis
- Present quarterly and yearly financial results to the company's board of directors and respond to board members' questions about these results
- Act as a financial spokesperson and communicate with regulators, investors, and rating agencies
- Work with investment bankers in obtaining external financing
- Act as a final arbiter in resolving internal financial management issues
- Respond to financial management questions raised by the company's president or board of directors

activities. Combining all this information allows financial managers to make decisions that help ensure the company's financial soundness.

Basic Principles of Financial Management

In order to understand financial management in a life insurance company, you need to be familiar with certain accounting documents and with solvency and profitability goals and processes.

Basic Accounting Documents

Like most businesses, insurance companies use financial statements to measure their financial performance and financial condition. A *financial statement* is a report that summarizes a company's major financial events and transactions. The two primary financial statements of any business are the balance sheet and the income statement, both of which help determine an insurer's levels of solvency and profitability.

Balance Sheet

A *balance sheet* shows a company's financial condition as of a particular date. For this reason, the balance sheet is often referred to as a snapshot of the company's finances at a specific point in time. A balance sheet summarizes what a company owns (assets), what it owes (liabilities), and its owners' investment in the company (owners' equity). As we discuss shortly, insurance companies usually use the term *capital and surplus* rather than *owners' equity*. An example of a simplified balance sheet is shown in Figure 15-2.

As you learned in Chapter 3, *assets* are things of value that a company owns. Assets can include investments, cash, buildings, equipment, and amounts that others owe to the company. Life insurance companies own several different types of assets, primarily bonds, stocks, real estate, mortgage loans, and cash. We discuss particular characteristics of these investment assets in Chapter 16.

A *liability* is a debt or future obligation of a company. The most important liabilities for a life insurance company are policy reserves. As you learned in Chapter 8, policy reserves represent the amount that, together with future premiums and assumed rate of investment interest, is expected to be needed to pay the future benefits of the policies then in force. A company must always have an amount of assets that exceeds the amount of its liabilities. These assets are often said to be "backing up" the liabilities. Thus, an insurer maintains assets that back up its policy reserves.

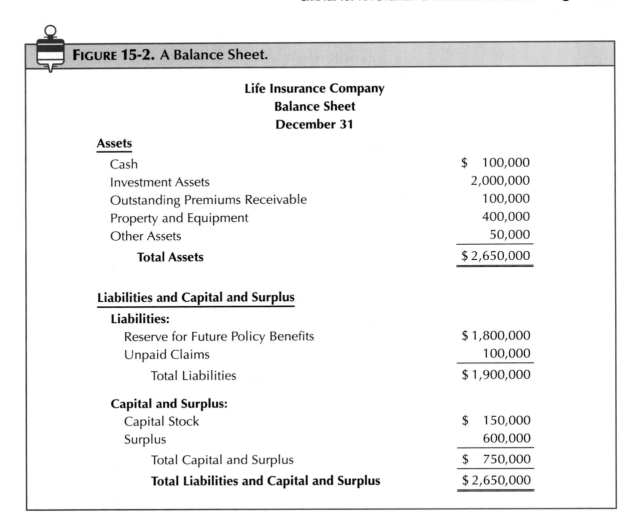

FIGURE 15-2. A Balance Sheet.

Life Insurance Company
Balance Sheet
December 31

Assets

Cash	$ 100,000
Investment Assets	2,000,000
Outstanding Premiums Receivable	100,000
Property and Equipment	400,000
Other Assets	50,000
Total Assets	**$ 2,650,000**

Liabilities and Capital and Surplus

Liabilities:

Reserve for Future Policy Benefits	$ 1,800,000
Unpaid Claims	100,000
Total Liabilities	$ 1,900,000

Capital and Surplus:

Capital Stock	$ 150,000
Surplus	600,000
Total Capital and Surplus	$ 750,000
Total Liabilities and Capital and Surplus	**$ 2,650,000**

Insurance laws in the United States and Canada require insurers to maintain at least a minimum level of policy reserves that will result in a high likelihood of payment of all policy obligations as they come due. Most insurers maintain a level of reserves that exceeds the required minimum. *Reserve valuation* is the process of establishing a value for an insurer's required policy reserves. An insurer's *appointed actuary*—an actuary who has been duly appointed by an insurer's board of directors to render an official actuarial opinion as to the insurance company's financial condition—is responsible for determining the amount of policy reserves that must be set aside each year to ensure that sufficient funds will be available in the future to meet the company's obligations. In making this determination, the appointed actuary makes conservative assumptions as to expected premium payments, expected investment income, anticipated claim experience, and anticipated expenses. In the United States, the methods of setting

required policy reserves are prescribed by law, although actuaries can use some discretion in determining whether reserves in excess of the required reserves are needed. In Canada, the reserve calculation method is not specified by law; instead, the appointed actuary establishes reserves according to a set of standards established by the Canadian Institute of Actuaries. For more on calculating reserve requirements, see Focus on Technology 15-1.

In addition to policy reserves, other required reserves insurers maintain include

- A reserve for policy dividends payable

- A reserve for premiums that policyowners have paid in advance

- A reserve for claims that have been incurred but not yet paid

- Two types of *asset fluctuation reserves*, which are designed to absorb gains and losses in the insurers' investment portfolio

- Various *contingency reserves*, which are created to act as a cushion against special risks that insurers face. One example is a group contingency reserve, which protects an insurer against greater-than-anticipated losses caused by an unusual concentration of risk under a group insurance program.

 Focus on Technology 15-1. | **Pru Cuts Reserving Challenge Down to Size.**

The estimated 600 million calculations it takes to figure out Prudential Life Insurance Company's quarterly reserve requirements used to take 64 people working for 35 days.

Now it is done on a monthly basis and takes five days and four people.

"It has gotten this group of individuals [actuaries] out of the data-gathering business and into the financial analysis business," says Jane Landon, vice president, life systems, who managed Prudential's changeover to a new reserving system.

During the changeover project, the reserving system had to come off a mainframe computer and onto a series of smaller computers in a massive parallel processing (MPP) network. Landon described MPP as "lots of computers with a very fast highway that is hooked together so the whole thing can operate very swiftly."

With actuaries now having most of the month to engage in the kind of planning that was not possible under the old system, Landon said the company can look forward to reserving figures ever more

accurate as more "what-if?" scenarios and differing assumptions are played out.

"Being able to know where you stand on a monthly basis puts you in a better position from a trending and control perspective," Landon said.

And its ultimate benefit may be felt in the policyholder's pocketbook.

"It will be protection for our policyholders all around," said Landon. "For example, if we are over-reserving, then we are not able to pass along as high a dividend as possible to our customers." •

Source: Excerpted from "Pru Cuts Reserving Challenge Down to Size," *Insurance Accounting* (29 March 1999): 1, 6. Used with permission.

As you learned in Chapter 3, *capital and surplus* refers to the excess of assets over liabilities. *Capital* represents the funds that a company's owners have invested by purchasing stock issued by the insurance company. *Surplus* represents the total net profits that have been earned from a company's operations and left to accumulate since the company's inception. For mutual insurers that do not issue stock, capital and surplus is known simply as *surplus*. For simplicity in this text, we use the term *capital and surplus* to refer to the excess of assets over liabilities for all insurance companies (stock and mutual). As you will see, capital and surplus are important determinants of an insurer's solvency.

For any insurer, the relationship of assets, liabilities, and capital and surplus on the balance sheet is based on the following basic accounting equation:

Assets = (Liabilities) + (Capital and surplus)

At all times, the amount of the insurer's assets must equal the sum of its liabilities and its capital and surplus. In other words, the balance sheet must balance. To help remember this concept, imagine a balance sheet as having two sides, with assets on the left side and liabilities and capital and surplus on the right side. The total of the left side *always* equals the total of the right side.

Income Statement

During an insurer's normal business activities, money continually flows into and out of the company. The income is typically in the form of **revenue**, which are funds that a company generates from its business operations. A life insurer's two main sources of revenue are (1) insurance premiums and (2) earnings from its investments. Most of the outgo is in the form of **expenses**, which are funds that a company spends to support its business operations. The majority of an insurer's expenses are contractual benefit payments to policyowners and beneficiaries. This category also includes changes in the value of the insurer's reserves from one period to the next. For example, if the value of an insurer's policy reserves has increased since the last period, the increase in reserves is considered a cost to the company and is treated as an expense.

In addition to policy benefits, other insurance company expenses are

- Agent commissions

- Employee salaries and benefits

- Product development and administration costs

- Marketing costs

- Facilities' maintenance costs

- Taxes

We have defined the insurer's *profit* as the excess of revenues over expenses during a defined period of time. If the amount of expenses exceeds the amount of revenue, the excess is known as a **loss**. Stock insurance companies generally use the terms **net income** (or *net gain*) and **net loss** in place of *profit* and *loss,* respectively. Mutual insurers generally use the term *contribution to surplus* in place of profit.

An insurer reports its revenues and expenses on an income statement. Whereas a balance sheet is a snapshot of a company's financial condition at a point in time, an **income statement**, also called a *statement of operations*, reports on an insurer's net income or net loss for a given period by summarizing the company's revenues and expenses during that period. Figure 15-3 shows a simplified income statement.

FIGURE 15-3. An Income Statement.

Life Insurance Company
Income Statement
For the Year Ended December 31

Revenues

Premium Income	$ 900,000
Net Investment Income	150,000
Total Revenues	**$ 1,050,000**

Benefits and Expenses

Policy Benefits and Claims	$ 700,000
Increase in Policy Reserves	50,000
Agent Commissions	150,000
Other Operating Expenses	50,000
Total Benefits and Expenses	**$ 950,000**
Net Income	**$ 100,000**

Linking the Income Statement to the Balance Sheet

The income statement is linked to the balance sheet through the capital and surplus account. At the end of each accounting period, the net income amount shown on the income statement is added to the amount of capital and surplus on the balance sheet. Note, however, if the income statement shows a net loss, the amount of the net loss is subtracted from the capital and surplus account on the balance sheet.

As a simple example, assume that at the beginning of one accounting period an insurer's balance sheet shows capital and surplus of $10 million. At the end of the accounting period, the insurer's income statement shows net income of $500,000. As a result, the balance sheet at the end of the accounting period is adjusted to show an increase to capital and surplus of $500,000, for a total of $10,500,000 in the capital and surplus account. Figure 15-4 illustrates this result. By contrast, had the income statement shown a net loss of $500,000, the capital and surplus account would be reduced by $500,000, leaving a total of $9,500,000 of capital and surplus.

Solvency and Profitability

You know that the dual goals of financial management for an insurer are to protect solvency while enhancing profitability. Both solvency and profitability can be measured by financial managers, and both are essential to an insurer's ability to remain in business and to meet the needs of its owners and policyowners.

FIGURE 15-4. Linking the Income Statement to the Balance Sheet.

Balance Sheet (End of Previous Period)		Income Statement (Current Period)		Balance Sheet (End of Current Period)	
Assets	$25,000,000	Revenues	$2,000,000	Assets	$26,000,000
		less			
		Expenses	$1,500,000		
Liabilities	$15,000,000			Liabilities	$15,500,000
Capital & Surplus	$10,000,000			Capital & Surplus	$10,500,000
		Plus	*Equals*		
Total Liabilities and Capital & Surplus	$25,000,000	Net Income	$500,000	Total Liabilities and Capital & Surplus	$26,000,000

Solvency

As you have learned, *solvency* in general terms is the ability of a business to meet its financial obligations on time. For an insurance company, **solvency** has a more specific definition; it refers to the ability to maintain capital and surplus above the minimum standard of capital and surplus required by law. Because this minimum standard is a legal requirement, insurer solvency is sometimes referred to as *statutory solvency*. In Canada, solvency is sometimes referred to as *capital adequacy*. Failure to satisfy this requirement could result in insurance regulators taking control of the insurer. The inability of an insurer to maintain the legally required minimum standard of capital and surplus is known as **insolvency**.

The legal minimum standard of capital and surplus varies from state to state and from insurer to insurer and is based on the degree of risk associated with an insurer's investments and the specific lines of business the insurer sells. An insurer that holds more risky investments has a higher legal minimum standard of capital and surplus than a comparable insurer that holds less risky investments. By establishing such risk-based minimum standards of capital and surplus, combined with the conservatism explicitly built into statutory policy reserves, insurance regulators attempt to ensure that each insurer has sufficient resources to pay policy benefits and other financial obligations on time.

Risks Affecting Solvency

In the normal course of conducting its business, an insurance company faces potentially serious risks that can threaten its statutory solvency. These risks can be grouped into four broad categories of risk, known as **contingency risks**, or *C-risks*. In order to protect an insurance company's financial strength, financial managers focus their attention on managing these risks.

- **C-1 risk** is **asset risk**, or the risk of loss on an investment for a reason *other than* a change in market interest rates. Examples of C-1 risk are the risk that stocks owned by an insurer will lose market value and the risk that the issuer of bonds owned by an insurer will default and not make scheduled bond payments. Insurers manage asset risk by evaluating potential investments carefully, investing a large percentage of their assets in high-quality investments, and allocating funds across diverse categories of investments.

- **C-2 risk** is **pricing risk**, also called *insurance risk*, which is the risk that the insurer's experience with mortality or expenses will

differ significantly from expectations, causing the insurer to lose money on its products. Life insurers manage C-2 risk by designing and pricing products sensibly, maintaining sound underwriting and reinsurance practices, and carefully controlling their expenses.

- *C-3 risk* is *interest-rate risk*, which is the risk of loss caused by a shift in market interest rates. Examples of interest-rate risk are (1) a loss on the sale of a bond when market interest rates rise, (2) the inability of an insurer to earn a rate of return on its assets that equals or exceeds the interest rates guaranteed in its insurance contracts, and (3) *disintermediation*, which is a phenomenon in which customers remove money from one financial intermediary (in this case an insurance company) and place the money in another intermediary to earn a higher return. Insurers manage C-3 risks through effective asset-liability management (ALM) practices, which we discuss later in this section.

- *C-4 risk* is *general business risk*, which is the risk of losses resulting from ineffective general business practices or environmental factors beyond the company's control. Examples of general business risks are inefficient management, losses from fraud and litigation, changes in tax laws, economic downturns, and natural disasters. Insurers can control some C-4 risks by using a high-quality and experienced management team that controls operating costs, exercises sound managerial judgment, supports ethical behavior, monitors financial results, and conducts regular internal and external audits.

The presence of the four C-risks helps explain why adequate capital and surplus are so important to an insurance company's solvency. Capital and surplus keep the company solvent by providing funds to cushion the losses resulting from these risks. Thus, an insurer's continued solvency usually depends on the adequacy of its capital and surplus. Best Case Scenario 15-1 discusses the importance of capital and surplus to an insurer's solvency. Although the example in this scenario is simplified, it illustrates how capital and surplus protect an insurer's solvency.

Measuring Solvency

To measure their solvency, insurance companies usually use capital ratios, rather than absolute capital and surplus amounts, such as shown in Best Case Scenario 15-1. A *ratio* is a comparison of two numeric values that results in a measurement expressed as a percentage or a fraction. A *capital ratio* is a ratio of some quantity of the insurer's

Best Case Scenario 15-1. Protecting Solvency with Adequate Capital and Surplus.

In order to see how capital and surplus cushion losses and help an insurer remain solvent, we will first review the terms in the basic accounting equation:

Assets = Liabilities + Capital and surplus

Rearranging these terms to isolate capital and surplus, we develop a new equation:

Assets – Liabilities = Capital and surplus

Next, let's compare this revised basic accounting equation for two insurance companies, the Best Friend Life Insurance Company and the No Fear Life Insurance Company. Each insurer has $900 million in assets. Best Friend has $750 million in liabilities and No Fear has $850 million in liabilities. As we can see from the following revised basic accounting equations for each company, Best Friend has a higher level of capital and surplus than No Fear ($150 million to $50 million):

Insurer	Assets	–	Liabilities	=	Capital and surplus
Best Friend	$900 million	–	$750 million	=	$150 million
No Fear	$900 million	–	$850 million	=	$50 million

Suppose that unexpected losses occur. For instance, economic conditions suddenly worsen, and many bond issuers default on the bonds owned by Best Friend and No Fear. As a result of these losses, the value of each insurer's assets falls by $75 million to $825 million. Assuming that the value of their liabilities remains the same, Best Friend has sufficient capital and surplus to absorb the losses and remain solvent. No Fear, on the other hand, does not have sufficient capital and surplus and could be declared insolvent:

Insurer	Assets	–	Liabilities	=	Capital and surplus
Best Friend	$825 million	–	$750 million	=	$75 million
No Fear	$825 million	–	$850 million	=	–$25 million

By maintaining a higher level of capital and surplus, Best Friend is better able than No Fear to protect its solvency (and its policyowners) from unexpected losses. •

capital and surplus to some quantity of the insurer's assets. For example, the basic capital ratio is

$$\text{Capital ratio} = \frac{\text{Capital and surplus}}{\text{Assets}}$$

The information necessary to calculate a capital ratio is contained on an insurer's balance sheet. The capital ratio is usually expressed as a percentage. Generally speaking, the greater the value of the capital ratio, the better the insurer's solvency. For example, a capital ratio of 15 percent generally shows greater solvency than a capital ratio of 10 percent.

The capital ratio in the preceding example is known as an *unweighted* ratio because it does not take into account the level of risk inherent in the insurer's operations. When an unweighted ratio is ad-

justed to take into account an insurer's level of risk exposure, the ratio becomes a *risk-weighted ratio.* Risk-weighted ratios are generally superior to unweighted ratios in determining whether an insurer has an adequate amount of capital and surplus given the riskiness of its operations.

Insurance regulators in the United States and Canada use risk-weighted capital ratios to monitor each insurer's solvency and to identify potentially impaired insurers. In the United States, **risk-based capital (RBC) ratio requirements**, modeled after the NAIC's *Risk-Based Capital (RBC) for Insurers Model Act,* enable state regulators to evaluate the adequacy of an insurer's capital relative to the riskiness of its operations. The RBC ratios are based on a prescribed risk-weighted formula. Although the actual ratio calculation is beyond the scope of this text, essentially the RBC ratios compare the insurer's actual amount of capital and surplus to the amount of capital and surplus the insurer should possess considering its risk exposure.

Each insurance company in the United States must perform the RBC calculations according to the prescribed formula and file an annual report of its RBC levels with the state insurance department and the NAIC. Regulators analyze the results and compare them with specified standards. If the ratio results fall below the standards, state regulators take action against the insurer. The lower the ratio results, the more severe the regulatory action. Figure 15-5 shows the required regulatory action under the NAIC's RBC monitoring system. For example, if an insurer's RBC ratio result is 175 percent, the insurer must submit a confidential plan of action to the insurance department in its state of domicile.

In Canada, the risk-weighted capital ratio tests that federally licensed insurers must perform annually are known as **Minimum Continuing Capital and Surplus Requirements (MCCSR)**, established by the Canadian Life and Health Insurance Association (CLHIA). As with RBC tests in the United States, if an insurer's MCCSR ratio falls below a stated minimum, the insurer becomes subject to closer regulatory scrutiny. Insurers incorporated in Quebec must meet a slightly different set of ratio requirements that are similar to the federal MCCSR.

In addition to regulators, an insurer's internal managers and insurance rating agencies evaluate risk-based capital ratios to monitor capital levels. A **rating agency** is an independent organization that evaluates the financial condition of insurers and provides information to potential customers of and investors in insurance companies.

Profitability

You have learned that profit is the excess of revenues over expenses. A company that consistently produces profits can stay in business, grow, and increase the wealth, or value, of the company. An increase

FAST FACT

In 1998, for the first time since RBC ratios were mandated in 1993, each of the 130 largest life insurers in the United States had RBC ratio results over 175 percent. The average RBC ratio for all 130 companies was 272.4 percent.[2]

FIGURE 15-5. Required Regulatory Action under the NAIC RBC Monitoring System.

Range of RBC Ratio Results	Prescribed Regulatory Action
250% and above	No regulatory action necessary.
200% to 249%	Life insurer must perform additional analyses. If the results of those analyses indicate a problem, the insurer must submit a confidential plan of action to the state of domicile.
150% to 199%	Life insurer must submit a confidential plan of action to the state of domicile.
100% to 149%	Life insurer becomes subject to confidential investigation by state of domicile.
70% to 99%	State of domicile is authorized to take insurer into receivership.
Below 70%	State of domicile is mandated to take insurer into receivership.

Source: Adapted from NAIC, Risk-Based Capital for Life and/or Health Insurers Model Act, Sections 3–6, 1993. Reprinted with permission from the National Association of Insurance Commissioners.

in the value of the company is indicated by such measures as an increase in the share price of the company's stock and an increase in the capital and surplus account on the company's balance sheet. In contrast, a company that consistently suffers losses will eventually go out of business.

Although profitability can be attained and measured over a short period of time, insurers typically strive for long-term profitability. Long-term profitability enables an insurer to

- Provide funds for investments

- Pay policy dividends on participating policies

- Pay cash dividends to stockholders and increase the attractiveness of the company's stock to investors

- Generate high-quality ratings from insurance rating agencies

- Provide funds to develop products, product lines, and distribution channels

- Provide funds for expansion and acquisitions

Measuring Profitability

The income statement provides some insight into an insurer's profitability, at least over the short term, because it shows the company's net income or net loss during a specific period. However, the income statement cannot provide insight into the company's profitability over the long term. For this information, companies rely on the balance sheet.

Insurers prepare income statements on a regular basis (such as quarterly). Each time an insurer prepares an income statement, it transfers the resulting net income or net loss figures to the balance sheet. As a result, the capital and surplus account on the balance sheets over a period of time reflects the cumulative effects of a company's operations. If the company's operations have been profitable, the capital and surplus account shows continuing growth, unless all net income has been paid out as dividends.

A profitability measure that makes use of both the income statement and the balance sheet is known as the ***return on capital ratio***, which is a ratio that compares some measure of an insurer's earnings during a stated period to some measure of its capital and surplus. This ratio is usually expressed as

$$\text{Return on capital} = \frac{\text{Earnings}}{\text{Capital and surplus}}$$

The result of the return on capital ratio indicates how effectively an insurer has employed its capital and surplus in generating a profit during a given period. Generally, the higher the return on capital ratio, the more effectively the company used its resources to earn a profit. Like the capital ratio discussed earlier, return on capital can be unweighted or it can be weighted to take into account the insurer's level of risk. Return on capital ratios can be calculated for the company as a whole, for a line of business, for a specific product, or for a distribution system. Instead of a return on capital ratio, some insurers use a *return on surplus ratio*, which is a measure of earnings to a measure of surplus.

Planning Financial Goals and Strategy

Senior financial officers assist an insurer's president in (1) establishing corporate goals for profitability and solvency, (2) planning the strategies

the company will use to meet these goals, and (3) monitoring and managing the plans that are implemented. Financial managers also help the president explain the financial goals and strategies of the firm to the company's board of directors, stockholders, rating agencies, and policyowners.

Financial Goals

General financial goals of all insurers are to earn a sufficiently high return on investments while maintaining a high level of solvency. These goals are much easier to state than to achieve. Pursuing profitability involves a certain amount of risk taking, whereas protecting solvency involves risk avoidance. The tradeoff between solvency and profitability requires an insurer to balance solvency requirements and profitability goals. Finding the correct balance between solvency and profitability is crucial to the financial success of an insurance company.

Solvency Goals

Goals related to an insurer's solvency usually are expressed as targeted financial results, such as a specific risk-weighted capital ratio. Typically, insurers set their capital targets well above the minimum levels required by insurance regulators. Another solvency-related goal is to maintain the company's industry rating, or achieve a higher rating, from an insurance rating agency. Rating agencies place considerable emphasis on solvency, and their ratings generally reflect the adequacy of insurers' capital.

Profitability Goals

Insurers usually establish a number of profitability goals. For example, many insurers set goals that specify the target rates of return on capital they want to earn; such targets are set for the company as a whole and for each of the insurer's lines of business. Another common profitability goal specifies a target rate of growth. For example, an insurer may set a goal of increasing its revenues or of increasing the value of its assets by a stated percentage each year. A stock insurer may set a growth-rate goal of increasing the share price of its stock.

Planning Financial Strategies

Once financial goals are established, financial managers implement strategies designed to achieve these goals. Financial strategies may be

characterized as aggressive strategies, conservative strategies, or some combination of aggressive and conservative.

- A company that places a strong emphasis on strategies that could enhance its rate of return (profitability) but potentially threaten its solvency generally pursues an ***aggressive financial strategy***. Elements of an aggressive financial strategy include investing in relatively high-risk assets, developing many new and unusual products, expanding into new lines of business, and instituting new distribution systems.

- An insurer that places a strong emphasis on avoiding strategies that could threaten its solvency but enhance its rate of return generally pursues a ***conservative financial strategy***. Elements of a conservative financial strategy include investing in relatively low-risk assets, developing traditional products for existing markets, and using existing distribution systems.

Generally, a life insurance company should not employ financial strategies that are overly aggressive or overly conservative. An insurer that is overly aggressive may jeopardize its solvency position by taking on excessive risk. An insurer that is overly conservative may maintain an unnecessarily high level of capital and surplus and could miss opportunities for growth and also limit the potential returns for its owners and its ability to remain competitive in the insurance industry. Many insurers use a combination of aggressive and conservative strategies, shifting between them as market conditions change.

Monitoring and Measuring Financial Results

In order to determine whether it is meeting its financial goals, an insurer must have a way of measuring its financial results. Financial managers make sure that suitable measurement systems are in place to achieve the effective management of capital and other financial objectives. Usually, the heads of the company's lines of business work with the company's chief financial officer to develop appropriate performance measures.

An insurer typically establishes uniform ground rules and standardized performance measures for gauging financial results among business units. The CFO collects performance results from the various business units of the company. By using a system of standardized performance measures, the CFO can impartially monitor the company's business practices and the results of operations.

Managing the Insurer's Capital and Surplus

Effective management of capital and surplus is one of an insurer's most important financial management responsibilities because capital and surplus directly reflect the company's solvency and profitability. At a minimum, managing capital and surplus involves maintaining at least the minimum level of capital and surplus required by law. Managing a life insurance company's capital and surplus is extremely complex, and a comprehensive discussion is beyond the scope of this text. Instead, we provide a brief overview of the essential steps in the capital and surplus management process. These steps include the following:

- **Analyze the company's capital and surplus needs.** The first step involves determining the amount of capital and surplus needed for internal risk management purposes, regulatory requirements, and rating agency requirements. Financial managers calculate the amount of capital and surplus needed to ensure the survival of the company in a wide variety of adverse conditions. These managers must also take into consideration (1) the capital needed to fund the desired level of business growth and (2) the capital needed for strategic uses, such as for the acquisition of another company or the development of a new information system. Typically, financial managers determine the amount of capital and surplus needed for the organization as a whole and for each business unit.

- **Measure the projected return generated by this capital and surplus.** Insurance companies can measure projected return in several ways, such as different variations of the basic return on capital ratio. These measures are usually adjusted for risk.

- **Compare the projected return on capital with the company's hurdle rate.** *Hurdle rate* is the minimum percentage rate of return on capital that a company must earn for a given level of risk. The hurdle rate can be thought of as a benchmark or goal. A company bases its hurdle rate on the overall rate of interest the company pays for the funds it employs and the rate of return on capital expected by the company's owners. As we discuss in detail in the next chapter, an investor invests funds with the intention of achieving a return that is commensurate with the risk associated with the investment. By comparing the return generated by the capital and surplus with an appropriate hurdle rate, financial managers can determine whether the company is achieving an acceptable reward for the risks it is taking with its capital and

surplus. The rate of return on capital must exceed the hurdle rate in order for the return to be considered acceptable.

- **Determine whether capital and surplus should be used in a more effective way.** If the rate of return being earned on the capital is below the hurdle rate, the company needs to look for more profitable ways to use its capital. Financial managers may need to abandon unprofitable investments and lines of business in order to improve the return on capital and maximize the wealth of the company.

- **Arrange for financing any required additional capital.** If needed, an insurer can raise additional funds in two general ways: internal financing and external financing. *Internal financing* involves raising funds through the core business operations of the company. For an insurance company, internal financing comes from the accumulation of net income. *External financing* involves raising funds from outside the company. The most common means of external financing for stock life insurers is issuing stock to the public. Insurers also have certain means of raising funds through borrowing.

Managing Cash Flows

The life insurance business involves many cash flows. A *cash flow* is any movement of cash into or out of an organization. A *cash inflow*, also called a *source of funds,* is a movement of cash into an organization. An insurer's cash inflows come from (1) revenues generated by product sales and investment income, (2) sales of existing assets, and (3) external financing. A *cash outflow*, also called a *use of funds,* is a movement of cash out of an organization. Most of an insurer's cash outflows are payments to policyowners and beneficiaries for insurance benefits, cash surrenders, and withdrawals. Other cash outflows are payments for operating expenses and for purchases of new assets.

The basic goal of managing these cash flows is to have, at all times, enough assets in the form of cash to meet financial obligations as they come due and also to have the remaining assets invested wisely in order to earn the most favorable return possible. Cash-flow management is a critical financial management responsibility because the pattern of an insurance company's cash flows directly affects its solvency and profitability. The pattern of cash flows refers to the timing and the amount of flows into and out of the company.

FAST FACT
In 1998, life insurers in the United States generated $444.3 billion in premium income and $176.8 billion in investment income.[3]

The Effect of Cash Flows on Solvency and Profitability

For an insurer, being solvent is more than having assets that exceed liabilities. A sufficient amount of an insurer's assets must always be in the form of cash so that the insurer can pay its obligations as they come due. An insurer that has more assets than liabilities can still have difficulty meeting its obligations if the insurer has insufficient cash assets. When an insurer cannot pay its current obligations, the insurer must either sell assets—possibly at a loss—or borrow funds.

In order to protect its solvency, an insurer maintains adequate asset *liquidity*, which is the ease and speed with which an asset can be converted to cash at nearly the asset's true value. The more liquid an asset, the easier it is to convert the asset to cash at close to the asset's true value. Cash is obviously the most liquid of all assets, because no conversion is necessary. Certain short-term securities, such as United States Treasury bills, are considered highly liquid because they can be sold almost instantly. A piece of commercial real estate is a less liquid asset because finding a buyer who will pay the asset's true value and finalizing the sale are much more time consuming.

"Well, gentlemen, there's your problem."

You might think that an insurer would want to keep most or all of its assets in cash to avoid a cash shortfall. However, an insurer cannot afford to keep excessive amounts of cash on hand because cash and other highly liquid assets generally earn low or no returns. Insurers need to earn higher returns on their investments to achieve their financial goals. Longer-term and less liquid assets generally offer higher rates of return. Financial managers seek to find a level of liquidity that allows the company both to pay current obligations and to earn a favorable investment return.

Asset-Liability Management (ALM)

Theoretically, an insurance company can balance the need for solvency with the desire for profitability by maintaining cash inflows that are at least equal to its cash outflows. In the ideal situation, the insurer's premium income and investments provide cash inflows that match in both timing and amount the cash outflows for policy benefit payments and operating expenses. The company can fulfill all of its financial obligations and still keep the maximum amount of its assets invested to earn a favorable return. In reality, perfectly matching cash inflows to cash outflows is not possible, but financial managers strive to match these flows of funds as closely as they can.

In order to match cash inflows and cash outflows, and to support the insurer's strategic objectives for solvency and profitability, financial managers manage assets and liabilities together. *Asset-liability management (ALM)* is a cash-flow management program for coordinating the financial effects of the insurer's product liabilities with the financial effects of the insurer's investments. Through ALM, financial managers identify the patterns of the company's cash outflows and then construct a portfolio of assets that will produce patterns of cash inflows which, when combined with the cash inflows from operations, are sufficient to meet the company's obligations on time. In applying ALM principles, an insurer estimates the timing and amount of claims that a product will generate in a specific period. These claims represent future cash outflows. The insurer then determines the amount of money that it must invest today to grow to a sum that will provide the cash inflows needed to pay those future claims.

The concept of ALM is relatively straightforward, but ALM applications are extremely complex. Asset-liability management has become a day-to-day financial risk management activity for most insurance companies. Many insurers have created ALM technical teams and have adopted a formal system of internal financial reports for communicating ALM information to the managers who need the information to make financial decisions. Some insurers outsource their ALM to specialized consulting firms.

Effective asset-liability management requires the involvement of, and extensive communication among, the insurer's president, chief financial officer, chief investment officer, product actuaries, and investment managers, as shown in Figure 15-6.

- The president and chief financial officer make the final determination of the products the company will develop, according to market attractiveness and rating agency constraints. They consult with the investment area and product development area to determine whether the products can produce desired returns within the company's tolerance for risk. Once the product decision has been made, the president and CFO oversee the management of the assets backing the liabilities of the product through a joint effort of the investment area and the product development area.[4]

- Product actuaries attempt to design and price products so that the resulting cash flows will be predictable and the insurer can

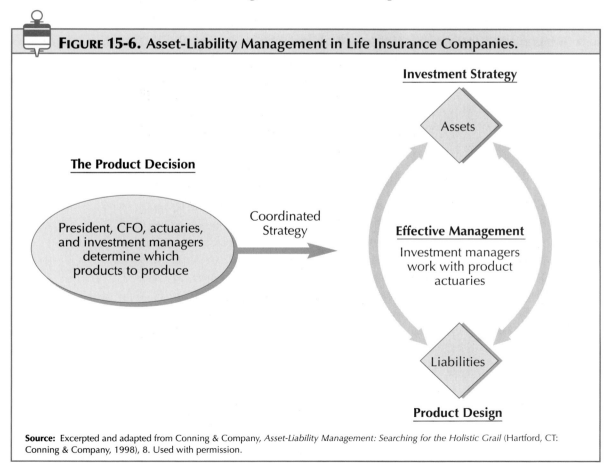

FIGURE 15-6. Asset-Liability Management in Life Insurance Companies.

Investment Strategy

Assets

The Product Decision

President, CFO, actuaries, and investment managers determine which products to produce

Coordinated Strategy

Effective Management

Investment managers work with product actuaries

Liabilities

Product Design

Source: Excerpted and adapted from Conning & Company, *Asset-Liability Management: Searching for the Holistic Grail* (Hartford, CT: Conning & Company, 1998), 8. Used with permission.

meet its liabilities. For example, product actuaries incorporate into the products certain features intended to (1) encourage customers to keep the policies in force for the long term and (2) discourage policyowners' demands for withdrawals and surrenders.

- Investment managers determine the probable timing and amount of net cash inflows from various asset types, based on a given interest-rate scenario. Investment managers are concerned with matching the timing and amount of cash inflows with the liability outflows projected by the product actuaries. Investment managers must be able to respond to mismatches in aggregate cash flows from changes in the business environment. Investment managers must also ensure that the insurer's investments are sufficiently liquid so that financial obligations can be paid on time in almost any economic environment. If ALM has been effective, the company's assets and operations will provide sufficient cash inflows to pay off liabilities as they come due and also will provide the insurer a profit.

Forecasts and Simulations

ALM makes use of forecasts and simulations. As you learned in Chapter 8, a *forecast* is an estimation of a possible future scenario. Actuaries make forecasts about the amount, duration, and timing of their product-related cash flows (premium revenue, benefit payments, cash surrenders, and withdrawals), and investment managers make forecasts of asset-related cash flows (investment income and purchases and sales of securities). These forecasts are based on sets of assumptions about future conditions or events, such as the following:

- The movement of interest rates

- Rates of inflation

- The behavior of various types of investments

- Regulatory, social, and political factors

- The competitive environment

- Sales of products

Forecasts, of course, are uncertain. To understand how and to what extent forecast results may vary, insurance companies use simulations to predict how altering various assumptions will affect operating results. A **simulation** is a model used to represent a complex system in

order to study how the system behaves under various circumstances. The objective of using a simulation is to explore a number of "what if" scenarios, from "best" to "worst." Simulations help answer questions such as

- What happens to our asset and liability cash flows if interest rates rise or fall by a percentage point next year?

- What happens to our cash flows and financial position if new product sales are 10 percent above or below expectations?

- What is the effect on our cash flows and financial position if we increase agent compensation for a line of business to match competitors' rates?

Cash-Flow Testing

Asset-liability management is mainly concerned with interest-rate risk. Changes in market interest rates can have substantial effects on the insurer's assets and liabilities, and, consequently, on the insurer's cash flows. Interest-rate changes affect the number of policy lapses, surrenders, and withdrawals, all of which can have a significant effect on an insurer's cash outflows. Interest-rate changes also affect the performance of most of an insurer's investments and therefore affect cash inflows.

Insurance companies undertake periodic cash-flow testing to evaluate the effect of changing interest-rate assumptions on projected cash flows. *Cash-flow testing* is the process of projecting and comparing, as of a given date, the timing and amount of asset and liability cash flows. Financial managers project the company's cash inflows and cash outflows under many different interest-rate scenarios and then analyze the results. Using cash-flow testing, the insurer can identify interest-rate scenarios that would threaten the company's financial position so that the insurer can take precautions and make adjustments as necessary.

Most jurisdictions require insurers to undergo certain cash-flow tests. In the United States, most states have adopted the *NAIC's Revised Standard Valuation Law,* which requires insurers to test cash flows under seven interest-rate scenarios, such as interest rates rising or falling gradually, interest rates rising or falling rapidly, and interest rates reversing directions. After the insurer completes the cash-flow tests, the insurer's appointed actuary signs a declaration attesting to the adequacy of the insurer's reserves based on the results of the cash-flow tests. Required cash-flow testing is a way for regulators to identify potentially impaired insurance companies.

Life insurers in Canada are required to annually test the adequacy of their reserves and capital using ***dynamic solvency testing (DST)***, which is similar to the cash-flow testing required in the United States. DST is the use of simulation modeling to project the company's future financial condition under a number of business-growth scenarios and a number of interest-rate scenarios. Each insurer in Canada must file a statement prepared annually by its appointed actuary that attests to the insurer's financial prospects based on the results of the dynamic solvency tests.

Key Terms

profitability
return
financial management
financial statement
balance sheet
reserve valuation
appointed actuary
asset fluctuation reserve
contingency reserve
revenue
expenses
loss
net income (net gain)
net loss
income statement (statement of operations)
solvency (statutory solvency, capital adequacy [Canada])
insolvency
contingency risks (C-risks)
asset risk (C-1 risk)
pricing risk (C-2 risk) (insurance risk)
interest-rate risk (C-3 risk)
disintermediation

general business risk (C-4 risk)
ratio
capital ratio
risk-based capital (RBC) ratio requirement
Minimum Continuing Capital and Surplus Requirements (MCCSR)
rating agency
return on capital ratio
aggressive financial strategy
conservative financial strategy
hurdle rate
internal financing
external financing
cash flow
cash inflow (source of funds)
cash outflow (use of funds)
liquidity
asset-liability management (ALM)
simulation
cash-flow testing
dynamic solvency testing (DST)

Endnotes

1. ACLI, *1999 Life Insurance Fact Book* (Washington, D.C.: American Council of Life Insurance, 1999), 145; CLHIA, *Canadian Life and Health Insurance Facts*, 1999 ed. (Toronto: Canadian Life and Health Insurance Association, 1999), 23.

2. "Distribution of RBC Ratios for 130 U.S. Life Insurers," *National Underwriter*, Life & Health/Financial Services ed. (26 April 1999): 1.

3. ACLI, 88.

4. Conning & Company, *Asset-Liability Management: Searching for the Holistic Grail* (Hartford, CT: Conning & Company, 1998), 28.

Managing Investments

LEARNING OBJECTIVES

After reading this chapter, you should be able to

- Identify who is responsible for establishing an insurer's investment policy, and describe aspects of the typical investment policy

- Discuss the risk-return tradeoff of investing

- Explain what is meant by diversification and why diversification of investments is important

- Explain the factors that investment analysts consider when evaluating and selecting investments

- Distinguish between debt investments and equity investments, and give examples of each

- Describe the general characteristics of the typical investments that insurance companies make

- Discuss the characteristics of conservative investment strategies and aggressive investment strategies

*L*ife insurance companies in the United States and Canada are among the most important institutional investors in the world. In 1998, life insurance companies invested $204 billion in the U.S. capital markets (financial markets for long-term funds), ranking third among all institutional investors behind commercial banks and mutual funds.[1] By investing in a wide range of businesses and industries, insurance companies help provide the impetus for economic growth. The ways insurance companies manage their investments affect not only policyowners and stockholders, but also many other people throughout the societies in which insurers operate.

All investments involve potential risks and potential rewards. An *investment* is any expenditure of money or assets made in an attempt to earn a return. As you have learned, a *return* is the reward or compensation received for taking a risk. We have defined *risk* as the probability of a financial loss. In the context of investments, **risk** is the possibility that the investor will fail to earn a return or will lose all or part of the initial investment, or **principal**. Life insurance companies make investments primarily for the benefit of their policyowners. The returns earned on investments enable insurers to reduce the cost of insurance, and the insurers use investment income to pay policy benefits and operating expenses and to generate profits.

Through asset-liability management (ALM), which we discussed in Chapter 15, financial managers of a life insurance company identify the patterns of the company's cash outflows and then construct portfolios of investments (assets) to produce patterns of cash inflows that, when combined with the cash inflows from operations, are sufficient to meet the company's obligations on time. A **portfolio** is a collection of financial assets assembled to meet an investment goal. Investment professionals study the behavior and the risk and return characteristics of many different investments in order to identify the assets that are likely to produce the desired return patterns.

We begin this chapter by examining the organization of the investment department and the investment guidelines to which investment staff must adhere. Then we explain some of the basic principles of investing. Finally, we identify and describe the types of assets that make up the typical life insurance company investment portfolio and the types of investment strategies that insurers follow.

Organization of Investment Operations

A life insurance company's investment operations are under the direction of a chief investment officer, who directs a team of portfolio managers. The insurer's investments are separated into portfolios by type—such as stocks, bonds, mortgages, and real estate—and a portfolio manager is assigned to each portfolio and makes investment decisions according to the company's general investment guidelines.

Remember that actuaries specify the financial resources needed to support each insurance product. Many insurance companies have found that they need a close link between the portfolio managers and the actuaries in order to clarify asset-liability management goals. The person responsible for this link, the ***asset manager***, monitors the investment-related cash inflows and cash outflows of a specific line of the insurer's business and makes sure sufficient funds are available for that line. The asset manager is responsible for matching investments to product liabilities and adjusting the company's investment holdings so that cash is available as needed to pay liabilities. A typical investment department's organizational structure is shown in Figure 16-1.

In addition to the chief investment officer, asset managers, and portfolio managers, other employees in the typical investment department include

- *Investment analysts,* who conduct research into specific investment opportunities

- *Economists,* who forecast economic trends

- *Traders,* who buy and sell investments for the portfolios

Some insurers also hire outside investment managers to manage all or part of the investment portfolios.

Establishing an Investment Policy

By law, a life insurance company's board of directors is responsible for adopting a written investment policy and for supervising and directing the insurer's investment function and its portfolio construction process. The board usually delegates the responsibility for writing the investment policy to an investment committee or finance committee that is made up of members of the board of directors and certain company executives, such as the chief financial officer, the chief investment officer, and the chief actuary. The board must approve and adopt the investment policy for the company.

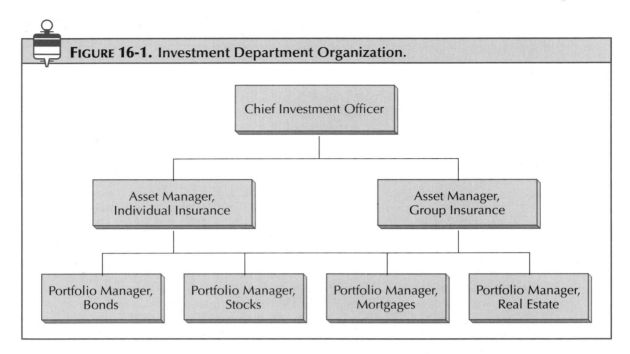

FIGURE 16-1. Investment Department Organization.

In setting the investment policy, the investment or finance committee researches the company's financial position, its current investments, and any conditions that can influence investment operations, such as the economic environment. The investment policy typically incorporates the following factors:

- The insurer's investment objectives, including (1) creating an investment portfolio with cash-flow properties that are consistent with the insurer's asset-liability management strategy, (2) meeting obligations to policyowners, (3) contributing to the growth of the insurer's earnings and surplus, and (4) maintaining an adequate *spread*, or difference between the yield (rate of return) earned on the insurer's investments and the interest rate guaranteed on its products

- The types of investments needed to achieve the insurer's investment objectives

- Minimum standards for the safety of the principal invested and for the level of investment earnings

- The types of risks that investment staff can and cannot take in making investments

FAST FACT

In 1998, 59 percent of insurers hired outside managers to manage their investment portfolios.[2]

- The dollar amount of investments that each level of investment staff can authorize without having to seek approval from a higher level of authority within the company

- Applicable federal, state, and provincial regulations that constrain the insurer's investment activities

Investment Department Operations

Staff members in the investment department carry out the company's day-to-day investment activities according to the investment policy adopted by the board of directors. These day-to-day activities are based on operational plans established by the chief investment officer, the asset managers, and the portfolio managers. The chief investment officer and the asset managers monitor the company's liabilities and generate specific information about the asset requirements needed to manage the liabilities. The chief investment officer and the asset managers also determine the amount of money available for portfolio managers to invest during a specific time frame.

Insurers sometimes divide a large investment portfolio into smaller portfolios and specify that the earnings from the smaller portfolios will back the liabilities (cash outflows) of certain product lines. For example, an insurer may assign the earnings from a portfolio of bonds to support one of its decreasing term life insurance products. Such assignment of earnings is helpful in asset-liability management. By assigning all or part of each investment portfolio, investment managers can match specific assets with specific liabilities and can monitor and manage the cash flows of each product line.

Investment analysts assigned to each portfolio conduct research into specific investment opportunities. For example, investment analysts examine and evaluate annual reports of companies issuing stocks and bonds, interview the management of such companies, read financial publications, and screen potential investments using specialized investment-tracking software and systems. Analysts also collect information about promising mortgage loan and real estate investment opportunities. The portfolio managers and other members of the investment staff examine this research and evaluate the various investments and investment strategies needed to achieve the company's investment goals.

When evaluating a specific investment, a portfolio manager generally considers the following factors:

- The investment's cash flow characteristics

- The investment's expected **rate of return**, which is the expected return of an investment expressed as a percentage of the purchase

price. For example, if an insurer invests $1,000 and earns a return of $100 on the investment, the rate of return is 10 percent ($100 return ÷ $1,000 investment = 10 percent). Rate of return incorporates any gain in the value of the asset, any income earned on the asset, and deduction of any taxes payable on the investment income.

- The risk characteristics of the investment

- The liquidity of the investment

- General economic conditions, such as expected movements in interest rates and the expected inflation rate

- Regulatory requirements that constrain the insurer's investment activities

After reaching an investment decision, the portfolio manager tells a trader in the investment department which investments to buy or sell, the price limitations for buying and selling, and the deadline for the transactions. Periodically, the investment committee evaluates the company's investment results.

Returns on Insurers' Investments

Before we describe the types of investments insurers generally hold in their portfolios, we will explain the kinds of returns an insurer can earn and several factors that can affect investment returns. Some types of returns an insurer may earn from an investment include interest, capital gain, rental income, and dividends.

- *Interest* is a fee paid for the use of someone else's money. *Simple interest* is interest paid only on an original sum of money, whereas *compound interest* is interest paid on both the original sum and on any previously accumulated interest. Compound interest is standard in most investments and business transactions.

- A *capital gain* is the amount by which the proceeds of the sale of an investment exceed the amount that the investor originally paid for the investment. For instance, if an insurer purchases an asset for $1,000 and later sells the asset for $1,200, the insurer has earned a $200 capital gain ($1,200 sales price – $1,000 purchase price = $200 capital gain). When the purchase price exceeds the selling price, the result is a *capital loss*.

- The investor may earn income in the form of rent or lease payments. Further, the owner of stock may receive cash dividends at specified times.

If an investment earns more than one type of return, the total return on the asset is the sum of the earnings from the various sources.

Return, Inflation, and Deflation

An insurer that invests money is letting another party use the insurer's money. In exchange, the insurer expects to receive a return. The value of an investment can increase or decrease over time, depending on the return earned. Further, the value of the invested amount can change according to other factors, such as *inflation*, which, as you have learned, is an increase in the average level of prices in an economy, or **deflation**, which is a decrease in the average level of prices. Even when an investment is earning a positive return, the actual value of the investment can remain relatively the same or even decrease if inflation is simultaneously fairly high. Insurers cannot control inflation or deflation, but they can monitor and measure investment returns to try to generate earnings that remain ahead of these factors.

Return and Risk

In addition to considering the potential returns from an investment, the insurer must consider the risks presented by the investment. Some investments are very safe—in other words, the probability of failing to earn a return or losing all or part of the principal is small—whereas other investments are quite risky. In investing, risk and return are fundamentally linked. The relationship between risk and return can be expressed as follows: All other factors being equal, the higher the risk associated with an investment, the greater the expected return on the investment. Similarly, the lower the risk associated with an investment, the lower its expected return.

Because of the relationship of risk and return, a person who takes on considerable risk when making an investment expects to be compensated with a greater return; if enhanced return is not likely, the person has no reason to take the risk. The interplay between risk and return is known as the **risk-return tradeoff**, and it is a factor in every investment decision—and virtually every financial decision—that an insurer makes.

As you learned in our discussion of contingency risks (C-risks) in Chapter 15, sources of risk include an insurer's products, specific investments, and the general economic environment. Risk can be higher

or lower, and so can expected return. Figure 16-2 gives some examples. Later in this chapter, we discuss the risk and return characteristics of typical insurance company investments.

Return and Diversification

In order to manage the overall risk levels of their portfolios, insurance companies invest in a variety of different assets. **Diversification** is an investment strategy of holding in a portfolio many assets with various risk and return characteristics in order to reduce the overall risk the investor faces. Diversification helps an insurer achieve the expected overall investment returns that are consistent with the level of its tolerance for risk.

Suppose that an insurer invested all of its money in one asset, and that asset's return was worse than the insurer had expected. The insurer would suffer a financial loss. However, if the insurer also held many other investments in its portfolio, the poor return of the one investment would have only a minimal effect on the return of the entire portfolio. The losses of one investment can be offset by the gains of other investments. Similarly, an insurer can construct a variety of investment portfolios, each representing a slightly different total risk level. Taken together, the portfolios represent a generally balanced level of risk.

Insurers pursue diversification by holding different types of investments, such as bonds, stocks, mortgages, and real estate, and also by

---

FIGURE 16-2. Risk and Return.

Lower risks that generally provide lower expected return	Higher risks that generally provide higher expected return
• A short-term investment that will allow an invested sum to be released fairly quickly	• A long-term investment that will not allow the invested sum to be released fairly quickly
• A borrower with a good credit rating	• A borrower with a poor credit rating
• An investment with good liquidity or marketability—one that is easy to sell	• An investment with poor liquidity or marketability—one that is difficult to sell
• A loan that is secured by collateral	• A loan that is unsecured by collateral
• A new product that has low initial costs	• A new product that has high initial costs
• The selling of a new product in a familiar market	• The selling of a new product in an unfamiliar market
• A loan that is repaid on a specified due date	• A loan that can be repaid any time

holding many different investments of each type. Insurers further diversify by holding some investments issued in the home country and some issued abroad. Focus on Technology 16-1 illustrates a relatively new asset that some insurers are holding as a means to further diversify their portfolios.

Regulation of Insurer Investments

Unlike most investors, insurers must comply with regulatory requirements that impose limits on the types and amounts of investments they may make. These regulatory requirements are designed to (1) require insurers to exhibit reasonable behavior with respect to prudent diversification of their investment portfolios and (2) protect consumers from the threat of insurer insolvency as a result of taking on too much risk in search of high returns. Such regulatory requirements as a general rule place limits on the investments in an insurer's general account, and not its separate account.

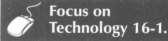

Focus on Technology 16-1. | **Catastrophe Bonds.**

Many life insurance companies have discovered a new way to add diversification to their investment portfolios: buy *catastrophe bonds,* otherwise known as *cat bonds.* Cat bonds are a means for property/casualty (P/C) insurers to transfer some of the risk associated with catastrophic events, such as hurricanes, earthquakes, floods, and tornadoes.

Catastrophe bonds are issued by reinsurance companies that are affiliated with P/C insurers. A reinsurer issuing cat bonds places the proceeds from the bond offering into a trust. If the P/C insurer's claim costs related to catastrophes are below a specified level during a defined time period—usually one year—then bond investors (such as life insurance companies) are paid

back their entire amount of principal from the trust, plus interest. However, if the P/C insurer suffers catastrophic losses above a certain level, the reinsurer uses some or all of the money in the trust to pay the claims. In this case, the bondholders lose some or all of their investment.

Determining the offering price of a cat bond involves the use of sophisticated statistical models to determine the probability that losses on the business underlying the bonds will be high enough to trigger payments from the trust. For example, if the underlying business is a block of homeowners' insurance policies in Florida (a hurricane-prone area), modeling data would include levels of policy deductibles, the current value of the insured

properties, construction characteristics of the insured properties, and exact location of the properties, including distance from the ocean.

For life insurers, the attraction of cat bonds as investments is that the risk associated with cat bonds—property catastrophe risk—is uncorrelated with the risk in the rest of investors' portfolios. Changes in economic conditions and the changes in the business community can affect the value of virtually all of the insurer's other investments. However, changes in the economy or the business community have no effect on the likelihood of a hurricane, flood, tornado, or earthquake occurring and thus have no effect on the value of catastrophe bonds. •

Sources: Susan Hodges, "Catastrophe Bonds: Your New Port in a Storm?" *NAMIC Online,* 12 November 1997, http://www.namic.org/n/pb/pc/111297/catastro.htm (15 November 1999). Sally Whitney, "How Much Is That Cat Bond?" *Best's Review,* Life/Health ed. (April 1999): 52–53.

- A **general account** is an account composed of assets that support the life insurer's contractual obligations for guaranteed products the insurer has issued, such as traditional whole life insurance policies.

- By contrast, a **separate account**, known as a **segregated fund** in Canada, is an account composed of assets that support the liabilities associated with the variable products the life insurer has issued, such as variable life insurance policies.

The investments held in an insurer's separate account are not subject to the same regulatory restrictions as the investments in the general account, because the investment risk associated with separate account products is assumed by the policyowners of the products rather than the insurer. For general account investments, however, the insurer bears the investment risk, and, thus, insurance regulators seek to assure that an insurer's general account investments are reasonably safe so that policyowners are protected.

In the United States, life insurers must comply with state requirements that govern their general account investments. Such regulatory requirements define which assets an insurer may include when reporting its statutory assets—the assets that back its required reserves—on the Annual Statement. The assets that may be reported as statutory assets are known as **admitted assets**. All other assets, known as **nonadmitted assets**, are reported separately and may not be applied to support an insurer's required reserves. For example, furniture, automobiles, and most office equipment are treated as nonadmitted assets, because the value of such assets is not considered to affect whether the insurer can meet its future obligations. We discuss these admitted assets and the Annual Statement in detail in Chapter 17.

The states also require insurers to follow specified safety guidelines in selecting their investments. These safety guidelines require the insurer's investment portfolios to be diversified and composed of high-quality assets that present relatively low investment risks. Such regulatory requirements take two general forms:

- Most states impose quantitative limitations on the amount of each type of asset an insurer may treat as admitted assets. For example, a state may prohibit insurers from investing more than 20 percent of their admitted assets in common stock.

- A few states impose a prudent person approach, establishing statutory guidelines that insurers are to follow in making investment decisions. Rather than placing quantitative limits on insurer investments, these states require an insurer to act as a prudent person would in making decisions about which assets it includes in its investment portfolio.

The states also regulate how insurers determine the value of their assets for statutory reporting purposes. The process of setting reported values for invested assets is known as **asset valuation**. Requirements concerning asset valuation are designed to assure that all insurers use the same standards in valuing assets and that valuations are accurate.

Canadian life insurance companies must abide by federal and/or provincial laws regarding their investments. As a general rule, these laws require insurers to follow a prudent person approach to investing. Insurers also must follow diversification guidelines that state the maximum allowable amount of each type of investment they may hold.

Insurance Company Investments

Life insurance companies, like other investors, can choose from many different types of investments. The assets in an investment portfolio can be classified according to whether the assets represent debt or equity.

- **Debt** represents the investor's loan of funds to the debt issuer in exchange for the promised repayment of the principal loaned and the payment of interest on the amount of the principal loaned. Bonds are the most common type of debt instrument in which insurers invest. Mortgage loans are another debt investment for insurers.

- **Equity** represents the investor's ownership or share of ownership in an asset such as a business or a piece of property. Common stock is an important example of an equity asset.

Most assets held by life insurance companies also can be classified as securities. A **security**, also called a *financial instrument*, is a document that represents either (1) an ownership interest in a business or (2) an obligation of indebtedness owed by a business, government, or agency. A security that represents an ownership interest in a business, such as a share of stock, is known as an *equity security*. A security that represents an obligation of indebtedness—for example, a government bond—is known as a *debt security*.

In this section, we describe how life insurers buy and sell securities and the types of assets in which they tend to invest—bonds, stock, mortgages, and real estate. Figure 16-3 shows the percentage of these investments held by U.S. and Canadian insurers. Note that the insurer's general account contains a greater proportion of lower-risk investments (such as bonds), and the separate account contains a greater proportion of higher-risk investments, such as stocks. The management of each type of investment requires special expertise.

FIGURE 16-3. Distribution of General Account and Separate Account Assets Held by Life Insurance Companies.

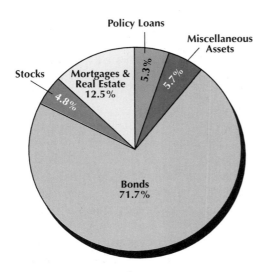

U.S. General Account Assets

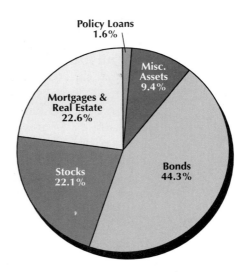

Canadian General Account Assets

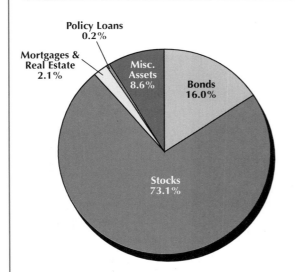

U.S. Separate Account Assets

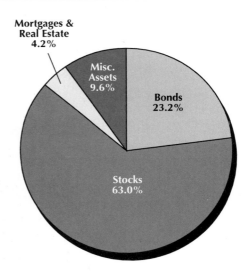

Canadian Segregated Funds Assets

Sources: Data from ACLI, *1999 Life Insurance Fact Book* (Washington, D.C: American Council of Life Insurance, 1999), 116–17. Used with permission. Data also from CLHIA, *Canadian Life and Health Insurance Facts*, 1999 ed. (Toronto: Canadian Life and Health Insurance Association, 1999), 21, 24.

Buying and Selling Securities

Insurers purchase new issues of securities through public offerings or private placements. Insurers purchase or sell previously issued securities on securities exchanges and through over-the-counter markets.

New Issues of Securities

In a *public offering*, the security issuer makes a new security available for sale to the public. Usually, an investment bank facilitates the offering. The issuing firm must register the security with the appropriate government agency, such as the Securities and Exchange Commission (SEC) in the United States or the securities commissions of the various provinces in Canada. The security registration document requires information about the type of security being offered and the issuing company's financial condition, management, industry competition, and experience. After being registered, the securities are distributed to investors through the investment bank's network of securities brokers and dealers.

Private placements have become a preferred way for insurers and other large institutional investors to purchase new issues of securities. A *private placement* is a method of issuing securities in which the security is sold directly from the issuer to an institutional investor. The issuer and the investor negotiate the price and terms of the private placement. Private placements are not required to be registered with government agencies, and an investment bank is not needed to act as a liaison between the issuer and the purchaser. As a result, issuing private placement securities is quicker and less costly than making a public offering.

Previously Issued Securities

Insurance companies can sell securities they own and purchase previously issued securities by placing orders on organized securities exchanges or over-the-counter markets. A *securities exchange* is a market in which buyers and sellers of securities (or their agents or brokers) meet in one location to conduct trades. The New York Stock Exchange and the Toronto Stock Exchange are well-known exchanges.

An *over-the-counter (OTC) market* is a market in which dealers at different locations who have an inventory of securities stand ready to buy and sell securities. OTC dealers are linked together by a vast computer network. The National Association of Securities Dealers Automated Quotation System (NASDAQ) is a well-known OTC market for stocks. The majority of bonds are traded as over-the-counter investments through bond dealers.

Bonds

A **bond** is a security that represents a debt the issuer of the bond owes to the investor who owns the bond, known as the **bondholder**. Businesses and governmental entities issue bonds as a method of raising funds. Local governments, for example, often issue bonds to finance major projects such as for building schools or transportation systems.

The business or government that issues a bond is legally obligated to pay the bondholder a specified amount of money on a specified date, known as the **maturity date**. The amount owed on the maturity date is specified on the bond and is known as the bond's **par value**, *face value*, or *maturity value*. Typically, bonds are issued with par values of $1,000, $10,000, or $100,000.

In addition to repaying a bond's par value, the bond issuer usually is obligated to make periodic—typically semiannual—interest payments to the bond owner. Such interest payments are referred to as *coupon interest payments* because the amount of the interest payments is based on an interest rate, known as the **coupon rate**, specified in the bond. Because the coupon rate generally is fixed for the life of the bond, bonds are a type of *fixed-income investment*. If the issuer does not meet the repayment terms of the bond, the bondholder has a legal claim on the assets of the issuer. A bondholder can earn a return from (1) the receipt of coupon interest payments and (2) a capital gain upon the sale of the bond before it matures.

A bond's market price—that is, the price at which the bond can be traded in the open market—is not necessarily the same as its par value. In fact, during much of a bond's life, the market price differs from the par value. The price of a bond changes as market interest rates change. As interest rates rise, bond prices fall, and as interest rates fall, bond prices rise. For this reason, bond prices and interest rates are said to be inversely related.

You can see the explanation for this inverse relationship with a simple example. Suppose an insurance company purchased a bond with an 8 percent coupon rate that matures in 10 years. The insurer purchased the bond when it was issued and paid the par value of $1,000. This bond provides annual income of $80 ($1,000 par value × .08 coupon rate = $80).

One year later, market interest rates rose, and new bonds were being issued with coupon rates of 10 percent. Because of this change in interest rates, the insurer's bond became less desirable, and, therefore, less valuable in the marketplace. That is, if the insurer tried to sell its bond for $1,000, it would have trouble finding a buyer; buyers would instead purchase newly issued 10 percent bonds because they provide $100 in annual income ($1,000 par value × .10 coupon rate = $100), rather than the $80 that the insurer's bond pays. To find a buyer for its

8 percent bond, the insurer would have to reduce the price below $1,000. As you can see, the rise in market interest rates has resulted in a drop in the price of bonds.

The same principle works in reverse. If interest rates had fallen to 6 percent one year after the insurer purchased its 8 percent bond, the insurer's bond, which pays $80 in annual income, would be more valuable than newly issued bonds that pay only $60 in income. Therefore, if the insurer wished to sell its 8 percent bond, it could demand a price above the $1,000 par value. In other words, the fall in interest rates caused a rise in the price of bonds. A bond is always worth its par value on the maturity date, and the bond always pays the same coupon payment, regardless of how much an investor pays to purchase the bond. For more on the mechanics of a bond, read Best Case Scenario 16-1.

Bonds are the largest investment holding in the general accounts of insurance companies because they are relatively safe investments that have extremely predictable cash-flow properties from the periodic coupon payments and the lump-sum payment of principal at maturity. Bonds are important for successful asset-liability management because an insurer can match the cash flows of various bonds with specific liability cash flows. Insurance companies hold many bonds until their maturity date and use the cash proceeds to pay benefits under insurance contracts and to provide guaranteed rates of return on whole life policies. Some insurers also actively trade bonds to take advantage of bond market segments that increase or decrease in value.

Best Case Scenario 16-1.   A Bond Issue.

To finance the construction of a new bridge, the government of State A issued $10 million worth of bonds to the public. These bonds were issued with a par value of $100,000 and had a 10-year term to maturity and a 5 percent coupon rate. The Best Friend Life Insurance Company purchased one of the $100,000 bonds for its investment portfolio.

As a result of this transaction, State A was obligated to pay Best Friend interest of $5,000 ($100,000 par value × 0.05 coupon rate = $5,000) each year for 10 years. Interest payments were due semian-

nually, and, thus, State A paid $2,500 every six months ($5,000 ÷ 2 payments = $2,500). On the bond's maturity date at the end of the 10-year period, the government made the last of the interest payments and also repaid the $100,000 par value to Best Friend.

If Best Friend had not wished to hold the bond until the bond's maturity date, Best Friend could have sold it on the open market. Suppose that after holding the bond for five years and receiving 10 of the semiannual interest payments, Best Friend sold the bond for $100,100.

(We can assume that interest rates had fallen, causing the bond price to rise.) The bond was purchased by Mountaintop Bank. Best Friend received the $100,100 sales price and had no further rights in the bond. Mountaintop became the new bondholder and held the bond until maturity. Mountaintop received the final 10 semiannual bond interest payments from State A and, on the maturity date, received State A's repayment of the $100,000 par value. •

Bond Risk and Return Characteristics

Several characteristics of a bond determine the degree of risk it presents to the purchaser. These characteristics include the bond's term to maturity, default risk, call provision, convertibility, and collateral. Generally, the riskier the bond, the higher the coupon rate the bond has.

Term to Maturity. A bond's term to maturity—the length of time until the bond matures—is one of the most important factors in determining its balance of risk and return. Bonds are subject to interest-rate risk because changes in market interest rates affect the price of bonds. Bonds with long terms to maturity (such as 10 years or more) are more susceptible to interest-rate risk than are bonds with short terms to maturity because interest rate changes are likely to occur at some time during the lengthy period before a long-term bond's maturity date. Long-term bonds generally offer higher coupon rates than short-term bonds to compensate investors for the higher risk.

Default Risk. *Default risk* is the risk that the issuer of a bond will be unable to make interest payments or to pay the par value of a bond when the bond matures. Financially strong issuers are less likely to default on a bond than are financially weak issuers, and so bonds issued by financially strong issuers have less risk and can offer lower returns than bonds issued by financially weak issuers. The safest of all bonds are those issued by the federal government, because the federal government can always raise taxes and even print money to pay off its debts.

Bond ratings help insurance companies and other bond purchasers determine the creditworthiness of bond issuers and the default risk of their bonds. A ***bond rating*** is a letter grade assigned by a bond rating agency to indicate the credit quality of a bond issue. Bond ratings are based on a variety of factors, such as the earnings record and financial strength of the issuing entity, the total amount of the issuer's bond indebtedness, and the property (if any) pledged to back up the bonds.

Two of the best-known bond rating agencies are Moody's Investors Service and Standard and Poor's Corporation. Figure 16-4 shows a sample of the bond ratings and descriptions published by these two rating agencies. The meanings and interpretations of the ratings vary only slightly from agency to agency. The higher the rating, the lower the default risk, the safer the bond investment, and the lower the expected rate of return. Bonds that are rated in the highest categories—above Baa (Moody's) or BBB (Standard & Poor's)—and that have the lowest risk of default are known as ***investment-grade bonds***. Almost all of the bonds held in the general accounts of life insurance companies are investment grade.

FIGURE 16-4. Bond Ratings.

Moody's Rating	Standard and Poor's Rating	Description
Aaa	AAA	Highest quality (lowest default risk)
Aa	AA	High quality
A	A	Upper medium grade
Baa	BBB	Medium grade
Ba	BB	Lower medium grade
B	B	Speculative
Caa	CCC	Poor
Ca	CC	Highly speculative
C	C	Lowest grade (highest default risk)

Call Provision. Some bonds contain a ***call provision*** that states the conditions under which the bond issuer has the right to force the bondholder to sell the bond back to the issuer at a date earlier than the maturity date. The call provision specifies when a bond can be called and the price that investors receive if the bond is called. A call provision increases the risk to the investor because the investor may be forced to part with the bond at an inopportune time.[3] Because of this increased risk, bonds with call provisions offer higher coupon rates than comparable noncallable bonds.

Convertibility. A ***convertible bond*** can be exchanged for shares of the issuing company's common stock at the option of the bondholder. This feature allows the bondholder to share in the firm's good fortunes if the price of the company's stock rises. Because a conversion feature offers a bondholder an additional way to generate a return on the investment, a conversion feature reduces the risk that the bondholder assumes. Because they have lower risk, convertible bonds also have lower coupon rates than do comparable nonconvertible bonds.

Collateral. Bonds may be either secured or unsecured, depending upon whether or not the bond is backed by ***collateral***—property that is pledged by the issuer to the investor until the debt obligation is satisfied. If a bond is secured by collateral, the bondholder can seize the collateral if the bond issuer fails to make bond payments when due. The seized property can then be sold to meet the bond obligations.

Unsecured bonds are not backed by collateral. Instead, they are backed only by the full faith and credit of the issuer. Unsecured bonds are more risky than comparable secured bonds and, consequently, unsecured bonds tend to have higher coupon rates than do secured bonds.

Types of Bonds

Bonds are often categorized by the type of entity or organization that issued them. Four categories of bonds in which insurers invest are corporate bonds, federal government bonds, agency bonds, and municipal bonds. Many other types of bonds exist, and new types of bonds are regularly created.

- *Corporate bonds* are issued by corporations, typically very large corporations. Corporate bonds may be secured or unsecured, and many are callable. Life insurance companies have been the largest institutional investors in the U.S. corporate bond markets since the 1930s.

- *Federal government bonds* are issued by the federal government and help pay government expenditures and finance the national debt. These bonds are backed by the credit and taxing authority of the federal government. Federal government bonds, such as *U.S. Treasury bonds* and *Government of Canada bonds* typically have maturities of 10 to 30 years and are regarded as low-risk, low–coupon-rate investments.

- *Agency bonds* are bonds issued by agencies of the federal government, such as the Federal National Mortgage Agency ("Fannie Mae") and the Federal Home Loan Mortgage Corporation ("Freddie Mac") in the United States and The Farm Credit Corporation in Canada. Federal agencies issue bonds to raise funds to buy or originate loans, such as home mortgage loans, farm loans, and educational loans. Agency bonds tend to have low risk, because most investors feel that a federal government would not allow a federal agency to default on its obligations.

- In the United States, *municipal bonds* are issued by state and local governments to finance projects such as school and road construction and other large programs. An important characteristic of most municipal bonds in the United States is that the interest paid to bondholders is exempt from federal income taxation. Municipal bonds may be backed by the credit and taxing authority of the issuing government, or they may be backed by the cash flow of a particular revenue-generating project for which the bonds were issued, such as a toll road or a public university

> **FAST FACT**
>
> In 1997, the Prudential Insurance Company of America purchased a $55 million bond secured by the royalty income of recording artist David Bowie.[4]

dormitory. In Canada, only bonds issued by city governments are known as *municipal bonds.* Bonds issued by provincial governments are known as *provincial bonds.*

Figure 16-5 shows the yields for several different types of bonds. Notice that, consistent with the risk-return tradeoff, bonds with lower risk have traditionally provided relatively lower returns than higher-risk bonds.

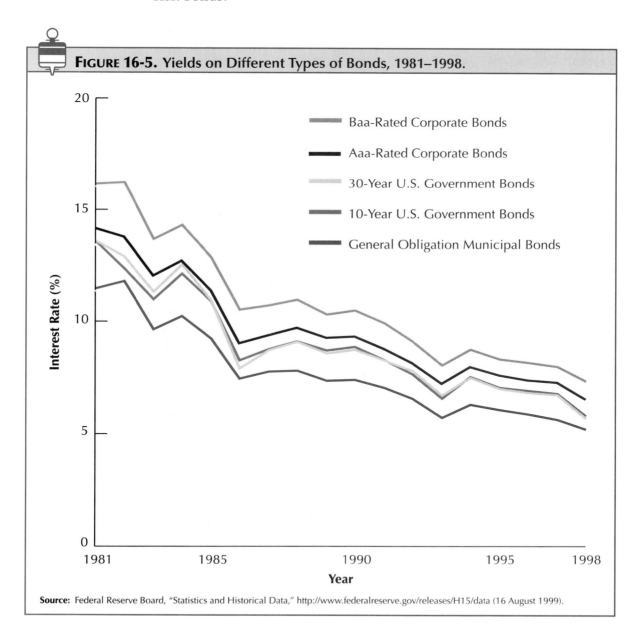

FIGURE 16-5. Yields on Different Types of Bonds, 1981–1998.

Source: Federal Reserve Board, "Statistics and Historical Data," http://www.federalreserve.gov/releases/H15/data (16 August 1999).

Stock

We have said that a share of stock represents an ownership interest in the issuing company and thus is an equity investment. Stocks, like bonds, are a form of financing for corporations that issue stock. During their organization phase, many companies issue stock as a way to raise cash to begin operations. Other companies operate as privately owned organizations for a period before "going public" and offering ownership shares in the form of stock.

A stockholder earns a return from stock through (1) capital gains upon the sale of the stock and (2) the receipt of cash dividends paid by the issuing corporation. Cash dividends are periodic distributions of the issuing company's earnings.

As a general rule, stocks are riskier than bonds for several reasons. First, the cash-flow characteristics associated with stocks are more variable than the cash-flow characteristics of bonds. For most stocks, the amount of a cash dividend can be changed over time and may not be paid at all, whereas the coupon payments of bonds are fixed in amount and timing. Second, stock prices tend to fluctuate much more than bond prices, because stocks have no maturity date and no maturity value. Third, stockholders have a lower priority claim than bondholders do on the issuing company's assets if the company goes out of business. Stockholders will be paid only if funds remain after bondholders and other creditors of the company have been paid.

Because of the higher risks and irregular cash-flow characteristics associated with stocks, insurers are limited by law as to the amount of their general account assets they can invest in stocks.

Mortgages

People and businesses use mortgages to finance the purchase of real estate. A ***mortgage*** is a loan, typically a long-term loan, secured by real estate. The borrower pays off the loan through the process of ***amortization***, which is the reduction of a debt by regular payments of principal and interest that result in full payment of the debt by the maturity date. If the borrower does not make the mortgage payments as they come due, the lender has the right to seize the property pledged for the loan and sell the property to satisfy the loan.

Life insurance companies have always been an important source of mortgage loans in the United States and Canada. The vast majority of insurers' mortgage holdings are commercial mortgages that finance retail stores, shopping centers, office buildings, factories, hospitals, and apartment buildings. Many of the mortgages that insurers originate are used to pay off short-term, bank-financed construction loans that

come due when the construction is completed. As with privately placed bonds, the insurer and the borrower of a commercial loan negotiate the terms of the loan. These terms include the loan amount, duration, and interest rate. By negotiating the loan terms, an insurer can match asset cash flows with expected liability cash flows.

Like bonds, mortgages are generally considered to be fixed-income investments, because the insurer receives interest payments of the same amount at regular intervals until a specified maturity date. Such a predictable stream of cash inflows is appealing to insurers. Mortgages are also appealing to insurers because they are secured debt instruments, and, thus, the insurers' investments are protected in the event of a default. As a general rule, however, mortgages tend to be somewhat riskier investments than bonds. This increased risk is the result of a number of characteristics of mortgages, including the following:

- Mortgage loans are not standardized. Each mortgage loan has a specific interest rate, maturity date, and contract terms. Although mortgages that vary from one another can be packaged for resale, individual mortgages are generally too small to be attractive investments for insurance companies. As a result, many mortgage loans are more difficult to resell than bonds. This relative lack of liquidity makes mortgages more risky than bonds.

- Changing market interest rates present significant risks to insurers that hold mortgages with fixed interest rates. If interest rates rise considerably, the interest an insurer earns from its mortgage investments will lag behind the interest the insurer could earn on new investments. If interest rates fall considerably, borrowers are likely to refinance their mortgage loans by paying off their existing loans and taking out new loans at lower interest rates. When a borrower refinances, the insurer loses the income stream it had planned to receive from the investment.

- Mortgages, like bonds, present a risk that the debtor may default and not repay the loan. Whereas bonds are rated by bond rating agencies, mortgage loans do not have such a rating. Thus, evaluating the default risk presented by a mortgage is more difficult than evaluating the risk presented by a bond.

Most insurers today also invest in residential mortgages. Rather than holding many individual mortgage loans, however, insurers participate in the residential mortgage market by buying mortgage-backed bonds, known as *collateralized mortgage obligations (CMOs)*, which are bonds secured by a pool of residential mortgage loans. Insurers favor CMOs because they can be bought and sold like bonds and thus are relatively liquid.

Real Estate

In addition to financing other people's purchases of real estate through investing in mortgage loans, life insurance companies directly purchase real estate. Because ownership is involved, real estate is classified as an equity investment. Most of insurers' real estate holdings are investment properties, such as office buildings, apartment complexes, and shopping centers in which available space is rented to generate income for the insurer. The remainder of an insurer's real estate holdings are (1) land and buildings that the company uses for its home office and regional offices and (2) real estate acquired through default on mortgage loans held by the insurer.

Real estate investments provide insurers with a return in the form of rental income and the opportunity for appreciation in the value of the investments. The rate of current income received on real estate generally exceeds the rates of cash dividends paid on common stock. However, the income stream from a real estate investment is unpredictable because of the possibility of vacancies in the properties. The unpredictable nature of real estate cash flows makes real estate investments less suited than bonds in meeting an insurer's asset-liability management needs. Also, the value of a piece of real estate can fluctuate considerably over time. As a result, real estate typically represents only a small portion of life insurers' general account assets.

Insurers can acquire real estate through several methods. The simplest method of acquiring real estate is outright purchase. The insurer may make the purchase directly, or it may form a subsidiary company that specializes in real estate investments. Another option is for the insurer to join with other companies (insurers or noninsurers) in purchasing the property. The partnering companies then share the rental income from the property.

Another method of investing in real estate is to participate in a **sale-and-leaseback transaction**, under which the owner of a building sells the building to an investor (in this case an insurance company) but immediately leases back the building from the investor. The individual or organization that leases the building from the insurer is known as the **lessee** and is responsible for the maintenance and operation of the building. The insurer, as **lessor**, is freed from administration of the property—such as collecting rent from the building's tenants and maintaining the property. However, the insurer receives regular income in the form of lease payments from the lessee.

Policy Loans

When a policyowner borrows against a policy's cash value, the insurer classifies the loan as an investment. Although insurers charge

customers interest on policy loans, the interest rate is relatively low compared to the rates of interest insurers earn on their other investments. Policy loans make up a relatively small portion of the assets held by life insurance companies. A higher-than-expected level of policy loans can limit the insurance company's overall portfolio investment returns because, by loaning the money, the insurer is deprived of the opportunity to invest it elsewhere for a higher return.

Policy loans differ in a number of respects from other insurance company investments.

- An insurer cannot control the timing of a policy loan; the decision to take out a policy loan is made by the policyowner.

- Policy loans, unlike other loans, do not require the borrower to establish a systematic repayment plan. Thus, an insurer cannot count on a steady stream of cash inflows from its outstanding policy loans.

- In contrast to other debt instruments, policy loans do not have contractual maturity dates. A customer need not pay back the policy loan or the loan interest so long as the policy has sufficient cash value to secure the loan plus any accrued interest. However, any outstanding policy loan and accrued interest are deducted from the benefit payable when the insured person dies.

Investment Strategies

Life insurance companies develop investment strategies that correspond to their solvency and profitability goals and their asset-liability management practices. One way to describe an investment strategy is by its level of aggressiveness. Within the constraints of regulatory limitations on general account investments, life insurers choose whether to pursue an aggressive investment strategy, a conservative investment strategy, or a strategy in between. Insurance companies that are financially strong and that have a large amount of capital and surplus can, if they choose, take a relatively aggressive approach with their investments. Such a strategy involves taking more investment risks in order to earn potentially higher returns and increase the wealth and profitability of the company.

As you have seen, equity investments are generally riskier than debt investments. In order to boost its potential returns, an insurer pursuing an aggressive investment strategy may maximize its investment in equities, such as corporate stocks and real estate, and its investment in lower-quality (below investment-grade) debt investments, as al-

lowed by regulatory requirements. The insurer also might choose longer-term debt investments over shorter-term debt; as a general rule, the longer the term to maturity of a debt investment, the riskier the investment.

A conservative investment strategy focuses on safeguarding the company's capital rather than on earning high returns. Earning adequate returns is still important for an insurer following a conservative strategy, but such an insurer is willing to give up some potential returns in exchange for reducing the possibility of significant investment losses. A conservative investment strategy involves maximizing holdings of high-quality, shorter-term bonds and minimizing holdings of equity securities. As Insight 16-1 explains, an insurance company's corporate form can influence the aggressiveness of its investment strategy.

Another way to categorize investment strategy is by the amount of trading done in a portfolio. With regard to debt investments, the two

 Insight 16-1. **Study: Greater Investment Risk Increases Rewards for Mutuals.**

When it comes to investing assets, mutual life insurers are more willing to take on risk than their publicly owned counterparts, according to a study. The additional risk from investing more aggressively brought additional earnings for mutual life companies in 1997, according to PriceWaterhouseCoopers' Fourth Annual Intercompany Investment Performance study.

Mutual life companies tend to invest in higher-risk markets than stock life companies, according to Jack Lutkowitz, director of the study. For example, mutual life companies invested more in private placements—24 percent vs. 16 percent for stock life insurers—and less in public bonds—26 percent vs. 38 percent for publicly owned companies.

Because of the differences in their products and reporting requirements, mutual companies can take a longer-term view of investments than stock companies, which are under more pressure from stockholders for immediate performance, Lutkowitz said.

Unlike stock companies, mutual companies aren't required to disclose their quarterly financial information, which may lessen the pressure to produce immediate results and allow mutuals to pursue riskier, but potentially more profitable, long-term returns, he said.

Lutkowitz said that stock companies focus more on annuity business, which tends to have shorter liabilities, while mutual companies sell predominantly long-term products such as traditional life insurance. Because mutual company investments are aligned more to liabilities with longer durations, mutuals can invest more aggressively, Lutkowitz said.

For stock companies, 70.8 percent of their 1997 gross investment income came from bonds. Invest-

ments in mortgage loans accounted for 11.3 percent, while preferred and common stocks accounted for 4.1 percent. Policy and collateral loans accounted for 4.9 percent, other investments accounted for 4.1 percent, real estate accounted for 2.9 percent, and cash and short-term investments accounted for 1.9 percent.

For mutual companies, 62.2 percent of their 1997 gross investment income came from bonds, and investments in mortgage loans accounted for 15.1 percent. Real estate accounted for 8.2 percent, policy and collateral loans accounted for 5.6 percent, other investments accounted for 3.1 percent, preferred and common stocks accounted for 3 percent, and cash and short-term investments accounted for 2.8 percent of gross investment income. •

Source: Excerpted from Meg Green, "Study: Greater Investment Risk Increases Rewards for Mutuals," *BestWeek*, Life/Health ed. (8 March 1999): 9. © A.M. Best Company. Used with permission.

extremes are a buy-and-hold strategy and an active management strategy. Under a ***buy-and-hold strategy***, asset managers carefully select debt securities and expect to hold them until they mature, are prepaid, or default. The total mix of the asset portfolio remains fairly static. Selection of appropriate securities is crucial to the success of this strategy, because the asset manager bases investment success largely on original selections for the portfolio. Under an ***active management strategy***, the asset manager views any investment in the portfolio as potentially tradable, if doing so would improve the portfolio's performance. Theoretically, the entire mix of assets in the portfolio can be changed at any time.

In reality, most insurers' investment strategies fall somewhere between the two extremes of buy-and-hold and active management. A strict buy-and-hold strategy is generally too inflexible, because asset managers may need to make changes in the portfolio as necessitated by changes in economic conditions, investment performance, or asset-liability management requirements. Similarly, an excessively active management strategy is undesirable because selling a large portion of the company's assets at any time is risky, and a high rate of asset turnover can produce high brokerage commission expenses and potentially unfavorable tax consequences. Active management also requires more management time than a buy-and-hold strategy.

Key Terms

investment
risk
principal
portfolio
asset manager
spread
rate of return
interest
simple interest
compound interest
capital gain
deflation
risk-return tradeoff
diversification
general account
separate account (segregated fund)
admitted asset
nonadmitted asset

asset valuation
debt
equity
security (financial instrument)
public offering
private placement
securities exchange
over-the-counter (OTC) market
bond
bondholder
maturity date
par value (face value, maturity value)
coupon rate
default risk
bond rating
investment-grade bond
call provision
convertible bond

Key Terms, continued

collateral

mortgage

amortization

collateralized mortgage
  obligation (CMO)

sale-and-leaseback transaction

lessee

lessor

buy-and-hold strategy

active management strategy

Endnotes

1. ACLI, *1999 Life Insurance Fact Book* (Washington, D.C.: American Council of Life Insurance, 1999), 114.

2. "More Insurers Outsourcing Investment Management," *Best's Review*, Life/Health ed. (June 1999): 79.

3. Bond issuers typically call bonds when market interest rates drop. In this way, issuers can issue new bonds with lower coupon rates. If the bond that an insurer is holding is called, and the insurer wishes to re-invest the proceeds in another bond, it will probably have to purchase a bond with a coupon rate that is lower than the original bond's coupon rate.

4. Ron Panko, "Going for the Big Picture," *Best's Review*, Life/Health ed. (October 1998): 43.

Accounting and Financial Reporting

LEARNING OBJECTIVES

After reading this chapter, you should be able to

- Give examples of the internal users and external users of accounting information

- Describe the differences between financial accounting and management accounting

- Describe the differences between generally accepted accounting principles (GAAP) and statutory accounting practices, and explain how each of these accounting standards is used

- Name and describe the central activities of the typical financial accounting operations in life insurance companies

- State the purposes of an Annual Statement, an Annual Return, and an annual report

- Understand how and why insurers prepare budgets and undertake cost accounting

- Explain the purposes of auditing

CHAPTER OUTLINE

So far in our discussion of financial management in life insurance companies, you have learned how insurers set financial goals; establish financial strategy; and manage capital, cash flows, and investments. This chapter concludes our discussion of financial management with a look at the accounting and financial reporting functions in a life insurance company.

Accounting is a system or set of rules and methods for collecting, recording, summarizing, and analyzing a company's financial operations. *Financial reporting* is the process of presenting financial data about a company's financial position, the company's operating performance, and its flow of funds for an accounting period. Financial reporting includes the preparation and filing of financial statements, many of which are required by law.

The accounting function of any business traditionally has been thought of as scorekeeping. Businesses measure their performance in financial terms: assets owned, net income earned, expenses incurred, and so forth. But accounting and financial reporting are also essential for planning an insurer's solvency and profitability goals and for determining whether the company is meeting these goals. In other words, managers use information provided through accounting and financial reporting to help answer the questions, "How has the company performed up to now?" and "How can the company perform better in the future?"

We begin this chapter by explaining who uses financial accounting information and how the accounting department is usually organized. Then we discuss the laws and accounting conventions that guide insurers' accounting and financial reporting activities. We distinguish between financial accounting and management accounting, and we examine the essential aspects of each of these types of accounting. The chapter concludes with an explanation of internal and external auditing.

Users of Accounting Information

Many people use accounting information to make decisions related to a company. The users of accounting information fall generally into two groups: internal users and external users, as shown in Figure 17-1.

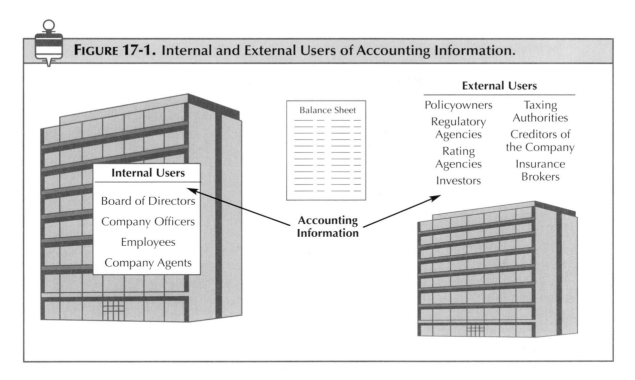

FIGURE 17-1. Internal and External Users of Accounting Information.

Internal Users

Internal users of accounting information range from company officers and members of the board of directors, who conduct strategic planning and financial management, to agents and internal marketers. Managers in all functional areas also use accounting information to set departmental or team guidelines and procedures.

For example, the managers in product development use accounting information to help evaluate the sales patterns and the types of purchasers of various insurance and financial services products, and then to plan new products and additional features for existing products. In the actuarial department, managers use accounting information to determine whether the premiums received for each product are adequate to pay the insurer's costs for product development, distribution, administration, benefit payments, and commissions and to provide a profit for the company. Other functional areas, such as underwriting, claims, customer service, legal, human resources, and information systems, also evaluate accounting information and use it as a guide for day-to-day operations and for long-term planning.

External Users

External users are people outside of an insurance company who have a need for information contained in the company's financial statements. External users of financial information about an insurance company include

- Insurance regulatory agencies, such as state and provincial insurance departments that oversee insurers' operations and analyze their solvency

- Insurance rating agencies that need financial information to rate companies on their financial strength and claim-paying ability

- Current and potential policyowners of the company

- Current and potential investors in the company

- Government taxing authorities

- The company's competitors, including other insurers and competing brokers and agents

- Creditors of the company

Responsibilities and Organization of the Accounting Department

Generally, the accounting department of a life insurance company is responsible for gathering, recording, analyzing, and distributing information about the company's financial operations. The accounting department carries out the following activities:

- Establishing a system of *accounts*, which are basic storage units used to record, group, and summarize similar types of business transactions

- Maintaining the company's accounting records

- Recording cash receipts and cash disbursements

- Preparing and analyzing financial statements

- Overseeing the preparation of tax returns. In some companies, the accounting department prepares the returns; other insurers establish a separate tax department for this responsibility.

- Assisting managers with interpreting financial results

- Analyzing the company's operating costs and allocating costs to the areas that incur them

- Assisting financial managers with developing long-term financial plans for the entire organization

- Compiling budgets and preparing reports of performance that deviates from budgets

An audit committee of the company's board of directors usually oversees an insurer's accounting operations, which typically are centralized in a single accounting department. The person in charge of the accounting department usually holds the title *controller* (or *comptroller*), reflecting the fact that the accounting area is responsible for controlling the company's operations and protecting its resources. Reporting to the controller are a number of assistant controllers or assistant managers, each overseeing a different unit of the accounting department. Typical units include policy accounting, financial reporting, cash accounting, cost accounting, budgeting, investment accounting, and tax accounting. Employees within each unit include senior accountants, accounting analysts, and accounting clerks. Figure 17-2 shows these typical relationships.

One area—internal auditing—deserves special mention. Internal auditing examines the company's accounting operations, financial statements, and systems of internal controls. Depending on the insurer, internal auditing may be considered part of accounting, part of compliance, or an independent department. Even when considered part of accounting or compliance, internal auditing usually reports directly to the audit committee. This reporting relationship maintains the independence and objectivity of the internal auditing staff and is necessary to ensure internal auditors are impartial when they examine the company's operations and financial statements.

You should be aware that every department in an insurance company performs tasks involving business transactions that must be accounted for, so a great deal of interaction occurs between the accounting department and other functional areas throughout the company. For example, the accounting department works with the actuarial department to complete the financial statements the insurer must file

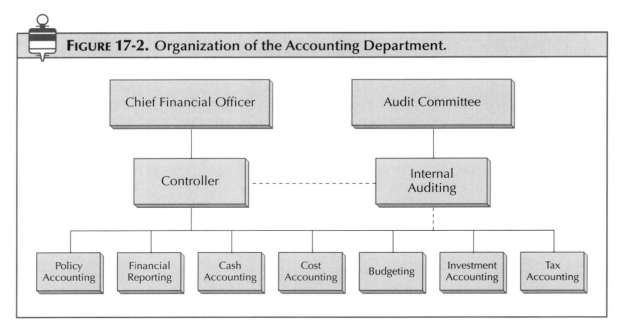

FIGURE 17-2. Organization of the Accounting Department.

with insurance regulators. The accounting department provides the investment area with information about the tax consequences of making certain investments. Accounting also helps plan and control operating budgets for each of the company's divisions. Typically, accounting serves mainly as an advisory area to the other departments and leaves final business decisions with the departments.

Financial Accounting

Each insurance company establishes accounting systems that are designed to provide reliable and consistent tracking and reporting of financial information. However, users of accounting information have different uses for the information, and they need to answer different questions with regard to a company's finances. As a result, two general types of accounting—financial accounting and management accounting—have been developed to meet the diverse needs of the company's users of accounting information. ***Financial accounting*** focuses primarily on gathering and summarizing data to meet financial reporting and tax requirements. ***Management accounting***, also called *managerial accounting,* is the process of identifying, measuring, analyzing, and communicating financial information so that internal managers can decide how best to use the company's resources. The subject of this section is financial accounting. We will describe management accounting in the next section of this chapter.

Much of financial accounting is mandated by law. Life insurance companies must prepare numerous financial statements according to specific accounting conventions and regulatory requirements, and must file these financial statements with specific regulatory and governmental agencies at prescribed times. Financial accounting must be precise, accurate, and timely. The perspective of financial accounting is historical because it is most concerned with events that have already taken place. Although an insurer's financial accounting reports are prepared primarily for external users, these reports also provide internal managers with valuable information about the company's current financial condition.

Accounting Standards

Insurers are required by law to conduct their financial accounting activities in accordance with certain accounting standards. These standards advise, among other things, how and when accountants recognize revenues and expenses and how they value assets and liabilities. In accounting, **recognition** is the process of (1) classifying items in a financial transaction as assets, liabilities, capital and surplus, revenue, or expenses, and (2) recording the transaction in the company's accounting records. (Read Best Case Scenario 17-1 for more on recognition in accounting.) Two important accounting standards for life insurers are generally accepted accounting principles (GAAP) and statutory accounting practices.

Generally Accepted Accounting Principles

Generally accepted accounting principles (GAAP) are a set of financial accounting standards, conventions, and rules that U.S. stock insurers and all Canadian insurers follow when summarizing transactions and preparing financial statements. The underlying premise of financial statements prepared in accordance with GAAP is the ***going-concern concept***. Under this concept, accounting processes are based on the assumption that a company will continue to operate for an indefinite period of time. Financial statements prepared according to GAAP provide users with financial information that is based on standardized definitions, valuation methods, and formats. As a result, users can effectively evaluate the financial performance of one company from year to year and can compare the financial performances of several companies.

To provide uniform financial reporting in most of the business community in the United States, the Securities and Exchange Commission

Best Case Scenario 17-1.

Recognition of Financial Transactions.

The Best Friend Life Insurance Company and Bob's Hobby Shop recognize financial transactions differently. Best Friend recognizes a financial transaction when the company incurs a financial obligation as either the payor or the payee. In contrast, Bob's Hobby Shop recognizes financial transactions only when cash actually changes hands. As a result, Best Friend's financial statements generally present a more accurate picture of the company's current financial position than the financial statement's for Bob's Hobby Shop present about its current condition.* To illustrate, consider the following example.

December 20: Best Friend and Bob's Hobby Shop each purchased computer equipment on account from the same computer store.

Under the terms of the transactions, Best Friend and Bob's Hobby Shop were each required to make full payment for the equipment within 30 days.

Best Friend

> Best Friend, December 20
> Computer Equipment Owned ⟶ Increase
> Debts Owed ⟶ Increase

Best Friend's accountants recognized the computer purchase by recording an accounting entry. The entry documented two facts about Best Friend's financial condition:

1. The dollar value of computer equipment owned by the company was greater after the purchase than it was before the purchase.

2. The company owed money for the new computer equipment.

Because Best Friend recognized the transaction in this way, Best Friend's financial statements prepared immediately after the purchase reflected the increases in (1) the dollar value of the company's computer equipment owned and (2) amounts owed on account.

Bob's Hobby Shop

> Bob's Hobby Shop, December 20
> No Entry

Because no cash changed hands on the day of the purchase, the accountant for Bob's did not recognize the transaction with an accounting entry. As a result, the company's financial statements on that date did not show either an increase in the dollar amount of computer equipment owned by the company or the amount owed to the computer store.

January 10: Best Friend and Bob's each paid the computer store to settle their accounts.

Best Friend

> Best Friend, January 10
> Cash ⟶ Decrease
> Debts Owed ⟶ Decrease

Best Friend's accountants recorded this payment with an accounting entry that (1) reduced the company's cash balance by the amount paid to the computer store and (2) eliminated the debt owed to the computer store.

Bob's Hobby Shop

> Bob's Hobby Shop, January 10
> Computer Equipment Owned ⟶ Increase
> Cash ⟶ Decrease

The accountant at Bob's made an accounting entry that recorded both the purchase of and the payment for the computer equipment. •

* Assume that these financial statements are prepared according to generally accepted accounting principles (GAAP).

(SEC) mandates that all stock insurance companies and any company that sells variable life insurance must prepare general-use financial statements according to GAAP. The Financial Accounting Standards Board (FASB), a private organization funded by the accounting profession, establishes U.S. GAAP requirements. All life insurers in Canada must prepare their financial statements according to Canadian GAAP. The Canadian Institute of Chartered Accountants (CICA), an association of professional accountants, establishes Canadian GAAP requirements. The requirements for U.S. GAAP and Canadian GAAP are not identical, but they are very similar. Specific differences between the two are beyond the scope of this text.

Statutory Accounting Practices

In addition to preparing financial statements according to GAAP, insurance companies in the United States must prepare a second set of financial statements. State insurance laws require all insurers to prepare financial statements for insurance regulators according to ***statutory accounting practices***, which are a set of financial accounting standards that implement current statutes and regulations. Statutory accounting practices are designed to provide insurance regulators with information about an insurer's solvency.

Insurance companies have to satisfy the statutory accounting requirements for each state in which they write business. Traditionally, statutory accounting requirements have varied—in some cases considerably—from state to state. However, in 1998, the National Association of Insurance Commissioners (NAIC) approved the Codification of Statutory Accounting Principles, which creates one set of written standards for statutory accounting. Although each state still has authority over the statutory accounting guidelines in the state, the state may adopt Codification as its own statutory guidelines. If uniformly adopted by all states, Codification would replace the disparate sets of accounting standards used by the states. The effective date for Codification was set for January 1, 2001. For more on Codification, read Insight 17-1.

Statutory accounting is not a requirement in Canada. However, Canadian insurance companies that operate in the United States follow statutory accounting practices when preparing financial reports of their U.S. business.

Generally, statutory accounting is perceived as a more conservative approach than that of the going-concern concept used by GAAP. ***Accounting conservatism*** is the choice of a financial reporting method that results in the projection of lower values for a company's assets, higher values for its liabilities and expenses, and a lower level of net

Insight 17-1. | **Codification of Statutory Accounting.**

Statutory accounting practices needed an overhaul. Too much variation in accounting standards and practices existed from state to state.

For each state, statutory accounting requirements could be found in (1) the existing *Accounting Practices and Procedures Manual* of the National Association of Insurance Commissioners (NAIC), (2) the state's own variations of statutory accounting procedures, often documented in many forms, (3) the instructions accompanying the state's Annual Statement form, and (4) many other sources. Adding to the complexity of statutory accounting was the introduction of new insurance products for which no accounting rules were available.

Codification—the development of a uniform set of account rules for all states—was the solution, but achieving this goal was a difficult, seven-year process. The NAIC assembled a working group—a panel of regulators—to study Codification. The working group wrote a statement of concepts for statutory accounting. Disparate accounting practices were collected, modified into a single standard, revised, dis-

cussed and debated by insurers and regulators, modified and debated again, and finally approved. At times the debates become contentious, but compromises were eventually reached, and Codification became a reality in the spring of 1998.

The written rules for Codification were assembled in the *Accounting Practices and Procedures Manual, version effective January 1, 2001*. To be effective in a state, Codification must be adopted by the state's legislature. The NAIC anticipates that most states will adopt Codification in full or with specific exceptions.

Codification creates change for insurance companies operating in the United States. For example, insurers may have to modify their accounting systems in order to abide by the new accounting rules. Also, Codification includes new procedures for valuing certain assets and liabilities, and these new valuation methods can affect an insurer's financial condition. The amount of change for each company is largely a function of how much current state accounting statutes differ from the codified *Accounting Practices and Procedures Manual*.

Areas of accounting in which change is likely to be felt most significantly include the following:
• Valuation of assets
• Estimation of liabilities, in particular, contingency reserves
• Calculation of income taxes
• Treatment of transactions between affiliated companies
• Disclosure of information in the notes accompanying financial statements

The likelihood of states adopting Codification as their own statutory guidelines will increase if the NAIC makes Codification an accreditation requirement. The NAIC's accreditation program consists of model laws, regulations, and other tools that states must have in place to regulate for solvency. Only the states that have these tools in place receive accreditation from the NAIC. Between 1999 and 2001, state regulators and insurers are to consider Codification as an accreditation requirement. A final vote by the NAIC on the matter is to occur in early 2002. If the measure is approved, states will have until 2004 to adopt Codification. •

Sources: "NAIC Codification—An Overview of Statement of Statutory Accounting Principles No. 54," *The Financial Reporter* (January 1999): 3–4. Mark A. Parkin and Steven M. Butters, "Codification: A New Era Begins," *National Underwriter*, Life & Health/Financial Services ed. (June 8, 1998): A18, A45. Henry W. Siegel, "Laws and Sausages: How Statutory Accounting Was Codified," *Contingencies* (September/ October 1998): 36–39.

income than would be the case if the company used a less conservative reporting method. Conservatism is fundamental to statutory accounting because it focuses on demonstrating to regulators that the insurer is able to meet its policy obligations even under adverse circumstances. In contrast, GAAP is oriented more toward demonstrating the company's profitability.

Financial Accounting Operations

The basic financial accounting operations in life insurance companies can be classified as follows:

- Policy accounting

- Investment accounting

- General accounting

- Tax accounting

In this section, we'll discuss each of these areas of accounting and the challenges they pose to life insurance accountants.

Policy Accounting

Each year, an insurance company processes millions of transactions related to life insurance policies. *Policy accounting* is the accounting operation that is responsible for recording all financial transactions related to the policies an insurer has issued, including accounting for premiums, commissions, policy loans, policy dividends, and claim payments.

- Premium accounting systems ensure that (1) policyowners are properly billed, (2) premium payments from policyowners are properly accounted for, and (3) premium income is recorded by appropriate categories so that the company can use the data to compute premium taxes, prepare financial statements, and prepare management accounting reports (discussed later in this chapter).

- The basic policy record used for premium accounting usually identifies the producer who is to receive the commission and the amount of the commission. Accounting systems used by most insurers are programmed to automatically update both the policy record and the commission record upon the insurer's receipt of a premium payment.

- Accounting for policy loans requires recording the principal (the initial amount borrowed) and interest on each policy loan the insurer makes. If the policyowner does not pay the interest when due, the company adds the unpaid interest to the amount of the outstanding loan.

- Once each year, an insurer's board of directors declares a policy dividend on participating policies according to a dividend sched-

ule recommended by the company's chief actuary. Accounting for policy dividends involves recording the amount of each policy dividend and applying the dividend according to the dividend option that each policyowner has chosen.

- When a claim payment is authorized and the correct payee identified, the accounting area records the transaction and issues a check to be mailed to the appropriate person. If the policy proceeds are left with the insurance company under a settlement option, accountants note the amount of the proceeds and the conditions of the settlement option.

Investment Accounting

The accounting area is responsible for recording all accounting entries related to the assets in an insurer's investment portfolios. Accounting for investments includes tracking and recording the following amounts:

- The cash inflows and cash outflows associated with the insurer's investments. The cash inflows include investment income (bond and mortgage interest payments, cash dividends on stocks owned, and rental income) and sales of securities. The cash outflows typically are for purchases of securities and investment expenses such as brokerage commissions and money management fees. Tracking these investment cash flows is critical to the company's asset-liability management efforts.

- Investment valuations that will be used in the company's financial statements. The differences between GAAP and statutory accounting require accountants to maintain separate accounting records in which they assign different valuations to their assets.

- Realized and unrealized gains and losses from investments. An ***unrealized gain (or loss)*** is one that has not become actual. When an investment matures or is sold, any gain or loss on the investment becomes a ***realized gain (or loss)***.

In addition, the accounting area establishes the accounting records necessary to divide the insurer's general account by product line. Many insurers segment the general investment account so that they can evaluate cash flow patterns of different product lines and can conduct asset-liability management. Accountants usually establish an investment account—a segment—for each product line within the general account.

Keep in mind that the segments within the general account are *not* the same as separate accounts, which contain the assets backing the insurer's variable life insurance and pension products. All of the assets in the general account are available to support any of the liabilities that are backed by the general account. Segmenting the general account by product line helps financial managers track and manage cash flows effectively.

General Accounting

As business entities, life insurance companies undertake some of the same basic accounting operations that all businesses undertake. One example is payroll accounting, which involves calculating employees' wages, preparing paychecks, maintaining payroll records, and producing payroll reports for internal management and government agencies. Each employee's payroll record typically contains information such as salary rate, number of dependents claimed, deductions from income, and year-to-date totals of income and deductions. Accountants record federal, state, provincial, and local payroll tax deductions for each employee so that this information can be included in quarterly reports to the government and in periodic and annual withholding statements to employees. Paychecks are produced before the actual payroll date so that employees will receive them on the payroll date. Many companies use electronic systems to transfer paychecks directly into an employee's bank account or into several accounts if the employee so directs.

Another type of general accounting that all businesses undertake is disbursement accounting. The objectives of disbursement accounting are to (1) provide a permanent record of all cash disbursed, (2) confirm that all cash disbursements are properly authorized, and (3) ensure that all disbursements are charged to the proper account. Large expenditures must usually be supported by a **voucher**, which is a check request signed by someone with the authority to disburse the amount involved. Large, continuous disbursements, such as payroll checks, commission checks, and policy dividends, are generally made electronically.

Tax Accounting

The accounting area keeps records related to all the company's taxes and prepares tax returns and filings. In addition to income taxes, unemployment taxes, and property taxes that all businesses pay, insurance companies also pay **premium taxes**, which are taxes on the premium income an insurer earns within a state or province. Premium taxes are calculated as a percentage of premium income. For financial reporting purposes, insurers maintain separate accounting records of premiums for each state and province in which they write business.

Many insurers' accounting systems are automated so that premium taxes are automatically calculated at the end of the year on the basis of premium income recorded in each state or province during the year.

The definition of premium income for premium tax purposes varies from state to state. Some states impose a tax on gross premiums, whereas other states and all Canadian provinces allow an insurer to deduct the amount of policy dividends from gross premiums before calculating the amount of premium taxes owed. Some states require insurers to pay the greater of the premium tax or the state income tax. Accountants must make sure they follow the applicable premium tax rules in each state or province before calculating the premium taxes due.

Financial Reporting

The culmination of financial accounting is financial reporting—the preparation and filing of required financial statements that communicate summaries of a company's numerous financial transactions. Accountants use financial accounting to organize and summarize a company's business transactions so that the company can satisfy financial reporting requirements. As noted earlier, the accounting department oversees all of the company's financial reporting. The primary purpose of financial reporting is to present an organization's financial data in a meaningful way to external users. Two important financial statements that all types of businesses prepare are the balance sheet and the income statement, which we discussed in Chapter 15. Two other important financial statements are

- The *statement of cash flows*, which provides information about the company's cash receipts, cash disbursements, and net change in cash during a specified period

- The *statement of surplus*, which provides information about the change in value of the company's surplus account during a specified period

The accounting standard—GAAP or statutory accounting—that a company uses to prepare these financial statements depends on the purpose of the statements, the external users for whom the statements are intended, and the applicable laws. Insurers must prepare special financial reports that are required by insurance regulators in the United States and Canada. In the remainder of this section, we describe these reports—the Annual Statement in the United States and the Annual Return in Canada. Finally, we describe the annual report.

FAST FACT

Life insurance company financial reporting in the United States dates back to 1828 when an act of the New York legislature required "all monied corporations" to file annual reports with the state controller on a prescribed form. The State of New York thus became the originator of what we now know as statutory accounting for the insurance business.[1]

The Annual Statement in the United States

As you learned in Chapter 2, the statutory *Annual Statement* is a document that presents information about an insurer's operations and financial performance, with an emphasis on demonstrating the insurer's solvency. The Annual Statement must be prepared according to statutory accounting practices. Each year, life insurers in the United States must file an Annual Statement with the NAIC and the insurance department of every state in which they write business. Canadian insurers that operate in the United States must file an Annual Statement of their U.S. business with the appropriate states. (Read Focus on Technology 17-1 for more on Annual Statement filing.) An insurer's senior officers must attest to the accuracy of the information contained in the Annual Statement.

The general form for the Annual Statement was developed by the NAIC, although each state's insurance commissioner specifies the exact format and contents of that state's Annual Statement. The Annual Statement typically includes the following reports and other information:

- A balance sheet in the form of an *Assets* page and a *Liabilities, Surplus, and Other Funds* page. We have provided examples of these pages in Figures 17-3 and 17-4.

- An income statement in the form of a *Summary of Operations* page

- A *Capital and Surplus Account* page

- A *Cash Flow* statement

- Other exhibits, schedules, and supplemental reports that support the totals shown in the primary financial statements. Such sup-

---

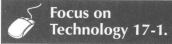

Focus on Technology 17-1.

Internet Filing of the Annual Statement.

In 1998, the National Association of Insurance Commissioners (NAIC) began accepting Annual Statement filings from insurance companies via the Internet. A total of 739 insurers took advantage of the online filing system in the first year.

The Internet-based filing system reduces the time for processing and receiving filings, according to NAIC staff. The result was that Annual Statement filings came in earlier than usual. Overall, the filing and processing went smoothly in the first year. •

Source: Rick Pullen, "NAIC's First Filing Period over Internet Runs Smoothly," *BestWeek,* Life/Health ed. (19 April 1999): 6.

FIGURE 17-3. The Annual Statement Assets Page.

	ASSETS	1 December 31, 2001	2 December 31, 2000
1.	Bonds (less . . . . $0 liability for asset transfers with put options)	 316,689,427	 312,135,670
2.	Stocks:		
2.1	Preferred stocks		
2.2	Common stocks	 2,000	
3.	Mortgage loans on real estate	. . . 71,428,839	 64,547,665
4.	Real estate:		
4.1	Properties occupied by the company (less . . . . $0 encumbrances)		
4.2	Properties acquired in satisfaction of debt (less . . . . $0 encumbrances) .	 5,816,146	 7,534,676
4.3	Investment real estate (less . . . . $0 encumbrances)		
5.	Policy loans	. . . 51,740,233	 50,719,951
6.	Premium notes, including . . . . $0 for first year premiums		
7.	Collateral loans		
8.1	Cash on hand and on deposit	 2,460,584	 2,544,758
8.2	Short-term investments		
9.	Other invested assets		
10.	Aggregate write-ins for invested assets	 654,485	
10A.	Subtotals, cash and invested assets (Lines 1 to 10)	. . . 448,791,714	 437,482,720
11.	Reinsurance ceded:		
11.1	Amounts recoverable from reinsurers	 1,708,484	 182,664
11.2	Commissions and expense allowances due	 143,958	 2,122
11.3	Experience rating and other refunds due	 50	 1,597
12.	Electronic data processing equipment	 205,714	 182,229
13.	Federal income tax recoverable	 485,562	 1,349,091
14.	Life insurance premiums and annuity considerations deferred and uncollected	 6,170,771	 6,322,794
15.	Accident and health premiums due and unpaid		
16.	Investment income due and accrued	 6,498,487	 6,637,745
17.	Net adjustment in assets and liabilities due to foreign exchange rates		
18.	Receivable from parent, subsidiaries and affiliates		
19.	Amounts receivable relating to uninsured accident and health plans		
21.	Aggregate write-ins for other than invested assets	 268,811	 219,296
22.	Total assets excluding Separate Accounts business (Lines 10A to 21)	. . . 464,273,551	 452,380,258
23.	From Separate Accounts Statement		
24.	Totals (Lines 22 and 23)	. . . 464,273,551	 452,380,258
	DETAILS OF WRITE-INS		
1001.	Accounts receivable — sale of securities	 654,485	
1002.	. . . .		
1003.	. . . .		
1098.	Summary of remaining write-ins for Line 10 from overflow page		
1099.	Totals (Lines 1001 thru 1003 plus 1098) (Line 10 above)	 654,485	
2101.	State guarantee fund	 260,902	 214,907
2102.	Other miscellaneous assets	 7,909	
2103.	Leasehold improvements		 4,389
2198.	Summary of remaining write-ins for Line 21 from overflow page		
2199.	Totals (Lines 2101 thru 2103 plus 2198) (Line 21 above)	 268,811	 219,296

FIGURE 17-4. The Annual Statement Liabilities, Surplus, and Other Funds Page.

LIABILITIES, SURPLUS AND OTHER FUNDS

		1 December 31, 2001	2 December 31, 2000
1.	Aggregate reserve for life policies and contracts . . . . $359,410,607 (Exh. 8, Line H) less . . . . $0 included in Line 7.3 (including . . . . $33,233 Modco Reserve)	359,410,607	353,310,073
2.	Aggregate reserve for accident and health policies (Exhibit 9, Line 17, Col. 1) (including . . . . $0 Modco Reserve) . . .		
3.	Supplementary contracts without life contingencies (Exhibit 10, Line 11, Col. 1) (including . . . . $0 Modco Reserve) . .	2,485,520	2,715,088
4.	Policy and contract claims:		
	4.1 Life (Exhibit 11, Part 1, Line 4d, Column 1 less sum of Columns 9, 10 and 11)	6,597,034	4,522,038
	4.2 Accident and health (Exhibit 11, Part 1, Line 4d, sum of Columns 9, 10 and 11)		
5.	Policyholders' dividend and coupon accumulations (Exhibit 10, Line 16, col. 1).	11,711,422	12,041,237
6.	Policyholders' dividends . . . . $126,012 and coupons . . . . $0 due and unpaid (Exhibit 7, Line 10). . . .	126,012	116,809
7.	Provision for policyholders' dividends and coupons payable in following calendar year — estimate amounts:		
	7.1 Dividends apportioned for payment to . . . . April 30, 1996.	1,370,721	1,425,894
	7.2 Dividends not yet apportioned	2,877,502	3,214,400
	7.3 Coupons and similar benefits.		
8.	Amount provisionally held for deferred dividend policies not included in Line 7.		
9.	Premiums and annuity considerations received in advance less . . . . $0 discount; including . . . . $0 accident and health premiums (Exhibit 1, Part 1, Col. 1, sum of Lines 4 and 14).	86,019	151,919
10.	Liability for premium and other deposit funds:		
	10.1 Policyholder premiums, including . . . . $0 deferred annuity liability	96,413	126,503
	10.2 Guaranteed interest contracts, including . . . . $16,735,681 deferred annuity liability	16,735,681	18,149,937
	10.3 Other contract deposit funds, including . . . . $1,477,990 deferred annuity liability. . . .	11,858,087	9,488,495
11.	Policy and contract liabilities not included elsewhere:		
	11.1 Surrender values on cancelled policies		
	11.2 Provision for experience rating refunds, including . . . . $0 A&H experience rating refunds . . .		
	11.3 Other amounts payable on reinsurance assumed		
	11.4 Interest maintenance reserve (Page 48, Line 6).	3,422,631	2,749,515
12.	Commissions to agents due or accrued — life and annuity . . . . $0 accident and health $0		
12A.	Commissions and expense allowances payable on reinsurance assumed.	219	(181)
13.	General expenses due or accrued (Exhibit 5, Line 12, Col. 5)	2,334,481	1,896,544
13A.	Transfers to Separate Accounts due or accrued (net)		
14.	Taxes, licenses and fees due or accrued, excluding federal income taxes (Exhibit 6, Line 9, Col. 5)	205,879	365,975
14A.	Federal income taxes due or accrued, including . . . . $391,037 on capital gains (excluding deferred taxes)		
15.	"Cost of collection" on premiums and annuity considerations deferred and uncollected in excess of total loading thereon	859,042	1,132,601
16.	Unearned investment income (Exhibit 2, Line 10, Col. 2).	56,478	36,762
17.	Amounts withheld or retained by company as agent or trustee.	632,428	842,957
18.	Amounts held for agents' account, including . . . . $0 agents' credit balances	94,390	165,591
19.	Remittances and items not allocated	393,553	145,827
20.	Net adjustment in assets and liabilities due to foreign exchange rates		
21.	Liability for benefits for employees and agents if not included above	1,517,240	1,395,083
22.	Borrowed money . . . . $0 and interest thereon . . . . $0.		
23.	Dividends to stockholders declared and unpaid		
24.	Miscellaneous liabilities:		
	24.1 Asset Valuation Reserve (Page 49, Line 12, Col. 7).	5,071,383	4,462,724
	24.2 Reinsurance in unauthorized companies		29,192
	24.3 Funds held under reinsurance treaties with unauthorized reinsurers		
	24.4 Payable to parent, subsidiaries and affiliates	297,427	
	24.5 Drafts outstanding		
	24.6 Liability for amounts held under uninsured accident and health plans		
	24.7 Funds held under coinsurance		
25.	Aggregate write-ins for liabilities	1,513,481	1,224,034
26.	Total liabilities excluding Separate Accounts business (Lines 1 to 25)	429,753,650	419,709,017
27.	From Separate Accounts Statement		
28.	Total Liabilities (Lines 26 and 27)	429,753,650	419,709,017
29.	Common capital stock	6,600,000	6,600,000
30.	Preferred capital stock		
31.	Aggregate write-ins for other than special purpose funds		
32.	Surplus Notes		
33.	Gross paid in and contributed surplus (Page 3, Line 33, Col. 2 plus Page 4, Line 44a, Col.1).	13,835,804	12,085,872
34.	Aggregate write-ins for special purpose funds.	400,000	400,000
35.	Unassigned funds (surplus)	13,684,097	13,585,369
36.	Less treasury stock, at cost:		
	(1) . . . . 0 shares common (value included in Line 29 . . . . $0)		
	(2) . . . . 0 shares preferred (value included in Line 30 . . . . $0)		
37.	Surplus (Total Lines 31 + 32 + 33 + 34 + 35 − 36).	27,919,901	26,071,241
38.	Totals of Lines 29, 30 and 37 (Page 4, Line 48)	34,519,901	32,671,241
39.	Totals of Lines 28 and 38 (Page 2, Line 24)	464,273,551	452,380,258

	DETAILS OF WRITE-INS		
2501.	Post retirement benefit	747,611	536,711
2502.	Due to reinsuring company	160,000	206,000
2503.	Miscellaneous liabilities	605,870	481,323
2598.	Summary of remaining write-ins for Line 25 from overflow page.		
2599.	Totals (Lines 2501 thru 2503 plus 2598) (Line 25 above)	1,513,481	1,224,034
3101.	. . . .		
3102.	. . . .		
3103.	. . . .		
3198.	Summary of remaining write-ins for Line 31 from overflow page.		
3199.	Totals (Lines 3101 thru 3103 plus 3198) (Line 31 above)		
3401.	Reserve for state guaranty funds	400,000	400,000
3402.	. . . .		
3403.	. . . .		
3498.	Summary of remaining write-ins for Line 34 from overflow page.		
3499.	Totals (Lines 3401 thru 3403 plus 3498) (Line 34 above)	400,000	400,000

porting documents provide details about the company's lines of business, premiums, reinsurance ceded and assumed, policy dividends, investments, nonadmitted assets, and expenses.

An important feature of the Annual Statement concerns the treatment of an insurer's assets. Statutory accounting practices prescribe specific rules that life insurance companies must follow in valuing assets. For the purposes of Annual Statement reporting, life insurers divide their assets into two categories: admitted assets and nonadmitted assets. As you learned in Chapter 16, *admitted assets* are those assets that state insurance laws permit to be included in the Annual Statement. These assets are admitted because they are considered to back the insurer's policy reserves. Some typical admitted assets are

- Cash

- Investment-grade securities

- Computer equipment

- Accounts receivable due in 90 days or less

Nonadmitted assets are those assets that state insurance laws prohibit from being included in the Annual Statement. Because they are not admitted on the Annual Statement, these assets are presumed not to back the company's policy reserves. Examples of nonadmitted assets are

- Furniture, machines, and equipment (except computer equipment)

- Office supplies

- Advances to agents

- Speculative or low-quality securities

- Accounts receivable due in more than 90 days

The value of some nonadmitted assets is completely omitted from the Annual Statement, whereas the value of other nonadmitted assets is partially omitted from the Annual Statement. The effect of not admitting certain assets is to reduce an insurer's reported surplus. Requiring that certain illiquid assets be omitted from the Annual Statement is one way insurance regulators ensure conservatism in insurers' accounting operations.

The Annual Return in Canada

Similar to the U.S. Annual Statement, the *Annual Return* is a document that presents information about an insurer's operations and performance, with an emphasis on demonstrating the insurer's solvency. Life insurance companies registered under the federal Insurance Companies Act are required to file an Annual Return with the Office of the Superintendent of Financial Institutions (OSFI) and with the provincial insurance regulators of each province in which they write business. Insurers authorized under provincial legislation must file an Annual Return with provincial regulators. U.S. insurers operating in Canada must file with OSFI an Annual Return of their Canadian business.

Whereas the U.S. Annual Statement is prepared according to statutory accounting practices, the Canadian Annual Return is prepared according to Canadian GAAP. Unlike the Annual Statement, the Annual Return does not distinguish between admitted assets and nonadmitted assets.

The basic financial statements and supporting exhibits and schedules of the Annual Return include

- A balance sheet in the format of a *Statement of Assets* and a *Statement of Liabilities, Policyholders' and Shareholders' Equity*

- An *Income Statement*

- A *Reconciliation of Surplus*

- Exhibits, schedules, and supplemental reports

The Annual Report

The Annual Statement and the Annual Return are required financial reports that provide insurance regulators with information about an insurer's solvency. An annual report, on the other hand, is a general-use document intended for external parties other than insurance regulators. An **annual report** is a GAAP-based publication that a company's management sends to its owners and other interested parties to report on the company's financial condition and performance during the past year.

The annual report typically includes a balance sheet, an income statement, a statement of cash flows, and a statement of owners' equity for the past year and at least one prior year. The annual report may also include other financial data, charts, graphs, and notes. The annual report usually includes a letter from the chief executive of the

company. This letter summarizes the year's activities, describes current conditions and operations, and discusses the company's future prospects and plans.

In the United States, the Securities and Exchange Commission (SEC) requires all publicly traded companies (including stock life insurers) and companies that sell variable life insurance products to prepare an annual report for their stockholders so that they and other investors can compare the relative merits of alternative investments. Publicly traded Canadian insurers are also required to provide an annual report to their owners. Although not required to do so, many mutual insurers that do not sell variable products or pension products also prepare an annual report for interested users.[2]

Management Accounting

Whereas financial accounting focuses on providing information to meet financial reporting requirements, management accounting focuses on providing financial information solely for a company's managers. Managers need this information to plan and implement business strategies and to control and evaluate operations. Management accounting is not a substitute for financial accounting. Management accounting systems use the accounting information captured by the company's financial accounting system and then present the information in ways that are useful for company managers.

Management accounting differs from financial accounting in several important ways, which are summarized in Figure 17-5. Because management accounting reports are for internal users only, no specific laws or conventions govern management accounting. Whereas financial accounting is required by law, management accounting is elective. Also, the focus of financial accounting is primarily historical, while management accounting is concerned with planning and establishing guidelines for future performance. In short, the objective of financial accounting is to "tell it like it was," and the objective of management accounting is to "tell it like it will be."[3]

Management accounting also tends to be less precise than financial accounting. Managers would rather have an immediate report that is reasonably accurate than wait for a report that is exact. Insurers are free to design any type of management accounting reports they choose, or they can elect not to undertake management accounting at all. However, virtually all companies undertake some forms of management accounting. In this section, we will discuss two aspects of management accounting: budgeting and cost accounting.

FIGURE 17-5. Distinctions Between Financial Accounting and Management Accounting.

Financial Accounting	Management Accounting
Provides data for *external* users	Provides data for *internal* users
Is required by law	Is not required by law
Is subject to specific accounting principles	Is not subject to specific accounting principles
Must generate accurate and timely data	Emphasizes relevance and flexibility of data
Has a backward-looking focus	Has mainly a forward-looking focus
Reports on the business as a whole	Can focus on the business as a whole or on individual parts of the business
Culminates in the presentation of financial statements and so is an end in itself	Helps managers make decisions, and so is a means to an end

Budgeting

Fundamental to business planning is **budgeting**, which is the process of creating a financial plan of action that an organization believes will help it achieve its goals. A **budget** is a financial plan of action expressed as assets, liabilities, revenues, and expenses that covers a specified time period. Budgets typically project income or expenses for the company as a whole and for departments, products, lines of business, or profit centers. In addition to being central to the planning process, budgets become control devices when actual operating results are compared with budgets.

The format and content of budgets vary widely from company to company and are based on management preferences. A budget can cover a relatively short time period, such as a month or a year, or it can cover a period of several years. Generally, the longer the time period covered, the less precise the budget.

Budgets are essentially statements about expected future performance. During the budgeting process, life insurance managers and other staff make forecasts about the following amounts:

- Number of policies the company will sell during the budget period

- Amount of income the company expects to earn during the budget period

- Cost of the work that must be done to sell and administer the desired number of products and to conduct other company operations

- Cost of anticipated capital expenditures

- Amount of benefits paid

Methods of projecting sales and income can range from relatively simple estimates based on prior experience to complex forecasts using computer models.

The budgeting process requires a great deal of cooperation throughout the company. A budget committee comprised of various executives and senior managers usually oversees the budgeting process, and each department or business unit is usually responsible for drafting its own budget. Insight 17-2 briefly describes the budgeting process in one company.

Three types of budgets that insurance companies typically prepare are operational budgets, cash budgets, and capital expenditure budgets.

Operational Budgets

A budget covering part or all of a company's operations is referred to as an *operational budget*. Operational budgets set forth the income and expenses the company anticipates during a stated time period. The first type of operational budget that a company prepares is a *revenue budget*, which indicates the amount of anticipated income from policy sales and investments. The revenue budget is usually prepared first because it determines the financial limits of the other budgets.

Following the preparation of the revenue budget, budget planners prepare *expense budgets*, which are schedules of expenses expected during the given period. Examples of expense budgets are budgets for benefits (claims, cash surrenders, and policy dividends), budgets for sales and marketing expenses, including agent commissions, and

 Insight 17-2. Budgeting in the Client Service Department at First Colony Life.

The officers in the Client Services department prepare the department's budget, which includes staffing costs and capital expenditures for the department. Department managers are asked for their input into the department's staffing needs and equipment needs for the coming budget period. This information is used as the basis for the budget. The departmental budget is submitted to the Budget Planning and Analysis area for review and approval.

Each month, department officers compare the budgeted costs to the actual costs incurred. They compare the *full-time equivalent rate*— generally the number of employee hours that should be needed to complete the current workload—with the actual staff hours worked. Current and future overtime needs and costs are also reviewed monthly. Any additions to the budget are requested along with the reasons for the additional expense. •

Sources: Mary K. Bryant, Project Manager—Quality Department, First Colony Life Insurance Company; Robert Harvey, Associate Vice President—Client Services Department, First Colony Life Insurance Company.

budgets for general and administrative expenses needed to operate the company.

Cash Budgets

Cash budgets project a company's beginning cash balance, cash inflows, cash outflows, and ending cash balance for a particular period. Cash budgets provide information the insurer needs to develop its investment strategy and to conduct effective asset-liability management. Many insurers prepare an annual cash budget that is divided into quarterly, monthly, weekly, and even daily budgets so that they can monitor their cash flows more closely.

Capital Expenditure Budgets

Capital expenditure budgets show a company's plans for the financial management of capital investments. These *capital investments* can include the purchase of another company, the launch of a new product, the purchase of a new computer system, or the purchase of new office space. Financial managers use capital expenditure budgets to analyze decisions about investing in such long-term projects and to help monitor the financial status of the company's capital investments.

Budgets as Evaluation and Control Devices

Budgets have important uses in the areas of performance evaluation and control. A basic step in using management accounting as a control tool is to establish a standard of performance and to use that standard as a benchmark against which actual performance is compared. Budgets serve as useful benchmarks because they describe an expected level of future performance expressed in quantifiable terms—policies sold, income earned, expenses incurred, and so on. By com-

paring actual results to budgets, companies evaluate their performance in many areas.

The difference between actual results and budgeted results is a **budget variance**. Management accountants prepare regular reports showing budget variances for the company, for individual departments, and for each product line. By analyzing its variances, a company can isolate substandard performance or problem areas, such as costs that exceed budgets or revenues that fall short of budgets. Budget variances also indicate where performance surpassed expectations. When a company experiences large variances, it may revise its budgets or change its operations.

Cost Accounting

A key to improving the solvency and profitability of an insurer's operations is to understand and control the company's costs. **Cost accounting** is a system by which a company accumulates expense data in order to control costs and manage assets. The system enables a company's managers to plan operations, organize employee work loads, and evaluate current financial performance so that the company can make appropriate financial management decisions.

To be a valuable management tool, a cost accounting system should accumulate and allocate costs accurately and fairly. Specifically, the cost accounting system should categorize all of the company's costs in meaningful ways and then assign each cost to the departments, products, and lines of business that are responsible for generating the cost. Only when costs are properly allocated and assigned will financial managers be able to accurately evaluate the performance of the company and its various segments.

Financial managers can use several different methods to analyze costs. Three methods are change analysis, functional cost analysis, and activity-based costing.

Change analysis is the process of comparing an expense in one period to the same expense in a different period. For example, an insurer may compare its claim department's costs incurred during the month of January this year with the claim department's costs from January one year ago. Change analysis can help the insurer spot cost trends, fluctuations, peaks, and valleys, but it does not explain the reasons for the changes.

Functional cost analysis is a method by which an insurer assigns costs to each company function. Financial managers can then analyze the costs of specific processes, such as policy issue, collection of renewal premiums, and claim processing, rather than the costs of organizational structures. Functional cost analysis is especially helpful in making pricing and staffing decisions.

Activity-based costing (ABC) is a method by which an insurer links its costs to its products based on the activities required to produce each product. Like functional cost analysis, ABC traces costs to various functions or activities. Activity-based costing then goes a step further by tracing the activity costs to specific products or lines of business. For example, whereas functional cost analysis helps determine the cost of processing claims, ABC identifies the cost of each activity within the claim processing function and assigns those activity costs to the insurance products for which claims are processed. Activity-based costing results in more appropriate pricing and more effective cost control than do other cost-accounting methods.

Auditing

To conclude our discussion of financial management, we'll look at the important topic of *auditing*, the process of examining and evaluating company records and procedures to ensure that the company's financial statements are presented fairly and reasonably, that quality is maintained, and that operational procedures and policies are effective. Auditing is included in this chapter because it has traditionally been associated with the accounting function. However, you should be aware that auditing extends well beyond the accounting area. Any investigation of records, policies, or procedures to ensure that they conform to established policies can be considered an audit. For example, insurance companies use audits to evaluate their operating procedures, management efficiency, and compliance with specified rules and regulations. We discuss these aspects of auditing more in Chapter 18.

With respect to accounting and financial reporting, the most common type of audit is a *financial audit*, which is an examination of the company's financial statements and an examination of individual accounts and accounting records. The scope of a financial audit can be limited to one aspect of the insurer's finances—such as an examination of premium accounting—or can cover all financial transactions in an accounting period—such as an audit of the insurer's Annual Statement or Annual Return. Auditors from both the internal audit department and from outside the organization periodically examine the company's financial statements and accounting procedures in order to

- Verify the reliability of the company's accounting records and financial reports

- Verify that the company's assets are accounted for and are safeguarded from loss

- Assess the soundness of and the employees' adherence to the company's accounting controls

In most jurisdictions, an insurer's required financial statements must undergo an external audit by an auditor who is not associated with the company. An **external audit**, also called an *independent audit*, includes (1) an evaluation of the company's financial statements, (2) the issuance of an opinion as to whether those financial statements present fairly the company's operations through adherence to GAAP, statutory accounting, or other accounting principles, and (3) a recommendation of changes to the company's system of internal control. External audits are performed primarily for the benefit of interested third parties, such as stockholders, policyowners, creditors, regulators, and government authorities that rely on the information contained in the insurer's financial statements. At the conclusion of an external audit, the auditor issues an **auditor's report** that expresses the auditor's opinion as to whether the financial statements present fairly the company's financial position.

In the United States, federal securities laws require publicly traded insurance companies to undergo annual external audits of their GAAP-based financial statements. Insurance laws in many states require that each insurer's Annual Statement undergo an external audit each year. Canadian insurers undertake an annual external audit of the Annual Return in accordance with requirements of the Office of the Superintendent of Financial Institutions (OSFI).

Related to an external audit is a **financial condition examination**, which is a formal, on-site investigation that is carried out by insurance regulators and is designed to identify and monitor any threats to an insurer's solvency. During a financial condition examination, examiners from the applicable regulatory agency

- Examine the insurer's accounting records and evaluate whether the insurer is being operated on a sound and lawful basis

- Investigate the insurer's financial and business activities to assure that they do not contain any hazards to the insurer's solvency

In the United States, virtually every state requires each insurer domiciled in the state to undergo a financial condition examination at least every five years. Many states require insurers to be examined every three years. More frequent examinations are conducted if the state insurance commissioner believes they are warranted. In Canada, OSFI examines the financial condition of each federally licensed insurer at least once every three years.

During a financial condition examination, an insurer is required to provide examiners with access to relevant materials and business

records. If an insurer refuses to be examined or to comply with reasonable requests from examiners, the insurer's license to conduct business in the jurisdiction may be suspended or not renewed.

Upon completion of the examination, examiners file an examination report with the state insurance commissioner and send a copy of the report to the insurer under study. The examination report emphasizes any adverse conditions, significant changes in the insurer's operations or financial condition since the previous examination, and violations of state solvency laws or regulations. The report may suggest causes for any problems and recommend solutions to the problems. The insurer has a specified time, usually 30 days, within which to respond in writing to the examination report and to specify how any problems discovered by the examiners will be corrected.

If the examination report indicates that the insurer is financially impaired, the insurance department takes any action necessary to protect the insurer's policyowners, ranging from ordering the insurer to take specified corrective actions to seizing control of the insurer for the purpose of selling off the insurer's business and terminating the company's operations.

Key Terms

accounting
financial reporting
account
financial accounting
management accounting
   (managerial accounting)
recognition
generally accepted accounting
   principles (GAAP)
going-concern concept
statutory accounting practices
accounting conservatism
policy accounting
unrealized gain (or loss)
realized gain (or loss)
voucher
premium tax
statement of cash flows
statement of surplus

annual report
budgeting
budget
operational budget
revenue budget
expense budget
cash budget
capital expenditure budget
budget variance
cost accounting
change analysis
functional cost analysis
activity-based costing (ABC)
auditing
financial audit
external audit (independent
   audit)
auditor's report
financial condition examination

Endnotes

1. Edward P. Brunner, "Development of the Insurance Industry and Its Accounting Principles," *Life Insurance Accounting* (Durham, NC: Insurance Accounting & Systems Association, Inc., 1994), 10.

2. Mutual insurance companies may provide an annual report that is based on statutory accounting rather than GAAP.

3. Robert N. Anthony, James S. Reece, and Julie H. Hertenstein, *Accounting: Text and Cases* (Chicago: Richard D. Irwin, 1995), 515.

4. Lucy Barnes McDowell, "Budgeting & Planning: Still a Long Way to Go?" *Resource* (May 1999): 46.

Legal Operations and Compliance

As you have seen throughout this book, the business operations of a life insurance company involve many activities that are subject to regulation in each jurisdiction in which the insurer operates. These activities include product design and development, sales and marketing practices, underwriting, claim administration, financial management, financial reporting, employment practices, and employee conduct. The laws and regulations govern the financial stability of insurers, the products insurers offer, and the manner in which insurers conduct their business. In addition to insurance laws, many other types of laws affect the operations of life insurers.

In order to assure that they comply with applicable laws and protect their own legal rights, life insurance companies must rely on the advice of lawyers and other specialists in the regulatory environment. Most insurance companies have a *legal department*, also known as a *law department*, and a *compliance unit* or *department* which review company actions to ensure that the company fulfills its obligations to all parties, including its agents, policyowners, beneficiaries, and owners.

This chapter examines the legal and compliance operations in a life insurance company. We begin by discussing some organizational structures for the legal and compliance functions. Then we examine the legal department's role in several insurance company operations. Last, we explore the important topic of regulatory compliance, and we describe the people and procedures involved in an insurance company's compliance efforts. In our discussion, we use the general term **compliance**, or *regulatory compliance*, to mean an insurer's adherence to applicable regulatory requirements.

Organization of Legal and Compliance Operations

Life insurance companies can choose to organize their legal and compliance operations in many ways. Virtually all insurers have a legal department that is in charge of handling all of the company's legal matters. In some companies, members of the legal department are also responsible for regulatory compliance matters. In other insurers, a separate department or unit is devoted solely to compliance. This compliance department may report to the head of the legal department, or it may report to the chief executive officer. In other companies, compliance is one unit of

another department, such as internal audit, agency operations, or marketing. For simplicity, this text presents compliance as one unit of the insurer's entire legal operations. Regardless of structure, a close relationship exists between the legal function and the compliance function. For example, if the compliance area discovers a case of misconduct in the company, it typically confers with company lawyers to determine the appropriate course of action.

Generally, the person in charge of an insurance company's legal function is known as the *general counsel* or *chief counsel.* In some companies, the general counsel is also the company's chief compliance officer. The general counsel usually advises the company's board of directors on important legal issues affecting the company. This person manages the company's lawyers, paralegals, clerks, and law librarians, and may manage compliance managers and compliance specialists. A ***paralegal*** is a person specially trained in techniques of legal research and the procedures for various legal transactions. Unlike lawyers, paralegals have not passed a state or provincial ***bar examination***, which is a licensing test that a person must pass before practicing law.

Life insurance companies generally organize their legal staff according to one of a few basic structures, depending on the size of the company, the extent of its operations, and its marketing territory. Four typical structures are organization by legal specialty, geography, company function, and product line.

- In a legal department organized by specialty, legal staff members are responsible for specific operations. For example, some staff members are assigned to handle contract law matters, while other staff handle litigation, tax law, securities law, compliance, and so on.

- In a structure organized by geographic region, some legal operations are carried out by lawyers in each of the company's regional offices. Examples of these regional activities are (1) handling legal requirements that are specific to the region, (2) assisting the regional claim department in resolving claim disputes, and (3) arranging for local counsel to handle a lawsuit in which the company is involved. Other legal operations are generally handled in the central legal department at the insurer's home office.

- When the legal department is organized by function, lawyers are assigned to specific functional areas within the company. For example, a lawyer or group of lawyers handles all legal matters for the marketing department, another group handles legal matters for the claim administration department, another handles legal matters for the investments department, and so on.

- When the legal department is organized by product, one lawyer or group of lawyers is assigned to individual life insurance products, another lawyer or group of lawyers is assigned to group life insurance products, and so on.

Responsibilities of the Legal Department

An insurance company's legal department has some involvement in virtually every insurance company operation. Figure 18-1 graphically illustrates the legal department's relationships with other company departments. In some cases, the legal department serves primarily in an advisory capacity. In other cases, lawyers have specific duties and responsibilities. In this section, we briefly discuss the legal department's role in many of an insurer's operations.

Incorporation and Changes in Corporate Structure

An organization that is forming for the purpose of operating as a life insurance company must meet a number of requirements and must file many documents with governmental and regulatory agencies. We described many of these requirements in Chapter 3. For example, in the United States, lawyers draft the articles of incorporation that must be filed with the government of the state in which the insurer wishes to incorporate. And lawyers apply for the license, also called a *certificate of authority,* that the insurer must obtain from the state insurance department of each state in which it plans to conduct business.

The legal department is closely involved whenever an insurance company changes its corporate form, such as through a demutualization or a conversion from a mutual company to a mutual holding company. The legal department advises the company's board of directors on (1) the differences in the regulation of stock companies, mutual companies, and mutual holding companies (discussed in Chapter 19), (2) the legal issues involved in the change in corporate form, (3) the structure that would be most beneficial to the insurer, and (4) the best way to accomplish a change in corporate form.

Company lawyers play an important role when an insurer is involved in a merger or partnership with or an acquisition of another company. Lawyers help to negotiate the terms of the agreement, and they help in explaining to the company's board of directors and senior officers the terms of various offers and counteroffers. Lawyers also draft and review the contracts and other legal documents associated with mergers, acquisitions, and changes in corporate form.

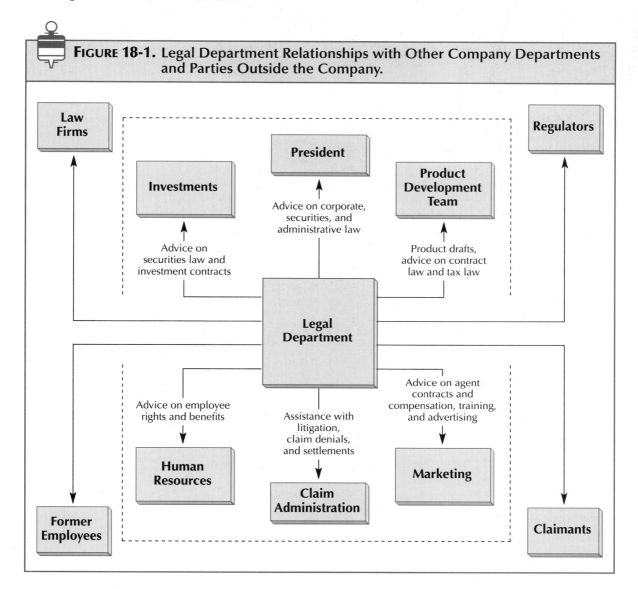

FIGURE 18-1. Legal Department Relationships with Other Company Departments and Parties Outside the Company.

Product Development

Numerous state and provincial insurance laws regulate the products that insurance companies sell. Tax laws and legal requirements can influence the development of a new product. An insurer's legal department advises the product development team on relevant laws to assure that new products comply with the laws of each jurisdiction in which the company will sell the products. Lawyers also help draft the wording of new insurance contracts.

Contracts

In order to conduct business, an insurance company must enter into a variety of contractual agreements with its owners, agents, policy-owners, beneficiaries, and third parties that do business with the insurer. A **contract** is a legally enforceable agreement between two or more parties. A body of law, known as **contract law**, governs the requirements the parties must meet in order to form an agreement that is legally binding on the parties and that specifies the rights and duties of the parties to a contract. One of the legal department's most important roles involves the formation and performance of the contracts into which the insurance company has entered.

A life insurer enters into a contract each time it issues a policy, because insurance policies are legally binding contracts. An insurer's marketing specialists and actuaries usually write the initial drafts of insurance policies. Company lawyers review these drafts to ensure that they comply with laws of the jurisdictions in which the company intends to sell the policies. Life insurance companies also rely on the advice of lawyers as they carry out—or *perform*—the terms of a contractual agreement with the policyowner.

As we stated earlier, lawyers are involved in the negotiation and review of contracts associated with mergers and acquisitions. The legal department also assists with the legal requirements of private placement investments, real estate investments, and mortgage loans. For example, lawyers help negotiate the terms of a private placement purchase of bonds that the insurer's investment managers have recommended. Lawyers also draft the private placement contract that sets forth the terms of the agreement between the insurance company and the issuer of the private placement securities.

Because many insurance companies invest in real estate, an insurer's lawyers must be skilled in **real property law**, a branch of law that deals with the ownership and transfer of rights in real estate. The legal department handles the contracts and deeds for the purchase and sale of property, and it advises the company's investment specialists about the best way to handle a particular real estate asset. For example, the company may benefit more by entering into a sale-and-leaseback arrangement for a new office building than by purchasing the building outright. You learned about sale-and-leaseback arrangements in Chapter 16.

An insurer's lawyers negotiate the terms of mortgage loans and draft the mortgage loan contracts. Lawyers also negotiate the purchase and sale of blocks of mortgages, and they handle the foreclosure proceedings when a borrower defaults on a mortgage loan owned by the insurer.

Product Distribution

In Chapter 9, you learned about the agency relationship that exists between a principal (in this case, a life insurance company) and its agents, who are appointed to act on behalf of the principal to sell the principal's products. The body of law that has been developed to regulate the relationship between principals and their agents is known as *agency law*. The legal department is responsible for overseeing the legal aspects of the agency relationship, including writing the agency contracts that spell out (1) the scope of the agent's authority, duties, and responsibilities, and (2) the method the insurer will use to compensate the agent for carrying out those duties. Company lawyers advise the insurer whenever legal questions arise about an agency contract. The legal and compliance areas also help the insurer make sure its agents comply with applicable regulatory requirements as they conduct business.

Claim Administration

A small percentage of claims are denied for reasons such as that the policy was not in force at the time of the insured's death, the deceased was not covered under the policy, or the cause of death was excluded from the insurance coverage. When a claim analyst believes there is cause to deny a claim, or if the claim analyst has a question about the insurer's liability for the claim, typically the claim analyst consults the legal department. The insurer's lawyers assist the claim analyst in interpreting the language of the policy and analyzing the facts of the situation to determine the insurer's liability. If the decision is to deny the claim, the legal department advises the claim analyst about the legal aspects of the denial. If the claimant disputes the insurer's decision to deny the claim and files a lawsuit for the policy proceeds, the legal department handles the litigation process or attempts to reach a settlement with the claimant. For more on claim disputes, see Focus on Technology 18-1.

Employee Relations

As employers, life insurance companies must abide by numerous state, provincial, and federal laws that govern the relationship between an employer and an employee. This body of law is known as *employment law*. Generally, employment laws (1) protect employees against discrimination in the workplace, (2) guarantee employees certain minimum workplace standards, and (3) ensure that certain minimum requirements are included in employee retirement and health benefit plans.

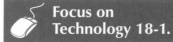

Focus on Technology 18-1. | **Settling Claims Online.**

The traditional ways to resolve disputed claims—such as litigation and trading paper settlement offers and counteroffers—can be time consuming and expensive. Some insurers have found that the Internet provides an efficient and cost-effective alternative.

One provider of online claim dispute resolution is Cybersettle, which was started by two attorneys. With Cybersettle, the insurer initiates the dispute resolution process by filing three rounds of confidential offers through the Cybersettle internet site. The claimant is notified by e-mail that the insurer is attempting an online settlement, and the claimant is prompted to file three rounds of confidential demands. Cybersettle compares the offers and corresponding demands. If the two sides are within an agreed-upon formula of one another, a match is considered to have been made, and the case settles for the median amount. If the two sides are not within those parameters, no settlement is reached. The parties can pursue traditional methods of litigation without prejudice because the amounts of offers and demands are not revealed. •

Source: "How It Works," *Cybersettle.com,* http://www.cybersettle.com/how/index.htm (10 November 1999).

The insurer's legal department advises the company's human resources area in fulfilling employee rights, establishing and implementing sound employment practices and policies, and complying with various employment laws.

Nondiscrimination in the Workplace

The federal governments in the United States and Canada have enacted laws that prohibit employment discrimination on the basis of several factors, such as a person's age, race, national origin, color, religion, sex, or marital status. Discrimination is prohibited for a wide range of employment practices. Important federal laws in the United States that prohibit employment discrimination, and the employment practices covered under these laws, are shown in Figure 18-2.

In Canada, the federal *Canadian Human Rights Act* protects the employees of federally regulated companies against unfair discrimination in employment. Most provinces have enacted similar human rights acts.

Employment Standards Legislation

The U.S. Department of Labor administers several federal laws that mandate certain employment standards for covered employees, including employees of life insurance companies. For example, the ***Fair Labor Standards Act (FLSA)*** establishes minimum wage, overtime pay, record keeping, and child labor standards that affect workers of federal, state, and local governments and employees of companies that meet an annual dollar volume of business test.

FIGURE 18-2. U.S. Laws Prohibiting Employment Discrimination.

Title VII of the *Civil Rights Act of 1964* prohibits employment discrimination on the basis of race, color, sex, religion, or national origin. Title VII includes broad prohibitions against sex-based discrimination and prohibits sexual harassment.

Title I of the *Americans with Disabilities Act of 1990 (ADA)* prohibits employment discrimination against people with disabilities, including hearing and vision impairments, paraplegia, epilepsy, alcoholism, past drug use, and AIDS, among many other conditions.

The *Age Discrimination in Employment Act of 1967 (ADEA)* protects people who are 40 years of age or older from being discriminated against in the workplace because of their age.

Under Title VII, the ADA, and the ADEA, discrimination in the following aspects of employment is illegal:

- Hiring and firing
- Compensation, assignment, or classification of employees
- Transfer, promotion, layoff, or recall
- Job advertisements
- Recruitment
- Testing
- Use of company facilities
- Training and apprenticeship programs
- Fringe benefits
- Pay, retirement plans, and disability leave
- Other terms and conditions of employment

Source: "Federal Laws Prohibiting Job Discrimination—Questions and Answers," The U.S. Equal Employment Opportunity Commission, 10 December 1998, http://www.eeoc.gov/facts/qanda.html (12 January 2000).

Another important workplace standards law administered by the Department of Labor is the *Family Medical Leave Act (FMLA)*, which requires employers with 50 or more employees within a 75-mile radius to allow eligible employees in specific circumstances to take up to 12 weeks of unpaid leave within any 12-month period. An employer subject to the Act must maintain group health insurance coverage for an employee on leave at the same level and in the same manner as if the employee had continued to work.

In Canada, many employment standards, such as minimum wage rates, overtime pay, and maximum hours of work, are mandated in the federal *Canada Labour Code* and in provincial statutes typically known as *Labour Standards Acts* or *Employment Standards Acts*. In addition, legislation in all jurisdictions requires employers to give covered employees a stated minimum amount of vacation after the

employees have completed a specified period of employment. Finally, all jurisdictions require employers to provide a stated number of weeks of unpaid leave for the birth of a child.

Retirement and Health Benefit Standards

In the United States, the federal **Employee Retirement Income Security Act (ERISA)** ensures that certain minimum plan requirements are contained in employee welfare benefit plans established by employers. Administered by the Department of Labor, ERISA typically covers *pension plans* and *welfare plans*. Pension plans provide income for employees when they retire. Welfare plans provide some or all of the following employee benefits: health benefits, disability benefits, death benefits, prepaid legal services, vacation benefits, payment for child care, scholarship funds, and apprenticeship and training benefits.

ERISA sets uniform minimum standards with respect to enrollment, vesting, accrual of benefits, and maximum benefits to assure that employee benefit plans subject to the Act are established and maintained in a fair and financially sound manner. An insurer's lawyers work with the human resources staff to make sure that the company's employee benefit plans comply with ERISA requirements. Company lawyers also work with the product development team to ensure that group life insurance and other benefit plan products that the company sells are in compliance with ERISA.

In Canada, the *Pension Benefits Standards Act* sets forth requirements for private pension plans of companies that are subject to federal legislative control. The pension plans of all other companies are subject to provincial legislation. The federal legislation and provincial legislation cover design provisions required of pension plans and the funding and solvency of pension plans. The Act also lists the requirements that pension plans must meet to receive tax-favored status.

Handling Litigation

At times, a person or organization may institute a legal proceeding against a life insurance company, or the insurer may institute a legal proceeding against another party. These proceedings may ultimately lead to **litigation**, which is the process or act of resolving a dispute by means of a lawsuit. The legal department represents the company or arranges for legal representation whenever the company is involved in a lawsuit. Lawyers handling litigation for an insurance company are responsible for

- Instituting or responding to the lawsuit

- Researching the facts of the case

- Taking statements from the involved parties

- Researching relevant court cases

- Representing the company in all trial court proceedings

- Filing for or defending an appeal of the original trial decision

A lawsuit may include issues that are governed by any number of areas of the law. Lawsuits can be time consuming and costly to defend, and a verdict against the insurer can result in negative publicity for the company as well as liability to pay damages to the other party. Typically, insurance companies try to settle legal disputes before cases go to trial. The legal department may offer to settle the dispute through arbitration or mediation. **Arbitration** is a method of resolving a conflict in which an impartial third party, known as an **arbitrator**, evaluates the facts in dispute and renders a decision that is binding on both parties. **Mediation** is a method of conflict resolution in which an impartial third party, known as a **mediator**, facilitates negotiations between the parties in an effort to create a mutually agreeable resolution to the dispute. In most instances, insurers go to trial only as a last resort.

Regulatory Compliance

Insurance companies are generally subject to two types of regulatory requirements: (1) laws enacted by federal, state, or provincial legislatures, and (2) rules and regulations adopted by administrative agencies, such as state or provincial insurance departments. Both types of requirements are legally binding on insurance companies. Failure to comply with an insurance law or regulation carries potentially high penalties, including fines levied by insurance departments, amounts paid to customers in order to settle lawsuits, and loss of the privilege to conduct business in a jurisdiction. Insurers also risk the negative publicity generated by noncompliance.

Although every employee in a life insurance company has a duty to be law abiding, a specific unit of the company, known as *compliance,* generally is designated to ensure that the company follows applicable insurance laws and regulations. As we noted earlier, this unit may be part of the legal department or it may be a self-contained department.

The compliance area has an important enforcement responsibility. But an equally important function of compliance is to provide business units in the company with information so that they can make the best possible business decisions. Staff in the compliance area

keep abreast of regulatory changes, review the changes to determine their effect on the company's operations, communicate the new requirements to all affected employees, and follow up later to ensure that the company is abiding by the new requirements.

To effectively meet their regulatory obligations, insurers typically establish compliance management programs. Such a program enables an insurer to know which laws affect its business and to ensure that the company complies with these laws. A comprehensive compliance program includes elements of prevention, monitoring, and education and training. Although presented individually here, these three elements overlap in many ways.

Prevention

The starting point of a compliance program is to establish company policies and procedures that comply with the regulatory requirements of the jurisdictions in which the company operates. If the insurer's policies and procedures are in compliance, and if employees follow these policies and procedures, then problems with non-compliance are prevented. An insurer must also establish internal control systems. *Internal control* is a system or method designed to assure the implementation of a program, promote operational efficiency, and safeguard the organization's assets. In a broad sense, internal control extends beyond the compliance area and includes accounting controls, management efficiency controls, and other types of controls. Figure 18-3 lists examples of internal controls. Proper internal control helps ward off potential misconduct and establishes accountability for compliance throughout the company.

Monitoring

The monitoring element of the compliance program enables the insurer to observe whether employees and producers are following the insurer's policies and procedures. A common way of monitoring compliance is through auditing. In Chapter 17, you learned that any investigation of records, policies, or procedures to ensure that they conform to established policies is considered an *audit*. Simply, internal control involves putting policies and procedures in place, and auditing ensures that these policies and procedures are followed. An *internal audit* is an examination of the company's records, policies, and procedures conducted by a person associated with the organization. An insurer's internal audit department conducts audits of the compliance program. Internal audit typically works independently of

FIGURE 18-3. Types of Internal Controls.

Internal Control	Insurance Examples
Approval, review, checking, or recalculation	• Randomly recalculating premiums charged to policyowners • Requiring senior management approval of disbursements above a certain amount
Comparing information on independently generated documents	• Comparing a policy application to a policy master file • Comparing an applicant's medical information received from several sources
Prenumbering	• Prenumbering checks and purchase orders • Numbering applications and claims when received
Comparison with third-party information	• Reconciling bank statements with internal accounting records • Reconciling internally generated listings of securities held in safekeeping with listings provided by the custodian of the securities • Totalling the amount of policyowner complaints and reconciling this total with the amount of complaints shown in the state insurance commissioner's records
Soliciting third-party information	• Periodically sending to agents statements requesting notification of errors in payment • Confirming amounts receivable from persons or companies owing money to the insurer
Cancellation of documentation	• Voiding, rather than discarding, checks that contain errors
Timeliness of operation	• Depositing cash daily • Reviewing the claim register bi-weekly for unresolved claims • Reviewing the new business register bi-weekly for applications that have not been underwritten within a specified time

all other departments and reports directly to the audit committee of the insurer's board of directors. Insurers also undergo external audits of their compliance programs. Some of these external audits are voluntary and are performed by independent assessors hired by the company. A type of external audit is a compulsory market conduct examination performed by insurance regulators. We discuss this kind of examination later in this chapter.

Education and Training

Education and training are necessary to make employees aware of relevant laws and the company's policies and procedures to comply with these laws. Many companies provide their employees and producers with compliance manuals that contain information about the insurers' compliance programs and the market conduct rules that producers and employees must follow. For example, state laws place specific requirements on the way insurers handle customer complaints. Customer service representatives and any other employees who are likely to receive customer complaints must be trained in the insurer's complaint handling procedures, including how to interact with the customer, how to investigate the validity of the complaint, and how to respond to the complaint. Insurers generally are responsible for the activities of their producers and thus must provide producers with adequate compliance training. The compliance program also includes a system for revising procedures and for informing employees when regulatory requirements or company policies change.

For a description of one company's compliance program, read Insight 18-1.

Market Conduct Compliance

Insurance laws can be divided into two general types—*market conduct laws* and *solvency laws*—which we first described in Chapter 2. Market conduct laws are designed to assure that insurers conduct business fairly and ethically. Solvency laws, which in Canada are also known as *prudential laws,* are designed to assure that insurers are financially able to meet their debts and pay policy benefits as they come due.

The compliance unit generally has responsibility for compliance with market conduct laws, whereas the actuarial and accounting departments generally manage solvency compliance. We have discussed many elements of insurer solvency and solvency regulation throughout the text. For example, insurers must (1) prepare and file an Annual Statement (or Annual Return in Canada), (2) maintain reserves, assets, and capital and surplus at levels that are at least equal to those required by law, and (3) adequately diversify their investment portfolios. Insurers in the United States and Canada also must submit to periodic financial conduct examinations performed by insurance regulators.

In this chapter, our focus is on market conduct compliance, which involves adhering to all of the applicable market conduct requirements in each of the jurisdictions in which an insurer is licensed to conduct business. Market conduct requirements generally seek to

Insight 18-1. Compliance Program at Standard Insurance Company.

The comprehensive compliance program at Standard Insurance Company includes education and training, monitoring, and enforcement.

Compliance training at The Standard is a vital part of the training and professional development curriculum available for company employees. The overall company compliance program is divided among the seven business divisions. In each division, a senior officer is designated the divisional compliance officer and is responsible for reviewing and revising the division compliance program at least annually and for promoting the program's goals and employee awareness of the program. Additionally, each division has an Ethics Advisory Council (EAC) that reviews, investigates, and reports any alleged instances of unethical conduct.

Compliance training and awareness at The Standard is part of every new employee's orientation program. In the initial new employee orientation session, the company's Code of Ethical Conduct and the Corporate Policy Statement on Ethical Conduct are read and discussed. Each year, all employees participate in a review session on compliance and ethics issues, and they must sign a statement in which they commit to uphold the principles of the Corporate Policy Statement.

When new field representatives sign their contract with The Standard, they must also sign an Ethical Commitment Statement in which they commit to abide by a standard of ethical behavior relating to sales practices and disclosure of information to customers.

Employees and field representatives receive the following types of compliance training:

- They receive quarterly newsletters from the Ethics Advisory Council.
- They receive *The Edge,* a quarterly magazine from Individual Sales and Marketing, which includes in each issue at least one article about ethics, the compliance program, or related topics.
- They receive annual written reminders from the EAC concerning the confidentiality of policyowner information and company information.
- They attend New Product Orientation sessions before each new product is introduced. During New Product Orientation, employees who will be administering and servicing the new product and field representatives who will be selling the new product are trained in the mechanics of and uses for the product. The orientation includes training in compliance issues that affect the new product.
- They attend annual division meetings devoted to discussing the division's compliance program. The meetings remind employees about the importance of (1) detecting and reporting fraud and (2) disclosure and reporting of ethical violations.
- Field representatives receive compliance training manuals, edu-

cational pieces, and a copy of the Compliance Program. They also attend annual sales seminars or production club meetings in which they review ethical, compliance-sensitive selling practices and sound business practices.

- New management personnel participate in a five-day Leadership Education training program, a portion of which is devoted to compliance training.
- All home office employees identified under compliance laws (and others) receive fraud training that is conducted by the company's Special Investigative Unit. The training helps employees identify fraud and outlines procedures for reporting fraud. Many states require insurers to provide their employees with a minimum of one hour of fraud training per year.

Compliance Teams track and disseminate information regarding legislative and regulatory updates using an electronic tracking service to keep apprised of all applicable issues in the 50 jurisdictions in which the company operates. Compliance analysts review the statutes and regulations and, with help from a reviewing attorney, assess how they relate to The Standard's ongoing business. The statutes and regulations are then routed to the appropriate departments, and Compliance Bulletins are prepared and sent to affected departments. This process ensures that affected departments are aware of regulatory changes and their potential impact. •

Source: Janice F. Spradlin, Director—Training, Standard Insurance Company.

ensure that insurance companies treat policyowners fairly with respect to marketing practices, policy provisions, claim handling, and customer service functions, and charge premiums that are reasonable in relation to the benefits provided. Traditionally, the focus of market conduct compliance has been on producers. However, home office employees also must be knowledgeable about market conduct rules. For example, a customer service representative who misleads a policyowner can subject the insurer to regulatory sanctions.

The specific activities involved with market conduct compliance for each company vary depending on the types of products that the company sells and the way the company organizes its compliance function. We describe some of these specific activities in this section. Figure 18-4 lists some typical activities of the compliance function.

Market Conduct Compliance in the United States

Life insurance companies must comply with the market conduct requirements of each state in which they are licensed to sell insurance. Each insurer must undergo periodic examinations of its operations so that state regulators can determine whether the insurer has complied with applicable market conduct requirements. Specific market conduct requirements can vary considerably from state to state, and compliance staff must be trained and experienced in all of these requirements in order to ensure the company's compliance. In this section, we briefly discuss market conduct requirements relating to policy form filing

FIGURE 18-4. Typical Activities of the Compliance Function.

- Disseminating information about regulatory and legislative updates
- Overseeing the licensing, training, and conduct of producers
- Monitoring and tracking advertising materials
- Filing policy forms with regulators
- Monitoring the way the company protects the privacy and confidentiality of customer information
- Preparing for market conduct examinations
- Overseeing proper handling of customer complaints
- Working with regulatory agencies to demonstrate the company's compliance with applicable laws
- Coordinating internal and external audits

and approval, producer licensing, marketing and sales, underwriting and policy issue, claim administration, complaint handling, and consumer privacy. We will also discuss market conduct examinations.

As you learned in Chapter 6, much of an insurer's market conduct is governed by provisions of unfair trade practices laws that have been enacted in almost all states. These laws define certain business practices as unfair and prohibit those practices in the business of insurance if they (1) are committed flagrantly in conscious disregard of the law or (2) occur so frequently as to indicate a general business practice.

In addition to complying with market conduct laws and regulations, insurers that are members of or that aspire to be members of the Insurance Marketplace Standards Association (IMSA) must abide by requirements that, in some cases, are more rigorous than similar regulatory requirements. As you learned in Chapter 1, IMSA is an association of insurers that implements a voluntary market conduct compliance program for the life insurance industry. In order to qualify for IMSA certification, an insurer must have in place policies and procedures that assure compliance with the American Council of Life Insurance's (ACLI's) Six Principles of Ethical Market Conduct (see Figure 1-6). The insurer's market conduct policies and procedures must pass a stringent assessment by an independent assessor.

Policy Form Filing and Approval

In the United States, a life insurer generally may not begin to sell an insurance product in a state until the product's policy form has been filed with and approved by the state insurance department. Such filing and approval requirements enable state insurance regulators to assure that policies comply with all applicable regulatory requirements, which range from requirements concerning the provisions that may and may not be included in policy forms to requirements regarding the readability of policy language. Some states also require insurers to provide state regulators with projections of anticipated claims and premium income for each new product. The compliance area generally is responsible for filing policy forms with state insurance regulators and, if necessary, working with members of the product development team to revise policy forms so that they meet regulatory requirements. Once an insurer obtains approval of a policy form, the compliance area develops issue instructions for business units that are affected by the new product. As you learned in Chapter 7, issue instructions list the approved policy forms for each jurisdiction and other requirements that the company must follow when selling or administering the product.

In addition to complying with state filing and approval requirements, life insurance companies that issue variable life insurance products in the United States must comply with federal securities laws that govern all types of securities. The body of law known as *securities law*

governs the purchase and sale of securities. The agency that administers federal securities laws is the Securities and Exchange Commission (SEC). Company lawyers advise the insurer's product development team about laws that govern the sale of securities. The compliance area ensures that, before being offered for sale to the public, each variable product that the company markets complies with federal requirements and is registered with the SEC. The insurer registers the security by filing a registration statement with the SEC and paying a filing fee.

Producer Licensing

Insurance producers must obtain a license to sell insurance from the state insurance department of each state in which they conduct business. These licensing requirements are intended to allow the states to oversee the activities of the people who sell insurance products. Each insurance company develops a system of policies and procedures to ensure that its producers have been properly appointed by the company to sell insurance on its behalf and are appropriately licensed to do so. The insurer must also develop procedures for terminating a producer's appointment. The agency operations unit usually manages the producer licensing and termination system, with oversight from the compliance department.

In addition to state licensing requirements, insurers and agents that sell variable life insurance products in the United States must comply with licensing requirements imposed by federal securities laws. A person selling variable life insurance must be a registered representative with the National Association of Securities Dealers (NASD) and must be associated with a broker-dealer firm that has registered with the Securities and Exchange Commission (SEC) and is a member of the NASD. The agency operations and compliance units are generally responsible for ensuring that the people who will be selling the company's variable life insurance products are properly registered with the NASD.

Marketing and Sales

Both lawyers and compliance specialists usually are involved in assuring that the company and its agents comply with all applicable state and federal regulatory requirements for the marketing and sale of insurance. These requirements include the following:

- Producers must abide by a range of requirements designed to ensure that they conduct their businesses honestly, fairly, and ethically. Courts and insurance regulators hold insurance companies responsible for the conduct of their producers, regardless of the producer's relationship to the insurer. To fulfill regulatory

requirements, an insurance company typically develops a producer compliance program that (1) explains the company's expectations of its producers regarding market conduct compliance, (2) explains the applicable market conduct laws and regulations, (3) trains producers in proper market conduct practices, and (4) audits the activities of producers. The insurer must have mechanisms in place to supervise agents and to deal promptly with potential difficulty before the problems become too complex for a simple resolution. An insurance company that fails to properly oversee its agents' activities or whose agents violate market conduct regulations is subject to fines by state insurance departments and, in extreme cases, could lose its license to conduct an insurance business.

- Advertising and sales materials that companies and agents use to market insurance must comply with requirements designed to ensure that consumers receive accurate information about the insurance products they are considering buying. An insurer is ultimately responsible under the law for all of its advertising, and, thus, it must establish a method to ensure that all advertising is reviewed and approved by the company's legal department before it is used. Focus on Technology 18-2 describes how one insurer complies with such requirements by controlling the content of its agents' Internet sites.

- Insurers and agents are required to disclose specific types of information to applicants for and owners of certain products. Disclosure requirements vary depending on the type of product. For example, most states require life insurers to provide specified types of information to prospective purchasers of individual life insurance. The required information includes a Buyer's Guide that educates consumers about life insurance and shows consumers how to compare the cost of similar types of life insurance policies. Many states require insurers to provide periodic reports to owners of certain types of policies, most notably variable life insurance contracts.

Insurers that market variable life insurance must comply with securities laws that govern how variable products are marketed. For example, we have already explained that insurers must register their variable insurance products with the SEC and that prospective purchasers of a variable product must be given a prospectus of the product that has been filed with and approved by the SEC. Registered representatives must comply with NASD rules that impose a variety of requirements on how NASD broker-dealers and their registered

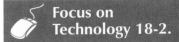

Focus on Technology 18-2. **Controlling the Content of Agents' Internet Sites.**

In 1999, the New York Life Insurance Company began a program to help its agents establish their own Internet sites that could be used to attract customers. In order to assure compliance with state insurance laws regarding the content of the sales and advertising materials used by producers, New York Life strictly controls the content of the agents' Internet sites.

New York Life's agents can include on their Web sites only information about the areas of insurance in which they specialize and the products they sell. For New York Life agents, this information is already printed on personal marketing brochures that have previously been approved by the company's compliance department.

"The general rule is, if we don't allow something to be printed on the agent's personal brochure, we won't allow it on the agent's Web site," said Louis H. Adasse, Corporate Vice President—Corporate Compliance for New York Life.

The insurer hired an Internet vendor to design a single Web template according to the insurer's compliance specifications. Agents interested in participating in the program supply the vendor with content information for the personal Internet page. The vendor imports the information into the template and submits a copy of the Internet page to New York Life's compliance department for review and approval. Any updates to an agent's site must go through the approval process at the home office.

Agents pay a one-time fee for the page design and a monthly fee for the vendor to maintain the site. Each agent's site includes a direct hyperlink to New York Life's main Internet site. Visitors to New York Life's site can also link to a particular agent's page.

The program is advantageous for the company and the agents. For the company, the single template and content review help guarantee uniformity of the Internet sites and help ensure compliance with regulations governing agents' sales materials. For agents, the sites offer a new way to reach potential customers without the time and expense of designing their own Internet sites. •

Source: Louis H. Adasse, Corporate Vice President—Corporate Compliance, New York Life Insurance Company, 1999.

representatives conduct their business. Broker-dealers must supervise the activities of their registered representatives to ensure that they serve their customers properly and deal fairly with the public.

Underwriting and Policy Issue

Insurance companies establish underwriting guidelines that direct their own risk-assessment decisions. In Chapter 11 you learned that an insurer's underwriting activities are constrained by laws designed to protect consumers against unfair discrimination—that is, underwriting decisions based on factors such as the proposed insureds' race, sex, marital status, national origin, or religion. Insurance companies are also required to apply premium rates to their underwriting decisions in a consistent manner and in accordance with their established rating methods. Compliance specialists make sure that underwriters are aware of and are following relevant laws and procedures and that the insurer's underwriting guidelines are filed with the state insurance department, if so required.

Claim Administration

Most states have enacted laws based on the NAIC Unfair Claims Settlement Practices Act that require insurance companies to investigate and pay claims promptly and fairly. The compliance area regularly monitors the company's claim practices to ensure compliance with claim settlement practices laws.

Complaint Handling

The unfair trade practices laws in most states require insurers to maintain records of customer complaints and to respond promptly and fairly to them. Some states impose a time limit within which insurers must respond to each customer's complaint. The compliance staff develops and supervises the company's complaint handling procedures to ensure that complaints are dealt with promptly and fairly. The compliance area also makes sure that the insurer's records reflect all complaints (1) received directly by the company and (2) submitted to the state insurance department.

Many insurers take additional steps with respect to complaint handling. For example, some insurers survey new policyowners to learn their opinion of the insurer's sales and policy issue processes. These surveys help to uncover problems and head off possible future complaints. Insurers also regularly analyze their complaints and seek explanations for complaints that have not been resolved within a stated time. A requirement of IMSA certification is for an insurer to use complaint information to analyze and eliminate the root causes of complaints.

Consumer Privacy

As part of its underwriting, claim administration, and customer service processes, an insurer collects a large amount of personal information about its customers. Insurers in the United States must comply with the federal Fair Credit Reporting Act (FCRA), which regulates the reporting and use of consumer credit information and seeks to ensure that consumer credit reports contain only accurate, relevant, and recent information. Insurers also must comply with state privacy laws that many states have patterned after the NAIC Model Privacy Act, which establishes standards for the collection, use, and disclosure of information gathered in connection with insurance transactions, such as underwriting and claim evaluations. To be in compliance with state privacy regulations, an insurer must follow certain stipulated procedures when a person (1) applies for new or renewal coverage or (2) submits a claim. The compliance area monitors the company's adherence to required procedures.

Also, the Financial Services Modernization Act (FSMA) of 1999 requires financial institutions (including insurers) to establish written procedures for protecting consumers' private information and to disclose these privacy policies to their customers each year. The FSMA also requires insurers to follow specific procedures for sharing their customers' personal data.

Market Conduct Examinations

The insurance departments in all states are required by law to conduct periodic, on-site investigations of insurance companies operating within their jurisdictional boundaries. Insurance regulators make two general types of examinations—financial condition examinations and market conduct examinations. As you learned in Chapter 17, a *financial condition examination* is designed to identify and monitor threats to an insurer's solvency. The purpose of a **market conduct examination** is to determine whether an insurer's market conduct operations are in compliance with applicable laws and regulations. The state insurance departments have developed procedures for market conduct examinations. These procedures enable insurance department examiners to determine whether an insurer is engaging in unlawful activities, and if so, to decide what regulatory action should be taken.

© 1996 *Reinsurance Reporter.* Used with permission.

During a market conduct examination, a team of examiners from the state insurance department visits the insurer's home office or regional office. The examiners inspect samples of the insurer's business records, such as producer licensing records, underwriting records, and records of customer complaints. Examiners evaluate whether (1) the insurer has established standards to ensure that the activity is carried out effectively, (2) the insurer's standards comply with applicable regulatory requirements, and (3) the activity is being carried out according to the established standards. Examiners also evaluate the insurer's system of internal controls and its methods of detecting and correcting market conduct problems. The insurer provides space for the examiners to work, appoints an employee—usually a member of compliance or internal audit—to act as liaison between the company and the examiners, and delivers the requested records.

A market conduct examination can report on the company's operations as a whole or on specific areas of its operations. The scope of the examination determines the specific business records that the examiners request and inspect.

- A *comprehensive market conduct examination* is an examination of all of an insurer's market conduct operations. Most states require the insurance department to conduct comprehensive market conduct examinations of insurers every three to five years.

- A *target market conduct examination* is an examination of one or more specific areas of an insurer's operations. For example, a target examination can focus on an insurer's claim administration activities or its agent licensing practices. An insurance department can demand a target examination of an insurer whenever the department has reason to believe such an examination is necessary.

Upon completion of either a comprehensive examination or a target examination, the team of examiners prepares a report of its findings. The report lists any market conduct problems the examination has uncovered and specifies steps the insurer should take to correct the problems. As necessary, the state insurance department conducts a follow-up examination to determine whether the insurer has complied with the specified actions in the examination report.

The state insurance department may sanction an insurer that is found to have violated state insurance laws or regulatory requirements. Such a sanction generally takes the form of a fine, although in severe cases the insurance department may suspend or revoke the insurer's license to conduct business in the state. An insurer may also

face lawsuits filed by customers who believe they were harmed by the insurer's unlawful activities.

A market conduct examination can be stressful for an insurance company. Best Case Scenario 18-1 illustrates some of the steps an insurer can take to reduce anxiety and make an examination go as smoothly as possible.

Best Case Scenario 18-1.   Surviving a Market Conduct Examination.

The Best Friend Life Insurance Company, which operates in State A, received written notification from State A's insurance commissioner that a team of examiners would be sent to Best Friend in 45 days to perform a comprehensive market conduct examination. The examination was to include a review of the company's files, records, and practices to determine compliance with State A's insurance statutes and regulations. Best Friend took several steps prior to and during the examination to simplify the process.

Before the Examination

The first step was to assemble an exam team of employees who were knowledgeable about Best Friend's functions, procedures, and business philosophies. Team members included representatives from agency operations, actuarial, claims, legal, compliance, marketing, training, and information systems, along with the company's complaint coordinator, chief counsel, and the operations managers for each of the company's lines of business. Having a diverse and experienced team enabled the company to handle efficiently the examiners' requests for information.

The team members elected one member—compliance representa-

tive Patty Colucci—to be the examination coordinator. Patty served as the primary link between Best Friend and the state examiners. All of the examiners' requests for information went through Patty, who set up a computer database to track the requests. Each database record included the date of the request, a description of the request, the date the request was needed, the name of the Best Friend employee to whom the request was assigned, and the date the request was fulfilled.

The state insurance department sent Best Friend a list of the records, statements, forms, and other materials the examiners would need upon arrival at the company. Patty met with Best Friend's exam team to discuss the requested materials and the best way to present them to the examiners. Patty gathered the required material and labelled each piece of information with a description of the contents and an explanation for any requested material not included. Patty arranged with Best Friend's facilities manager for a workspace and equipment for the examiners to use while on site.

During the Examination

When the examiners arrived, Patty met with them to (1) orient them to the company and its operations, (2) clarify any questions about the

examination, (3) present the requested materials, and (4) discuss the timeline for the examination. Patty instructed the examiners to make all additional information requests through her. She was also to be the point of contact for arranging any meetings between the examiners and other Best Friend employees.

As the examiners made additional information requests during the examination, Patty recorded the requests in the tracking database and forwarded each request to the appropriate Best Friend employee for handling. She also kept a copy of all materials given to the examiners. Taking this step would help the company analyze the examiners' final report later.

After the Examination

The examiners completed their work at Best Friend and returned to the state insurance department to prepare the examination report. When Best Friend received the report, Best Friend's exam team met to analyze and discuss it. The team discussed actions Best Friend would take as a result of the examiners' findings. Best Friend then acted on the suggestions. •

Market Conduct Compliance in Canada

Life insurance companies operating in Canada have to abide by many of the same types of market conduct laws and regulatory requirements as do life insurers in the United States. Provincial regulators have considerable direct authority over the market conduct of insurance companies and their salespeople. Most market conduct laws of each common-law province are contained in the province's Insurance Act. All insurance companies and producers operating within the province must comply with the provisions of the Act. These provisions govern such matters as the licensing of insurers, the licensing and education of producers, the content and form of insurance contracts, marketing and sales practices, and customer complaint handling. Federally incorporated life insurers must also comply with guidelines developed and promoted through the Canadian Life and Health Insurance Association (CLHIA) that govern the care, handling, and protection of confidential information. Statutory requirements regarding the readability of policy documents are rare in Canada, unlike in the United States.

Although the federal Office of the Superintendent of Financial Institutions (OSFI) traditionally has been charged with regulating insurer solvency, OSFI is taking an increasing role in marketplace regulation, as Insight 18-2 discusses.

An important tool used to measure the compliance of insurers in Canada is the Standards of Sound Business and Financial Practices. As you learned in Chapter 2, insurers must comply with the provisions of the Standards, which require insurers to perform a series of self-assessment tests and file an annual report of the results with regulators. One category of test that relates to market conduct is internal controls. The regulators review and report on each institution's compliance with the Standards. Full responsibility for compliance with the requirements of the Standards rests with the senior officers and the board of directors of each insurer.

Insurers in some provinces are required to take an active role in monitoring the activities of their producers, much the same way U.S. insurers are required to do so. These provinces have enacted "duty of care" statutes that obligate insurance companies operating in the province to take reasonable care to prevent misconduct by producers selling on their behalf. According to the Ontario duty of care legislation, which was the model for other provinces, an insurance company must

- Thoroughly screen all prospective producers for suitability before offering them appointments with the company

- Establish a monitoring system to prevent violations of laws and ethical standards regarding sales of insurance

Insight 18-2.   OSFI's Role in Marketplace Regulation.

In 1999, Canada's life and health insurance industry began working with the Office of the Superintendent of Financial Institutions (OSFI) on a common checklist for compliance with provisions of the Insurance Companies Act, the primary federal legislation affecting the operations of life insurance companies. The OSFI is interested in compliance with marketplace regulation because of the adverse effects that questionable sales practices may have on the financial soundness of an insurance company.

The foundation for this work is OSFI's Legislative Compliance Management System for life and health insurers, which is based on an existing framework for banks and trust companies. This program requires each insurer's board of directors to (1) implement a compliance management system that includes policies and procedures governing the insurer's compliance activities and (2) periodically review the system's operations. An insurer's management is responsible for revising the system when necessary, devoting appropriate resources to the system, and ensuring that controls are implemented to monitor the company's compliance with the Insurance Companies Act.

In order to be reasonably assured that an insurer is complying with the Act, OSFI periodically reviews the company's legislative compliance management system. During a review of an insurance company, OSFI seeks answers to the following questions:

• What is the company policy on "market conduct" practices, and who in the company is accountable for ensuring that compliance standards and processes are followed?

• Is the company's top management supporting the compliance efforts?

• Is compliance monitoring independent of the company's marketing and sales functions?

• Does the officer in charge of compliance management report to the company's board of directors and the chief executive officer?

• Are prospective agents subject to a thorough background review, and are agents properly informed about their ethical and legal duties?

• How are market conduct practices monitored?

• What is the protocol regarding product description and disclosures?

• What type of complaint handling procedures are in place in the company?

• How are consumers protected in cases in which insurance is marketed electronically? •

Sources: J-P Bernier, *Regulation of Life Insurance Around the World* (Toronto: Canadian Life and Health Insurance Association, 1999), 31–32. Memo to Federally Regulated Life Insurance Companies from John R. Thompson, Deputy Superintendent—Regulation, Office of the Superintendent of Financial Institutions, 31 May 1999.

• Take reasonable steps to ensure that producers comply with all laws and regulations[1]

An insurer breaching its obligation to monitor its agents' conduct is subject to civil liability or regulatory penalties.

In Canada, a life insurance company is required to submit all of its policy forms to provincial insurance regulators before the company can receive a license to conduct an insurance business within the province. After receiving a provincial license, a life insurer is required to file only its variable insurance policy forms with provincial regulators before using those forms. Finally, provincial insurance regulators have the authority to conduct market conduct examinations of the insurers operating in the province. Typically, provincial regulators perform examinations only when they have questions or concerns about an insurer's market conduct compliance.

Key Terms

compliance (regulatory
  compliance)
paralegal
bar examination
contract
contract law
real property law
agency law
employment law
Fair Labor Standards Act (FLSA)
Family Medical Leave Act
  (FMLA)
Employee Retirement Income
  Security Act (ERISA)

litigation
arbitration
arbitrator
mediation
mediator
internal control
internal audit
securities law
market conduct examination
comprehensive market conduct
  examination
target market conduct
  examination

Endnote

1. Section 15.2 of Regulation 760 under the *Insurance Act of Ontario.*

Strategic Planning for Long-Term Growth

Consolidation, competition, shifting consumer needs, and many other factors are changing the financial services industry and forcing life insurance companies to closely examine their operations, corporate structures, and the businesses in which they are engaged. To succeed in this ever-changing environment, an insurer must be able to perform effectively and efficiently the operations we have discussed in this book. However, an equally critical component of corporate success is the ability of senior management to plan and guide the strategic direction of the company, and to fend off new threats and exploit new opportunities so that the company can grow and remain profitable.

A goal of most insurers is long-term growth—an increase in the wealth, or value, of the company as measured by factors such as the value of the company's stock and its capital and surplus. Growth allows an insurer to

- Build enough capital and surplus to ensure its long-term ability to pay policy benefits

- Diversify the sources of its revenues in order to protect against future economic downturns

- Provide a suitable return for the company's owners

- Generate the funds it needs to invest in new technology and new distribution systems, and to undertake other large projects

- Fortify the company's financial position in the face of increased competition

This chapter examines some of the strategic changes a life insurer might consider undertaking in order to provide growth opportunities and to compete in the changing financial services industry. We begin by describing strategic planning in life insurance companies. Then we discuss several growth strategies that insurers can follow and the benefits and drawbacks of each strategy. These strategies include (1) developing new marketing strategies that can increase sales of the company's products, (2) changing the structure of the organization in order to increase revenues and/or decrease expenses, (3) entering into strategic alliances with other companies, and (4) expanding the geographic area in which the company operates in order to increase its customer base.

FAST FACT

According to a LIMRA International survey, corporate growth is the main issue concerning chief executive officers of U.S. life insurers.[1]

Strategic Planning in Life Insurance Companies

Insurance companies have different operating goals. Some insurers focus on providing a wide variety of products for a great number of customers. Other insurers specialize in a particular *niche market*—a small, specialized market segment in which consumers share similar needs—and become dominant players in this market. Whatever an insurer's goals, the cornerstone of successful operations is effective planning. *Planning* is the process of preparing for the future by establishing appropriate goals and formulating the strategies, tactics, and other activities necessary to achieve those goals. Planners determine which strategy is most appropriate by taking into consideration the company's goals, resources, strengths and weaknesses, and the environmental conditions in the insurance industry.

The focus of this chapter is on the issues an insurer considers as part of its *strategic planning,* which, as we defined in Chapter 4, is the process of determining an organization's major long-term corporate objectives and the broad, overall courses of action that the company will follow to achieve these objectives. Insurers conduct strategic planning to answer questions such as

- Should we expand the current whole life insurance product line or create a new product line?

- Should we begin selling universal life products in a new state, province, or country?

- Should we sell a line of business or acquire another company?

- Should we change the corporate form of the company?

- Should we open a new distribution channel?

- Should we outsource our investment function to an asset management firm?

An insurer's senior management usually is responsible for strategic planning. A strategic plan covers a fairly long time horizon, such as three or five years. However, a strategic plan typically evolves as the insurer's environment changes. It is important that a strategic plan provide broad guidance for the company's future operations, but the plan also should be flexible enough to allow the company to respond to changes in its economic and social environment.

New Marketing Strategies

One way an insurer can generate growth is by increasing the sales of its products. The company's marketing executives and other senior officers regularly monitor the company's marketing strategies and consider whether new strategies might be appropriate. For example, an insurer might develop new products or modify existing products to increase their appropriateness, availability, and profitability. The following are examples of marketing growth strategies that a life insurance company might implement:

- Increasing sales of existing products to current customers or potential customers. For example, the company might increase advertising for its existing term life products and train its producers to cross-sell term life products to customers who already own whole life coverage.

- Increasing sales of existing products by introducing them into new geographic markets. For example, an insurer may begin selling its existing products in new states, provinces, or countries.

- Increasing overall sales by modifying existing products or developing new products. For example, an insurer that had sold traditional individual life insurance products may enter the market for variable life insurance.

- Developing new distribution channels in an effort to reduce expenses, enhance sales and profitability, and reach new customers. For example, an insurer that previously had used only a career agency force might begin to distribute some of its products through worksite marketing, fee-based financial planners, banks, securities firms, or online insurance marketplaces.

- Purchasing a line of business from another insurer as a way of (1) increasing its share of a market or (2) entering a new market. For example, an insurer that has not previously sold variable life coverage may buy a block of business from another insurer.

- Selling a line of business. An insurer chooses to exit a certain product market or geographic market when the insurer finds the market to be unprofitable or too costly to service. The insurer can use the proceeds from the sale to pursue other growth opportunities, such as those mentioned above.

Change in Corporate Structure

Many life insurance companies have pursued growth strategies that involved changing their corporate structures. Such structural changes may result from the linking of two or more companies through a merger or an acquisition. Figure 19-1 shows the merger and acquisition activity of the U.S. life insurance industry in a given period. The result of so many structural changes is to consolidate the life insurance industry into one of fewer and bigger companies than ever before. This trend is expected to continue. Another type of structural change is the demutualization of a mutual insurer. We describe these structural changes in this section.

Mergers and Acquisitions

Most of the structural changes taking place in the financial services industry involve the linking of two or more companies through a merger or an acquisition. A *merger*, known as an *amalgamation* in Canada, is a transaction wherein the assets and liabilities of two companies are combined, one of the companies survives as a legal entity, and the other company ceases to exist. Stock insurers and mutual insurers can participate in mergers. However, if one of the companies involved in a merger is a mutual company, the resulting company must also be a mutual.

An *acquisition* is a transaction wherein one company purchases a controlling interest in another company.[2] Sometimes the acquiring company holds the acquired company's stock only as an investment, and the original management team of the acquired company continues to direct the company. In other cases, the management of the acquiring company takes over the operation of the acquired company. Although a mutual insurer may purchase stock in a stock insurer, a mutual insurer does not issue stock, and, thus, cannot be acquired by another company.

Each life insurance company periodically assesses its current situation and determines its standing in the life insurance industry. Company executives examine whether or not the company can compete effectively and achieve its strategic goals, and if not, whether it has the resources and structural flexibility to acquire other companies. Insurers that do not have the capacity to acquire another company often search for merger partners or, in the case of stock insurers, become acquisition targets themselves.

Ideally, a merger or an acquisition should result in the new company's having a higher value to its owners than the old companies had. For example, if an insurer with a market value of $100 million merges

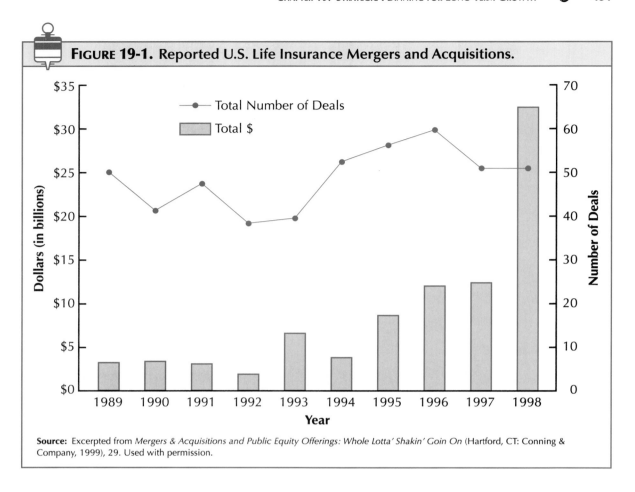

FIGURE 19-1. Reported U.S. Life Insurance Mergers and Acquisitions.

Source: Excerpted from *Mergers & Acquisitions and Public Equity Offerings: Whole Lotta' Shakin' Goin On* (Hartford, CT: Conning & Company, 1999), 29. Used with permission.

with a company valued at $200 million, the value of the combined company should exceed $300 million in order for the merger to be acceptable to both companies. For the combined company to be more valuable than the sum of its original parts, combined operations should be more efficient and more profitable.

Due Diligence

Before merging with or acquiring another company, a life insurer undertakes *due diligence*, which is a careful investigation into (1) the details of a potential merger or acquisition and (2) the operations and management of the other company or companies involved. During due diligence, an insurer carefully analyzes the other company's assets and liabilities, market conduct compliance record, past financial results, distribution systems and product mix, any pending litigation in which the company is involved, and general risks to the company's competitive position. The insurer must balance the need

to gather a great deal of information about the proposed transaction with the desire to complete the process quickly and confidentially.

Benefits of Mergers and Acquisitions

Life insurance companies have many reasons for merging with or acquiring other companies, but often mergers and acquisitions are aimed at allowing an insurer to quickly build its size. Mergers and acquisitions are generally regarded as relatively quick and efficient ways to achieve significant growth. Internally generated growth through increased sales activity is usually a more gradual process than growth through merger or acquisition.

A merger or an acquisition can benefit a financially troubled insurer that seeks a stronger partner or acquirer in order to overcome its own financial difficulties or to obtain enough surplus to help it expand. (Insight 19-1 discusses one insurer's acquisition of a financially troubled insurer.) An insurance company may need new products and services

Insight 19-1.   MetLife's Purchase of General American.

In the summer of 1999, General American Life Insurance Company encountered financial difficulty when several of its large institutional customers (primarily pension funds and money market funds) exercised their rights to withdraw several billion dollars in cash from funding agreements issued by the insurer.

A *funding agreement,* also called a *guaranteed investment contract (GIC),* is a short-term, bond-like financial instrument in which the issuer—usually an insurance company—accepts a single deposit from another financial institution and promises to pay a specified interest rate on the funds deposited during a specified time period. Under most funding agreements, the depositor has the right to redeem its money by providing a specified notice to

the issuer, such as seven days. General American's problem was that it could not meet the sudden demand for cash without selling a large portion of its bond portfolio at a loss, an action that would have jeopardized the position of its policyowners. General American notified the state insurance department of the situation and was placed under administrative supervision.

With the state insurance department's approval, GenAmerica, the parent company of General American, announced itself as an acquisition target for a company that could help GenAmerica out of its financial difficulty. The Metropolitan Life Insurance Company (MetLife) stepped forward with an offer of $1.2 billion in cash for GenAmerica and

its subsidiaries, including General American. The boards of directors of GenAmerica and MetLife quickly approved the deal.

The transaction was mutually beneficial. MetLife paid $5.1 billion in cash to the General American funding agreement holders who had requested withdrawals of their money. In return, MetLife found in General American an acquisition target that fit its growth strategy. General American, the 41st-largest insurer in the United States (1) provided MetLife with a strong geographical presence in the midwestern United States, (2) added to MetLife's core businesses of life insurance and asset management, and (3) provided MetLife with an entry into the life reinsurance business. •

Sources: "St. Louis Insurance Company Falters after Credit Rating Drops," *St. Louis Post-Dispatch* via NewsEdge Corporation, 16 August 1999, http://www.newspage.com/cgi-bin (17 August 1999). "MetLife to Acquire General American for $1.2 Billion," *General American,* 26 August 1999, http://www.genam.com/genam/topstory (10 September 1999). "Most General American Holders Seek Payment from MetLife," *The Wall Street Journal Interactive Edition,* 27 September 1999, http://interactive.wsj.com (27 September 1999).

"This is your first merger isn't it?"

© 1997 Frank Monahan. Used with permission.

to offer its customers, but rather than spend the time and money to develop these new products and services itself, the company can seek a merger partner whose products, sales force, or territories complement its own. For example, a company selling individual life insurance may merge with a company that specializes in group insurance, or a company that concentrates in the Midwest may merge with or acquire a company that concentrates in the Southeast. Some insurance companies buy investment brokerage firms in order to be able to offer their own customers a wider range of financial services products and to gain access to the customers of the acquired firms.

Companies also engage in mergers and acquisitions in order to obtain the advantages of economies of scale. ***Economies of scale*** are the reduction in a company's unit costs as the size of its operations increases. Economies of scale exist because some operations are more efficient when done on a large scale. In theory, when two or more companies are combined into one, the resulting larger company should be able to combine many functions, such as accounting, underwriting, claim administration, and customer service. The larger company can then spread those costs over a larger revenue base—in other words, the

combined company can reduce the amount of some expenses as a percentage of its sales.

Other advantages of mergers and acquisitions are that customers often feel that larger companies are more stable than smaller ones, and companies that appear to be growing usually find it easier to attract and retain good employees.

Drawbacks to Mergers and Acquisitions

Mergers and acquisitions also have certain disadvantages, which insurers consider before making a deal.

- A merger or an acquisition is a complicated process that involves significant legal, accounting, actuarial, and investment costs. The companies involved in the transaction have to develop a proposal for the transaction, and that proposal must be approved by the boards of directors and owners of both companies and by the regulatory authorities of the states and/or provinces in which the companies involved are domiciled. In the United States, the companies must file all required legal documents with the secretary of state and the insurance department in the state of domicile of each insurance company involved. Typically, the companies must file such documents with the Securities and Exchange Commission (SEC). In Canada, a transaction involving a federally regulated insurance company must be approved by the Minister of Finance.

- The employees of combining companies often experience a great deal of anxiety about the transaction. Employees wonder if their jobs will be eliminated or changed. They also wonder if the corporate culture and the management style of the new company will be different from the previous management style. Some employees leave the company during the transition rather than wait to see how their jobs fit into the new structure.

- Combining the sales operations, distribution systems, and information systems of the merging companies can be an enormous and difficult challenge. Focus on Technology 19-1 discusses the merging of information systems.

- Typically, at least one of the companies involved in a merger will have to relocate its headquarters to the headquarters of one of the other parties to the transaction. Some employees may resign rather than move, and the company may have to hire new employees at the new location. The company that is moving may have to provide severance pay to certain employees, relocate key employees, and sell buildings that it owns in the old location.

Focus on Technology 19-1.

Merging Technologies when Merging Companies.

Insurance company mega-mergers create mega-challenges for those who must combine disparate information systems into a single system capable of propelling the new entity into a new age of financial services.

"When you make a decision to merge two companies, there is a lot of due diligence, but not concerning how you write your programs or what the premise of your source code is," said Dominick Cavuoto, partner-in-charge of the Insurance-Financial Service Division of KPMG Peat Marwick. "And once there is a merger, it is a major task to see how we are going to shake this out. Which is going to be the surviving [information] system?"

Since every merger presents unique challenges, solutions are equally diverse. With one-stop financial shopping the goal, companies often find that separate information systems may be the initial path of least resistance, but not the most rewarding one in the end.

Sometimes there are more than two information systems to merge. "You may have 22, because sometimes in situations somebody has built a product that has had its own little feature generating its own little statement," said Cavuoto. "So there is a huge amount of technology necessary to make this happen."

In some mergers, information systems are relatively compatible, but other times they are "worlds apart," according to Cavuoto. But whether to go through the effort and expense of conversion can depend on factors not readily available.

"[The merging companies] may know that in a year or two they are planning on buying another major entity, and once they have that piece they will be complete, so it will make sense to convert all three [systems at once]," Cavuoto said. "So what is key is knowing who the strategic thinkers are at the organization at the highest level and what the strategic vision is going forward."

Cross-country mergers add a new dimension to combining information systems "because there are so many cultures we are dealing with. We have different views of what an employee is, of what timely IS is, and different views on how to structure performance and return," Cavuoto said. •

Source: Excerpted from "Technology on Fast-Breaking Wave," *Insurance Accounting* (5 April 1999): 3. Used with permission.

Holding Company Systems

As a result of the many mergers and acquisitions that have taken place in the insurance industry, many life insurers are now part of holding company systems. As you learned in Chapter 2, a holding company has a controlling interest in one or more other companies, known as subsidiaries. The holding company and the subsidiaries operate as distinct corporate entities under their own names. The holding company usually leaves operating decisions to the management of each subsidiary, but the management of the holding company is responsible for long-range planning for the entire holding company system and for allocating financial resources among the companies in the holding company system.

A holding company approach to the consolidation of two or more insurers has several advantages.

- A holding company structure eliminates some of the potential corporate culture clashes and other problems that can occur when a new company is created from the combination of two or more existing companies.

- A subsidiary insurer can borrow funds through the holding company.

- Within limits established by law, an insurer can transfer funds to the holding company that owns it, eliminating the need for the holding company to look outside the holding company family for necessary funds.

- A holding company arrangement can be used to control subsidiaries in widely differing industries, thus diversifying the products and services provided to customers, diversifying the interests of the holding company, and protecting the holding company from the risks involved in concentrating on just one kind of business.

- A holding company may have an easier time than subsidiary companies in accessing the capital markets.

Insurance regulators have been wary of potential abuses in holding company arrangements. Regulators are concerned that a holding company could raid the surplus of an insurance subsidiary to help finance the operations of the holding company or its other subsidiaries. In order to protect insurers, policyowners, and beneficiaries from financial difficulty resulting from potential abuses, all states have enacted laws that separate the assets and liabilities of an insurance subsidiary from the assets and liabilities of the holding company that owns it and the holding company's other subsidiaries. States also impose a number of filing and reporting requirements on companies that are part of an insurance holding company system. These requirements govern the approval to engage in holding companies, the disclosure of financial transactions between entities within a holding company system, and limitations of the amounts that a domestic insurer can invest in its subsidiaries.

Downstream and Upstream Holding Companies

Holding companies can be created either downstream or upstream. A **downstream holding company** is a holding company that is owned or controlled by the corporation that forms it. In turn, the downstream holding company owns or controls another subsidiary company or companies. Both stock insurers and mutual insurers can own subsidiaries in a downstream holding company arrangement. Mutual holding companies (discussed later in this chapter) are one type of downstream holding company.

An **upstream holding company** is a holding company that controls the corporation that formed it and can also own other subsidiaries.

Only stock insurers can form, or be purchased by, an upstream holding company. Mutual insurers cannot be owned or purchased by other companies because they do not issue stock. For more on the difference between downstream and upstream holding companies, read Best Case Scenario 19-1.

Demutualization

Stock insurers can participate in any of the structural changes discussed thus far—mergers, acquisitions, and upstream and downstream holding companies—to help meet growth and profitability objectives. As we have noted, however, mutual insurers are not able to undertake all of the structural changes available to stock insurers. Some mutuals have found themselves at a competitive disadvantage compared with stock insurers and have made the strategic decision to demutualize—that is, to convert from a mutual form of ownership to a stock form of ownership.

The decision to demutualize is an important one for a mutual insurer, its employees, and its policyowners. Demutualization can affect the company's operations and corporate culture, as well as its perception among policyowners, competitors, and rating agencies. Figure 19-2 lists some questions that mutual insurers face when considering demutualization.

Advantages of Demutualization

Mutual insurers generally cite a number of reasons for pursuing demutualization.

- **Improved access to capital.** Because a mutual insurer's access to capital is limited, the insurer is also limited in its expansion opportunities and its participation in mergers and acquisitions. By converting to a stock insurance company, the insurer can increase its capital by issuing shares of stock and selling that stock to investors. The cash that stock companies receive from a stock issue can then be used to (1) pursue growth through mergers and acquisitions, (2) develop new technologies, or (3) increase the company's surplus.

- **More flexible corporate structure.** Stock companies have greater flexibility than mutual companies in forming holding companies to buy and operate other types of companies, including companies that are not in the insurance business, without restricting those companies to regulations meant only for insurers. As noted earlier,

Best Case Scenario 19-1. **Downstream and Upstream Holding Companies.**

Downstream Holding Company

The Best Friend Life Insurance Company acquired the MountainView Company and the Large Life Insurance Company. Rather than merging the three companies into one, Best Friend created a holding company, Best Holdings, Inc., that owns MountainView and Large Life. MountainView and Large Life are considered to be subsidiaries of Best Holdings, but the two companies continue to operate under their own names.

This holding company arrangement is known as a downstream holding company because the holding company (Best Holdings) is owned by the company that created it (Best Friend). Best Friend effectively controls MountainView and Large Life through Best Holdings. The presidents of MountainView and Large Life report to the president of Best Holdings. The president of Best Holdings reports to the president of Best Friend.

Downstream Holding Company

(Insurer owns holding company)

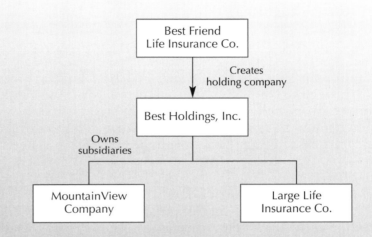

Upstream Holding Company

The Best Friend Life Insurance Company acquired the MountainView Company and the Large Life Insurance Company. Best Friend then created Best Holdings, a holding company, to control Best Friend, MountainView, and Large Life. This holding company arrangement is known as an upstream holding company because the holding company (Best Holdings) controls the corporation that created it (Best Friend). The presidents of Best Friend, MountainView, and Large Life all report to the president of Best Holdings. •

Upstream Holding Company

(Holding company owns insurer)

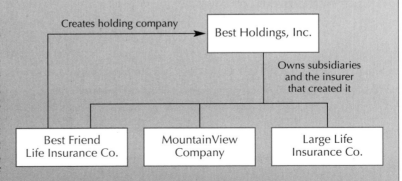

> **FIGURE 19-2.** Important Questions for a Mutual Insurer That Is Considering Demutualization.
>
> 1. What is the best type of corporate organization for this insurance company?
> 2. Will a corporate reorganization put the company on an equal competitive footing with stock insurance companies?
> 3. Can the company's organizational structure ensure its success?
> 4. Is access to additional capital sufficient to enable the company to change its operations?
> 5. Can the company use new capital effectively to earn competitive returns?
> 6. How will potential affiliations with other companies enable the company to enhance its standing in the marketplace?
> 7. How will the company's conversion to a stock company affect its ratings?
>
> **Source:** Adapted from Michael A. Cohen, Larry G. Mayewski, and Michael L. Albanese, "End of an Era?" *Best's Review*, Life/Health ed. (August 1998): 42. © A.M. Best Company. Used with permission.

mutual insurers cannot be part of upstream holding companies. Also, if a mutual insurer acquires a company from another industry, that company must conform to the regulatory requirements imposed on a mutual insurance company.

- **Improved efficiency and competitiveness.** By merging with or acquiring other companies, a stock insurer may be able to achieve economies of scale, which can make it more efficient and competitive in the industry.

- **More attractive employment incentives.** Stock companies can offer shares of company stock or stock options as part of their compensation packages. These incentives can help attract and retain managers and employees. Mutual companies cannot compensate employees in this way.

- **More active interest of the company's owners.** Stock insurance company stockholders tend to take a more active interest in company operations than do the policyowners of mutual insurers. Some executives believe that, because of this active stockholder interest, the management of stock companies tends to be more aggressive, growth-oriented, and adaptable to changes in the economy than the management of mutual companies.

Disadvantages of Demutualization

Some mutual companies have considered demutualization but have not proceeded with the process for a number of reasons.

- Demutualization involves complex financial and legal reporting and disclosure requirements. When the demutualized insurance company issues stock to the public, the insurer becomes subject to oversight from federal and provincial securities regulators. As a result, the insurer must comply with specific financial reporting requirements that can be more extensive than the requirements imposed on mutual insurance companies.

- Demutualization requires the distribution of a mutual company's excess surplus among its policyowners, and determining the most equitable and efficient way to distribute this surplus can be difficult. For example, should all policyowners—past and present—share in the distribution of surplus, or should only current policyowners share in the surplus? Also, should policyowners receive the distribution in cash, shares of stock in the converted company, or both?

- In the United States, a demutualized company can become the target of a takeover in which another company purchases a controlling interest in the insurer. In Canada, no single entity can own more than 10 percent of a demutualized insurer, so demutualized insurers are protected from takeover bids.[3]

- The process of demutualization can be lengthy and complex. The time and expense associated with demutualization can be enormous and difficult to estimate in advance. Costs include legal fees, accounting and actuarial consulting fees, and printing and postage costs.

- The morale of the converting company's employees may decline because of uncertainty about the direction of the new company. Demutualization involves changes in corporate culture that may worry or unnerve employees. For example, employees could fear that a more intense focus on the company's corporate earnings could possibly lead to a reduction of the workforce as a way to reduce costs and improve profits.

- Demutualized companies have to balance the interests of policyowners and stockholders. As a mutual company, management's role was to serve the interests of policyowners only.

Methods of Demutualization

In the United States, a mutual insurer that decides demutualization is in the best interest of the company, its policyowners, its producers, and its employees can undertake the demutualization in one of two general ways: (1) standard demutualization or (2) conversion to a mutual holding company. Under both demutualization methods, a policyowner's policy rights, or contractual rights, are transferred to the new stock insurance company. An important difference between the two methods concerns the treatment of policyowners' membership rights, which are ownership rights in the mutual company. Mutual holding company conversions are not permitted among Canadian insurers.

Standard Demutualization. Under *standard demutualization*, a mutual insurance company reorganizes as a stock insurance company. To accomplish a standard demutualization, policyowners surrender their membership rights in exchange for "valuable consideration," such as a portion of the company's surplus (in the form of cash) or shares of stock in the new corporation. Policyowners maintain their policy rights through the new stock insurance corporation. Figure 19-3 graphically illustrates a standard demutualization.

Mutual Holding Company Conversion. A relatively new method of demutualization is through conversion to a mutual holding company. A *mutual holding company conversion* is a demutualization method by which a mutual insurance company reorganizes itself into three distinct entities: (1) a parent holding company organized as a mutual company, (2) an intermediate holding company organized as a stock

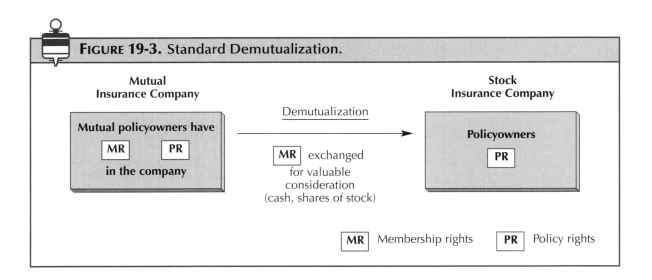

FIGURE 19-3. Standard Demutualization.

company and owned by the mutual holding company, and (3) a subsidiary operating company organized as a stock insurer. The membership rights of the mutual insurer's policyowners are transferred to the new mutual holding company, and their policy rights are transferred to the new stock insurance operating subsidiary. The newly formed mutual holding company is generally required to maintain at least a 51 percent interest in the intermediate stock holding company, and the intermediate stock holding company must control 100 percent of the newly formed stock insurance operating subsidiary. If it so desires, the mutual holding company can offer up to 49 percent of the intermediate stock holding company for sale to investors. A mutual holding company conversion is illustrated in Figure 19-4.

A mutual holding company conversion can be viewed as a compromise between remaining a mutual company and undergoing standard demutualization. The mutual insurer's policyowners become the owners of the mutual holding company. As owners, the policyowners are entitled to vote for the directors of the mutual holding company, and they are allowed to purchase shares of stock in the intermediate stock holding company. During the conversion, the original mutual insurer's policyowners typically do not receive cash or shares of stock as policyowners do in a standard demutualization, because all assets and liabilities of the original mutual insurer are transferred to the new stock insurance subsidiary. As with a standard demutualization, a mutual holding company conversion requires the approval of the

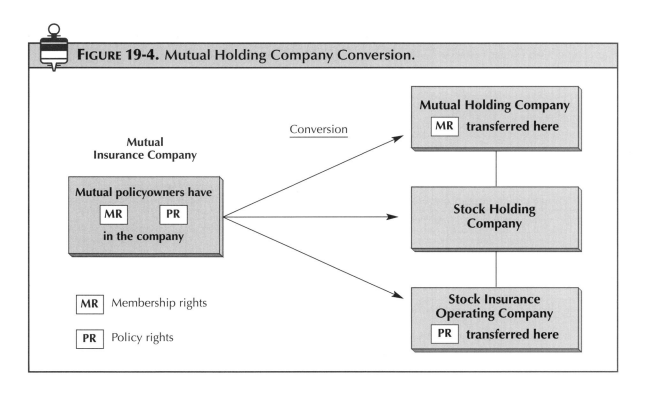

FIGURE 19-4. Mutual Holding Company Conversion.

mutual insurer's board of directors, policyowners, and the state insurance department in the insurer's state of domicile.

Current laws in a number of states do not allow mutual holding company conversions. Some mutual insurers domiciled in these states have redomesticated or announced their intention to redomesticate to states that do permit mutual holding companies.

The choice between a standard demutualization and a mutual holding company conversion has been a controversial one since mutual holding company conversions became possible in some jurisdictions in the 1990s. Mutual insurers considering demutualization carefully consider the advantages and disadvantages of each, which are described in Figure 19-5.

Strategic Alliances

Because mergers and acquisitions can be expensive and time consuming, some life insurance companies instead choose to develop strategic alliances that will strengthen their competitive position and provide new opportunities for growth. A *strategic alliance* is a prolonged relationship involving risk and reward sharing by two or more independent firms that are also pursuing their own strategic goals. Through a strategic alliance, a life insurance company can gain the resources or expertise of other firms and still retain its own independence. Insurance companies form strategic alliances with third-party administrators, securities firms, foreign insurance companies, domestic insurers, commercial banks, technology firms, Internet marketers, and medical firms, among others.

Life insurers enter strategic alliances for many reasons, including the following:

- To gain access to new geographical markets

- To gain new distribution channels

- To maximize return on existing operations

- To improve customer service

- To enhance a product line

Insurance industry strategic alliances usually take one of two legal forms: joint ventures and partnerships. A *joint venture* is an agreement by two or more parties to work together on a project. An example of a joint venture is an agreement between an insurer and a bank in which the insurer develops, underwrites, and administers an insurance prod-

FIGURE 19-5. Advantages and Disadvantages of Traditional Demutualization and Mutual Holding Company Conversion.

Demutualization	Mutual Holding Company Conversion
Advantages	
Greater amount of capital can be raised in the public markets than can be raised by a mutual holding company. Mutual holding companies can offer only 49 percent of the stock holding company for sale to investors.	The public offering of stock issued by the stock subsidiary may be held at any time or not at all, depending on market conditions.
Company valuations tend to be higher than in a mutual holding company conversion.	The amount of capital sought in a public offering can be tailored for a specific opportunity, avoiding a build-up of un-needed capital.
A company that can be fully acquired is more attractive to prospective suitors.	Mutual holding company conversion is much less expensive and less time consuming than a demutualization.
A complete conversion to a stock company is perceived to bring a greater sense of urgency to company management.	The mutual company heritage is preserved for policyowners who may find the policy dividends paid by mutuals a desirable feature.
	Existing management does not risk losing control of the stock company as is possible in a standard demutualization in the United States.
Disadvantages	
The process is more expensive and time consuming than a mutual holding company conversion.	Management's loyalties are divided between the interests of policyholders and the stockholders.
The timing of an initial public offering lacks flexibility.	Some people see this conversion as only a temporary step toward demutualization.
Significant cultural changes need to take place in order for the company to be successful as a public company.	Less capital can be raised through mutual holding company conversion than through traditional demutualization.

Source: Adapted from Michael A. Cohen, Larry G. Mayewski, and Michael L. Albanese, "End of an Era?" *Best's Review,* Life/Health ed. (August 1998): 43. © A.M. Best Company. Used with permission.

uct and supplies the product to the bank for distribution. A ***partnership*** is a contract between two or more organizations that agree to pool their funds and talents and share in the profit and loss of the enterprise. An example of a partnership is two insurance companies that work together to develop, underwrite, distribute, and administer an insurance product. A partnership is generally a continuing relationship that can be the

basis of many projects, whereas a joint venture is usually limited to one project with a specified duration. Once the project is completed, the joint venture terminates.

In a changing financial services environment, strategic alliances are flexible and cost-efficient ways for an insurer to access the technology of or make use of the management or distribution expertise of another company. Participants in strategic alliances can move quickly into new and potentially profitable situations.

International Expansion

The life insurance markets in the United States and Canada are considered to be *mature*—that is, relatively few new potential customers exist. Competition from domestic and foreign insurers has increased, and profit margins have shrunk.[4] These conditions have prompted many insurers to look for new opportunities in a number of foreign countries whose insurance markets are largely undeveloped. In particular, U.S. and Canadian life insurers see much promise in many Asian and Latin American countries.

Since the 1990s, many North American life insurers have expanded their operations to other countries and become multinational corporations in pursuit of growth and profitability. A **multinational corporation** is a business that owns or controls product or service facilities outside the country in which it is headquartered, known as its **home country**.

In addition to maturing insurance markets at home, other conditions have shifted to make global expansion attractive. For example,

- Many countries are more politically stable than in the past

- Many countries are more willing than in the past to engage in trade with other nations

- In several countries, insurance industries that were run by the federal governments have become privatized

- Insurance markets of many countries contain fewer regulatory restrictions than do the insurance markets in the United States and Canada

- Advancements in technology have improved global communications and facilitated international commerce

- Solvency regulations are beginning to become more standardized around the world

FAST FACT

In December 1997, the World Trade Organization (WTO), the international agency that oversees rules of international trade, finalized a financial services agreement involving 97 countries that represent approximately 95 percent of world trade in banking, insurance, and securities. The participating countries agreed to (1) open their financial services markets to foreign companies, (2) allow foreign companies to hold a controlling interest in their operations overseas, and (3) uphold most-favored-nation guarantees that prohibit a member country from providing special favors to only certain other member countries.[5]

Motivations for Expanding Internationally

International operations offer insurers several attractive marketing and financial opportunities. International expansion also offers many opportunities for an insurer's employees.

Marketing Opportunities

Insurers around the world are taking advantage of the marketing opportunities that emerging markets offer. For example, insurers can increase sales of their existing products by selling them in the foreign country. In some cases, these products may have never been available in that country.

An insurer may be able to sell a product in another country that, for regulatory reasons, could not be sold in the insurer's home country. For example, an insurer may develop a product line that is supported by investments that are not permitted in the home country. International expansion also allows an insurer to test a new product, a new marketing strategy, or a new distribution method in another country on a small scale before attempting a full-scale launch in the home country. Finally, international expansion allows an insurer to keep pace with multinational competitors.

Financial Opportunities

An insurance company operating internationally has the opportunity to increase its profits and add to its surplus, thus leading to an increase in financial resources that can benefit the entire company, including its domestic business. International expansion also enables an insurer to diversify its operations, which generally has a positive effect on the company's financial position. Just as insurers invest in many different types of assets in order to diversify their investment portfolios, insurers can also operate in many different countries in order to diversify several types of risk. International operations allow an insurer to

- Spread its underwriting risks over a larger, more diverse customer base, thereby offsetting unusually high losses among one customer segment

- Reduce the adverse effect that an economic downturn in any one country will have on the entire company's financial performance

- Reduce the adverse effect of business losses associated with political upheaval in any one country in which the insurer operates

Employee Opportunities

By becoming a multinational corporation, an insurer can provide new challenges for its current employees and managers who wish to take on an international assignment. If the company has long-term plans for a particular international market, this opportunity is valuable for the overall development of the employees and the company's long-term success in that market.

Considerations in Expanding Internationally

Establishing international operations offers an insurer many potential rewards, such as a vast source of potential new customers and higher levels of profitability than are available at home. But with these attractive rewards come substantial risks. International expansion requires an investment—sometimes a significant one—but an organization generally is not as knowledgeable about the people, regulations, business customs, economic conditions, and political conditions of foreign countries as it is of those of its home country. An insurer's inexperience with these factors increases the chance that the expansion will not produce the desired results or may fail altogether.

To help ensure a successful international expansion, extremely careful planning and research are necessary to determine which country or countries to enter and how best to undertake the foreign operation. Figure 19-6 lists 12 questions one writer suggests an insurer should ask and answer before expanding abroad.

Characteristics of the Host Country

For a multinational corporation, the **host country** is a foreign country in which the multinational does business. When considering an international expansion, an insurer carefully evaluates the following types of factors about each potential host country:

- The economic climate and stability of the host country, including the standard of living of its residents

- The regulatory climate in the country, including investment limitations, required minimum capital and surplus amounts, financial reporting requirements, permissible corporate structures, limitations on allowable distribution systems, and limitations on international employers' choices in hiring employees

- The level and nature of insurance competition in the country

> **FIGURE 19-6. Twelve Questions to Ask When Expanding Abroad.**
>
> 1. Do local laws in the target country protect foreign investors?
>
> 2. Does the target country have adequate reserve regulations to protect policyowners?
>
> 3. Is the target country politically stable?
>
> 4. Is the target country economically stable?
>
> 5. Does the target country maintain records and statistics, and are they reliable?
>
> 6. Does the target country have investment laws with restrictions?
>
> 7. Are people in the target country familiar with the concept of profit?
>
> 8. Will the company have to bend its standards too far to accommodate a foreign culture?
>
> 9. Is the target country friendly to security transactions? For example, some political, cultural, or religious customs prevent charging interest.
>
> 10. Will foreign professionals be able to provide the standard of service that the company is used to?
>
> 11. Are there any cultural or religious taboos against marketing the company's products?
>
> 12. Does the target country welcome foreign companies?
>
> **Source:** Adapted from Jerry Warshaw, "Twelve Questions to Ask When Expanding Abroad," *On the Risk* (Fall 1998): 85–86. Used with permission.

- Any political barriers to entering the country, including taxation policies and laws relating to the removal of money from the country

- Demographic characteristics of the country, including the literacy rate of the residents, size of the population, rate of population growth, and age distribution of the citizens

- Cultural traits in the country, including the residents' attitudes toward insurance and toward the presence of foreign businesses

- The types and amount of private insurance in force in the country

- The availability of statistical information on insured lives in the country. If insured lives statistics are unavailable, insurance products must be priced using general population mortality information, which can be less reliable than insured lives statistics.

- Differences in the way the underwriting process is carried out in the host country and the way it is carried out in the home country

Methods of Establishing International Operations

Two methods that U.S. and Canadian insurers may use to enter foreign markets are joint ventures and acquisitions. In the context of international operations, a joint venture involves the insurer entering into an agreement with an insurer or financial services company domiciled in the host country. With the help of such a host company, the multinational insurer can sell its products in the host country, but in exchange must share the profits earned from the joint venture with the host company.

A joint venture can be advantageous for both the multinational insurer and the host company. The multinational insurer gains the host company's experience with local laws, markets, and business conventions. A joint venture is also a relatively inexpensive way for the insurer to sell insurance in the host country because a relatively small amount of start-up money is necessary to begin the operation. A joint venture is also advantageous for the host company, which can (1) benefit from the multinational insurer's technological or marketing expertise, (2) possibly enter into a similar joint venture in the other insurer's country in the future, (3) share in the profits of the joint venture, and (4) increase its market share in the host country.

A second method of entering a foreign market is by acquiring a controlling interest in an insurer already operating in the host country. By acquiring an existing firm, the multinational insurer establishes an immediate presence in the foreign market. Compared with a joint venture, acquiring a controlling interest enables the insurer to gain greater control over operations and to keep a greater share of the profits in the business.

The disadvantages of an acquisition include the potentially high cost of acquiring a foreign subsidiary and the increased risk that the insurer assumes in the operation. Potential barriers to acquisitions include the fact that some countries do not allow foreign ownership of insurance companies, and in some countries, attractive acquisition targets may not be available.

Staffing Considerations

Once an insurer decides to establish an operation in a foreign market, the operation must be staffed. An insurer can staff the foreign office with residents from the insurer's home office, citizens of the host country, citizens of a third country, or some combination of these.

Each staffing option has a number of advantages and disadvantages for a multinational insurer. For example, sending current employees to work in the host country is advantageous because the insurer is already familiar with these employees, the insurer can exert consider-

able control over the employees, and elements of the corporate culture of the home office will be maintained in the foreign office. However, moving employees is expensive—both in physically moving the employees and their families and in recruiting and training their replacements in the home office. Also, employees may have a difficult time adjusting to living in the new country.

Staffing the international office with host country employees is less expensive for the multinational insurer and can help improve relations with the host country. Also, the employees are already familiar with the local customs, manners, and ways of doing business. However, the home office may not be able to exert control over these employees, and communication between the home office and the foreign office can be difficult, especially when language barriers must be overcome.

Key Terms

niche market

planning

merger

amalgamation

acquisition

due diligence

economies of scale

downstream holding company

upstream holding company

standard demutualization

mutual holding company
conversion

strategic alliance

joint venture

partnership

multinational corporation

home country

host country

Endnotes

1. Joseph D'Allegro, "Growth Is #1 Concern of CEOs," *National Underwriter*, Life & Health/Financial Services ed. (18 October 1999): 3.

2. As you learned in Chapter 2, controlling interest is ownership of more than 50 percent of a corporation's voting shares of stock. Practical control of a company's operations can take place with as little as 10 percent of a company's stock, however, if the remaining stock is widely distributed.

3. In 2001, Canadian regulators are to review the necessity of the widely held rule.

4. *Profit margin* is the ratio of net profit to gross sales and is usually expressed in percentage form.

5. "Successful Conclusion of the WTO's Financial Services Negotiations," World Trade Organization, 15 December 1997, http://www.wto.org/wto/archives/press86.htm (9 March 2000).

Glossary

ABC. *See* **activity-based costing.**

accidental death benefit. A supplementary life insurance policy benefit under which the insurer pays the beneficiary an amount of money in addition to the basic death benefit if the insured dies as a result of an accident. [14]

account. A basic storage unit used to record, group, and summarize similar types of business transactions. [17]

accountability. The fact that employees are answerable for how well they use their authority and how effectively they carry out their responsibilities. [4]

accounting. A system or set of rules and methods for collecting, recording, summarizing, reporting, and analyzing a company's financial operations. [17]

accounting conservatism. The choice of a financial reporting method that results in the projection of lower values for a company's assets, higher values for liabilities and expenses, and a lower level of net income than would be the case if the company used a less conservative reporting method. [17]

ACD. *See* **automatic call distribution.**

acquisition. A transaction wherein one company purchases a controlling interest in another company. [19]

active management strategy. An investment strategy in which an asset manager views any security in the portfolio as potentially tradable, if doing so would improve the portfolio's performance. [16]

activity-based costing (ABC). A cost accounting method by which an insurer links its costs to its products based on the activities required to produce each product. [17]

actuarial assumptions. The values—for such elements of product design as mortality rates, investment earnings, expenses, and policy lapses—on which an insurer bases its product pricing and policy reserve calculations. [8]

actuary. An expert in the mathematics of insurance, annuities, and financial instruments. [8]

adequate rates. Premium rates that are high enough to provide the insurer with enough money on hand to pay operating expenses and policy benefits when they come due. [8]

admitted asset. Assets that may be reported as statutory assets. [16]

advanced underwriting department. A department that assists agents with estate planning and business insurance cases; this department (1) prepares proposals based on the information the agent has collected; (2) accompanies the agent, if requested, on sales presentations; (3) provides computer support services; and (4) conducts seminars and counsels agents regarding tax laws and methods of using insurance products to solve estate planning problems. [10]

adverse selection. *See* **antiselection.**

agency-building distribution system. A distribution system in which the insurance company recruits and trains sales agents, finances those agents, and provides them with office facilities. [9]

agency contract. A legal document that defines an agent's role and responsibilities, describes the agent's compensation, and specifically states the agent's right to act for a principal. [9]

agency law. The body of law that has been developed to regulate the relationship between principals and their agents. [18]

agency office. A field office in a general agency system that is established and maintained by a general agent. [9]

agency relationship. A legal relationship by which one party is authorized to perform certain acts for another party. [9]

agency system. *See* **ordinary agency distribution system.**

agent. In an agency relationship, an individual who is authorized to perform certain acts for another party. [9]

agent-broker. A career agent who can place business with her primary insurance company and with insurers other than her primary company. [9]

agent's statement. A portion of the insurance application in which an agent can comment at length on any factors relevant to the case and the risk it involves. [12]

aggressive financial strategy. A financial management strategy which takes risks that could enhance the company's profitability and threaten its solvency. [15]

AI. *See* **artificial intelligence.**

alien corporation. From the point of view of any state in the United States, an insurance company that is incorporated under the laws of another country. [3]

ALM. *See* **asset-liability management.**

amalgamation. *See* **merger.**

amortization. The reduction of a debt by regular payments of principal and interest that result in full payment of the debt by maturity. [16]

annual report. A GAAP-based publication that a company's management sends to its stockholders and other interested parties to report on the company's financial condition and performance during the past year. [17]

Annual Return. In Canada, a report of an insurer's operations and financial performance. [2]

Annual Statement. In the United States, a document that reports information about the insurer's operations and financial performance. [2]

antiselection. The tendency of people who believe they have a greater-than-average likelihood of loss to seek insurance protection to a greater extent than do those who believe they have an average or less-than-average likelihood of loss. Also called *adverse selection* or *selection against the insurer.* [11]

application software. A type of software that helps users solve a particular type of problem. [5]

appointed actuary. An actuary who has been duly appointed by an insurer's board of directors to render an official actuarial opinion as to the insurance company's financial condition. [15]

appointment. A written statement that accompanies the application for an agent's license; made by an officer of an insurer that is licensed to do business in the state; indicates that an insurer appoints the applicant as an insurance agent for the line(s) of insurance

the applicant is authorized to write for the insurer. [10]

APS. *See* **attending physician's statement.**

arbitration. A conflict-resolution method by which an impartial third party evaluates the facts in a dispute and renders a decision that is binding on the parties. [18]

arbitrator. In arbitration, the impartial third party that evaluates the facts in dispute and renders a decision that is binding on the parties. [18]

articles of incorporation. A document that describes the essential features of a proposed company. [3]

artificial intelligence (AI). A field of technology that involves computer systems modeled on the characteristics of human intelligence. [5]

asset fluctuation reserve. In the United States, a statutory reserve designed to absorb gains and losses in an insurer's investment portfolio. [15]

asset-liability management (ALM). A cash-flow management program for coordinating the financial effects of the insurer's product liabilities with the financial effects of the insurer's investments. [15]

asset manager. An investment department employee who monitors the investment-related cash inflows and cash outflows of a specific line of the insurer's business and makes sure sufficient funds are available for that line. [16]

asset risk (C-1 risk). The risk of loss on an investment for a reason *other than* a change in market interest rates. [15]

assets. All things of value owned by a company. [3]

asset share. The amount of assets per unit of coverage that an insurance product has accumulated at a given time. [8]

asset share model. A financial simulation model used to indicate how a product's assets can be expected to grow and when the product can be expected to become profitable for the company. [8]

asset valuation. The process of setting reported values for an insurer's invested assets. [16]

assignment. An agreement under which one party transfers some or all of his ownership

rights in a particular policy to another party. [13]

assuming company. *See* **reinsurer.**

attending physician's statement (APS). An underwriting report by a physician who has treated, or who is currently treating, the proposed insured. [12]

auditing. The process of examining and evaluating company records and procedures to ensure that the company's financial statements are presented fairly and reasonably, that quality is maintained, and that operational procedures and policies are effective. [17]

auditor's report. A statement by an external auditor that expresses the auditor's opinion as to whether the financial statements present fairly the company's financial position. [17]

authority. The right of an employee to make decisions, take action, and direct others in order to carry out a responsibility. [4]

authorization to release information. A section of the claimant's statement that permits an insurer to obtain claim-specific information from medical caregivers and institutions, government agencies, other insurers, consumer reporting agencies, and other sources. [14]

automated workflow. An information management system that both enhances the flow of work within an organization and generates data about the procedures used to accomplish work. [12]

automatic call distribution (ACD). A type of computer/telephony integration that automatically routes calls to available telephone representatives. [13]

automatic reinsurance. A reinsurance agreement in which an insurer must cede specified types of cases or a block of business to a reinsurer, and the reinsurer must accept the risk for those cases up to a predetermined maximum. [12]

balance sheet. An accounting statement that shows a company's financial condition as of a particular date. [15]

bankinsurance. Insurance coverage that is manufactured and underwritten by a commercial bank's own insurance company and distributed through the bank's distribution channels. [2]

bar examination. A licensing test that a person must pass before practicing law. [18]

basic mortality table. A mortality table that has no safety margin built into the mortality rates. [8]

benchmark. A performance standard for a specific process that has been achieved by a recognized leader in that process and that represents the company's goal for its own performance of the process. [13]

binding limit. The dollar amount of risk that a reinsurer obligates itself to accept under an automatic agreement without making its own underwriting assessment of the risk. [12]

blended rating. A premium-calculation method in which the insurer uses a combination of experience rating and manual rating to set a group's premium rate. [8]

block of policies. A group of policies issued to insureds who are all the same age, the same sex, and in the same risk classification. [8]

board of directors. In a corporation, the primary governing body, elected by the owners and shown on the top level of the organization chart. [4]

bond. A security that represents a debt owed by the issuer to the bondholder. [16]

bondholder. The investor who owns a bond. [16]

bond rating. A letter grade assigned by a bond rating agency that indicates the credit quality of a bond issue. [16]

branch manager. *See* **general manager.**

branch office. A field office that is established and maintained by the insurance company. [9]

branch office system. A career agency system in which an insurance company establishes and maintains branch offices in key areas throughout its marketing territory. [9]

break-even period. *See* **validation period.**

break-even point. *See* **validation point.**

brokerage company. An insurance company that uses the brokerage system exclusively and does not establish a career agency force. [9]

brokerage distribution system. A type of personal selling distribution system that relies on the use of agent-brokers, licensed life in-

surance brokers, and independent property/casualty agents and brokers to distribute a company's products. [9]

broker-dealer. A firm that (1) provides information or advice to its customers regarding the sale and/or purchase of securities, (2) serves as a financial intermediary between buyers and sellers by underwriting or acquiring securities in order to market them to its customers, and (3) supervises the sales process to make sure that salespeople comply with applicable securities regulations. [9]

budget. A financial plan of action expressed as assets, liabilities, revenues, and expenses that covers a specified time period, such as one year. [17]

budgeting. The management accounting process that includes creating a financial plan of action that an organization believes will help it achieve its goals. [17]

budget variance. The difference between actual results and budgeted results. [17]

build. The shape or form of the body, including the relationships among height, weight, and the distribution of weight. [11]

business cycle. A process of cumulative changes in the total economic activity of a nation over a time span longer than a year. [6]

business market. *See* **organizational market.**

buy-and-hold strategy. An investment strategy in which an asset manager carefully selects debt securities and expects to hold them until they mature, are prepaid, or default. [16]

C-1 risk. *See* **asset risk.**

C-2 risk. *See* **pricing risk.**

C-3 risk. *See* **interest-rate risk.**

C-4 risk. *See* **general business risk.**

call abandonment rate. The rate at which customers who telephone a company and are put on hold to wait for assistance hang up before receiving assistance. [13]

call center. A customer service unit composed of telephone representatives trained to handle questions about the insurer's product lines. [13]

call provision. A provision that states the conditions under which a bond issuer has the right to force the bondholder to sell the bond back to the issuer. [16]

Canadian Council of Insurance Regulators (CCIR). In Canada, the committee of provincial insurance regulators that looks at emerging trends and works toward harmonizing legislation through model codes and standardized reporting requirements. [2]

capital. The funds that a company's owners have invested in the company. [3]

capital adequacy. *See* **solvency.**

capital and surplus. The amount by which a company's assets exceed the amount of its liabilities. [3]

capital expenditure budget. A type of budget that shows a company's plans for the financial management of capital investments. [17]

capital gain. The amount by which the proceeds of the sale of an investment exceed the amount originally paid to purchase the investment. [16]

capital ratio. The ratio of some quantity of an insurer's capital and surplus to some quantity of the insurer's assets. [15]

captive agent. A career agent who is under contract to only one insurer and who is not permitted to sell the products of other insurers. Also called an *exclusive agent.* [9]

career agency system. *See* **ordinary agency distribution system.**

career agent. A full-time salesperson who holds an agency contract with at least one insurance company and is compensated by commissions. [9]

case assignment system. A method an insurer uses to distribute underwriting cases to an appropriate person or group based on certain characteristics of the case. [12]

cash budget. A type of budget that projects a company's beginning cash balance, cash inflows, cash outflows, and ending cash balance for a particular period. [17]

cash flow. Any movement of cash into or out of a business. [15]

cash-flow testing. The process of projecting and comparing, as of a given date, the timing and amount of asset and liability cash flows. [15]

cash inflow. A movement of cash into an organization. Also called a *source of funds.* [15]

cash outflow. A movement of cash out of an organization. Also called a *use of funds.* [15]

cash value. For a permanent life insurance policy, the amount of money, before adjustments for factors such as policy loans, that the policyowner will receive if the policy does not remain in force until the insured's death. [8]

CCIR. *See* **Canadian Council of Insurance Regulators.**

ceding company. In a reinsurance relationship, an insurance company that transfers all or part of a risk. [12]

centralized organization. Organization in which top management retains decision-making authority for the entire company. [4]

central processing unit (CPU). The computer circuitry that performs the processing or data manipulation and that controls all other parts of a computer. [5]

certificate of authority. *See* **license.**

certificate of incorporation. A document that grants a corporation its legal existence and its right to operate as a corporation. Also known as a *corporate charter.* [3]

chain of command. The structure of authority that flows downward in an organization from the higher levels to the lower levels. [4]

change analysis. A type of cost accounting that involves the comparison of an expense in one period to the same expense in a different period. [17]

claim analyst. A person who is trained to review each claim and determine the insurance company's liability. Also known as *claim examiner, claim specialist,* and *claim approver.* [14]

claimant. A person who submits a claim to an insurance company. [14]

claimant's statement. A document in which a claimant provides information concerning the deceased insured, including the date, place, cause, and circumstances of death. Also called a *claim form.* [14]

claim approver. *See* **claim analyst.**

claim examiner. *See* **claim analyst.**

claim form. *See* **claimant's statement.**

claim fraud. An action by which a person intentionally uses false information in an unfair or unlawful attempt to collect benefits under an insurance policy. [14]

claim investigation. The process of obtaining additional information necessary to make a claim decision. [14]

claim philosophy. A precise statement of the principles the insurer will follow in conducting claim administration. [14]

claim specialist. *See* **claim analyst.**

client-server architecture. A network architecture in which users (clients) connected to the network make service requests from other computers (servers) that are dedicated to special functions. [5]

CMO. *See* **collateralized mortgage obligation.**

coaching. An on-the-job training and development technique in which a junior employee or junior manager is assigned to work with an experienced employee or manager and is given some of the work of the experienced person. [4]

cold calling. A prospecting method in which an agent writes, calls, or visits prospects with whom she has had no prior contact. [9]

collateral. Property that is pledged by the issuer of a bond to the bondholder until the debt obligation is satisfied. [16]

collateralized mortgage obligation (CMO). A mortgage-backed bond that is secured by a pool of residential mortgage loans. [16]

commission. The amount of money, usually a percentage of the premiums, that is paid to an insurance agent for selling and servicing an insurance policy. [9]

committee. A group of people chosen to consider, investigate, or act on matters of a certain kind. [4]

committee underwriting. A risk selection approach in which a group of highly qualified people from inside and outside the underwriting area is called together for a case assessment. [12]

competitor. Another company that can provide a product or service to satisfy the needs of a specific market. [6]

compliance. An insurer's adherence to applicable regulatory requirements. Also known as *regulatory compliance.* [18]

compound interest. Interest that is earned on both an original sum of money and on any previously accumulated interest. [16]

comprehensive business analysis. The phase of product development in which initial product specifications are developed and the product's market potential is closely examined. [7]

comprehensive market conduct examination. An examination of all of an insurer's market conduct operations. [18]

computer/telephony integration (CTI). A technology that unites computer systems with telephone systems so that the two can work together as one system. [13]

concentrated marketing. A target marketing strategy by which a company focuses all of its marketing resources on satisfying the needs of one segment of the total market for a particular type of product. [6]

concept testing. A marketing research technique designed to measure the public acceptability of new product ideas, new promotion campaigns, or other new marketing elements before a company incurs the expense of actually producing these items. [7]

conducting a pilot program. *See* **test marketing.**

conservative financial strategy. A financial management strategy that avoids risks that could threaten the company's solvency and enhance its profitability. [15]

constraint. A factor that limits the marketing activities of a company. [6]

consumer market. A market that consists of people who buy products for themselves or their families. [6]

consumer reporting agency. A person or organization that regularly prepares consumer reports and furnishes them to other people and organizations. [11]

contestable claim. A claim that arises when an insured dies during the contestable period of a life insurance policy. Also called a *resisted claim.* [14]

contestable period. The time during which an insurer has the right to cancel or rescind a policy if the application for insurance contained a material misrepresentation. [14]

contingencies. Unexpected events that cause actual expenses, investment earnings, mortality rates, or persistency rates to deviate significantly from company forecasts. [8]

contingency reserve. Under statutory accounting in the United States, a reserve created by an insurer to act as a cushion against a special risk. [15]

contingency risks. Four broad classifications of risk that could threaten an insurer's solvency. Also known as *C-risks.* [15]

contract. A legally enforceable agreement between two or more parties. [18]

contract law. A body of law that governs the requirements the parties must meet in order to form an agreement that is legally binding on the parties and specifies the rights and duties of the parties to a contract. [18]

contractual savings institution. A financial intermediary that acquires funds at periodic intervals on a contractual basis. [2]

contribution to surplus. In a mutual insurance company, the excess of revenues over expenses before payment of policy dividends. *See also* **profit.** [8]

contributory plan. A group insurance plan under which insured group members must contribute some or all of the premiums required for their coverage. [11]

controlling interest. Ownership of more than 50 percent of another company's voting shares of stock. [2]

convertible bond. A bond that can be exchanged for shares of the issuing company's common stock. [16]

coordination. The orderly arrangement of the activities of various parts of the company so that the company can achieve its goals. [4]

corporate charter. *See* **certificate of incorporation.**

corporate ethics office. A corporate office in which company employees can (1) receive advice or counsel to help resolve ethical dilemmas and (2) report ethical misconduct. [1]

corporation. A legal entity, separate from its owners, that is created by the authority of a government and that continues beyond the death of any or all of its owners. [3]

cost accounting. A system by which a company accumulates expense data in order to control costs and manage assets. [17]

cost basis. The sum of the premiums paid for a life insurance policy plus accumulated dividends less any withdrawals. [13]

cost center. An area of an organization that is responsible for costs but not for revenues. [4]

cost of benefits. The total amount of contractually required benefits and cash surrender values an insurance product is expected to pay. [8]

coupon rate. The rate of interest that determines the amount of the periodic interest payments on a bond. [16]

CPU. *See* **central processing unit.**

credit life insurance. A type of life insurance designed to pay off a debt to a creditor if the debtor-insured dies. [2]

C-risks. *See* **contingency risks.**

CRM. *See* **customer relationship management.**

cross-selling. The process of offering a variety of insurance and financial services products to a customer. [9]

cross training. *See* **job rotation.** [4]

CTI. *See* **computer/telephony integration.**

customer relationship management (CRM). A combination of strategies and technology that allows an organization to manage all aspects of its relationship with a customer. [13]

customer service. The broad range of activities that a company and its employees undertake in order to keep customers satisfied so they will continue doing business with the company and speak positively about the company to other potential customers. [13]

data. Raw, unprocessed facts. [5]

database. An organized collection of information. [5]

database management system (DBMS). A group of programs that manipulates a database and allows users to obtain the information they need. [5]

data mining. The analyzing of data in a data warehouse to discover patterns, trends, and relationships. [5]

data warehouse. A type of database management system that is designed specifically to support management decision making. [5]

DBMS. *See* **database management system.**

death certificate. A document that attests to the death of a person and that bears the signature—and sometimes the seal—of an official authorized to issue such a certificate. [14]

debit agent. *See* **home service agent.**

debt. An investor's loan of funds to another entity in exchange for the promised repayment of the principal loaned and the payment of interest on the amount of the principal loaned. [16]

decentralized organization. Organization in which top management shares decision-making authority with employees at lower hierarchical levels. [4]

decision support system (DSS). An organized collection of people, procedures, software, databases, and devices used to support decision making. [5]

declined class. In risk assessment for individual life insurance, a risk class that generally includes only proposed insureds whose impairments and anticipated extra mortality are so great that the insurer cannot provide coverage at an affordable cost for them. [11]

default risk. The risk that the issuer of a bond will be unable to make interest payments or pay off the face value of a bond when the bond matures. [16]

deflation. A decrease in the average level of prices in an economy. [16]

delegation. The process of assigning to another employee accountability for completion of specific tasks. [4]

demographics. Measurable characteristics that define or describe a given population. [6]

demutualization. The process of a mutual insurance company's conversion to a stock company. [3]

depository institution. A financial intermediary that accepts deposits from individuals and businesses and makes loans. [2]

development. An activity directed toward learning and improving the skills needed for future job performance. [4]

differentiated marketing. A target marketing strategy by which a company attempts to satisfy the needs of different segments of the total market by offering a number of products and marketing mixes designed to appeal to the different segments. [6]

direct response distribution system. A distribution system in which the consumer purchases products directly from the insurance company by responding to the company's advertisement or telephone solicitations. [9]

discretionary group. Any type of group that is not a single employer group, a debtor-creditor group, a labor union group, a multiple-employer group, an association group, or a credit union group. [11]

disintermediation. A phenomenon in which customers remove money from one financial intermediary and place the money with another intermediary to earn a higher return. [15]

distribution. The activities and resources involved in making products available to consumers. [6]

distribution channel. *See* **distribution system.**

distribution system. A network of organizations and people that, in combination, performs all the marketing activities required to transfer products from the insurer to the consumer. Also called a *distribution channel.* [6]

diversification. An investment strategy of holding in a portfolio many assets with different risk and return characteristics to reduce the overall risk that an investor faces. [16]

divisible surplus. The amount of surplus that is available for distribution to owners of participating policies. [3]

domestic corporation. From the point of view of a particular state in the United States, an insurance company that is incorporated under the laws of that state. [3]

domiciliary state. The state in which an insurance company incorporates and has its principal legal residence. [3]

downstream holding company. A holding company that is owned or controlled by the corporation that forms it and that in turn owns or controls other companies. [19]

DSS. *See* **decision support system.**

DST. *See* **dynamic solvency testing.**

due diligence. A careful investigation into (1) the details of a potential merger or acquisition and (2) the operations and management of the other companies involved in the merger or acquisition. [19]

dynamic solvency testing (DST). The use of simulation modeling to project the company's future financial condition under a number of business-growth scenarios and a number of interest-rate scenarios. [15]

economies of scale. The reduction in a company's unit costs as the size of its operations increases. [19]

economy. A system for producing, distributing, and consuming goods and services. [6]

EDI. *See* **electronic data interchange.**

electronic business (e-business). *See* **electronic commerce.**

electronic commerce (e-commerce). The use of the Internet and other information technologies to perform or facilitate the performance of business transactions. Also known as *electronic business (e-business).* [5]

electronic data interchange (EDI). The computer-to-computer exchange of standardized business transaction data between two or more organizations. [5]

electronic mail (e-mail). A telecommunication system that allows users to type messages or memos into computers and send those messages to other people who are connected to a network. [5]

employee loyalty. An employee's commitment of energy and efforts to an organization. [4]

Employee Retirement Income Security Act (ERISA). In the United States, the federal law designed to ensure that certain minimum plan

requirements are contained in employee welfare benefit plans. [18]

employer-employee group. A group that consists of the employees of a single employer. [11]

employment law. The body of law that governs the relationship between an employer and an employee. [18]

endorsement. A document that is attached to a policy and becomes part of the policy. [13]

equitable rates. Premium rates that vary from policy to policy based only on factors affecting the policy's costs. [8]

equity. An investor's ownership or share of ownership in an asset such as a business or a piece of property. [16]

ERISA. *See* **Employee Retirement Income Security Act.**

error rate. A measure of the accuracy of the work done by either an individual or a team. [13]

estate planning. A type of planning to help a client conserve, as much as possible, the personal assets that the individual wants to pass on to his heirs at his death. [10]

ethical dilemma. A situation in which a person is uncertain about the best ethical decision. [1]

ethics. A system of accepted standards of conduct and moral judgment that combines the elements of honesty, integrity, and fair treatment. [1]

evidence of insurability. Documented proof that an applicant is an insurable risk. [12]

exclusive agent. *See* **captive agent.**

expense budget. An operational budget that is a schedule of expenses expected during the given period. [17]

expenses. Funds that a company spends to support its business operations. [15]

experience rating. A method of setting group insurance premium rates using a particular group's experience. [8]

expert system. A system of hardware and software that stores knowledge in the form of rules and uses that knowledge to make inferences, similar to a human expert. [5]

external audit. An audit conducted by an auditor not associated with the organization; the audit includes (1) an evaluation of the company's financial statements, (2) the issuance of an opinion as to whether those financial statements present fairly the company's operations through adherence to GAAP, statutory accounting, or other accounting principles, and (3) a recommendation of changes to the company's system of internal control. Also called an *independent audit.* [17]

external customer. Any person or business who (1) has purchased or is using the insurance company's products, (2) is in a position to buy or use the company's products, or (3) is in a position to advise others to buy or use the company's products without being paid by the company to do so. [13]

external financing. Raising funds from outside a company. [15]

extranet. A portion of an organization's internal computer network that uses Internet technology but is accessible only to selected parties outside the organization, such as other organizations and business partners, with which the insurer needs to exchange information. [5]

face value. *See* **par value.**

facultative reinsurance. A reinsurance agreement in which a ceding company may choose whether to submit a case or a block of cases to a reinsurer, and the reinsurer may choose whether to accept each case or block of cases. [12]

Fair Credit Reporting Act (FCRA). In the United States, a federal law that regulates the reporting and use of consumer credit information and seeks to ensure that reports from consumer reporting agencies contain only accurate, relevant, and recent information. [11]

Fair Labor Standards Act (FLSA). In the United States, a federal law that establishes minimum wage, overtime pay, record keeping, and child labor standards that affect workers in most private companies and federal, state, and local governments. [18]

Family Medical Leave Act (FMLA). In the United States, a federal law that requires employers with 50 or more employees within a 75-mile radius to allow eligible employees in specific

circumstances to take up to 12 weeks of unpaid leave within any 12-month period. [18]

FCRA. *See* **Fair Credit Reporting Act.**

feedback. The part of a system that watches over and monitors the rest of the system. [5]

fiduciary. An entity or individual who holds a special position of trust or confidence when handling the business affairs of another and who must put the other's interests above his or her own. [1]

field force. The term for the collection of agents in an ordinary agency system. [9]

field office. A sales office located in an insurer's marketing territory. [9]

field underwriting. In underwriting, the process of gathering initial information about a proposed insured and screening applicants who have requested coverage. [11]

field underwriting manual. A document, developed by an insurance company, that (1) presents specific guidance for an agent's assessment of the risk represented by a proposed insured and (2) guides the agent in assembling and submitting the evidence of insurability needed for the underwriter to evaluate the risk. [12]

financial accounting. A type of accounting that focuses on gathering and summarizing data to meet financial reporting and tax requirements. [17]

financial audit. An examination of the company's financial statements and an examination of individual accounts and accounting records. [17]

financial condition examination. A formal, on-site investigation that is carried out by insurance regulators and is designed to identify and monitor any threats to an insurer's solvency. [17]

financial institution. A business organization that collects funds from the public and places these funds in financial assets, such as stocks, bonds, insurance policies, annuities, real estate, bank accounts, and loans. [1]

financial instrument. *See* **security.**

financial intermediary. An institution that moves money from businesses and people who have excess funds to businesses and people who have a shortage of funds. [1]

financial management. The process of managing an insurance company's financial resources in order to meet its solvency and profitability goals. [15]

financial planner. A professional who analyzes a client's personal financial circumstances and goals and prepares a program, usually in writing, to meet the client's financial goals. [9]

financial planning. A process in which a client's lifetime financial goals are reviewed and a plan is developed to help the client attain those goals. [10]

financial reporting. The process of presenting financial data about a company's financial position, the company's operating performance, and its flow of funds for an accounting period. [17]

financial services industry. The industry comprised of financial institutions that help consumers and business organizations save, borrow, invest, and otherwise manage money. [2]

financial statement. A report that summarizes a company's major financial events and transactions. [15]

firewall. A device that sits between a company's internal network and the outside Internet and limits access into and out of the network. [5]

first-year commission. A commission paid to an agent who sells a policy and is equal to a stated percentage of the amount of the premium the insurer receives during the first policy year. [10]

FLSA. *See* **Fair Labor Standards Act.**

FMLA. *See* **Family Medical Leave Act.**

forecast. An estimation of a possible future scenario. [8]

foreign corporation. From the point of view of any state in the United States, an insurance company that is incorporated under the laws of another state. In Canada, an insurance company that is incorporated under the laws of another country. Also called a *nonresident corporation.* [3]

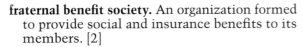

fraternal benefit society. An organization formed to provide social and insurance benefits to its members. [2]

fulfillment kit. In a direct response distribution system, a package of materials designed to address or "fulfill" a respondent's request. [10]

function. A distinct type of work, an essential step in a process, or an aspect of operations or management that requires special technical knowledge. [4]

functional authority. A staff unit member's formal or legitimate authority over line units in matters related to the staff member's functional specialty. [4]

functional cost analysis. A method of cost accounting by which an insurer assigns costs to each company function. [17]

functional regulation. The principle that similar financial activities should be regulated by a single regulator, regardless of which type of financial institution engages in the activity. [2]

GA. *See* **general agent.**

GAAP. *See* **generally accepted accounting principles.**

general account. An undivided investment account in which life insurers maintain funds that support contractual obligations for guaranteed insurance products such as traditional whole life insurance. [16]

general agent (GA). An independent businessperson who is under contract to an insurance company and whose primary function is to build and manage a field office of full-time career agents focused on distributing the products of a single company within a defined territory. [9]

general business risk (C-4 risk). The risk of losses resulting from ineffective general business practices or environmental factors that are beyond the company's control. [15]

general manager. The head of a branch office; the general manager's responsibilities include (1) increasing the sales of products that the company wishes to market and (2) recruiting, selecting, and developing career agents to help the company achieve its corporate growth and profit objectives. Also called a *branch manager.* [9]

generally accepted accounting principles (GAAP). A set of financial accounting standards, conventions, and rules that U.S. stock insurers and all Canadian insurers follow when summarizing transactions and preparing financial statements. [17]

going-concern concept. The accounting concept that states that accounting processes are typically based on the assumption that a company will continue to operate for an indefinite period of time. [17]

gross premium. The amount of money the insurer charges for an insurance policy. [8]

group representative. A salaried insurance company employee who is specifically trained in the techniques of marketing and servicing group insurance products. [9]

guaranteed-issue basis. A form of underwriting for a group of products in which every eligible member of a particular group of proposed insureds who applies and meets specified conditions is automatically issued a policy, and no individual underwriting takes place. [9]

hardware. The machinery and mechanical devices that make up a computer-based information system. [5]

heaped commission system. A commission system that features relatively high first-year commissions and lower renewal commissions. [10]

holding company. A company that has a controlling interest in one or more other companies. [2]

home country. The country in which a multinational corporation is headquartered. [19]

home office. The headquarters of an insurance company and usually the location of the company's executive offices. [3]

home service agent. An exclusive or captive agent who works for an insurance company that uses the home service distribution system. Also called a *debit agent.* [9]

home service distribution system. A personal-selling distribution system that relies on commissioned sales agents to sell specified products and to provide policyowner service within a specified geographic area. [9]

host country. A foreign country in which a multinational corporation does business. [19]

hurdle rate. The minimum percentage rate of return on capital that a company must earn for a given level of risk. [15]

illustration. As defined by the Life Insurance Illustrations Model Regulation, a presentation or depiction that includes nonguaranteed elements of a life insurance policy over a period of years. [7]

impaired risk. *See* **substandard class.**

impairment. Any aspect of a proposed insured's present health, medical history, health habits, family history, occupation, or other activities that could increase that person's expected mortality risk. [11]

implementation. The product development phase that includes establishing all of the administrative structures and processes necessary to take the product to market. [7]

IMSA. *See* **Insurance Marketplace Standards Association.**

income statement. An accounting statement that reports on the net income or net loss of a company for a given period by summarizing the company's revenues and expenses during that time. Also called a *statement of operations.* [15]

independent audit. *See* **external audit.**

independent contractor. A person who performs services for another business under a contract between them. [9]

inflation. A rise in the average level of prices in an economy. [6]

information. A collection of data organized so that it can be used. [5]

information management. The process of using a combination of systems and technology designed to ensure that information users get the right information at the right time in the right format. [5]

information system. A set of interrelated components that collects, manipulates, and disseminates information and provides a feedback mechanism to meet an objective. [5]

initial business plan. *See* **product proposal.** [7]

initial public offering (IPO). The first offering by a corporation to issue (sell) its stock to the public. [3]

input. An item or element that needs to be worked on by a system in order to achieve the system's objective. [5]

inside directors. Members of the board of directors who hold positions with the company in addition to their positions on the board. [4]

insolvency. The inability of an insurer to maintain capital and surplus above the minimum standard of capital and surplus required by law. [15]

inspection report. A type of investigative report that is prepared by a consumer reporting agency and that contains information about a proposed insured. [12]

installment certificate. A document that a claim analyst sends to a life insurance beneficiary when the policy proceeds are to be paid in installments during a fixed or lifetime period or for fixed amounts. [14]

institutional advertising. A form of advertising that promotes an idea, a philosophy, or an industry, rather than a specific product or service. [10]

insurable interest. The likelihood that a policyowner or beneficiary of an insurance policy will suffer a genuine loss or detriment if the event insured against occurs. [11]

Insurance Companies Act. The Canadian legislation that sets out federal insurance laws and the regulatory system for federally regulated life insurance companies. [2]

Insurance Marketplace Standards Association (IMSA). An insurance industry association, established by the American Council of Life Insurance (ACLI), that implements a voluntary market conduct compliance program for the life insurance industry. [1]

insurance risk. *See* **pricing risk.**

integrated image processing. A computer-based approach to capture, index, store, retrieve, and distribute documents in electronic form. [12]

interactive voice response (IVR) system. A type of computer/telephony integration that answers a telephone call, greets the caller with a

recorded or digitized message, and prompts the caller to respond to a menu of options. [13]

interest. A fee paid for the use of someone else's money. [16]

interest-rate risk (C-3 risk). The risk of loss caused by a shift in market interest rates. [15]

internal audit. An examination of a company's records, policies, and procedures conducted by a person associated with the organization. [18]

internal control. A system or method designed to assure the implementation of a program, promote operational efficiency, and safeguard the organization's assets. [18]

internal customer. An insurance company employee who receives service from other employees of the company. [13]

internal financing. Raising funds through the normal operations of a company. [15]

Internet. A collection of interconnected networks, all freely exchanging information. [5]

interpleader. A procedure by which the insurer pays the policy proceeds to a court, advises the court that the insurer cannot determine the correct recipient of the proceeds, and asks the court to determine the proper recipient or recipients. [14]

intranet. An organization's internal network that uses Internet technology but is accessible only to people inside the organization. [5]

investment. Any expenditure of money or assets made in an attempt to earn a return. [16]

investment-grade bond. A bond that is rated higher than Baa (BBB) by a bond rating agency. [16]

IPO. *See* **initial public offering.**

irrevocable beneficiary. A life insurance policy beneficiary whose designation as beneficiary may not be cancelled by the policyowner unless the beneficiary consents. [13]

issue instructions. Guidelines that show the approved policy forms for each jurisdiction, any variations or options in a jurisdiction's forms, and other requirements that various company areas must follow when selling or administering a new product. [7]

IVR. *See* **interactive voice response system.**

jet unit underwriting. A risk selection approach in which employees screen applications that meet specific criteria and are authorized to approve certain types of applications for immediate policy issue. [12]

job rotation. An on-the-job training and developing technique in which an employee moves from one position to another at regular intervals in order to develop expertise in a variety of jobs. Also called *cross training.* [4]

joint venture. An agreement by two or more parties to work together on a project. [19]

LAN. *See* **local area network.**

lapse rate. The percentage share of an insurer's business that customers voluntarily terminate over a specified period. [8]

law of large numbers. A probability theory that states that the more times a particular event is observed, the more likely it is that the observed results will approximate the "true" or calculated probability that the event will occur. [8]

legal reserve. *See* **policy reserve.**

lessee. The individual or organization that leases a building from a lessor. [16]

lessor. The individual or organization that leases a building to a lessee. [16]

letters patent. In Canada, a document certifying that the federal government and the governments of certain provinces have given an insurer the right to incorporate. [3]

level commission schedule. A commission schedule that provides the same commission rate for the first policy year and renewal policy years. [10]

levelized commission schedule. A commission schedule in which first-year commissions are higher than renewal commissions, but the gap between first-year and renewal commissions is smaller than the gap in the traditional heaped commission system. [10]

liabilities. A company's debts and future obligations. [3]

license. A document providing legal authority for an insurer to conduct an insurance business in a particular state. Also known as *certificate of authority.* [3]

licensed broker. A broker who is licensed to sell insurance and is not under an agency contract with any insurance company. Also known as a *pure broker.* [9]

life insurance company. A company that underwrites and issues life insurance. [1]

Life Insurance Illustrations Model Regulation. An NAIC model regulation that contains detailed rules for the use of life insurance policy illustrations and prohibits producers from using any illustration that does not comply with its requirements. [7]

line authority. Direct authority over subordinates. [4]

line unit. Area of an organization that produces and administers the organization's products or services. Also called *production departments* and *operating departments.* [4]

liquidity. The ease and speed with which an asset can be converted to cash at nearly the asset's true value. [15]

litigation. The process or act of resolving a dispute by means of a lawsuit. [18]

loading. An amount of money added to the net premium that covers an insurer's sales and operating expenses and that provides a profit. [8]

local area network (LAN). A network that connects computer systems and devices located within the same geographical area. [5]

location-selling distribution system. A distribution system designed to generate consumer-initiated sales at an insurance facility located in a store or other establishment at which consumers conduct personal business or shop for other products. [9]

loss. The excess of expenses over revenue. *See also* **net loss.** [15]

mainframe computer. A company's large central computer shared by hundreds of users connected through terminals. [5]

management accounting. The process of identifying, measuring, analyzing, and communicating financial information so that internal managers can decide how best to use a company's resources. Also called *managerial accounting.* [17]

management information system (MIS). A type of decision support system that provides information about the company's daily operations and helps employees and managers make day-to-day decisions and control routine activities. [5]

manager of agency operations. The home office person who is the link between an insurer's home office and its agency offices. Also called the *superintendent (director) of agencies.* [10]

managerial accounting. *See* **management accounting.**

manual rating. A method of setting group insurance premium rates by using an insurer's own claim experience—and sometimes the experience of other insurers—to estimate a group's expected claim and expense experience. [8]

market. A group of individuals or companies within the total population that make up the actual or potential buyers of a product. [6]

market conduct. All of the actions taken in the performance of an organization's business operations. [2]

market conduct examination. A formal investigation that is carried out by one or more state insurance departments and is designed to determine whether an insurer's market conduct operations are conducted in compliance with applicable laws and regulations. [18]

market conduct laws. Insurance laws that are designed to ensure that life insurance companies conduct their businesses fairly and ethically. [2]

market-driven organization. A business organization that responds to the needs of the marketplace and the consumers who make up the marketplace. [1]

marketing. The process of planning and executing the conception, pricing, promotion, and distribution of ideas, goods, and services to create exchanges that satisfy individual and organizational objectives. [6]

marketing mix. The four variables (product, price, promotion, and distribution) that marketers manipulate to fulfill marketing's role. [6]

marketing plan. A set of specific, detailed, action-oriented tactics that deal primarily

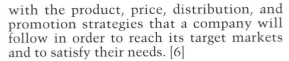

with the product, price, distribution, and promotion strategies that a company will follow in order to reach its target markets and to satisfy their needs. [6]

marketing research. The systematic gathering, recording, and analyzing of specific information that is essential in selling a company's goods and services. [6]

marketing territory. The geographical area in which an insurance company distributes its products. [9]

market segment. A submarket, or group of customers with similar needs. [6]

market segmentation. The process of dividing large, heterogeneous (dissimilar) markets into smaller, more homogeneous (similar) submarkets that have relatively similar needs. [6]

mass marketing. *See* **undifferentiated marketing.**

master application. In group insurance, a document that contains the specific provisions of the plan of insurance being applied for and that is signed by an authorized officer of the proposed policyholder. [12]

master group insurance contract. An insurance contract that insures a number of people. [8]

material misrepresentation. A misrepresentation of fact such that, had the insurer known the truth at the time of application, it would have made a different underwriting decision. [14]

matrix organization. An organization with a structure that includes both vertical and horizontal lines of authority. [4]

maturity date. The specified date on which the par value of a bond must be repaid to the bondholder. [16]

maturity value. *See* **par value.**

MCCSR. *See* **Minimum Continuing Capital and Surplus Requirement.**

mediation. A method of conflict resolution in which an impartial third party facilitates negotiations between the parties in an effort to create a mutually agreeable resolution to the dispute. [18]

mediator. In mediation, the impartial third party that facilitates the negotiations between the parties in an effort to create a mutually agreeable resolution to the dispute. [18]

medical report. A type of report in Part II of the application for life insurance that reports on the proposed insured's health and that is designed to be completed by both the proposed insured and a physician. [12]

membership rights. Ownership rights in a mutual insurance company, such as the right to vote in elections for the company's board of directors on the basis of one vote for each policyowner. [3]

memorandum of association. In Canada, a document similar to letters patent that contains the fundamental terms for registering for incorporation in the provinces of British Columbia, Alberta, Saskatchewan, Ontario, Newfoundland, or Nova Scotia. [3]

merger. A transaction wherein the assets and liabilities of two companies are combined, one of the companies survives as a legal entity, and the other company ceases to exist. In Canada, known as an *amalgamation.* [19]

MIB, Inc. A nonprofit organization established to provide information to insurers concerning impairments that applicants have admitted to or that other insurance companies have detected in connection with previous applications for insurance. [12]

Minimum Continuing Capital and Surplus Requirements (MCCSR). In Canada, risk-based capital requirements established by the Canadian Life and Health Insurance Association for federally licensed companies. [15]

MIS. *See* **management information system.**

model bill. *See* **model law.**

model law. Sample legislation on which states may base their own insurance laws and regulations. Also called a *model bill.* [2]

moral hazard. The likelihood that a person involved in an insurance transaction may act dishonestly in that transaction. [11]

mortality. The relative incidence of death occurring among a given group of people. [11]

mortality experience. The actual number of deaths occurring each year among an insurance company's own insureds. [8]

mortality rate. The rate at which death occurs among a defined group of people. [8]

mortality risk. The likelihood that a person will die sooner than statistically expected. [11]

mortality table. A chart that displays the incidence of death by attained age among a given group of people. [8]

mortgage. A long-term loan secured by real estate. [16]

motor vehicle record. A record of information about a person's driving history, including traffic violations and arrests and convictions for driving-related incidents. [12]

multinational corporation. A business that owns or controls product or service facilities outside the country in which it is based. [19]

multiple-line agency (MLA) system. A personal-selling distribution system that uses full-time career agents and agent-brokers to distribute life, health, and property/casualty insurance products for groups of financially interrelated or commonly managed insurance companies. [9]

mutual holding company conversion. A demutualization by which a mutual insurance company reorganizes itself into three distinct entities: (1) a holding company that has a mutual form of ownership, (2) an intermediate holding company organized as a stock company and owned by the mutual holding company, and (3) a stock insurance operating company that is a subsidiary of the stock holding company. [19]

mutual insurance company. An insurance company that is owned by the policyowners of the company. [3]

mutualization. The process of a stock insurance company's conversion to a mutual company. [3]

NAIC. *See* **National Association of Insurance Commissioners.**

NAIC Insurance Information and Privacy Protection Act. A model act that established standards for the collection, use, and disclosure of information gathered in connection with insurance transactions. Also known as the *NAIC Model Privacy Act.* [11]

NAIC Model Privacy Act. *See* **NAIC Insurance Information and Privacy Protection Act.**

National Association of Insurance Commissioners (NAIC). A nongovernmental organization in the United States composed of insurance commissioners or superintendents from every state. [2]

national banks. Federally chartered banks that are regulated by the Office of the Comptroller of the Currency (OCC), an agency of the U.S. Treasury Department. [2]

needs analysis. A process by which a salesperson develops a detailed personal and financial picture of a prospect in order to evaluate the prospect's insurance needs. [9]

net gain. *See* **net income.**

net income. A stock insurer's operating profit, or the excess of revenues over expenses during a defined period of time. Also known as *net gain. See also* **profit.** [15]

net investment income. The excess of investment income over investment expenses. [8]

net loss. An insurer's operating loss, or the excess of expenses over revenues during a defined period of time. *See also* **loss.** [15]

net premium. The amount of money per unit of coverage that an insurer charges to cover a product's expected cost of benefits. [8]

network. A group of interconnected computers and computer devices, including the telecommunications hardware and software that connects them. [5]

new business. The general term used to describe all the activities required to market insurance, submit applications for insurance, evaluate the risks associated with those applications, and issue and deliver insurance policies. [6]

niche market. A small, specialized market segment in which consumers share similar needs. [19]

nonadmitted assets. Assets that are reported separately from admitted assets and may not be applied to support an insurer's required reserves. [16]

nonagency-building distribution system. Personal selling distribution system in which the insurer does not train, finance, or house

the salespeople. Also called *third-party distribution system.* [9]

noncontributory plan. A group insurance plan under which insured group members are not required to contribute any part of the premium required for their coverage. [11]

nonguaranteed elements. The premiums, benefits, values, credits, or charges under a life insurance policy that are not guaranteed or not determined when the policy is issued. [7]

nonmedical limits. The total amounts of life insurance that will be issued to an applicant at one time without requiring a medical examination. [12]

nonmedical supplement. A type of report in Part II of the application for life insurance that contains health history questions that an agent or teleunderwriting specialist asks a proposed insured. [12]

nonpar policy. *See* **nonparticipating policy.**

nonparticipating policy. Insurance policy under which the policyowner does not share in the insurance company's surplus. Also called a *nonpar policy.* [3]

nonresident corporation. *See* **foreign corporation.**

not taken. *See* **undeliverable.**

numerical rating system. A risk classification method in which each medical and nonmedical factor is assigned a numeric value based on its expected impact on mortality. [12]

Office of the Superintendent of Financial Institutions (OSFI). The chief federal regulatory body overseeing Canadian insurance companies, banks, trust and loan companies, *caisses populaires,* and pension plans. [2]

operating department. *See* **line unit.**

operational budget. A budget covering part or all of a company's operations. [17]

operational planning. *See* **tactical planning.**

order to commence and carry on insurance business. In Canada, a document, issued by the applicable insurance regulatory body, that authorizes an insurance company to begin insuring risks. [3]

ordinary agency distribution system. A personal-selling distribution system that relies on full-time or part-time agents to sell and service

insurance products. Also known as *career agency system* or *agency system.* [9]

organizational market. A market that consists of people, groups, or formal organizations that purchase products and services for business purposes. Also called *business market.* [6]

organization chart. A visual display of various job positions in a company and the formal lines of authority and responsibility among company employees. [4]

orphan policy. A policy for which the original agent is no longer available to provide service. [13]

OSFI. *See* **Office of the Superintendent of Financial Institutions.**

OTC. *See* **over-the-counter market.**

output. The result of the work done by a system. [5]

outside directors. Members of the board of directors who do not hold other positions with the company. [4]

outsourcing. The process of hiring a vendor to provide a service rather than having the company's own employees provide the service. [4]

override. *See* **overriding commission.**

overriding commission. A payment based on the amount of sales produced by the agents in a field office. Also called an *override.* [9]

over-the-counter (OTC) market. A market in which dealers at different locations who have an inventory of securities stand ready to buy and sell securities. [16]

paralegal. A person specially trained in techniques of legal research and the procedures for various legal transactions. [18]

paramedical report. A type of report in Part II of the application for life insurance that contains (1) the proposed insured's answers to medical history questions and (2) the results of certain physical measurements taken by a paramedical examiner. [12]

par policy. *See* **participating policy.**

par value. The amount that the issuer of a bond must pay to the bondholder on the bond's maturity date. Also known as *face value* or *maturity value.* [16]

Part I. The part of the life insurance application that identifies the proposed insured and the applicant (if different from the proposed insured), specifies the amount and type of coverage requested, and provides basic insurability information. [12]

Part II. The part of the life insurance application that consists of medical information about the proposed insured. [12]

participating policy. An insurance policy under which the policyowner shares in the insurance company's surplus. Also called a *par policy*. [3]

partnership. A contract between two or more organizations that agree to pool their funds and talents and share in the profit and loss of the enterprise. [19]

persistency. The retention of business that occurs when a policy remains in force as a result of the continued payment of the policy's renewal premiums. [9]

personal-producing general agent. A commissioned sales agent who generally works alone, is not housed in one of a company's field offices, and engages primarily in personal production. [9]

personal-producing general agent (PPGA) system. A distribution system that uses personal-producing general agents to distribute products. [9]

personal selling distribution system. A distribution system in which commissioned or salaried salespeople sell products through verbal and written presentations made to prospective purchasers. [9]

planning. The process of preparing for the future by establishing appropriate goals and formulating the strategies, tactics, and other activities necessary to achieve those goals. [19]

platform employee. A bank's own employee who is trained and licensed to sell the products of an insurance company. [10]

policy accounting. The accounting operation that is responsible for recording all financial transactions related to the policies an insurer has issued, including accounting for premiums, commissions, policy loans, policy dividends, and claim payments. [17]

policy dividend. A participating policyowner's share of divisible surplus, payable at the end of the policy year. [3]

policy filing. The process of obtaining all required regulatory approvals for a product from all applicable jurisdictions. [7]

policy form. A standardized form, drafted by an insurer and filed with insurance regulators, that shows the terms, conditions, benefits, and ownership rights of specific types of coverage. [2]

policy issue. The insurance company functional area that prepares the insurance contract and facilitates the delivery of the policy to the customer, usually by way of the agent who sold the insurance. [12]

policy lapse. The termination of an insurance policy because of nonpayment of renewal premiums. [8]

policy liability. *See* **policy reserve.**

policy loan. A loan made by a life insurance company to the owner of a life insurance policy that has a cash value. [13]

policy reserve. A liability identifying the amount that, together with future premiums and assumed rate of investment interest, is expected to be needed to pay benefits of in-force policies. Also called *policy liability*, *statutory reserve*, and *legal reserve*. [8]

policy rider. An amendment to an insurance policy that either expands or limits the benefits payable under the policy. [13]

policy rights. A policyowner's contractual rights, such as the right to the policy values, the right to assign the values to another party, and the right to designate the beneficiary of the policy proceeds upon the death of the insured. [3]

portfolio. A collection of financial assets assembled to meet an investment goal. [16]

positioning. The marketing activity that involves defining a certain place or market niche for a product relative to competitors and their products and then using promotion and other elements of the marketing mix to support that position. [6]

PPGA. *See* **personal-producing general agent.**

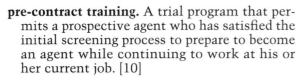

pre-contract training. A trial program that permits a prospective agent who has satisfied the initial screening process to prepare to become an agent while continuing to work at his or her current job. [10]

preferred class. In risk assessment for individual life insurance, a risk class that generally includes proposed insureds whose anticipated mortality is significantly lower than average and who represent a lower-than-average degree of risk. [11]

premium receipt. A receipt that a sales agent gives to an applicant for insurance in exchange for the initial premium payment and that provides a proposed insured with temporary insurance coverage while the application is being underwritten. [9]

premium tax. A tax on an insurer's premium income and annuity considerations earned within a state or province. [17]

price. The consideration that consumers give in exchange for a product. [6]

pricing objectives. Goals that specify what an organization wants to achieve as a result of its pricing strategy. [8]

pricing risk (C-2 risk). The risk that the insurer's experience with mortality or expenses will differ significantly from expectations, causing the insurer to lose money on its products. Also known as *insurance risk.* [15]

pricing strategy. The general guidelines that the company follows to achieve its pricing objectives. [8]

principal. In an agency relationship, a person or organization that authorizes an agent to act on his behalf. In the context of investments, the initial amount invested. [9, 16]

private placement. A method of issuing securities in which the security is sold directly from the issuing organization to an institutional investor. [16]

processing. The work performed by a system on its input. [5]

producer group. An organization of independent producers or firms that negotiates compensation, product, and service arrangements with insurance companies. [9]

product. The good or service that a seller offers to consumers to satisfy a need. [6]

product advertising. Advertising used to promote a specific good or service. [10]

production department. *See* **line unit.**

product mix. The range of products that a company makes available to customers. Also called a *product portfolio.* [6]

product portfolio. *See* **product mix.**

product proposal. An outline of a product's target market; market potential; technical specifications; and administrative, systems, and distribution requirements. Also called an *initial business plan.* [7]

profit. In a stock insurance company, the excess of revenue over expenses before stockholder dividends. *See also* **net income** and **contribution to surplus.** [8]

profitability. A business operation's degree of success at generating returns to its owners—including its ability to generate profit and to increase the value of the company. [15]

profit center. A line of business that (1) is evaluated on its profitability, (2) is responsible for its own revenues and expenses, and (3) makes its own decisions regarding its operations. [4]

program development. The process of using programming languages to code, test, and debug new application software. [5]

programmed instruction. An off-the-job training and developing technique in which educational devices are used to provide trainees with (1) information about a subject, (2) opportunities to apply their knowledge of the subject, and (3) feedback about their progress in gaining knowledge. [4]

project champion. *See* **project sponsor.**

project coordinator. The manager of the product development team who controls the day-to-day aspects of the project. Also called a *project manager.* [7]

project manager. *See* **project coordinator.**

project sponsor. A senior-level executive who authorizes a new product development project and who has ultimate authority over the project. Also called a *project champion.* [7]

promotion. The collection of activities that sellers use to communicate with consumers to influence them to purchase products. [6]

proposal for insurance. A document that provides a number of specifications for the insurance coverage approved by an insurer for a proposed group. [12]

prospect. A potential buyer of insurance products. [9]

prospectus. A written communication that offers a security for sale. [10]

public offering. A method of issuing securities in which the issuing entity makes the securities available for sale to the public. [16]

pure broker. *See* **licensed broker.**

RAA. *See* **retained asset account.**

rate of return. The expected return of an investment expressed as a percentage of the purchase price. [16]

rating. The act of approving an application for insurance on a basis other than the basis for which the policy was applied, including actions such as approving the application at a higher premium rate than applied for or with less coverage than applied for. [11]

rating agency. An independent organization that evaluates the financial condition of insurers and provides information to potential customers of and investors in insurance companies. [15]

ratio. A comparison of two numeric values that results in a measurement expressed as a percentage or a fraction. [15]

RBC. *See* **risk-based capital ratio requirement.**

realized gain (or loss). A gain (or loss) resulting from the actual sale or maturity of an investment. [17]

real property law. The body of law that deals with the ownership and transfer of rights in real estate. [18]

reasonable rates. Premium rates that do not exceed those rates needed to cover an insurer's expenses and provide the insurer with a fair profit. [8]

recognition. The process of (1) classifying items in a financial transaction as assets, liabilities, capital and surplus, revenue, or expenses, and (2) recording the transaction in the company's accounting records. [17]

registered representative. Any person who is a business associate of a National Association of Securities Dealers (NASD) member, engages in the securities business on behalf of the member by soliciting the sale of securities or training securities salespeople, and has passed a specified examination administered by the NASD. [9]

regulatory compliance. *See* **compliance.**

reinsurance. A form of insurance that enables an insurer to be indemnified or reimbursed in the event of covered losses claimed under insurance policies the insurer has issued. [12]

reinsurance treaty. A statement of the agreement between a ceding company and a reinsurer. [12]

reinsurer. A company that assumes a risk from a ceding company. Also called an *assuming company.* [12]

renewal commissions. Commissions paid to an agent (1) only for policies the agent sold and (2) for a number of years after the first policy year. [10]

replacement. The act of surrendering an insurance policy or part of the coverage provided by an insurance policy in order to buy another policy. [13]

Request for Proposal. A document that provides detailed information about requested insurance coverage and that requests a bid from an insurer for providing the coverage. [12]

rescission. The legal process under which an insurer seeks to have a contract declared void from the beginning on the basis of a material misrepresentation. [14]

reserve valuation. The process of establishing a value for an insurer's required policy reserves. [15]

resident corporation. In Canada, an insurance company that is incorporated under Canadian law. [3]

resisted claim. *See* **contestable claim.**

responsibility. The duties and tasks assigned to any given employee. [4]

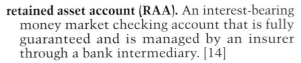

retained asset account (RAA). An interest-bearing money market checking account that is fully guaranteed and is managed by an insurer through a bank intermediary. [14]

retention limit. The amount of insurance that an insurer will carry at its own risk. [12]

retrocession. The act of transferring a risk from a reinsurer to a retrocessionaire. [12]

retrocessionaire. A reinsurer that assumes risks transferred from another reinsurer. [12]

return. The reward or compensation that an investor receives for taking a risk. [15]

return on capital ratio. A ratio that compares some measure of an insurer's earnings during a stated period to some measure of its capital and surplus. [15]

revenue. Funds that a company earns from its business operations. [15]

revenue budget. An operational budget that indicates the amount of income from operations—policy sales and investments—that the company expects during the budget period. [17]

risk. Generally, the probability of financial loss. In the context of investments, the possibility that an investor will fail to earn a return or will lose all or part of the initial investment. [1, 16]

risk-based capital (RBC) ratio requirement. In the United States, requirements that enable state regulators to evaluate the adequacy of an insurer's capital relative to the riskiness of the insurer's operations. [15]

risk class. A grouping of insureds that represent a similar level of risk to an insurance company. [11]

risk management. The practice of identifying risk, assessing risk, and dealing with risk. [1]

risk-return tradeoff. The interplay between risk and return: the greater the risk associated with an investment, the greater the potential return on the investment, and the lesser the risk associated with an investment, the lower the potential return on the investment. [16]

risk selection. *See* **underwriting.**

salaried sales distribution system. A distribution system that relies on the use of a company's salaried sales representatives to sell and service insurance products. [9]

sale-and-leaseback transaction. A method of purchasing real estate under which the owner of a building sells the building to an investor but immediately leases back the building from the investor. [16]

sales manager. The home office person who has direct authority over all of an insurance company's product distribution activities. [10]

savings bank life insurance (SBLI). In the United States, life insurance coverage sold by authorized savings banks to people who live or work in the state in which the insurance is sold. [2]

SBU. *See* **strategic business unit.**

Section 1035 exchange. In the United States, a tax-free exchange of specified types of insurance policies. [13]

securities exchange. A market in which buyers and sellers of securities (or their agents or brokers) meet in one location to conduct trades. [16]

securities law. The body of law that governs the purchase and sale of securities. [18]

security. A document or certificate representing either an ownership interest in a business or an obligation of indebtedness owed by a business, government, or agency. Also called a *financial instrument.* [16]

segregated fund. *See* **separate account.**

selection against the insurer. *See* **antiselection.**

selection of risks. *See* **underwriting.**

separate account. In the United States, an investment account maintained separately from the insurer's general account and that supports liabilities associated with variable products the insurer has issued. In Canada, known as a *segregated fund.* [16]

service department. *See* **staff unit.**

service fees. A small percentage of premiums payable on life insurance policies after renewal commissions have ceased. [10]

sex-distinct mortality table. A mortality table that shows different mortality rates for males and females. [8]

shareholders. *See* **stockholders.**

simple interest. Interest paid only on an original sum of money. [16]

simulation. A model used to represent a complex system in order to study how the system behaves under various circumstances. [15]

software. The programs that provide the sequences of instructions for a computer and that govern its operation. [5]

solvency. The ability of an insurer to pay its debts, policy benefits, and operating expenses when they come due. The ability of an insurer to maintain capital and surplus above the minimum standard of capital and surplus required by law. Also known as *statutory solvency*. In Canada, known as *capital adequacy*. [2, 15]

solvency laws. Insurance laws that are designed to ensure that insurance companies are financially able to meet their debts and pay policy benefits when they come due. [2]

source of funds. *See* **cash inflow.**

special risk. *See* **substandard risk.**

specialized medical questionnaire. An underwriting document that requests from the proposed insured's attending physician detailed information on a specific illness or condition. [12]

spread. The difference between the rate of return earned on an insurer's investments and the interest rate the insurer guarantees on its products. [16]

staff authority. Authority held by staff unit personnel to advise or make recommendations to line unit personnel. [4]

staff unit. Area of an organization that provides support services to line units and other staff units but does not itself produce or administer products and services. Also called *service department*. [4]

standard class. In risk assessment for individual life insurance, a risk class that generally includes proposed insureds whose anticipated mortality is average. [11]

standard demutualization. A demutualization in which a mutual insurance company reorganizes as a stock insurance company. [19]

standing committee. Permanent committee that company executives use as a source of continuing advice. [4]

state banks. State-chartered banks that are regulated by state banking authorities. [2]

statement of cash flows. A financial statement that provides information about the company's cash receipts, cash disbursements, and net change in cash during a specified period. [17]

statement of indebtedness. A document that a claim analyst sends to a life insurance beneficiary that specifies (1) a minimum interest rate that the insurer will pay on proceeds left on deposit with the insurer and (2) the frequency with which the insurer will make interest payments to the beneficiary. [14]

statement of operations. *See* **income statement.**

statement of surplus. A financial statement that provides information about the change in the company's surplus account during a specified period. [17]

statutory accounting practices. A set of financial accounting standards that is based on current statutes and regulations. [17]

statutory reserve. *See* **policy reserve.**

statutory solvency. *See* **solvency.**

stock. A security that represents an ownership interest in a company. [3]

stockholder dividends. Periodic distributions of a stock insurance company's net profit. [3]

stockholders. Owners of a company's stock. Also called *shareholders*. [3]

stock insurance company. An insurance company that is owned by the people who purchase shares of the company's stock. [3]

strategic alliance. A prolonged relationship involving risk and reward sharing by two or more independent firms that are also pursuing their own individual strategic goals. [19]

strategic business unit (SBU). An organizational unit that (1) serves a specific market outside the parent corporation, (2) faces outside competition, (3) controls its own strategic planning and new product development, (4) has its own

management and support functions, and (5) is responsible for its own costs and revenues. [4]

strategic planning. The process of determining an organization's major long-term corporate objectives and the broad, overall courses of action that the company will follow to achieve these objectives. [4]

subagent. A full-time soliciting agent recruited by a personal-producing general agent (PPGA). [9]

subsidiary. A company that is owned or controlled by a holding company. [2]

substandard class. In risk assessment for individual life insurance, a risk class that generally includes proposed insureds whose anticipated mortality is higher than average. Also called *special risk* or *impaired risk.* [11]

superintendent (director) of agencies. *See* **manager of agency operations.**

surplus. The total net profits that have been earned from a company's operations and left to accumulate since the company's inception. [3]

system. A set of components that interact to accomplish goals. [5]

systems analysis and design. The process of examining business processes, suggesting ways to improve the processes, and designing computer systems to enhance the processes. [5]

systems software. A type of software that coordinates the activities and functions of the hardware and various programs throughout a computer system. [5]

table of underwriting requirements. A document for an insurance product that specifies the kinds of information the underwriter must consider in assessing the insurability of a person who is proposed for coverage under that policy. [12]

tactical planning. The process of determining the specific tasks that need to be performed to carry out an organization's strategic plans. Also called *operational planning.* [4]

target market. A market segment on which a company focuses its marketing efforts. [6]

target market conduct examination. A market conduct examination of one or more specific areas of an insurer's operations. [18]

target marketing. The process of evaluating the attractiveness to the company of each market segment and selecting one or more of the segments on which to focus the company's marketing efforts. [6]

team underwriting. A risk selection approach in which underwriters form small groups to evaluate applications. [12]

technical design. The phase of product development that involves creating the product language, product provisions, pricing and dividend structures, and underwriting and issue specifications. [7]

telecommunications. The electronic transmission of communication signals that enables organizations to link computer systems into effective networks. [5]

telecommuting. *See* **teleworking.**

teleunderwriting. A method by which a home office employee or a third party administrator, rather than the agent, gathers most of the information needed for underwriting. [12]

teleworking. The act of working outside the traditional office or workplace, usually at home, by using electronic means of communication with the office, colleagues, and customers. Also called *telecommuting.* [5]

termination report. A report that states require insurers to file with the insurance commissioner whenever an agent's appointment is terminated. [10]

test marketing. The process of selling a product in a limited number of geographic areas and then measuring its level of success. Also called *conducting a pilot program.* [7]

third-party application. An insurance application submitted by a person or party other than the proposed insured. [11]

third-party distribution system. *See* **nonagency-building distribution system.**

third-party marketer. An independent general agency that sells insurance products for one or more banks. [10]

training. An activity directed toward learning, maintaining, and improving the skills necessary for current job performance. [4]

transaction. Any business-related exchange. [5]

transaction processing system. An organized collection of procedures, software, databases, and devices used to record high-volume, routine, and repetitive business transactions. [5]

turnaround time. The amount of time necessary to complete a particular customer-initiated transaction. [13]

undeliverable. A term used to describe an applied-for insurance policy that a consumer chooses not to accept when the agent attempts to deliver it. Also called *not taken.* [11]

underwriter. A person in an insurance company who evaluates risks, accepts or declines applications, and determines the appropriate premium amount to charge acceptable risks. [11]

underwriting. The insurance function that is responsible for (1) assessing and classifying the degree of risk a proposed insured represents and (2) making a decision concerning coverage of that risk. Also called *risk selection* or *selection of risks.* [11]

underwriting decision. The decision an underwriter makes regarding the classification of a risk and the premium amount to charge for insurance coverage. [11]

underwriting guidelines. The general standards that specify which applicants are to be assigned to the risk classes established for each insurance product. [11]

underwriting manual. A document that contains descriptive information on impairments and that serves as a guide to underwriting decision making. [12]

underwriting objectives. *See* **underwriting philosophy.**

underwriting philosophy. A set of objectives that generally reflect the insurer's strategic business goals and include pricing assumptions for products. Also called *underwriting objectives.* [11]

undifferentiated marketing. A target marketing strategy by which a company defines the total market for a product as its target market and produces only one product for that market. Also called *mass marketing.* [6]

Unfair Claims Settlement Practices Act. An NAIC model act that specifies a number of actions that are unfair claim practices if committed by an insurer transacting business in the state (1) in conscious disregard of the law or (2) so frequently as to indicate a general business practice. [14]

Unfair Trade Practices Act. An NAIC model act that defines certain practices as unfair and prohibits those practices in the business of insurance if they are committed (1) flagrantly in conscious disregard of the Act or (2) so frequently as to indicate a general business practice. [6]

unisex mortality table. A mortality table that shows a single set of mortality rates that reflect one mortality rate for both males and females at each age. [8]

unit of coverage. A basic amount of insurance coverage used to calculate premiums. [8]

unity of command. Principle that each employee should receive authority from only one person and be accountable to only that person. [4]

unrealized gain (or loss). A gain (or loss) that has not become actual because the investment has not matured or been sold. [17]

upstream holding company. A holding company that controls the corporation that formed it and can also own other subsidiaries. [19]

use of funds. *See* **cash outflow.**

validation period. The amount of time required for a product to become profitable or begin adding to surplus. Also called the *break-even period.* [8]

validation point. The point at which the product in an asset share model breaks even. Also called the *break-even point.* [8]

valuation mortality table. A mortality table that has a safety margin built into the mortality rates. [8]

vested commission. A commission that is guaranteed payable to an agent even if the agent no longer represents the company when the commission comes due. [10]

voice mail. A system that ties a company's phone system to its computer system so that verbal messages can be sent, received, stored, and retrieved. [5]

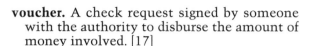

voucher. A check request signed by someone with the authority to disburse the amount of money involved. [17]

wait time. The average length of time that customers must stay on the telephone before they receive assistance. [13]

WAN. *See* **wide area network.**

wide area network (WAN). A network that ties together computers and computer devices located across large geographic regions. [5]

work division system. A method an insurer uses to divide underwriting cases according to the person or group that underwrites them. [12]

worksite marketing. The process of distributing individual or group insurance products to people at their place of work on a voluntary, payroll-deduction basis. [9]

Index

Numbers in *italics* indicate figures; *n* after a page number indicates an endnote

A

C

F

G

S

IMPORTANT—READ CAREFULLY BEFORE REMOVING THE QUIK REVIEW CD-ROM FROM ITS JACKET. *Use of the software program on the enclosed disk is subject to the terms of the license agreement printed below. By removing the disk from the jacket, you indicate your acceptance of the following LOMA License Agreement.*

LOMA LICENSE AGREEMENT

This is a legal agreement between you (individual or company) and LOMA. By removing the disk from its jacket, you are agreeing to be bound by the terms of this agreement.

Grant of License

LOMA grants to you the right to use one copy of the enclosed Quik Review (hereinafter "the software") on a single computer. The software is in "use" on a computer when it is loaded into temporary memory (RAM) or installed into permanent memory (hard disk, CD-ROM, or other storage device) of that computer.

Copyright

The software is owned by LOMA and is protected by U.S. copyright laws and international treaty provisions. Therefore, you must treat the software like any other copyrighted material (e.g., a book or musical recording) EXCEPT that you may either make one copy of the software solely for backup or archival purposes or transfer the software to a single hard disk provided you keep the original solely for backup or archival purposes. You may not copy the written material accompanying the software. The instructional material (hereinafter "the content") contained in the software is also owned by LOMA and protected by U.S. copyright laws and international treaty provisions. It is illegal to make any copy whatsoever of the content; to install the software on a network, intranet, or web site; to download the content to another computer or device; to print screens or otherwise cause the content to be printed; or to in any other way reproduce the content contained in the software.

Other Restrictions

You may not rent or lease the software. You may not reverse engineer, decompile, or disassemble the software or in any way duplicate the contents of the code and other elements therein.

Disclaimer of Warranty

LOMA MAKES NO WARRANTY EXPRESSED OR IMPLIED INCLUDING, WITHOUT LIMITATION, NO WARRANTY OF MERCHANTABILITY OR FITNESS OR SUITABILITY FOR A PARTICULAR PURPOSE. UNDER NO CIRCUMSTANCES SHALL LOMA BE LIABLE TO THE USER OR ANY THIRD PARTY FOR ANY INCIDENTAL OR CONSEQUENTIAL DAMAGES WHATSOEVER.

Limitation of Liability

You agree to indemnify and hold harmless LOMA, its employees, its agents, and their successors and assign against any loss, liability, cost or expense (including reasonable attorneys' fees) asserted against or suffered or incurred by you as a consequence of, or in the defense of, any claim arising from or based upon any alleged negligence, act or failure to act, whatsoever of LOMA, its employees, their successors, agents, heirs, and/or assigns with respect to the aforementioned software.

LOMA® is a registered trademark of LOMA (Life Office Management Association, Inc.), Atlanta, Georgia, USA. All rights reserved.